CW00950111

ANNALS OF COMMUNISM

Each volume in the series Annals of Communism will publish selected and previously inaccessible documents from former Soviet state and party archives in a narrative that develops a particular topic in the history of Soviet and international communism. Separate English and Russian editions will be prepared. Russian and Western scholars work together to prepare the documents for each volume. Documents are chosen not for their support of any single interpretation but for their particular historical importance or their general value in deepening understanding and facilitating discussion. The volumes are designed to be useful to students, scholars, and interested general readers.

Stalin and the Lubianka

A Documentary History of the Political Police and Security Organs in the Soviet Union, 1922–1953

David R. Shearer and Vladimir Khaustov

Yale UNIVERSITY PRESS

New Haven and London

Published with assistance from the foundation established in memory of Amasa Stone
Mather of the Class of 1907, Yale College.

Yale University Press books may be purchased in quantity for educational, business, or
promotional use. For information, please e-mail sales.press@yale.edu (U.S. office) or
sales@yaleup.co.uk (U.K. office).

Set in Sabon type by IDS Infotech, Ltd.
Printed in the United States of America.

Library of Congress Cataloging-in-Publication Data

Shearer, David R., 1952–. Stalin and the Lubianka : a documentary history of the
political police and security organs in the Soviet Union, 1922–1953 / David R. Shearer
and Vladimir Khaustov.
    pages   cm.—(Annals of communism)
Includes bibliographical references and index.
ISBN 978-0-300-17189-1 (hardback : alkaline paper) 1. Police—Soviet Union—History.
2. Police—Soviet Union—History—Sources. 3. Internal security—Soviet Union—History.
4. Lubianka (Prison : Moscow, Russia)—History. 5. Political prisoners—Soviet Union—
History. 6. Stalin, Joseph, 1879–1953—Influence. 7. Power (Social sciences)—Soviet
Union—History. 8. Social control—Soviet Union—History. 9. Soviet Union—Politics and
government—1917–1936. 10. Soviet Union—Politics and government—1936–1953.
I. Khaustov, V. N. (Vladimir Nikolaevich). II. Title.
    HV8224.S3757 2015
    363.20947'09041—dc23

                                                                    2014012361

A catalogue record for this book is available from the British Library.

This paper meets the requirements of ANSI/NISO Z39.48-1992 (Permanence of Paper).

10 9 8 7 6 5 4 3 2 1

Yale University Press gratefully acknowledges the financial support given for this publication by the John M. Olin Foundation, the Lynde and Harry Bradley Foundation, the Historical Research Foundation, Roger Milliken, the Rosentiel Foundation, Lloyd H. Smith, Keith Young, the William H. Donner Foundation, Joseph W. Donner, Jeremiah Milbank, the David Woods Kemper Memorial Foundation, and the Smith Richardson Foundation.

Contents

Contents

Preface

Vadim Staklo, of Yale University Press, first suggested a history of the Soviet political and security police. He was right to do so. Much has been written about particular aspects of the Soviet political police, but no single account existed of the Soviet political and security organs for the first thirty years of their existence. This volume is an attempt to provide such a history, at least for the first and formative decades of the Soviet state, from the early 1920s to the mid–1950s. It is both a narrative history and a document collection, combining interpretive text with translations of important as well as indicative documents from the period. Most of the documents, though not all, are taken from the four-volume series *Lubianka, Stalin*, published in Russia during the early and mid–2000s. Lubianka, of course, refers to the large nineteenth-century buildings on Lubianka Square, in downtown Moscow. That complex served as headquarters for the Soviet political and security organs throughout the twentieth century, and still serves as the headquarters of the Russian Federation security service, the FSB.

The documents in the *Lubianka, Stalin* series, and in this volume, come from a number of archives, but many are from collections in the still highly restricted archives of the security organs, and the Presidential Archive of the Russian Federation. Other major archival sources include the State Archive of the Russian Federation, the Russian State Archive of Social and Political History, the Russian State Archive of Contemporary History, and the State Archive of the Novosibirsk Oblast. Some of the documents in this volume were already published prior to the appearance of the *Lubianka, Stalin* series. Several have appeared in English translation, and these are noted. The great majority of the documents, however, appear here for the first time in English. Together, with the text, they tell a story previously untold, of the growth of the Soviet political and security organs, and the various and evolving functions of those organs in the realm of domestic and foreign spying, state security, and political and social repression.

This is more than a story of repression, however. During the first decades of the Soviet state, the history of the political police was inextricably tied to the rule of Joseph Stalin, the general secretary of the ruling Communist Party. Stalin became secretary in 1922, a position that became known as "general" secretary during the final illness of the founder of the Soviet state, Vladimir Lenin, and after the tumultuous years of revolution and civil war from 1917 to 1921. Stalin was not one of the early charismatic leaders of the Bolshevik Party, but he quietly asserted himself, and he did so largely through an alliance with key individuals in the political police. By the early and mid–1930s, Stalin rose to be the undisputed and ruthless leader of the country and, as this book shows, he did so largely through his ability to use the political police. He dominated the country, and the political police, until his death in early March of 1953. His rule became synonymous with the power of the political police, and in turn, the extent of power wielded by the police and security organs would have been impossible without Stalin. This power was never secure, however. Stalin manipulated the balance between the police and the ruling Communist Party, using each in turn to purge and maintain control over the other. The documents herein reveal this dynamic of Stalin's power, as well as the expanding, shrinking, and often changing functions of police activities over the decades of Stalin's rule.

Contrary to many perceptions, the Soviet political and security organs did much more than hunt and persecute Stalin's political rivals and supposed enemies of the regime. In a state plagued by weak civil institutions, the political police stepped into, and at times were pushed into, areas of social governance not usually associated with a political and state security agency. The documents here reveal the degree to which the police under Stalin fundamentally shaped the social, economic, and even geographical makeup of Stalin's peculiar brand of militarized socialism. Thus, this book is not just a history of police and repression, it is also a history of Stalinism, and of Soviet socialism.

We are grateful for the support of Yale University Press in making this book possible. We are also grateful to Marina Dobronovskaya for her invaluable help in translating both the words and the sense of the documents contained herein. Finally, our thanks go to Gavin Lewis, whose astute editing made a manuscript into a book.

David R. Shearer
Vladimir Khaustov

Note on Translation, Document Presentation, Transliteration, and Abbreviations

The great majority of documents in this collection are of an official nature. The language is highly bureaucratized, it is often stilted or convoluted, and almost all the documents were written in the passive voice. At times, the language in the documents is grammatically nonsensical. We have made no attempt to "clean up" the language into clear, readable English. On the contrary, we have made a conscious effort to retain the sense and tone of the language that strikes the reader in the original Russian. In a number of instances, this has required some judgment about what might sound normal or not normal to a Russian ear, and then to translate that into analogous English. In no case, however, have we allowed ourselves literary license. We have tried to stay as close as possible to the literal sense, phrasing, and word order of the Russian text. We have tried to retain in the English text some of the historical immediacy of the original language.

We have followed standard practice in using brackets and dots, [...], to indicate original text that we have excluded. The use of parentheses and dots, (...), indicates a break in the text of the original document. Text underlined by hand in the originals appears also underlined here, and wording crossed out by hand appears scored through; occasional typewritten underlining of headings appears here in italic; handwritten insertions, marginal annotations, and the like are interpolated in brackets at points corresponding to their positions in the originals.

In transliterating names, we have followed the standard Library of Congress system, with the following exceptions. In cases where a customary English-language spelling already exists, that version is used: Yagoda and Yezhov, for instance, are written as such, instead of as Iagoda and Ezhov, although Evdokimov remains as Evdokimov. In addition, for simplicity's sake personal names of both well-known and lesser-known personages are throughout spelled with "ya," "yu," and "-sky" rather than "ia," "iu," and "-skii": Karpovskaya, Trotsky, Yurovsky.

Abbreviations are a special problem in the highly bureaucratized language of Soviet documents. For the most part, and for the sake of accuracy, we have left them in transliterated form with translations in brackets. A list of abbreviations with glossary appears below.

Marina Dobronovskaya
David R. Shearer

Abbreviations and Glossary of Frequently Used Terms

AP RF	Presidential Archive, Russian Federation
ASSR	Autonomous Soviet Socialist Republic
BSSR	Belorussian Soviet Socialist Republic
c., cc.	comrade(s)
Cheka	acronym for the Extraordinary Commission to Combat Counterrevolution and Sabotage, the political police during the revolutionary war years 1917–22
Chekist	political police officer
c-r, c.r.	counterrevolutionary
DVK	Far East Territory
d.	*delo* (file) (in archive cites)
EKO (EKU)	Economic Crimes Department (Administration) of the political police
f.	*fond* ("collection") (in archive cites): archive designation, approximate equivalent of U.S. "record group"
GANO	State Archive of Novosibirsk Oblast
GARF	State Archive of Russian Federation
GKO (GOKO)	State Committee of Defense
GPU	State Political Administration, under the Russian Republic Commissariat of the Interior, 1922–23: preceded the OGPU
guberniia	a province of the Russian empire, still a government unit in the first years of Bolshevik rule

GUGB	Chief Administration for State Security: political police administration, 1934–41, under the Commissariat for Internal Affairs
GULAG	Chief Administration of Camps
INO	Foreign intelligence and espionage department, successively of the GPU, OGPU, and GUGB
Kadets	Constitutional Democrats: prerevolutionary political party
Kharbintsy	"Harbin people": Soviet reimmigrants who worked for the Chinese Eastern Railway, which ended at Harbin, Manchuria
kolkhoz	collective farm
Komsomol	Communist Youth League
KP(b)U	Communist Party (Bolshevik) of Ukraine
KPSS	Communist Party of the Soviet Union
krai	administrative territory, usually larger than an oblast, and associated with frontier status; also appears here in the plural as "krai"
kraikom	Communist Party krai committee
KRO	Department of Counterintelligence, State Political Administration
OO	Special Department
kulak	"rich" peasant
l., ll.	*list, listy* (folio[s]) (in archive cites)
LVO	Leningrad Military District
MGB	Ministry of State Security, March 1946–March 1953
militsiia	"militia": civil police
m-ks	Mensheviks
MTS	machine tractor station
MVD	Ministry of Internal Affairs, renamed successor to the Commissariat for Internal Affairs, from March 1946
Narkomiust	People's Commissariat of Justice
Narkomvnudel	People's Commissariat of Internal Affairs (see NKVD)
NEP	New Economic Policy, 1921–29: mixed state-market economic system, introduced by Lenin
NKGB	People's Commissariat of State Security, February 1941–March 1946
NKID (NKIDel)	Commissariat of Foreign Affairs

NKIu, NKIust	People's Commissariat of Justice
NKPS	People's Commissariat of Transportation
NKVD	People's Commissariat of Internal Affairs of the Russian Republic, 1918–30, and All-Union Commissariat for Internal Affairs 1934–46
ob.	*oborot* (reverse) (in archive cites): reverse side of a folio
obkom	Communist Party oblast committee
oblast	government administrative unit, larger than a region (raion), smaller than a district or territory (krai)
oblispolkom	oblast soviet executive committee
OGPU	United (Combined) State Political Administration: political police, 1922–34
okrug	district, usually referring to a military administrative district
op.	*opis'* ("inventory") (in archive cites): division of archive holdings below *fond*
osadnik	Polish farmer along the Polish eastern frontier, given land for military service
Osoboe soveshchanie	Special Board: highest sentencing board of the political police
OUN	Organization of Ukrainian Nationalists
Politburo	*Politicheskoe Biuro* (Political Bureau): executive body of the Central Committee of the Communist Party
politotdel	political department: used for political police administrations in machine tractor stations and on rail lines
PP OGPU	political police plenipotentiaries
privod	police detention
Procuracy	State prosecutorial agency
Procurator	Prosecutor
raion	government administrative unit, similar to a county
RGAE	Russian State Economic Archive
RGANI	Russian State Archive of Contemporary History
RGASPI	Russian State Archive of Social and Political History
RKKA	Red Army
RKP(b)	Russian Communist Party (Bolsheviks)
RO OGPU	Region (county level) office of the political police

RSFSR	Russian Soviet Federated Socialist Republic
s/ch	secret section (archive cite)
SKK	Northern Caucasus Territory
SMERSH	"Death to Spies": Counterintelligence directorate under the Commissariat of Defense
SNK	Sovnarkom
soviet	local governing council
sovkhoz	State farm, in which farmers were paid salaries as workers
Sovmin	Council of Ministers: replaced Council of People's Commissars from March 1946
Sovnarkom	Council of People's Commissars: highest government ruling body
spetspereselentsy	"special settlers": deportees
spetsy	"specialists" (professionals)
SPO	Secret Political Department, OGPU and GUGB
SR, s-r	Socialist Revolutionary
SSSR	Union of Soviet Socialist Republics
STO	Council of Labor and Defense
TO	Transport Department, GPU, OGPU, GUGB
Troika	Nonjudicial police sentencing board
TsA FSB RF	Central Archive of the Federal Security Service, Russian Federation
TsChO	Central Black Earth Oblast
TsIK	Central Executive Committee: highest executive organ of the Soviet government
TsK	Central Committee of the Communist Party
TsKK	Central Control Commission of the Communist Party
UkSSR (USSR)	Ukrainian Soviet Socialist Republic
UNKVD	district- or oblast-level NKVD administrations
VKP(b)	All-Union Communist Party (Bolshevik)
VMN	"the highest measure of punishment" (capital punishment)
VSNKh	Supreme Economic Council
VTsIK	All-Russian Central Executive Committee: highest government executive body of the Russian Soviet Federated Socialist Republic
VTsSPS	All-Union Central Council of Trade Unions

Stalin and the Lubianka

Introduction: Stalin and the Lubianka

On 20 December 1917, the revolutionary Bolshevik government of Russia created the Extraordinary Commission to Combat Counterrevolution and Sabotage. This political police became known by its Russian initials, ChK, or Cheka. It was created as a temporary agency in the exigencies of a brutal revolutionary war, but it grew into one of the most enduring and powerful institutions of the Soviet state. Originally subordinated to the executive council of the government, its power grew as its functions expanded. At its height, the political and security police was responsible for the protection of the country's leaders and the fight against political opposition and deviation, as well as against foreign and domestic spying. Chekists, as officials of the political police were called, were also responsible for border protection, internal population control and migration, residence registration of citizens, all prisons and labor camps, and a sprawling economic empire that included extractive industries, agriculture, and construction. The labor force for that empire consisted of hundreds of thousands of convicts, all under control of the political police. The agency commanded its own militarized fighting divisions, as well as the country's border forces. At times, organized as an independent All-Union ministry, it even threatened the power of the country's ruling Communist Party. This book explores the various incarnations and functions of the Soviet political and security forces from their beginnings to the 1950s, when their role and trajectory of development changed dramatically, and they entered a new era in their history.

1

The power of the Soviet political police was not a foregone conclusion.[1] Its rise to power was neither uncontested, nor the result of
an inexorable process of expansion. The power of the political police
waxed and waned as its functions expanded and shrank. Accordingly,
its organizational structure also changed, numerous times—so many
times, in fact, that its various acronyms make for awkward and
lengthy book titles.[2] In the early 1920s, critics nearly succeeded in
disbanding it. The political police rebounded, reaching its zenith
during the 1930s and World War II. Its power was severely curtailed,
once again, in the postwar era, especially in its domestic surveillance,
carceral, and economic functions.[3]

We often think of the Soviet political police as an agency that
existed to combat real and perceived enemies, and to protect Soviet
leaders and the security of the state, and in part it did so. From its
inception, the political police was officially subordinated to the
executive organs of the Soviet government, which meant the Central
Executive Committee (TsIK), the highest executive organ of the Soviet
government, and the Council of People's Commissars (Sovnarkom).
At the same time, the government could take no action that involved
the political police without it first being discussed by the Politburo
(Political Bureau) of the ruling Communist Party. In effect, then, the
political police functioned as more than a government security agency.
It was the "fighting arm of the Party," as Feliks Dzerzhinsky, the
founder of the Cheka, declared. Iosif Stalin, the general secretary of
the Communist Party from 1922 until his death in 1953, used the
political police very much in this capacity. And, to the extent that he
perceived his own power as identical to the interests of the Party, he
used the political police to strengthen his position within the ruling
elite, and to implement the kinds of policies, both domestically and
internationally, that he believed would further the goals of the Soviet
state.

As chapter 1 shows, Stalin, as general secretary, took quiet control
early on of operational direction, information flow, and strategic
leadership of the political police. If the Soviet political police became
a state within the state, it was surely Stalin's state. If the waxing and
waning power of the political police depended on its changing functions, it was primarily Stalin who defined those functions. The history
of the Soviet political police and the history of Stalin are inseparable.
The growth of police authority and prestige depended on Stalin's patronage and his use of it to achieve his goal of personal dictatorship,
and to implement policies that he believed furthered the interests of

Soviet power. Conversely, Stalin relied on the political police, first and foremost, to secure his undisputed power. In other words, Stalin's rise to power, and his dictatorship, cannot be understood apart from the history of the Soviet political police, and the development and power of the political police cannot be understood apart from Stalin's rise to power.

To say that Stalin's personal involvement had a profound effect on the way the police operated is not to say that the various heads of the police were passive. Each head placed his mark on the agency, especially in personnel choices, each bringing in his own "clan," administrative organization, and operational culture. Feliks Dzerzhinsky was a powerful Party leader in his own right. He fought relentlessly to maintain and expand the authority of the police throughout the period of budget and personnel cuts of the early 1920s. He fully supported and helped Stalin in strengthening the authority and scope of practice of the police, and he died before coming into serious conflict with Stalin. V. R. Menzhinsky, chosen by Dzerzhinsky as a deputy, was a cultured, even an effete man, often sickly, but still ruthless. Despite his debilitating bouts of angina, Menzhinsky masterminded some of the most successful Soviet espionage campaigns of the 1920s, and he scripted and stage-managed the first major show trials under Stalin in the late 1920s and 1930s.[4] Increasingly ill, Menzhinsky ceded many of his duties in the late 1920s and early 1930s to his deputy, Genrikh Yagoda. Yagoda, then Nikolai Yezhov, were competent administrators, but they were Stalin's creatures, even though Yagoda had originally been promoted by Dzerzhinsky. Yagoda and Yezhov did Stalin's bidding, and when they outlived their usefulness, or became a perceived threat, Stalin rid himself of them. In 1951, Stalin also executed A. S. Abakumov, whom he had appointed in 1946 to head the Ministry of State Security. As with Yagoda and Yezhov, Stalin concocted a conspiracy that implicated Abakumov and led to his arrest and death. Lavrentii Beria, the last of the state security heads under Stalin, proved a wary survivor of Stalin's machinations. He managed to outlive Stalin, as did his protégé, V. N. Merkulov, also head of state security during several years in World War II. Both Beria and Merkulov, however, were arrested and executed in 1953 as part of the power struggle among Stalin's successors in the ruling group of the Communist Party.[5]

During the late 1920s and the 1930s, as documents in chapters 2 and 3 reveal, the power of the political police in the Soviet Union grew rapidly during Stalin's dictatorial regime. Most histories explain

this power of the police during the 1930s as the consequence of Stalin's intensifying policies of political repression and of his personal
penchant to see enemies everywhere. Certainly, political repression
intensified under Stalin's style of personal despotism, but historians'
fixation on political forms of repression misses much of what the
political police actually did during the 1930s. As the documents in the
following chapters show, it expanded its jurisdiction and functions
during the 1920s and 1930s in a number of different areas. These
included revolutionary transformation of the countryside, social
order in urban areas, ethnic cleansing and border protection, residence and migration control, and forced labor policing.

The scope and scale of police activities expanded dramatically in the
very first years of the 1930s, during the collectivization drives. These
campaigns were designed to end private farming, and to bring arable
farm lands under state control. Farms and villages were gathered
together into large administrative units under Party and police control
as collective or state farms. Official propaganda described this process
as one of socialist reconstruction of rural life, and resistance was attributed to capitalist class hostility. Peasants who resisted were called kulaks
and, as part of the process of collectivization, they were "dekulakized."
Peasants' property was confiscated, and those identified as kulaks
were arrested and deported, or shot. As Lynne Viola and others have
described, resistance was widespread, and state violence brutal and systematic in response. Official propaganda described the violence of the
collectivization campaigns in terms of class war, but collectivization, as
chapter 3 shows, amounted to a broad social war to bring the countryside under the regime's control. During that war, the political police, the
OGPU, engaged in large-scale operations of mass suppression, arrest,
and deportation, aimed against the country's rural inhabitants.[6]

These campaigns of mass repression were part of a process designed
to extend state power into the countryside, and to eradicate, either
by shooting or by deportation, social opposition to Soviet power
among the country's peasantry. Once inaugurated, however, this revolutionary war mutated into a protracted and insidious social war on
a broad scale. Stalin's industrial revolution and class war in the countryside created social dislocation on an apocalyptic scale. Widespread
dispossession of property, wholesale deportations, and forced population migration characterized the early years of the 1930s. Dispossessed and often starving, hundreds of thousands of peasants and
other rural inhabitants, as well as those in former professional classes,
took to the rail lines and roads and streamed into and through the

cities and industrial sites. Famine conditions in the early 1930s and severe shortages of all goods, due to Stalin's industrial priorities, exacerbated the movement of masses of people—to escape famine-stricken areas, to find food and other necessities, to avoid political discrimination, to seek a better life, even just to survive. This unorganized movement of people drained economic resources and threatened to overwhelm the underdeveloped infrastructure of the cities and the social stability of the country. Large numbers of indigents and itinerants, criminals, unemployed youth, gypsies, the disenfranchised, and a range of other groups added to these mass migrations. Social displacement on such a scale heightened criminality and social disorder, and posed an imminent danger to the state and the goals of socialist construction.

The regime's policies created widespread social disorder, but the Soviet state possessed inadequate resources to deal with it. Social agencies were weak and quickly overwhelmed, and the state's civil policing agencies also experienced difficulty coping with the problems that suddenly confronted them. As a result, the country's leaders turned to the political police to bring order to the country. Under the command of Stalin's police chief Genrikh Yagoda, and with Stalin's backing, the political police expanded operational and administrative authority to take over institutions and problems of social governance, one after another—migration and trade, indigence, the unemployed, civil and residence registration and census taking, orphan children and related problems of juvenile delinquency, and a massive wave of petty criminality. Chapter 4 documents this political police involvement in social governance.

As political police were drawn deeper into upholding social order, they incorporated and subordinated the civil police in an attempt to create an integrated system of surveillance and control of the population. Encroachment of political police into areas of civil governance was not entirely new in the 1930s, but the scale of intervention during the 1930s was unprecedented for a peacetime period. This conflation of public order with state security was unique to the Stalinist era and fundamentally reshaped the repressive policies of the Soviet regime.[7] More than that, the forced removal, redistribution, or elimination of suspect populations reached a level of mass social engineering that was also unique to the Stalinist era. Neither in the 1920s, nor after Stalin's death in 1953, did the Soviet regime employ methods of mass police repression to try to maintain social order, or to restructure the social, ethnic, and territorial boundaries of the country.

There was an incremental logic to the escalating use of police and repression. Once Stalin used force, Stalin needed force. He began the decade with a state-sponsored revolutionary war in the countryside, but he then needed increasingly ubiquitous force to deal with the massive social dislocation and crises that resulted from the industrial and agrarian chaos of the early 1930s. Reading the successive documents in this collection gives a sense of a regime not so much building socialism by plan, but lurching from one crisis to another, each caused by official policies, but each unanticipated by the country's leaders. Given the concomitant breakdown of civil governance, it is understandable how police authority flowed in to fill the vacuum left by an undergoverned state and a fragmented and increasingly ungovernable society.[8]

Incrementalism notwithstanding, the merging of political and civil police and the conflation of state security and social order were not just the result of cumulative circumstances. There was an ideological basis for the politicization of social order, and it came about with Stalin's 1933 declaration of victory in the struggle to win the class war against socialism and Soviet power. In the plenary meetings of the Party's Central Committee of that year, Stalin declared that with the successful completion of his industrialization and agrarian policies, the socialist offensive had succeeded, the remnants of capitalism had been routed, and the victory of socialism had been assured. With that pronouncement, definitions of deviancy, criminality, or other unacceptable forms of behavior changed. If crime and deviancy could be accepted and even tolerated as part of the compromise with capitalism of the 1920s, such tolerance was no longer possible after Stalin's announcement of socialist victory. As the documents in chapter 4 show, social disorder could be explained as nothing else but class hostility toward the new Soviet order, and as sabotage of Stalin's grand project to build socialism. And in Stalin's famous dictum, the forces of disorder would intensify the further the country moved along the road to socialism, which, in turn, justified and required the increasing use of force and police authority. As the reproduction of Stalin's speech shows, the merging of political and civil policing functions resulted from more than the logic of historical circumstances. The ideology of socialist victory made social order a major priority of state security, and a part of the operational sphere of the political police during the 1930s.[9]

In 1934, in accordance with the broadened scope of OGPU activities, the political police was reorganized into a different organization, a

Chief Administration for State Security (*Glavnoe Upravlenie Gosudarstvennoi Bezopasnosti*), or GUGB. In turn, the GUGB was incorporated as the main administration into a new central state Commissariat for Internal Affairs, the NKVD (*Narodnyi Kommissariat Vnutrennykh Del*). The civil police, the *militsiia* (*Glavnoe Upravlenie Rabochekrest'ianskoi Militsii*, GURKM) was subordinated to the GUGB within the NKVD. Documents in chapter 4 follow this reorganization.

It is tempting to call what Stalin created a police state, but this is not an entirely accurate characterization. Although powerful, police and policing policies remained under the control of Stalin and the small group of ruling elite of the Communist Party. What evolved during the 1930s might be more appropriately called martial law socialism, or, literally, militarized socialism. "Militarization" (*voennizatsiia*) was the term that Yagoda and others used to describe the integration of the civil and political police, and it is an appropriate description. The merging of the two did, indeed, "militarize" the civil police, as well as bring the political police into the arena of social governance.[10] Specifically, this merging created a kind of militarized social gendarmerie, similar, in some ways, to the kinds of gendarme forces that existed in Russia prior to the Revolution, and which operated in European states during the nineteenth and early twentieth centuries. As documents in chapter 4 show, the task of Stalin's political and civil police was to maintain political and, more broadly, social order in the country.[11]

As the functions of the political police expanded, so did its numbers. Beginning with collectivization, the police never again under Stalin worried about cuts in budget or personnel. Both expanded, though never fast enough to keep pace with the increasing operational burdens. Systematic increases in numbers are difficult to document, and even more difficult to analyze for what they include and exclude, but documents give some idea of the expansion in police numbers and budgets, and in what areas, during the early and mid-1930s. As these documents show, high police officials put significant effort into reducing the top-heavy character of central police administration and strengthening the operational effectiveness of local police networks. Documents also show that police spent much time and effort attempting to perfect secret techniques of broad social surveillance. Although civil police administered the internal passport system, inaugurated in 1933, the political police utilized it to gather and catalog information about broad segments of the population. Similarly, they attempted to integrate material gathered from informant networks to augment surveillance, with the information compiled into registry catalogs (*kartoteki*). Neither the passport nor the informant system worked as effectively as police heads hoped. The informant system, in particular, proved ineffective, and state control surveys of police catalogs revealed many gaps and inadequacies. Still, as the documents in chapter 4 reveal, police during the 1930s moved from being an agency that targeted real or potential political opponents to an agency that attempted to develop surveillance systems to track and account for the whole of the population.

Developing technologies of mass surveillance went hand in hand with active shaping of the population through mass actions, such as deportations, the creation of restrictive settlements and regions, and the control of geographic space through restrictions on migration, residence registration, and work. Police enforced such restrictions mainly through the passport system, but political and civil police also engaged in specially approved campaigns of mass deportation of suspect populations in border zones and other strategic areas such as industrial and major urban centers, and even in resort areas of the political elite. In this way, the police came to play a significant role in forming the geographic as well as social and ethnic construction of Soviet socialism during the 1930s.

As documents in chapter 4 show, much of the activity of the police during the middle years of the 1930s revolved around forms of mass social and ethnic repression—the struggle against so-called social aliens and anti-Soviet elements—and in developing techniques of mass surveillance. The assassination of Sergei Kirov, the Leningrad party chief, in December 1934 altered police operational priorities. Police did not abandon social order forms of policing or mass forms of repression and surveillance, but, pressured by political leaders, Stalin in particular, police became increasingly consumed by, and then obsessed with, a frenzied hunt for spies, saboteurs, agents of hostile foreign powers, and conspiratorial organizations plotting to overthrow the Soviet regime. All these "enemies of the people" were supposedly linked to Stalin's former rivals, Leon Trotsky, Nikolai Bukharin, Grigorii Zinoviev, and others. Shaken by Kirov's assassination, Stalin unleashed and drove forward a relentless hunt for hidden enemies and conspirators. His focus became so obsessive that it overwhelmed and subsumed other state priorities, and led the Politburo to codify his fears in a new set of statutes for the political police. The new statutes, approved in April 1935, focused the chief task of the police on the struggle against "treason, spying, counterrevolution, terror, wrecking, subversive acts, and other antistate crimes ..."[12] This new directive did not entirely supplant Stalin's 1933 emphasis on socially alien and anti-Soviet social elements, but linked the social order campaigns to ever more urgent and ever more deadly political priorities.

As documents in chapter 5 reveal, through 1935 and into 1936 and 1937, political police investigations of supposedly conspiratorial organizations gained momentum and affected every branch of the state, the economy, the military, and cultural and social institutions. Purges, arrests, and interrogations followed by the hundreds and then the thousands as each purge, each arrest, each interrogation revealed an ever widening network of conspirators and secret oppositionists. Communist Party organizations were not immune from this spiral of suspicion and violence, as the police engaged in a systematic review of all card-holding members and all former members. The Politburo was careful to remind police not to act arbitrarily against Party members, and to work closely with local leaders, but this was a formality. Stalin was convinced that the Party was riddled with secret oppositionists, and directed police purges to investigate particular Party heads and whole organizations. No Party member was immune. Moreover, by decree of 27 July 1936, police no longer needed Party sanction or review to appoint investigators to local posts. Although some state prosecutors (*prokurory*) still challenged the legality of police methods, they too were subject to accusation and investigation if they interfered too much. By the end of 1936, the political police was nearing its zenith of power as an institution answerable to no one but Stalin.

With the political police protected by and working under Stalin's direct supervision, its power was unassailable, but that was not true of individual police officials. By the end of 1936, Stalin had grown suspicious of his own political police chief, Yagoda. Documents in chapters 5 and 6 depict Yagoda's fall from grace and power, the purge of his entourage, and his replacement by Nikolai Yezhov and a new cadre of officials. Despite the partial opening of archives, the reasons for Yagoda's purge are still unclear, although Yezhov's intrigues no doubt contributed to Stalin's suspicions. In the end, we can only accept at face value that Stalin, for his own reasons, truly believed that Yagoda had failed in his duties, and that he was connected with oppositionists, agents of foreign powers, and other anti-Soviet plots.[13]

The year 1936 brought not only an escalation in police activity and violence, but also the first of the three great Moscow show trials. More trials followed in 1937, both public and secret, and the final major trial of old Party leaders, and of Yagoda, in 1938. Yezhov headed the police apparatus from December 1936 until his own fall from power in late 1938, but during his two short years of tenure, Yezhov oversaw some of the bloodiest purges of the entire Stalinist era. These included not only arrests of so-called enemies, but widespread mass purges of certain categories of the population, among them various ethnic groups that the regime regarded as potentially hostile because of cross-border ties—what Terry Martin has called enemy nations within Soviet borders.[14]

Explaining the mass purges of the late 1930s is a problem, of course, since there is little documentation about their origins, and they directly contradicted the line put forward by Stalin's new head of police, Nikolai Yezhov, beginning in late 1936, to move the NKVD away from social policing functions.[15] There are many explanations that have recently been put forward, but the one that still makes the most sense is that put forward by Oleg Khlevniuk, namely that Stalin was increasingly convinced of a coming invasion. In that event, the Soviet leader feared an insurgency uprising among disaffected populations in the Soviet Union, which would repeat the success of insurgency movements in Spain that helped bring about the military defeat of the Loyalist forces. This is the well-known fifth column argument, and it is the only argument that makes sense of both the timing and the level of violence of the mass purges.[16]

Each of these supposed threats—class opposition, social disorder, underground political subversion, and national contamination—had generated separate political responses and operational policies throughout the 1930s. These concerns and policy lines converged in the great purges. By 1937, leaders were convinced that oppositionists, working with foreign agents, were actively organizing socially disaffected populations into an insurgency movement. Leaders worried that invasion, which seemed increasingly likely in the late 1930s, would be the signal for armed uprisings by these groups, as well as by purportedly disaffected ethnic minorities. Indeed, the threat of war was the final and key element, and it gave the mass purges their particular political urgency and virulence.

Domestic as well as international factors contributed to the organization of mass purges, and the documents in chapter 6 show the growing concern of leaders, especially at local levels, about renewed assertions of rights by groups regarded as potentially troublesome. Key here were returning kulaks, freed en masse in 1935 and 1936, after serving sentences in penal colonies. Officially banned from leaving their regions of exile, kulak peasants nonetheless found their way back to their home districts in large numbers, and demanded restitution of property and rights. Emboldened also were other marginal groups, especially clerical and religious ones, who believed, and rightly so, that the new constitution, promulgated in 1936, gave them protection from persecution. A new census process was begun in late 1936 and 1937, and the results shocked both local and national leaders by the impoverished and primitive conditions in which much of the population lived. Speeches at the Party's February and March 1937 plenum reveal a sense close to that of being besieged, and this sense gained urgency, not only in conditions of prewar tension, but also because of upcoming elections to a new national ruling body, the Supreme Soviet. There is no doubt that Stalin was secure in his political power, but for a number of reasons, leaders became convinced that a mass purge of the population was necessary and urgent.

The documents in chapter 6 lay bare the mechanisms and the phases of both the social and the nationality operations. They also show the haste that characterized the operations' preparation and execution. Only several weeks separated the first announcement of a general social purge, on 2 July 1937, and the onset of the purge process in late July and early August. During that time, and throughout the operations, central and local officials negotiated up and down the numbers to be purged, and in which category they were to be placed— the most dangerous to be shot, others to be sent to camps or exile. In the hectic weeks of July, meetings were arranged, briefings held, operational groups assembled, and sentencing boards, troikas, were named. As the documents show, these operations were monitored and controlled from the center, primarily by Stalin, but also by Yezhov. Nonetheless, purging was a chaotic as well as a bloody business, and the haste with which operations were implemented intensified the inherent chaos. Central authorities spent much time reprimanding and even removing and arresting local leaders either for lack of diligence or for overstepping their purge limits.[17]

The nationality operations overlapped and followed on from the mass social operations.[18] The latter peaked in December 1937 and early 1938, while the former intensified throughout 1938. Using a Politburo order, Stalin brought the mass operations to a halt on 17 November 1938, and soon after, the Politburo nullified the various operational orders that covered the purges. By this time, Stalin had already removed Yezhov and appointed a new political police head, Lavrentii Beria, who in turn oversaw the purge of Yezhov's command, and most of the major officers who had carried out the previous operations. This purge was carried out under the pretext of the illegality of the entire process and, unbelievably, on the basis of charges that Yezhov, and those around him, had operated as foreign agents dedicated to the subversion of the Soviet regime. In other words, Yezhov's command was purged for exactly the same reasons as Yagoda and his staff.

Beginning in 1939, Stalin and the Politburo reasserted the primacy of the Party and Procuracy organs in supervising the work of the NKVD, and in reviewing appointments at all levels. Procuracy officials, in turn, began to conduct mass reviews of sentencing and investigative practices from 1937 and 1938, but Stalin did not go from one extreme to another. Although Beria conducted a significant purge of the political police leaders, he also defended local organs against what he regarded as excessive interference by Procuracy officials, and from retribution by Party organs. Similarly, Stalin had to strike a delicate balance of relations between the military and the security police, and the police and the Party, since animosity ran high against the NKVD. Documents in chapter 7 reveal Stalin's attempt to reestablish a working governmental system after the great purges.

Mass repression by political police did not end with the great purges, of course, but campaigns targeted different populations after 1938, as documents in chapters 7 and 8 show. Categorical forms of mass deportations, for example, continued to hit ethnic communities hard inside the pre–1939 borders of the country, as they did in the new territories annexed in 1939 and reoccupied after 1945. Mass administrative repression of "socially dangerous populations" also continued in the new territories. In the occupied Baltic republics and in the post–1939 western border regions of Ukraine and Belorussia, security forces and civil police carried out the same kinds of mass social and political repression that had been characteristic of the mid–1930s.[19] Inside the country's pre–1939 borders, however, the role of the security forces shifted during and after the war years. Instead of mass social repression of "anti-Soviet elements," the NKVD returned to more traditional tasks of spying (abroad as well as domestically), seeking out supposed political enemies of the regime, and on expanded tasks of monitoring economic sectors and enterprises, especially in those supplying defense needs. Dealing with criminals, social marginals, and other supposedly "anti-Soviet elements" became, as it had been in the 1920s, the domain of the civil police, the *militsiia*, and fell under civil law jurisdiction rather than under the extrajudicial political powers of the state's security organs.

By the beginning of 1941, the NKVD was an unwieldy commissariat. It functioned as a state security organization, a major economic administration, an investigative organization, a social policing force, and a domestic surveillance organization. It protected borders, administered the civil police, oversaw a massive labor camp and colony system, and operated as an international espionage agency. The NKVD had indeed become Stalin's state within the state. Despite its size and power, however, the NKVD had suffered from the great purges in an analogous manner to the institutions that it had purged. The arrest of Yezhov and the purge of the command and operational structures had left the agency in disarray. This was especially true of its espionage systems abroad. Stories of individual spies, such as Viktor Sorge, operating in Japan, are well known, even legendary, but the regular networks in countries such as France, Germany, Britain, Canada, and the United States lacked staff and agents. Soviet spy networks had collapsed, and this left Moscow without a workable intelligence system. Counterespionage activities of foreign governments could not have disrupted Soviet intelligence gathering any more successfully than Stalin's purges. In order to streamline administration, and to rebuild an effective system, Beria recommended to Stalin a major overhaul, to separate operational sectors into a separate administration. Creation of a Commissariat of State Security (NKGB), separate from the Commissariat of Internal Affairs, the NKVD, occurred in February 1941. The newly proposed NKGB encompassed the state security organs, while the civil police remained within the NKVD.

Reorganization of the security agencies occurred almost on the eve of war. And while Stalin received reports of German intentions to invade the Soviet Union, he dismissed these as part of a British disinformation campaign designed to goad the USSR into a war with Germany. Stalin expected war, and he continued to build the country's military readiness at an intensive pace, but he knew none of the specifics of Hitler's Barbarossa plan of invasion, which came about on 22 June 1941. In October 1941, Stalin and the Politburo leaders reunited the internal and security commissariats, and postponed reorganization until 1943. In that year, the security organs were once again separated into a separate commissariat, the NKGB, while the civil police remained in the NKVD.

Many of the activities of the security police during the war are documented in chapter 7, especially the mass deportations of different nationalities and the infamous slaughter of Polish military personnel and other prisoners in 1940.[20] Stalin also relied on the security forces to purge territories in front of advancing or retreating German troops, and to round up and imprison or execute deserters from the Soviet military forces. Beria, as head of the NKVD and the Politburo member most concerned with security forces, kept Stalin informed about all the activities of the police and paramilitary security units. As the tide of the war turned, and as Soviet forces moved across Soviet borders, militarized security units followed, purging territories freed from German occupation. In the reoccupied Baltic and western border regions, as documents in chapters 7 and 8 show, Soviet security forces encountered serious armed opposition, which continued in these areas well into the postwar years. Opposition was so strong that special internal forces of the civil police and the NKVD were reintegrated under command of the state security agency, the NKGB. In 1946, this commissariat, like all commissariats, was renamed as a ministry, the Ministry of State Security (MGB), while the NKVD was renamed the Ministry of Internal Affairs (MVD). Suppressing resistance, purging, and sovietizing the new republics and the western border areas of Ukraine and Belorussia became a major preoccupation of both Soviet leaders and the state's security forces.[21]

As documents in chapter 8 show, much of the purging of new territories was carried out in the same way as the mass social operations of 1937 and 1938, but inside the 1939 borders of the Soviet Union, state security forces did not generally engage in the kind of politicized social policing and repression that characterized the prewar years. This is not to say that mass repression ended. On the contrary, it shifted focus and purpose. Millions of people found themselves under arrest and then convicted for infractions of labor discipline, antitheft, and other harsh laws associated with Stalin's extractive policies of economic reconstruction. However, these people were convicted by judicial courts rather than by police administrative boards, and for specific violations of laws rather than for potential disloyalty based on a suspect social or ethnic background. In the realm of social politics, people were repressed for what they did rather than who they were.

After the war, Stalin and other leaders employed political police methods—the kind of secret, extrajudicial policing that dominated the 1930s—primarily in the country's new territories, as well as in some regions of the Caucasus. In these areas, leaders perceived that the security of the state was at risk, as local authorities faced serious insurgency movements against Soviet rule all along the country's new borders. Inside the pre–1939 territories, in contrast, leaders depoliticized social order policing and the fight against criminality, even as they increased the role of civil police and courts in the effort to exert a kind of social and economic discipline over the population.

This shift in policies of repression reflected reforms designed to separate civil from political policing. In the postwar years, a series of bureaucratic reorganizations hived off the civil police from the state security organs and placed the former under the Ministry of the Interior, the MVD, which also operated most of the regime's labor camps. The state security ministry, MGB, operated only a new series of special regime camps for political prisoners. To those sentenced to prisons, camps, colonies, or penal settlements, the difference maybe mattered little between being arrested by political or civil police. But there was a difference, and a significant one. Social policing during the postwar years was not nearly as deadly as it was in the 1930s, and this change reflected a general demilitarization of the social sphere, if not a reduction in the numbers of people who experienced the coercive power of the state. So, the goal, and therefore the methods, of policing changed from the 1930s to the postwar years. No longer was social policing aimed at isolating or eliminating enemies of the state. Instead, leaders employed mass coercion to discipline a society in the service of the goals of state economic reconstruction.

Documents in the final chapter highlight the mechanisms of these changes, as well as the ongoing tensions between military intelligence organs and the state security departments assigned to monitor the military. As well, this chapter reveals the role played by the security police in Stalin's last major purge campaigns, especially that against Leningrad Party leaders, and the role of the MGB in the intensifying anti-Zionist and anti-Semitic policies and purges under Stalin. These policies culminated in the infamous Doctors' Plot, a fictitious plot by Kremlin physicians, most of whom were Jewish, supposedly to murder Stalin.

It is not clear how Stalin intended to use the last conspiracies that he concocted. The dictator died in the first week of March 1953, and his successors quickly dropped the fiction of the Doctors' Plot. Within weeks, they also acted, once again, to purge the security police, this time ridding themselves of Beria and dismantling the security organ's empire, subordinating it once and for all to the collective leadership of the Party and the government.

As the documents in this book attest, the history of Soviet state political and security organs is incontrovertibly tied to the history of Iosif Stalin and his rule. As such, this book is not just a story about police and repression; it is also a history of Stalinism, and a history of the Soviet Union in the first half of the twentieth century.

CHAPTER ONE

Expanding Power, Infiltrating the State
1922–1927

L ate in the evening of 24 October 1917, detachments of armed revolutionaries seized key points in Russia's capital city, Petrograd. The detachments operated under the authority of the Socialist Revolutionary Council of Workers, Soldiers, and Peasants. In fact, these revolutionary guards took orders from leaders of the major faction in the Council, the Bolshevik faction, especially Vladimir Lenin and Leon Trotsky. The actions of the guards on that October night deposed the weak provisional government, and Lenin and the Bolsheviks moved quickly to consolidate governmental power in their hands. The next day, Lenin announced the formation of an almost exclusively Bolshevik government, the beginning of a dictatorship. Lenin's actions precipitated a revolutionary war that the Bolsheviks managed not only to survive, but to win against considerable odds. They were able to hold and extend their power for a number of reasons, one of which was the formation and ruthless actions of the Cheka, the Extraordinary Commission to Combat Counterrevolution and Sabotage. Under Lenin's orders, the Cheka carried out systematic policies of "Red terror," that is, summary executions, against suspected enemies of the regime. The agency grew in size and number and became the "fighting arm" of the Bolshevik Party and government.

By spring 1921, the Bolshevik regime had defeated organized military opposition, but faced a range of difficult problems. After years of war, famine was killing millions of people, mass migration was emptying cities, and a militarized economy could not produce goods for civilian life. While the Bolsheviks had maintained political power primarily through military force, they ruled over a chaotic, nearly nonexistent state; the government had no constitutional form. Faced with these problems, Lenin and the Bolshevik Central Committee now had to manage the transition from a wartime to a peacetime government, economy, and society. This transition, begun in spring 1921, came to be known as the New Economic Policy, or NEP. It involved a dismantling of the nationalized and militarized war economy of the Civil War era, and creation of a mixed market and state-run economy. As a "partial retreat" from War Communism, the NEP also required the reintroduction of a money economy instead of state rationing, and this transition not only impoverished many people, it also placed economic and even state institutions in dire financial straits.

The Cheka Reborn

Among other issues, the transition to NEP required the demobilization of millions of fighting soldiers. The transition from a revolutionary government also raised the question of the Cheka. It had been created as an extraordinary institution in a time of revolutionary war. By contrast, NEP involved a partial relaxation of repression, and an attempt to create a legal structure appropriate for a socialist society at peace. What role would an extraordinary organ of revolutionary justice play in this new era? Was it needed, still? Should it take a different form? The defeat of the revolution's enemies left the agency with no further function, according to critics, especially under a government that had fought to overthrow a tyrannical police state. Those critics were no minor figures, but important Bolshevik leaders such as Nikolai Bukharin, one of the original revolutionary leaders, and one of the strong supporters of NEP. Other critics included the finance commissar, Georgii Sokol'nikov, and the justice commissar, Dmitrii Kursky.[1]

In 1922, these three, along with strong supporters of the Cheka including Iosif Unshlikht, its deputy head, and Iosif Stalin, the newly appointed general secretary of the Communist Party, were enjoined by the Politburo to form a commission that would eliminate the Cheka and reorganize it as a "political administration" under control of the governing state body, the Council of People's Commissars (Sovnarkom). At the local administrative level of the raion, this new political police was to be subordinated to the local Soviet government councils and, at the center, both to Sovnarkom and to VTsIK, the Central Executive Committee of the Russian Republic Supreme Soviet. These latter organs formed the main branch of the government. VTsIK was the chief governmental council of the Russian Soviet state and, formally at least, separate from the Communist Party.

The charter statutes of this new political administration redefined the name, image, and function of the Cheka. As the following documents show, the new State Political Administration (GPU) also retained broad powers, including the right to establish, or continue, extra-judicial sentencing boards.

DOCUMENT

· 1 ·

Note from I. S. Unshlikht to V. M. Molotov on delivery to the Politburo of statutes of the GPU, its province-level and transport departments, and its district-level plenipotentiaries. AP RF, f. 3, op. 58, d. 2, ll. 49–62.

6 March 1922

Herewith are attached 3 copies, confirmed by the commission, for the Politburo session: 1st, Statute of the Gospolitupravlenie (GPU); 2nd, Statute of province-level departments of the GPU; 3rd, Statute of transport departments of the GPU; 4th, Statute of district [*uezdnykh*] plenipotentiaries of province-level departments of the GPU. Statute of special departments of the GPU, sent to comrade Skliansky for agreement.

[...]

Deputy chairman of the GPU Unshlikht
Confirmed by the commission
22.1.22.

In addition, and for further development of VTsIK decision from 6 February 1922, the following was confirmed:

Statute of the State Political Administration (GPU)

I. General provisions

1. The State Political Administration (in abbreviated form, GPU) is subordinated to the NKVD [People's Commissariat of Internal Affairs].
2. The chairman of the GPU is the people's commissar of internal affairs or his deputy, appointed by SNK [Sovnarkom].
3. A Collegium under the chairman of the GPU, members of which are to be appointed by SNK, will resolve major issues and determine directions of work, as well as questions that require coordination between departments.
4. In order to accomplish goals assigned to the GPU, it will organize local offices:

a) Province-level departments of the GPU subordinated to the GIKs [executive committees of provincial soviets];
b) Oblast departments of the GPU subordinated to TsIKs of autonomous republics and oblasts;
c) Special departments of the GPU for military fronts, military districts, and armies; special departments for border protection units;
d) Transport departments of the GPU for railroads and waterways;
e) Plenipotentiary representatives of the GPU for unifying, leading, and coordinating work of local offices of outlying territories, and in autonomous republics and oblasts.

5. The GPU is an institution with strictly centralized management. It has the same rights as operating units of the Red Army in terms of using railroads and waterways, and state communication facilities (telegraph, telephone and radio communication); receiving supplies of rations and uniforms for its employees; and other advantages connected to this Statute (according to the decision of the STO [Council of Labor and Defense] from 17 September 1920).
6. All permanent employees of the GPU and its local organs are considered on active military duty and carry all the rights, duties, and advantages connected with that status.
7. Budget estimates of the GPU are to be affirmed by SNK; all estimates of local organs are to be included and affirmed within the general estimate of the GPU.
8. The GPU has at its disposal special forces, which are organized into a free-standing Army of the State Political Administration, and which are fully subordinated to the chairman of the State Political Administration. The strength of the army is to be determined by the STO. [...]

II. Goals of the State Political Administration

10. Goals of the GPU are:

a) Prevention and suppression of open counterrevolutionary actions (both political and economic);
b) Struggle against any kind of banditry and armed revolts;
c) Struggle against obviously criminal relations of employees toward their duties, as well as uncovering counterrevolutionary organizations and persons whose activities are directed toward undermining economic organs of the Republic;
d) Protection of state secrets and struggle against espionage in all of its forms (surveillance, wrecking, political, military, and economic);
e) Protection of railroads and waterways, struggle against theft of cargoes and against crimes that have goals of destroying transportation facilities or reducing the carrying capacity of transportation;

f)   Political protection of borders of the RSFSR, struggle against both economic and political contraband, and illegal border crossing;

g)   Implementation of special tasks, assigned by VTsIK and SNK, to protect revolutionary order.

III. Means to accomplish assigned tasks

11. In order to accomplish its tasks, the GPU is authorized to engage in the following activities: Use of informants, search and seizure, surveillance, arrest, confiscation, interrogation, preliminary investigative activities, and [surveillance] registration of individuals:

a)   Collection and communication of any information, political or economic, to appropriate state organizations, which may be relevant to the task of fighting counterrevolution.

b)   Agent surveillance of criminal or suspicious individuals, groups, or organizations within the territory of the RSFSR, and outside its borders.

c)   Issuing of exit and entrance permits to the RSFSR to foreign and Russian citizens;

d)   Deportation of unreliable foreign citizens from the RSFSR;

e)   Reading correspondence, both internal and foreign;
[...]

h)   Registration of persons apprehended or suspected of criminal activity and their affairs; registration of unreliable administrative and supervising personnel of state institutions, industrial enterprises, and command and administrative structures of the Red Army.

Statistical and political development of [surveillance] registry data. Registration and summarizing of abnormal phenomena of life in the RSFSR, in order to understand the reasons for, and consequences of, such phenomena.

12. The People's Commissariat of Justice is responsible for general oversight of the legality of actions of the GPU and its local bodies.

"Confirmed" 24.II.–22 Enukidze, Krylenko, Unshlikht
"Confirmed" 5.II.–22 Stalin, Kamenev, Kursky, Unshlikht

As the GPU charter noted, the new political administration came under control of Sovnarkom, as well as of VTsIK, which bodies appointed, or confirmed the appointment, of the agency's personnel. At the same time, the Party did not lose control over the GPU, the Politburo passing a secret rider that ensured its primacy over matters of the political police:

DOCUMENT

· 2 ·

Decision of the Politburo of TsK RKP(b) [Political Bureau of
the Central Committee of the Russian Communist Party (of Bolsheviks)].
On coordination of decisions of the Presidium of VtsIK, related to
the State Political Administration, with the Politburo. RGASPI, f. 17,
op. 3, d. 266, l. 5.
15 February 1922

Strictly confidential
No. 97, point 15-s—On coordination of the decisions of the Presidium
of VtsIK, related to the State Political Administration, with the Politburo.
(cc. [comrades] Enukidze, Unshlikht).
To charge c. Enukidze with personal responsibility to ensure that no
questions related to the State Political Administration be resolved by the
Presidium of VTsIK without preliminary approval by the Politburo.

Feliks Dzerzhinsky remained head of the GPU, and Unshlikht stayed
on as his active and energetic deputy. In several further riders, the
Politburo gave the GPU expanded authority to deal with banditry and
to strengthen civil police, drawing the latter under the influence if not
the administration of the political administration. From the beginning, then, political police became increasingly drawn into the sphere
of civil governance, due to the underdevelopment of Soviet institutions. This was to become a common pattern. Given the weakness of
civil police and the burden on the judicial system, leaders turned increasingly to the political police.

DOCUMENT

· 3 ·

Decision of the Politburo of TsK RKP(b). On extraordinary powers of the
GPU for struggle against banditry. RGASPI, f. 17, op. 3, d. 290. l. 4.
27 April 1922

On granting the GPU the right of immediate execution of bandit
elements at the place of a crime (c. Unshlikht's proposal) [...]

a) To authorize the GPU to execute bandit elements (i.e. partici-
    pants of armed robberies) captured at the moment of their crim-
    inal action, at the place of the crime.

b) To entrust the commission consisting of cc. Kursky, Krylenko, Kalinin, and Unshlikht with the juridical formulation of this decision on behalf of the Presidium of VTsIK.

c) To entrust the same commission with the juridical formulation of a decision to grant the GPU the right to exile criminal elements. [....]

DOCUMENT

· 4 ·

Note from I. S. Unshlikht to I. V. Stalin on additions to Statutes of the State Political Administration. AP RF, f. 3, op. 58, d. 2, l. 92.
10 May 1922

Considering the impossibility of resolving a whole variety of cases through legal procedures, and, at the same time, the necessity to rid ourselves of brazen and harmful elements, the State Political Administration suggests the following additions to our Statutes:

"In addition to and for further development of the Statute of the State Political Administration of the Republic, from 6 February 1922, to empower the State Political Administration with the following rights:

a) administrative exile to certain provinces for a term of up to two years for anti-Soviet activity, participation in espionage, banditry, and counterrevolution;

b) administrative deportation, outside the RSFSR borders, of ill-intentioned Russian and foreign citizens for a term of up to two years."

This decision should be published by the Presidium of VTsIK, so that deportation abroad would guarantee us from unwarranted return of the deportee. Simultaneously with the VTsIK decision, NKIu [the People's Commissariat of Justice] should add to the criminal code a statute on punishment for entering Russia without proper cause. I would think, up to two years in prison for illegal entrance, but if the purpose of entering is clearly counterrevolutionary—then all the way up to capital punishment.

Deputy chairman of the GPU Unshlikht

Early Struggles

The Cheka had been a feared and powerful agency during the Civil War era, but with the cessation of active military and revolutionary activities, and with the transition to NEP, its fortunes faded quickly.

As the following document shows, the new GPU was not immune to the same misfortunes as other parts of the new Soviet society, and although material conditions improved quickly, at the beginning, at least, GPU officials worried about the collapse of the organization.

DOCUMENT

· 5 ·

Letter of F. E. Dzerzhinsky to I. V. Stalin on the difficult conditions
of GPU personnel, with letter from V. N. Mantsev appended. RGASPI,
f. 76, op. 3, d. 245, ll. 4–5.
6 July 1922

(To all members of the Polit and Orgbiuro [Politburo and Organizational Bureau] of TsK RKP)

Yesterday, 3.VII, at the Orgbiuro session, Secretary of the Donetsk [Communist Party provincial committee's] Orgbiuro reported on the impossibly difficult conditions of personnel in the provincial GPU administration, on flight of communists from the GPU, of renouncing even their Party membership, etc. (Orgbiuro heard similar reports from impartial comrades.) The Kiev GPU administration, for example, survived from February until May on only the 1.4 billion [sic] allocated them each month. The [appended] memorandum from c. Mantsev pictures the situation in Ukraine, which is no worse than in the RSFSR. It is necessary to turn serious attention to this. GPU organs are still necessary for the security of the state.

At present, I have one request—to instruct Narkomfin [Commissariat of Finance], Narkomprod [Commissariat of Food Supply], and Narkomvoen [Commissariat of Military Affairs] to ensure that state allocations of food and materials to us, as well as financial [allocations], not be fictional, but be given to us in full, according to planned estimates. Only under these conditions can we fight with an iron fist against corruption and reduce staff to the maximum limit, selecting the best, and fulfilling our tasks.

With communist greetings, F. Dzherzhinsky
6 July 1922

[Letter from V. N. Mantsev]
20 June 1922
Respected comrade Dzherzhinsky
I am sending you this letter, in which I want to bring to your attention the difficult conditions of GPU organs and personnel in Ukraine. I think that this is a general issue, and in Russia the situation is hardly better. The

financial allocation that is paid to personnel is miserly, as is the food ra-
tion. An official, especially one with a family, can survive only by selling
everything he has on the open market. And he has very little. Because of
this, an official's general work capability is lowered, his morale weakens,
his discipline falls, and extraordinary conditions are necessary in order to
force him to work even at half his previous [ability]. Moreover, there
have been several instances of suicide as a result of hunger and extreme
exhaustion. I personally have received letters from female personnel, in
which they write that they are forced into prostitution in order not to die
from hunger.

Tens, if not hundreds [of GPU personnel], are arrested and shot for
assault and robbery, and in all cases, it is established that they turn to
robbery because of systematic starvation. There is mass flight from the
Cheka. The decline in numbers of communist personnel is especially dangerous. If, before, we had 60 percent communists, now we can barely
count 15 percent. Very often, if not daily, there are instances of [person-
nel] leaving the Party because of hunger and lack of material support.
And, those who are leaving are not the worst, the majority are of the
proletariat.

I do not think it necessary for me to draw conclusions from what is
written above. They are obvious. So, I must say the following. We have
tried all measures, along both Party and Soviet lines. We have gotten
some results. But it is just crumbs [*groshi*]. By the way, most help is
local. The Cheka lives mostly from its own means, rather than through
allocations from the center. The latter is so miserly, it cannot be taken
seriously.

Let me turn to the last [point]. The situation of the Cheka led the Southern Bureau of the VTsSPS [the All-Union Central Council of Trade Unions]
[…]to raise the question about [the Cheka] in one of its recent meetings,
which I attended. At the meeting, a mixed commission was chosen, from
us and from the Southern Bureau, to study the issue [of the Cheka]. And
this commission came to the following conclusion: the state cannot support
the Cheka apparatus to the full extent and, as a result, it is necessary to
reduce the [GPU] staff to the [minimum] limit and reduce the functions of
the GPU accordingly. But we already have reduced staff by 75 percent.
What else to cut? Do we have the authority to do that? Because the work
of the Cheka becomes more difficult and strained, and fulfilling it, even
with the current minimal number of personnel, has become more and more
difficult. There is only one way out—state power must understand, finally,
what kind of an institution the Cheka is, it [the Cheka] must be satisfied
fully [*udovletvoriat' polnost'iu*], allocations must come [in the form of]
fully satisfactory credits. And state power should do this.

I ask that you raise this issue, for the danger is close of a final dissolution of the Cheka. And if the Cheka is not needed, then that needs to be

said directly and firmly. And then, we will act accordingly. Let me know if you need material about the Cheka and its personnel.

With communist greetings

V. Mantsev

5.VII–22

Work conditions for GPU officials were, in fact, desperate, but no more so than for many officials, especially for those in militarized sectors of the state, such as in the police and the military. Apart from Bukharin, Sokol'nikov, and Kursky, other leading Bolsheviks criticized the GPU, and sought to cut it back. One of those critics was Leon Trotsky. In a 23 November 1923 memorandum to Stalin as general secretary, Trotsky criticized the appearance of GPU troops at a parade on Red Square celebrating the tenth anniversary of the October Revolution. He wrote that "During the parade, a glaring abnormality unfolded before the whole world," referring to the review of GPU forces—three infantry brigades, a unit of special forces, a mounted unit, and artillery. Trotsky noted that if the foreign correspondents at the parade understood that these were GPU forces, that fact alone could be used against the Soviet state. In his opinion, the very existence of a GPU military force was uncalled for and unjustifiable. The existence of a whole army with every kind of weapon belonging exclusively to the GPU compromised the country in front of its friends as well as enemies. Trotsky proposed severely cutting the GPU to no more than 20,000 persons, and border forces to no more than 25,000.[2]

Overall numbers of personnel were rarely discussed openly, and it is difficult to know how much of a cut Trotsky's proposals constituted, or to what extent they were implemented. The power of the Finance Commissariat carried more significant weight, as Sokol'nikov unilaterally cut the OGPU budget. As a result, the projected budget for the GPU for 1923 dropped from 72 million rubles in December 1922 to an actual allocation of 58 million. Dzerzhinsky complained that such cuts would lead to the complete disorganization of the organization, but the Politburo supported the cuts.[3]

The Intelligentsia, Mensheviks, and SRs: The First Large-Scale Operations

That year, 1923, was the low point for the OGPU. In the coming years, the situation improved, in part through rising wages and material support, and through a reduction in personnel, as Mantsev's letter reflected. It is interesting to note, however, the indication, as expressed by the Southern Trade Union Council, of at least some kind of popular sense in favor of eliminating the political police as no longer necessary. At the same time, the Politburo concurred with Dzerzhinsky's counterclaim that the GPU was still necessary for state security; indeed, even as Mantsev was warning of the GPU's dissolution, the Politburo was gearing up to use it in its largest operations since the Civil War. Those operations resulted from Lenin's concern about anti-Soviet attitudes among the professional and cultural elite, the intelligentsia. Lenin's directive about this, noted on the back of a letter of spring 1922 from N. A. Semashko (Document 6), set in motion a complex, but typical, process of responses by Politburo members— Lenin himself, Stalin, Dzerzhinsky, Unshlikht, and others—leading ultimately to a major operation by the GPU to infiltrate, monitor, and regulate the formation of key social and professional institutions. The process also reveals the continuing siege mentality of the Bolsheviks as they attempted to maintain their power within a semisocialist economy and society. The letter from N. A. Semashko, active in Soviet health and other social welfare issues, gives a flavor of Bolshevik wariness. The letter offers, as well, an example of the often stilted language of the Bolshevik revolutionaries:

DOCUMENT

· 6 ·

V. I. Lenin's proposal for a Politburo directive in connection
with N. A. Semashko's letter appraising the congress of medical
doctors. With a TsK cover letter. AP RF, f. 3, op. 58, d. 2, ll. 3–4.
23 May 1922

To all the Politburo members
    For voting
    On c. Stalin's recommendation, c. Lenin's proposal about a Politburo directive on the All-Russian Congress of Medical Doctors is forwarded to you for voting (see the attached letter by c. Semashko).
    C. Lenin's proposal is on the other side of c. Semashko's letter.

Rather secret
[Semashko's letter]
To c. Lenin and members of the Politburo:

Dear comrades. The recent All-Russian Congress of Medical Doctors has revealed such important and dangerous tendencies in our life that I consider it necessary not to leave members of the Politburo in ignorance about these trends, which are used successfully by Kadets [Constitutional Democrats], m-ks [Mensheviks, moderate anti-Bolshevik socialist party], and s-rs [Socialist Revolutionaries]; the more so, as far as I know, these tendencies are widespread not only among medical doctors, but also among other *spetsy* [specialists] (agriculturists, engineers, technicians, and lawyers), and even more so, many even high-ranking comrades not only do not understand this danger, but thoughtlessly lend their ear to the whisperings of such *spetsy*.

In the most general terms, the essence of the tendencies revealed at the congress may be reduced to: 1. A campaign against Soviet medicine and praise for the *Zemstvo* [pre–1917 local councils] and insurance types of medicine; 2. "further development [of medicine] to be based on "freely" elected independent organizations of the population, organized from the bottom up" (the exact resolution of the congress); on those patterns, which orators—Kadets, m-ks, s-rs—were drawing on this canvas. 3. Strong aspiration to stay out of general-professional worker movements and 4. Aspiration to strengthen their own organization by creating their own press publication.

For struggling against these trends, it seems to me, it is practically necessary: 1) to be extremely careful about the reorganization of our Soviet system. In this respect, the NEP has generated some kind of bygone nostalgic attitude [*likvidatorstvo*] when [we] with deeply thoughtful expression and irony begin … [text missing] … to *spetsy* about the basics of our Soviet way of life [*stroitel'stvo*]. Any idea of "Zemshchina" [local council movements] must be burned out with a red-hot iron.[4] No attempts should be [tolerated] to restore ("town councils") (c. Voreikis's idea). From this point of view, I personally consider that Narkomvnudel [the People's Commissariat of Internal Affairs], in my opinion, should be ordered to approve any reforms in the area of Soviet [administration] in town councils only after approval by the Politburo. 2) In particular, any attempts to replace Soviet (class) medicine with local ("popular") medicine and insurance ("not Soviet") should be considered politically inadmissible. 3. Gosizdat [State Publishing House] must not allow publication of any newspapers and journals of social-political (unscientific) character by *spetsy* and their societies. Otherwise, journals that are permitted now, such as [that of the] "Pirogov Society," will objectively degenerate into organs of anti-Soviet propaganda; permission for any periodical publication must be approved by the corresponding agency and the GPU. 4. VTsSPS should be extremely circumspect in the establishment of autonomy of [professional organizations] of specialists' sections (doctors, engineers) in general-professional unions, [and] in no event allow [creation of] separate independent specialists' unions. As to removal of the "top" m-k and s-r doctors who spoke at the congress (Drs. Granovsky, Magul, Vigdorchik, Levin), this question needs to be coordinated with the GPU (on what bases—administrative or judicial-investigative, [so as] not to give their tricks popular play, having in mind, that no more congresses should be held?).

Semashko.

[Annotations on the reverse:]

To c. Stalin. I think it necessary to show this as strictly secret (without making copies) to Dzerzhinsky, as well as to all members of the Politburo, and to issue a "directive." Dzerzhinsky (GPU) with the help of Semashko is entrusted to elaborate a plan of measures and to report to P/buro (2 week (?) deadline). 22. V. Lenin

In favor—Stalin
In favor—Trotsky
In favor—Kamenev
In favor—Rykov
In favor—Molotov

Tomsky—I abstain, since the question of the Congress of Medical Doctors requires a different approach. We ourselves, and c. Semashko, above all, are in many respects guilty.

DOCUMENT

· 7 ·

Note from F. E. Dzerzhinsky to the Politburo of TsK RKP(b), with attachment of the GPU report about anti-Soviet groupings among the intelligentsia. AP RF, f. 3, op. 58, d. 175, ll. 7–12.

3 June 1922

Herewith is forwarded the report about anti-Soviet groupings among the intelligentsia, with the *GPU* draft of a Politburo decision.

Chairman of the GPU, Dzerzhinsky

Absolutely secret

1. Introduction: The New Economic Policies of Soviet power have created a danger in favor of the unification and consolidation of power of bourgeois and petty bourgeois groups, based on the strengthening conditions of NEP development. The anti-Soviet intelligentsia widely utilizes the possibilities open to it for organization and strengthening its forces, which have been created by the peaceful course of Soviet power and the weakening of activities of the repressive organs. In the near future, the spontaneous renaissance of a significant number of private social unions (scientific,

economic, religious, etc.), which will draw anti-Soviet elements, will be the most disturbing symptom of a growing counterrevolutionary front. The might of the anti-Soviet intelligentsia, and the groups that rally around it, is strengthened still further by the widespread sense in Communist Party circles of a "peaceful" relaxed attitude, due to the liquidation of [military-political] fronts and the conditions of NEP. The weakening of repression has given wings to the hopes of the anti-Soviet intelligentsia and, in different forms, to the different strata of that intelligentsia to work in a determined way against Soviet power. *The main arenas of struggle against Soviet power by the anti-Soviet intelligentsia are occurring in the following: higher educational institutions, various societies, press, various professional conferences, theater, cooperatives, trusts [industrial administrations], trade organizations, and, more recently, religion, and other areas.*

2. [...] Both students and the anti-Soviet professorate in higher education institutions conduct counterrevolutionary work in two main directions: *a) struggle for "autonomous" higher education, and b) for improvement of the material conditions of the professorate and students, and the struggle for "autonomy,"* both circles of active anti-Soviet students and professors have an essentially political goal, which is directed against any influence in higher education of the Communist Party and the class principle.

[...]

4. *The permission granted by Soviet power to allow private publications and periodical press has put a powerful weapon into the hands of the anti-Soviet intelligentsia, which it has not hesitated to utilize.*

[...]

7. Removal of religious valuables and divisions among orthodox church groups is being used mainly by the Black Hundreds [a prerevolutionary anti-Semitic movement] intelligentsia.[5] Apart from the usual agitation against confiscation of valuables, and in addition to direct opposition, the elite Black Hundreds intelligentsia, including priests and a number of lay believers, have become energized and are preparing the ground for a united religious front for struggle against the atheism of Soviet power.

All of the above shows that, in the process of development of NEP, there is a definite crystalization and a rallying of anti-Soviet groups and organizations, which are informed by the political aspirations of a revived bourgeoisie. Given the current tempo of development, there is a possibility that these groups may come together into a dangerous force against Soviet power. The general situation in the Republic calls forth the necessity for decisive promulgation of a series of measures to prevent these possible political complications.

Special plenipotentiary GPU, Agranov
Moscow 1 June 1922.

DOCUMENT

· 8 ·

Decision of the Politburo of TsK RKP(b). On anti-Soviet groupings
among the intelligentsia. RGASPI, f. 17, op. 3, d. 296, ll. 2–3.
8 June 1922

No. 10. Item 8. [...] (c. Unshlikht)
  a) to accept (with amendments) the following proposal by c. Unshlikht:

1. In order to maintain order in higher educational institutions, to form a
    commission consisting of representatives of Glavprofobr [the Chief Ad-
    ministration of Professional Education] with the OGPU[6] (Yakovlev and
    Unshlikht), and of representatives of the Orgburo of the TsK to elabo-
    rate measures on the following questions:

    a) vetting of students by the beginning of the next academic year;
    b) establishing severe restriction on enrolment of students of non-
        proletarian origin;
    c) establishing certificates of political reliability for those students
        who were not sent by professional and Party organizations, and
        whose payments were not waived. C. Unshlikht has responsibility
        for calling the commission, deadline is one week.

2. The same commission (see point 1) is to elaborate rules for meetings
    and unions of students and the professorate.
    Recommend to the Political Department of Gosizdat to work jointly
    with the GPU to thoroughly check all publications published by pri-
    vate societies, by sections of *spetsy* of the trade unions, and by some
    narkomats [People's Commissariats]: (Narkomzem [People's Com-
    missariat of Agriculture], Narkompros [People's Commissariat of
    Education], and so forth).
    [... .]

    e) To create a commission consisting of cc. Unshlikht, Kursky, and
        Kamenev, to confirm a list of top leaders of hostile intellectual
        groupings to be deported [out of the country or to distant parts
        of Russia].
    f) To authorize the same commission in point 1 to address the issue
        of closing publications and press organs that do not fit the direc-
        tion of Soviet policy (journal of the Pirogovsky Society, etc.)

Secretary of TsK

Appendix to the protocol of the meeting of the Politburo of the TsK
RKP from 8.VI.22

[...]

3. To ensure that none of the congresses or the All-Russian meetings of *spetsy* (doctors, agriculturists, engineers, lawyers, and so forth) be called without the permission of the NKVD. Local congresses or meetings of *spetsy* are permitted by gubispolkoms [Soviet government executive committees of provinces], after preliminary approval by local organs of the GPU.

4. To assign the GPU the task to reregister all societies and unions (scientific, religious, academic, and so forth) [...], and to allow no new societies and unions without GPU permissions. To declare illegal, and subject to immediate liquidation, societies and unions that were not registered.

5. VTsSPS is not to allow formation and functioning of unions of *spetsy* outside the all-professional associations. To take into special account and special supervision the existing *spetsy* sections of trade unions. Charters of the *spetsy* sections must be revised with the assistance of the GPU. VTsSPS may give permission for formation of the *spetsy* sections at the professional associations only with GPU consent.

The documents above were part of an anti-intelligentsia campaign, spearheaded by the OGPU but initiated by Lenin and the Party leadership. This campaign to "sovietize" public intellectual life reached its greatest intensity in 1922 and 1923.[7] The most dramatic event of the campaign came in late 1922 with the expulsion from the country of some 217 professional intellectuals—teachers, scientists, writers—an event that resulted directly from the documents above.[8] The 8 June decision by the Politburo established the police's authority, for the first time, over censorship and control of all of Soviet public intellectual life. As the documents also show, much of the Party's concern about politically unregulated organizations involved the continuing and even reviving influence of rival socialist parties, particularly the Mensheviks, and the agrarian socialist party, the Socialist Revolutionaries (SRs).[9] One of the early and major preoccupations of the GPU was to ferret out Menshevik and SR sympathizers in workplaces and organizations, and this operation was tied to the Bolsheviks' decision to arrest and try key Menshevik leaders. As the following series of documents shows, it was primarily through their use of the political police, rather than through political means, that Bolshevik leaders hoped to destroy the organizational infrastructure and influence of these parties.

DOCUMENT

· 9 ·

Appendix to Politburo session No. 59, 29.III.23. Protocol of meeting,
23.III.23, on the question of measures to struggle against Mensheviks,
in accordance with instructions from the chairman of the GPU, c. Dzerzhinsky.
AP RF, f. 3, op. 59, d. 3, ll. 78–80.

Present: cc. Menzhinsky, Messing, Samsonov
Notes of the Chairman of the GPU on measures in the struggle against Mensheviks:

1. Measures of the struggle along Party lines:

1) To conduct a special campaign against Mensheviks in the press, specifically in places of vigorous Menshevik activity (plants, factories, workshops, etc.), and, in particular, in the Far East, Piter [Petrograd], and Moscow.

2) To select special comrades in gubkoms [province-level Party committees], who are newspaper workers, and to charge them with conducting the campaign against Mensheviks in the press.

3) Party organs are to pay particular attention to the struggle against Mensheviks' influence on the Komsomol [Communist Youth League].

Measures of struggle along GPU lines:

1) To receive sanction from the TsK RKP(b) for mass operations against Mensheviks, Bund [United Jewish Labor Movement], and Poalei Zion [Jewish Communist Labor Party] organizations.

2) As a rule, adult Mensheviks should be exiled to the Narym Krai [north-central Siberia], the Pechorsky Krai [in the Komi Republic] for youth under the age of 25, and Turkestan along the Kashgar border for the especially sick.

3) To coordinate removal of Mensheviks from offices and enterprises, with agreement of enterprise heads.

4) Recognize as necessary to expel Mensheviks, particularly, from all cooperative organizations.
   [... .]

6) Recognize as necessary to organize filtering commissions with representation of the GPU at VUZs [higher educational institutions] for students ... at the beginning of each academic year.

7) Remove active students-Mensheviks before the end of the current academic year.

8) Conduct extremely thorough expulsion of Mensheviks from NKPost [People's Commissariat of Post], NKPS [People's Commissariat of Transportation], Narkomvneshtorg [People's Commissariat of External

Trade], NKID [People's Commissariat of Foreign Affairs], VTsSPS, and Profintern [International Trade Union Organization] in order to sever Mensheviks' connections abroad.

9) Strengthen work of INO [the Foreign Department] of the GPU abroad to disrupt connections of Mensheviks with Russia. Komintern [Communist International] and Profintern must do the same.

10) Instruct localities about strengthening the TsK RKP(b), VTsSPS, and GPU struggle against Mensheviks.

11) Encourage Party comrades to give any reliable information and assistance to GPU organs in the struggle against Mensheviks.

12) Communists who cooperate with or render assistance to Mensheviks to be subject to severe Party sanctions

Secretary Samsonov
23 March 1923

Speculation, Banditry, and Institutional Conflicts

The anti-Menshevik campaigns were successful, at least as regards the leaders, although historians have noted that despite political repression, Menshevik influence remained strong in some economic sectors and trade union organizations.[10] In any case, the anti-Menshevik operations reinforced a reliance on the police, and this was true of measures to solve not only political problems, but problems of social disorder, as well. During the course of the early and mid–1920s, the political police pressed for and received broader authority to deal with two phenomena especially—"speculation" (profiteering) and banditry. The former threatened the state's control over the economy, and leaders perceived the latter as both a criminal activity and a potential base for anti-Soviet armed resistance. Expansion of political police jurisdiction in the area of criminality also resulted from the underdeveloped state of civil policing, at least according to political police officials. The civil police hardly existed during the 1920s, and local officers did not have the capability or manpower to fight widespread illegal trading and gang theft. In rural areas, especially, where bandit activity was most intense, local officials were often outnumbered and outgunned by bandit gangs operating in their territories.

Leaders usually granted extra powers to the political police, but this was not a foregone conclusion. Generally, resistance came from several important people and state institutions. As the following documents show, Nikolai Krylenko, chief prosecutor for the Russian Republic, clashed with the OGPU as early as 1922 over police authority.

The instance below, in which Krylenko and then deputy OGPU head Genrikh Yagoda came into conflict, was one of the first of many instances over the course of the 1920s and 1930s. As the documents below show, Krylenko objected to the right of the OGPU to investigate any crime other than those political crimes that fell strictly under its jurisdiction. He also objected to the exclusive right of the OGPU to investigate and try its own personnel. This, he believed, would turn the political police into a caste essentially outside the law.[11]

DOCUMENT

· 10 ·

Decision of the Politburo of the TsK RKP(b). On the authority of the GPU. AP RF, f. 3, op. 58, d. 2, ll. 99–100.
28 September 1922

Appendix to Politburo protocol No. 28, 28.IX.22. point 2

Draft decision by TsIK, supported by the Politburo 28.9.22, on additions to the authority of the Gospolitupravlenie [GPU]

[...]:

1. Grant the GPU authority a) to take extrajudicial action, even shooting, in relation to persons caught in the act of armed assault with the intent to rob; b) to give authority to exile and imprison in a kontslager [concentration camp] to the Board of Exile of the NKVD, [the latter] formed in accordance with the decree on expulsion, with a precise definition of categories of persons who are subject to expulsion, and for a limited period of time of confinement at the place of exile, up to three years.

2. Conduct investigations of cases of occupational crimes committed by GPU personnel, with the obligatory participation of a Procuracy oversight official, and to enact extrajudicial sentencing by the GPU Collegium, informing NKiust of the sentence.

3. Recognize the right of the GPU independently to decide whether to initiate or quash an investigation of those cases under its jurisdiction.

4. a) Establish, as a rule, that any Procuracy officials assigned to oversight of GPU activities be special deputies to either the republic-level or provincial-level Procuracy administrations, and that such officials be Party members for at least three years;

[... .]

Chairman VTsIK
Secretary VTsIK

DOCUMENT

· 11 ·

Memorandum of N. V. Krylenko to I. V. Stalin on authority of the GPU to impose extrajudicial sentences. AP RF, f. 3, op. 58, d. 2, l. 112.

Secret.

9 October 1922

This is to inform you that c. *Yagoda and I can find no mutual agreement* in connection with the Politburo decision of 28.IX on GPU authority to impose extrajudicial sentences on GPU personnel. *I insist on a clause that 1) allows the GPU this authority only in exceptional instances, and not "as a general rule," and 2) [that the GPU be required] to seek the "sanction" of NKIu, and not simply inform NKIu [of such a practice.]*

At the same time, I emphasize that a cardinal question needs to be resolved whether the GPU can investigate any crime or exclusively those within its legal jurisdiction, i.e. counterrevolutionary crimes, spying, banditry, or in connection with border defense.

I request that both questions be placed on the Politburo agenda, and that I and c. Kursky be present for the discussion.

With comradely greetings, Krylenko

In his exchange with Dzerzhinsky, Krylenko objected to the implicit and explicit criticisms that civil police and courts were weak and not doing enough to fight economic crimes and banditry. In making his request to the Politburo for expanded police powers, Dzerzhinsky used this argument as justification for expanded authority. Foreign Minister Chicherin also cautioned against expanded GPU powers, as did RSFSR Justice Minister Kursky. All three saw expansion of police powers as a threat to their own agencies and jurisdictions, as unconstitutional, or as excessive and unnecessary given current laws. In a letter objecting to expanded police powers, Krylenko succinctly summarized political police methods to act first and then seek a general sanction from the Central Committee.

In the meantime, Dzerzhinsky and the OGPU continued to seek special sanctions from the Politburo to conduct campaigns against both profiteering, or speculation as it was called, and banditry.

DOCUMENT

· 12 ·

Letter from F. E. Dzerzhinsky to I. V. Stalin on measures against
malicious speculators. TsA FSB RF, f. 2. op 1, d. 56, l. 99.
22 October 1923

One of the important factors inflating prices of products is malicious
speculators who chose as their profession inflating prices (especially of
foreign currencies) and entangling trusts and cooperatives, and their
workers, in their frauds. Moscow, in particular, attracts them, since the
major trusts, Tsentrosoiuz [the All-Russian Central Union of Consumer
Societies] and banks are located here. [They] gather here from every corner of the USSR.

They take over markets and black currency markets. Their methods—
payoffs and depravity. If one asks on what they live, they cannot tell you,
but they live in full chic. While Moscow has a housing hunger, plenty of
the most luxurious apartments are available to them. They are parasites,
seducers, bloodsuckers, malicious speculators, they corrupt and gradually
and imperceptibly draw in our enterprise executives ...

My suggestion is to broaden the authority of the Commission on Exile
to include the right to exile these malicious speculators, [...] in conjunction with reports from me, i.e. the Chairman of the OGPU.

I am convinced that within a month, we will cleanse Moscow of these
elements, and that will certainly have an effect on the whole of our economic life.[12]

DOCUMENT

· 13 ·

Memorandum from F. E. Dzerzhinsky to the Politburo of TsK RKP(b)
on the necessity to strengthen the struggle against banditry. AP RF, f. 3,
op. 58, d. 197, l. 78
29 January 1924

In the recent past, there has been an active increase in both criminal and
political [forms of] banditry, both in cities and in the countryside, [involv-
ing] assaults, and robbery, and wrecking trains.

We have already received a number of memos from c. Chicherin about
this, in connection with robberies of representatives of missions and diplomatic couriers: Polish, Italian, British, Persian.

It needs to be said directly that one of the reasons for lack of success in the struggle against banditry is the formalism and red tape in our courts, and the lack of coordination of efforts by courts, criminal investigation organs of the *militsiia* [civil police], and GPU organs.

Therefore I make the following recommendations:

1. To assign the OGPU and its local organs leadership in the struggle against banditry, both political and criminal, both in cities and in the countryside.
2. For this purpose, to subordinate criminal investigation organs and *militsiia* operationally to the OGPU.[13]
3. To give the OGPU authority of extrajudicial resolution of cases of banditry not only of persons captured with weapons, but in general, of those taking part in bandit attacks.
4. To entrust the OGPU to elaborate and, urgently, to put into practice a plan to free the peasant population from bandits, including horse thieves.

F. Dzerzhinsky

And again, attempts to limit the growing OGPU authority came from the foreign affairs commissariat as well as from Krylenko, who attempted to refute the implied accusation that civil police and courts were incapable of effective action.

DOCUMENT

· 14 ·

G. V. Chicherin's memorandum to the Politburo of the TsK RKP(b) concerning c. Dzerzhinsky's recommendations concerning the struggle against banditry. AP RF, f. 3, op. 58, d. 197, l. 80. 30 January 1924

Extremely secret

Concerning c. Dzerzhinsky's letter to the Politburo from 29 January No. 194/t, the Collegium of NKID considers it possible to implement the recommendations by c. Dzerzhinsky, granting the OGPU special powers for struggling against banditry, in the form he specified, but only in those areas where banditry is out of control [*svirepstvuet*], specifying precisely the boundaries [of those areas]. Granting the OGPU extrajudicial authority to resolve cases is, in the view of the NKID, possible only for bandits captured with weapons in their hands. The NKID Collegium would consider dangerous any further expansion of OGPU authority for extrajudicial resolution of cases.

Narkomindel [People's Commissar of Foreign Affairs] Chicherin

DOCUMENT
· 15 ·

Memorandum of N. V. Krylenko to the Politburo of the TsK RKP(b)
concerning F. E. Dzerzhinsky's recommendations on the struggle against
banditry. AP RF, f. 3, op. 58, d. 197, ll. 79–790b.
1 February 1924

———————————

Secret

Concerning c. Dzerzhinsky's recommendation on methods for the struggle against criminal and political banditry, I consider it necessary to communicate the following:

During ten months of the previous year, courts sentenced to execution 971 [people], and tribunals–296, for a total of 1,267 persons, which includes 721 persons, or 57 percent, for robberies and participation in gangs. Sentences for 497 persons were upheld [by higher courts], which is 39 percent of the total number.

During the same period, the GPU convicted 121 persons, including 16 for robberies and banditry. The total number of convicted people whose sentences were carried out was 604. This means two persons a day, on average. This percentage cannot be considered low. On the contrary, it should be considered excessively high. If all sentences were carried out it would increase twice and would reach four persons a day. Thus, one cannot complain that repression in relation to the struggle against banditry is weak.

In the main, c. Dzerzhinsky's explanation is incorrect that the growth in banditry is the result of formalism and red tape in our courts.

The general practice is that all cases of banditry are investigated by the GPU. A case goes to the court only after it has been marinated in the GPU. Cases are heard usually in military tribunals or at criminal courts at the provincial level. They do not sit long [since] investigations are always relatively simple and do not require any special additional actions.

After the recent decision of the Politburo about reduction of judicial red tape, issued on Dzerzhinsky's recommendation, instructions were sent to all courts not to let cases sit for more than three months. Also, provincial Procuracy and court officials are obliged to report the number of cases every two weeks.

For this reason c. Dzerzhinsky's recommendation to apply the right of extrajudicial reprisal [*rasprava*] in general to people involved in banditry leads in practice to extrajudicial reprisal against everybody who may become suspected, in accordance with "agent information." These may include anybody related to a banditry gang, such as bandits' informants, those who hide bandits, accomplices, etc.

Taking into consideration that, of late, the OGPU has been broadening its jurisdiction by appealing to the Presidium of TsIK for permission to resolve this or that case in an extrajudicial manner, and moreover, even resolves the case and passes the sentence first, and only then asks VTsIK to confirm this sentence—it becomes absolutely clear that even within the current legislation and practice, the GPU has sufficient space and enough possibilities for taking emergency measures in the struggle against banditry.

I consider it necessary to speak strongly against point three of c. Dzerzhinsky's proposal [to authorize GPU extrajudicial action against anyone associated with bandit gangs]. Points one and two, on operational submission of criminal investigation and *militsiia* organs to the OGPU, meet formal obstacles because of formal subordination of these organs to Narkomvnudel, and hence, they can be subordinated to the OGPU only by secret order. C. Dzerzhinsky's arguments, which are in principle correct, should be implemented in a general reform of Narkomvnudel, according to which the *militsiia* and criminal investigation organs would be included in the GPU system.

Finally, point 4, in the way it was formulated by c. Dzerzhinsky, can be accepted only under condition that this "plan for freeing the peasant population from bandits' abuse, including horse thieves" [...] must be discussed at the corresponding Party and Soviet levels for preliminary implementation.

With comradely greetings, Krylenko

As the following decision shows, the Politburo sided, for the most part, with Dzerzhinsky on the issue of OGPU authority over banditry.

DOCUMENT

· 16 ·

Decision of the Politburo of TsK RKP(b). On the struggle against banditry. RGASPI, f. 17, op. 3, d. 418, l. 3.
14 February 1924

No. 70, point 7 (Dzerzhinsky, Krylenko, Beloborodov, Chicherin).
To recognize as necessary strengthening the struggle against banditry, both political and criminal, both in cities and in the countryside, enjoining the OGPU and its local organs to carry out this decision: To subordinate criminal investigation and *militsiia* organs to [OGPU] operationally, and to recognize as necessary the temporary expansion of authority of the OGPU in the use of extrajudicial repressions; Also, to assign cc. Dzerzhinsky, Krylenko, and Beloborodov with presenting to the Presidium of the

TsIk of the USSR a concrete plan for the expansion of OGPU authority to enact extrajudicial repressions, and to free the peasant population from bandits, so that this plan would specify areas, terms, and methods of the struggle.

As the following document shows, the Politburo ceded other "temporary" measures to the OGPU, encroaching still further, in Krylenko's view, on the jurisdiction of the civil police and courts.

DOCUMENT

· 17 ·

Decision of the Politburo of TsK RKP(b). On struggle against thefts
in Moscow. RGASPI, f. 17, op. 162, d. 2, l. 6.
27 June 1924

8. a) To accept c. Dzerzhinsky's proposal authorizing the OGPU to take urgent measures for the elimination of thefts.
    b) To coordinate work of the OGPU with the same work of the *militsiia*.

In at least one instance, resistance from Kursky and Krylenko was so categorical that the OGPU backed away from a request to be granted jurisdiction. This instance involved a request to grant political police authority to make arrests and adjudicate cases of forgery of monetary instruments such as bills of exchange. In addition to Kursky, Finance Commissar G. Ia. Sokol'nikov also objected, arguing that forgery of such issues was relatively easy to detect and stop, compared to traffic in forged currency. Despite Stalin's support, the OGPU withdrew the request from Politburo consideration.

The simmering conflicts between state agencies and the OGPU continued throughout the 1920s, and even though Krylenko did not often win these conflicts, he did not give up. His arguments usually concentrated on the unconstitutionality of the OGPU's extrajudicial powers, but on at least one occasion, he focused on the damaging image abroad created by the OGPU's activities. In the memorandum below, Krylenko focused on the uproar caused by the Soviet government's execution of twenty individuals for alleged counterrevolutionary terrorist activities. The executions, ordered by the OGPU Collegium, the administrative sentencing board of the political police, resulted in a sharp negative reaction, internationally, especially among leaders of social democratic movements in several countries.[14] Arguing that the OGPU's administrative sentencing system only fueled anti-Soviet propaganda abroad, Krylenko advocated its abolition, and creation of a special court within the judiciary system.

DOCUMENT

· 18 ·

Note from N. V. Krylenko to the Politburo TsK RKP(b) about creating extraordinary courts within the OGPU of the USSR. AP RF, f. 3, op. 58, d. 3, l. 113.

1 July 1927

Events of the last days, and, in particular, the outcry of hypocritical indignation that the "execution of the 20" caused in all strata of the bourgeoisie, up to and including correspondence on this matter between c. Rykov and figures of the English Labour Party, make us raise the question again, to what extent it is expedient for Soviet power to give occasion for this hypocritical indignation, [to give] its class enemies propaganda material in the struggle against us, if it is possible to achieve the same purposes by punishing rigidly and severely class enemies of the revolution without giving unnecessary "arguments" against us to our opponents.

I believe that the proper organization of extraordinary courts provides a full possibility for the struggle against both spies and latent counterrevolution, without recourse to acts of extrajudicial reprisal, carried out by the OGPU, which, no matter how much one may wish, cannot be equated to judicial measures, if only because they lack a major component of any judicial action—that is, a personal deposition of the defendant in court, and his right to offer explanations personally.

At one time, C. Dzerzhinsky, now deceased,[15] had this point of view, when, in 1919, he established the Special Extraordinary Tribunal, under Cheka authority, for processing cases of the largest-scale speculators, swindlers of economic counterrevolution, unscrupulous suppliers of military uniforms, etc. This tribunal was abolished in 1920, in connection with an ongoing reform of all tribunals. His main principles, however, seem to me quite possible to restore now.

In other words, I recommend:

1. To create extraordinary courts within the All-Union OGPU and the GPUs of the republics for resolving cases of espionage, banditry, and counterrevolution, and the largest-scale cases that the Presidium of VTsIK considers necessary to resolve in a special order. The extraordinary courts will consist of 3 members: two from the OGPU Collegium, and one from the corresponding provincial court;

2. Sentences given by the extraordinary court are not subject to appeal, and must be carried out immediately;
3. Extraordinary courts are not restricted by any judicial procedures, and have the right to allow or not to allow depositions or redeposition of witnesses, at discretion. Each case must be completed within 24 hours after its arrival in this court;
4. There is no prosecution and no defense.
5. Supervision over the extraordinary courts is possible only through the current form of supervision of extrajudicial sentencing by the OGPU, that is, the prosecutor of the republic supervising the OGPU has the right to suspend a sentence, after which the question of re-trial is to be transferred to VTsIK or TsIK, respectively.

As for public attendance, although the special tribunals of the Cheka created by c. Dzerzhinsky acted publicly I personally believe that sessions of the extraordinary courts may be either open or closed, at the discretion of the OGPU, depending on the character of the case.

I think that such a form of punishment fully provides the necessary harshness of repression and swiftness of procedure, and gives the possibility of taking away from the hands of the counterrevolution the tool that it uses now, in the form of slanders about the "injustice" [*navety na "bessudnost"*] of the government of the working class.

In case of basic approval of this project, I would consider it expedient to create a special commission consisting of cc. Menzhinsky or Yagoda myself, and a third member chosen by the Politburo (say, c. Ordzhonikidze) for further elaborating.

With communist greetings, Krylenko

Despite Krylenko's efforts, the Politburo did not accept his recommendations.

Foreign Activity and Foreign Policy

Early on, the GPU became involved in foreign intelligence gathering, which was not inherently part of its activities, but was, nonetheless, an extension of its mission to protect the political interests of the Soviet state. GPU expansion into foreign affairs followed a step-by-step process similar to its extension into other spheres of state activity, and resulted in analogous kinds of institutional conflicts, in this case with the Commissariat of Foreign Affairs(Narkomindel). I. S. Unshlikht's memorandum to Stalin and Trotsky (document 19) began this process by recommending that the GPU organize systematic disinformation campaigns in foreign countries. Surprisingly, the Politburo accepted his recommendation apparently without the consultation of NKID officials. Maksim Litvinov, Deputy People's Commissar for Foreign Affairs, protested vigorously, and the division of responsibilities between the two agencies remained tense and unresolved. In a follow-up letter, Unshlikht recommended that full responsibility for information deployed abroad be concentrated in the OGPU. Using the same strategy that he employed successfully against the civil police, Unshlikht cited confusion over jurisdictions and working at cross-purposes—problems arising from GPU intervention in the first place—which Unshlikht now recommended resolving by giving full authority to the political police. He also, of course, attributed incompetency to the diplomatic corps as an excuse to expand OGPU jurisdiction in creating the kind of information that was to be disseminated to foreign governments. In effect, the OGPU would be creating foreign policy.

DOCUMENT

· 19 ·

Memorandum from I. S. Unshlikht to I. V. Stalin and L. D. Trotsky
on disinformation. AP RF, f. 3, op. 58, d. 2, ll. 131–32.
22 December 1922

Department of Counterespionage
  Absolutely secret
  With the transition of our republic to a state of peace, and with opening of borders to foreigners, intelligence services of the bourgeois states have intensified their activities using these new possibilities. Since, during the military period, enemy intelligence services were mainly interested in the location and conditions of our Red Army, now they redirect their attention mainly toward the conditions of our industry, gathering information about political work of our Party and Soviet organs, work of the NKID, etc.
  It is extremely important for the republic, during this current period of respite and diplomatic negotiations with the capitalist states, to disorient opponents, to mislead them.
  A skillful, regular encircling of our opponents with a network of disinformation will allow us somewhat to influence their policies in ways desirable for us, will allow us to force them to construct their practical conclusions on miscalculations. Besides, disinformation helps our direct struggle against foreign intelligence services, and [eases] the insertion of our agents into intelligence organs of bourgeois states, etc.

For the purpose of establishing systematic disinformation work, the GPU suggests to create a special bureau, consisting of representatives of the institutions that are most interested in this work—Razvedupr [Intelligence Administration], NKID, and the GPU.

Goals of the bureau must include: 1) Analysis of information arriving in the GPU and Razvedupr, and other institutions, about the level of awareness of foreign intelligence services about Russia. 2) Assessing the character of the information that interests our opponents.

3) Assessing the level of awareness of the opponent about us.

4) Creating and producing a variety of false information and documents that would give to opponents a misleading sense of the domestic situation in Russia, of organization and conditions in the Red Army, of political work of leading Party and Soviet organs, of work of the NKID, etc.

5) Supplying opponents with the above-stated materials and documents through corresponding organs of the GPU and Razvedupr.

6) Elaborating a number of articles and notes for the periodical press in order to prepare the background for release of different sorts of fictitious materials.

The GPU asks the Politburo of TsK RKP(b) to give its consent in principle for conducting disinformation work and for creation of the aforementioned bureau.

Deputy chairman of the GPU Unshlikht

Deputy Head of KRO [Department of Counterintelligence] Pilliar

On 11 January 1923, the Politburo issued a decision to enact Unshlihkt's recommendation and, in response, Litvinov sent the following memorandum to Stalin and other Politburo members.

DOCUMENT

· 20 ·

Statement from M. M. Litvinov to I. V. Stalin regarding the bureau of disinformation, with cover letter from the TsK RKP(b). AP RF, f. 3, op. 58, d. 2, ll. 135–136.
15 January 1923

On c. Stalin's instruction, the following statement from c. Litvinov from 11.1.23 [...] is forwarded to you all for your urgent consideration. You are requested to return the conclusion along with the material.

Deputy secretary of TsK, Nazaretian

Secret
11 January 1923

I have received the Politburo decision from January 11, No. 43 "On disinformation," along with c. Unshlikht's proposal. I consider it necessary to point out that NKID knows nothing about c. Unshlikht's proposal, and it is not clear from the decision itself what bureau is being considered, and who will be put in charge of this bureau. One may only guess that this is about active disinformation of foreign governments, and that the suggested bureau will be created within the GPU.

NKID realizes the necessity in some cases of circulating disinformation, and uses this frequently. However, NKID does not consider the GPU at all competent to decide when and how to spread [disinformation] data. In particular, I just recently ordered all the plenipotentiaries to refute regularly all false and doubtful information about Russia published in the foreign press. It might easily happen that our plenipotentiaries will refute immediately the information spread by this newly created bureau. However, since the Politburo already issued its decision, NKID is asking to add to this decision a point that will oblige the GPU to take no steps and to release no information without preliminary coordination with one of the members of the Collegium of NKID.

Deputy People's Commissar of Foreign Affairs, Litvinov

In return, Unshlikht sent the following notes to Stalin, first to answer Litvinov's complaint, and then to push for GPU control over all foreign intelligence activities.

DOCUMENT

· 21 ·

Letter from I. S. Unshlikht and R. A. Pilliar to I. S. Stalin
concerning M. M. Litvinov's letter regarding the disinformation
bureau. AP RF, f. 3, op. 58, d. 2, l. 133.
17 January 1923

Absolutely secret

It is clear from c. Litvinov's letter that NKID agrees with our point of view about the necessity for regular disorientation of opponents, and that NKID has been engaged in this kind of disorientation. As to c. Litvinov's suggestion about coordinating disinformation with one of the members of the Collegium of NKID—apparently this was prompted by c. Litvinov's lack of information that, according to the GPU suggestion, accepted by the Politburo of the TsK RKP(b), the Disinformation Bureau must include a competent representative of NKID.

Deputy chairman of the GPU Unshlikht
Deputy head of KRO of the GPU Pilliar

DOCUMENT

· 22 ·

Memorandum from I. S. Unshlikht to I. V. Stalin to concentrate all lines of
intelligence activity in the GPU. AP RF, f. 3, op. 58, d. 2, l. 140.
28 March 1923

Recently, there has been an increase in the number of suggestions of a
secret political character made to NKID representatives (for example,
suggestions made to c. Chicherin, and by the delegate Petrushevich),[16]
which coincide with the specialized activities of the GPU apparatus, and
result in parallelism and, inevitably, in both absolutely unnecessary currency expenditures and negative consequences of a political character for
the NKID organs.

For reasons of economic necessity, saving hard currency, and eliminating undesirable political consequences, the GPU asks the Politburo to
approve:

1. To concentrate exclusively in GPU organs all lines of intelligence
    work (diplomatic, political), in which NKID engages only occasion-
    ally.
2. In some instances, when NKID representatives take one or another
    promising initiative in the field of intelligence work, the NKID repre-
    sentative must first coordinate his steps with the GPU, or with its
    local organs.

Deputy chairman of the GPU Unshlikht

The Politburo approved the OGPU recommendation, consolidating
all foreign intelligence in the OGPU, and giving the political police
significant influence over diplomatic information to be given to other
governments.

Such Politburo decisions increased OGPU influence in foreign affairs, but did little to regulate relations between the foreign affairs
commissariat and the political police. Tensions continued between
diplomatic personnel and OGPU residents abroad, and this created
confusion and, at times, outright contradictions in Soviet foreign policy. In a 1925 memorandum, Litvinov, writing to Dzerzhinsky, enumerated Narkomindel's main grievances against the OGPU. In turn,
Dzerzhinsky passed on this list to his deputy, M. Trilisser. As Dzerzhinsky explained, Litvinov's main complaints were as follows:

48 Expanding Power, Infiltrating the State

DOCUMENT

· 23 ·

Memorandum of M. Litvinov to the TsK RKP(b). Late January or early
February 1925. RGASPI, f. 76, op. 3, d. 349, l. 2–20b.[17]

[... .] 1) Arrest of foreigners occurs without forewarning NKIDel. 2) Unjustified search and arrest of foreigners. 3) Inquiries by NKIDel remain
unanswered or are answered with inaccurate information, such that the
result discredits not only NKIDel, but also the USSR. This is the most
serious grievance. This is like a knife at our throat [*Vse ostrie ego protiv
nas*]. V. Ilich [Lenin] would berate us for this. And, as a result, we organize everyone against us, and give grounds for foreigners to start a campaign that, in the USSR, the GPU runs everything. Politically, this is the
most dangerous consequence. It allows enemies of the USSR to make of
the OGPU the main excuse for intervention and counterrevolution. 4)
Illegal refusal of visas to foreigners to enter the country. 5) Not to bring
criminal cases against foreigners through the GPU. 6) A more precise
definition of the term "economic espionage." 7) To regulate issues concerning material of the INO—to send by special courier.

In order to monitor ongoing concrete issues connected with NKIDel—
have with us a [specially appointed] plenipotentiary, who is fully responsible for this, but not like it is now, when it is unclear who is responsible
and who answers [...].

In his turn, Dzerzhinsky also attempted to regulate relations between the NKID and the OGPU, but in favor of the police. In February 1925, he requested his deputy, Trilisser, to work up a plan to
regulate relations with the foreign affairs commissariat, but, as the
excerpt shows, to do so by increasing OGPU influence.

DOCUMENT

· 24 ·

Memorandum, F. Dzerzhinsky to M. Trilisser. February 1925. RGASPI, f. 76,
op. 3, d. 349, ll. 2–20b.[18]

In view of current relations, the P/Buro [Politburo] needs to issue a decision to regulate our relations with NKID, and then to strictly enforce
those regulations. I cannot agree with our mutual relations in their present form, since, as a result of them, the interests of our state suffer in some
ways. NKIDel leads and carries out the foreign policy of the USSR and is

the only representative of the USSR for other countries. Therefore, our constant hostile relations with the NKIDel disorganize the prestige of Soviet power [...] abroad, and doom [us—the OGPU] to complete powerlessness. Our work and materials, therefore, are underutilized—with consequent damage to the state. And I demand that our mutual relations be put in order, by which I mean a necessary strengthening of our influence, and the significant [increased or more] use of the results of work by the INO and KRO. I ask that you brief c. Menzhinsky about this. [...] and I ask that you give me a draft of regulations based on decisions of the commission of c. Kuibyshev, the Politburo, and others.

To ensure further coordination of OGPU activity and foreign policy, Dzerzhinsky recommended, in 1925, that his deputy, V. R. Menzhinsky, be named an ex officio member of the collegium of the foreign affairs commissariat. This had a certain bureaucratic logic, and had been suggested by Litvinov, but the appointment also furthered political police intrusion into the highest levels of diplomatic policymaking.

DOCUMENT

· 25 ·

Note from F. E. Dzerzhinsky to I. V. Stalin with the suggestion to include
V. R. Menzhinsky on the Board of NKID. RGASPI, f. 76, op. 3, d. 349, l. 3.

23 May 1925

In connection with the information on foreign affairs organized by the OGPU, as well as with our struggle against espionage and counterrevolution organized by the capitalist countries, in the interests of the affairs of the country and its defense, closer contact of our work with NKID would be very desirable. For this purpose I suggest to include c. Menzhinsky on the NKID Collegium.

F. Dzerzhinsky

Stalin, the OGPU, and Trotsky

The authority of the OGPU as a punitive organ and an active counter-espionage agency continued to be a source of tension with other parts of the Soviet government, and the balance shifted back and forth depending on circumstances, personal power, and personalities, and on the policies and perceptions of the Politburo and Stalin. As the documents above show, Stalin worked closely, especially with Unshlikht, and to some extent with Dzerzhinsky, to extend GPU authority step by step into key areas of government and foreign policy. However, he was not always successful. In the early 1920s, Stalin was not the powerful dictator that he later became, and he was especially wary of Leon Trotsky, the charismatic and brilliant commander of the Red Army. Trotsky, who became Stalin's archenemy, had been second only to Lenin as a revolutionary figure, and after Lenin's incapacitating stroke in 1922 he was feared by the other leaders as a potential usurper of power, a Bonaparte of the Russian revolution. In the early 1920s, Stalin did not have the power to confront Trotsky in an open fight, but he found a willing ally in Dzerzhinsky, who, in the early 1920s, shared his dislike of Trotsky.[19] As the following documents show, the general secretary was ready to intrigue against Trotsky with the help of the GPU, but also quick to back down.

The following exchanges concern police investigation of anti-Soviet sentiment within the Baltic Fleet in the early 1920s. According to GPU statutes, the agency was required to inform and work with Party leaders of any government institution it was investigating. As the exchanges below imply, however, Stalin connived with Genrykh Yagoda, still a deputy head of the GPU, to conduct the investigation in secret. At the time, Trotsky was still the charismatic Commissar of Military and Naval Affairs, and he was not informed. Neither was his deputy V. I. Zof, commissar of the Russian Republic naval forces and member of the Baltic Fleet Revolutionary Military Council. Nor were other high-ranking Party and military officials consulted. When Trotsky got wind of this, he requested a report from Zof and, on the same day, accused the GPU of violating procedures in order to spring a "surprise." He addressed his complaints to Dzerzhinsky, as head of the GPU, but Dzerzhinsky referred him to Stalin, as the one who knew the most about the operation. The personal and political implications were all sub rosa, but the incident smacked of Stalinist intrigue to undermine Trotsky, using the GPU as a front. The series begins with Zof's report to Trotsky.

DOCUMENT
· 26 ·

Memorandum from V. I. Zof to L. D. Trotsky. AP RF, f. 3,
op. 58, d. 2, l. 117.
15 October 1922.

———————

[...]

In accordance with your order from 15 October of this year, I report:

Neither I, nor the Revvoensovet Baltflot [Revolutionary Military Council of the Baltic Fleet], nor the Naval Department, PUR [Political Administration of the Red Army], nor any other supervising political organs of the fleet—knew anything about materials on the fleet collected by the GPU, or [anything] about any investigation conducted by GPU organs of supposedly counterrevolutionary tendencies at Baltflot. [Typewritten note: "to c. Dzerzhinsky, Copy to c. Stalin—for members of the Politburo of TsK (for their information)."]

The OGPU brought this question to the Politburo at the very time of your absence from Moscow, and without informing Morved [the People's Commissariat of Naval Affairs of the RSFSR]. Already, after the first decision of the Politburo on this question, *I personally (27.IX–22) tried to find out the essence of the issue from c. Yagoda. However c. Yagoda did not give me a direct answer, alleging that Antonov-Ovseenko's commission* is dealing with this question.[20]

When Antonov-Ovseenko's commission was working in Petrograd, c. Naumov [chief of the Revolutionary Military Council of the Baltic Fleet], in his turn, tried to receive an explanation from c. Messing [GPU official]. However, again, he did not receive a clear and direct answer.

I confirm, again, that, despite all my attempts in Moscow, and attempts of experienced, leading officials of Baltflot in Petrograd, to establish normal permanent working relations between Morved and the GPU organs, the latter, apparently, has had a prejudiced attitude toward the Navy. Processing the information collected by the GPU organs, as well as all its operations concerning the Navy, have been conducted without Morved's knowledge. This has resulted in many errors and blunders.

Commissar of Naval Forces of the Republic, Zof

In turn, Trotsky wrote to Dzerzhinsky, sending a copy of his letter to Stalin, as general secretary, for distribution to all Politburo members.

DOCUMENT

· 27 ·

Memorandum from L. D. Trotsky to F. Dzerzhinsky. AP RF,
f. 3, op. 58, d. 2, ll. 114–15.

Absolutely secret
   To c. Dzerzhinsky
   Copies to Politburo members (for informational purposes)
   15 October 1922
The work of the GPU organs is completely abnormal and full of errors
in connection with the case of the Petrograd sailors, for which Antonov-
Ovseenko's commission was sent. These errors consist in the fact that
preliminary investigation, collection of evidence, surveillance, reporting to
higher authorities, and other [activities] are conducted completely without
participation of the most authoritative Party officials of Morved. For example, in Petrograd, all this was hidden from c. Naumov, a member of the
RVS [Revolutionary Military Council] of Baltflot, and in Moscow, c. Zof.
   In the specific case of Baltflot, there have already been, in the
past, enormous mistakes, for which the Politburo issued specific decisions. And so, now, one receives the impression that GPU officials consider it a matter of honor for themselves to present a "surprise," rather
than to work together with those officials who are closest to the case.
   15.X.22
   Trotsky

Two days later, Dzerzhinsky replied to Trotsky by referring him to
Stalin.

DOCUMENT

· 28 ·

Memorandum from F. Dzerzhinsky to L. D. Trotsky. AP RF,
f. 3, op. 58, d. 2, ll. 121–22.

Copy to c. Stalin
   The GPU coordinated the processing of the case about the mood of the
Kronstadt sailors with the secretary of the TsK, c. Stalin, who can best
say why the case was directed in one way as opposed to another.
   17.10.1922
On the same day, 17 October, Trotsky forwarded Dzerzhinsky's
reply to the Central Committee Secretariat, demanding that the issue
be placed on the Politburo agenda for discussion.

DOCUMENT

· 29 ·

Note from L. D. Trotsky to the Secretariat of TsK related to the
Morved case, in connection with F. E. Dzerzhinsky's answer. AP RF,
f. 3, op. 58, d. 2, ll. 121–22.
17 October 1922

Secret

I am forwarding, herewith, c. Dzerzhinsky's answer, and am asking to
schedule the question of the GPU work for the next possible session of
the Politburo.

[Appendix, Dzerzhinsky's letter, attached]

No stenographic record exists of that meeting, but Trotsky succeeded in his request that the Politburo censure the GPU for its violation of procedures and, at least temporarily, stopped a police campaign against the Party-military command structure.

DOCUMENT

· 30 ·

Decision of the Politburo of TsK RKP(b). On work of the GPU.
RGASPI, f. 17, op. 3, d. 17, l. 4.
26 October 1922

No. 33. Point 14. On Work of the OGPU. (Politburo No. 22 from 19.X).
(cc. Unshlikht, Messing, Naumov, Zof also in attendance).

To acknowledge the mistake of the GPU in not informing the political
leader of the fleet, Naumov, about new evidence concerning the fleet.

To request that, within a week, and on the basis of existing procedures,
the GPU develop, with the corresponding organs of the military and
military-naval administration, more concrete and precise forms of mutual communication and cooperative work, which will serve the full interests of the case. To request that c. Unshlikht provide a written affidavit
about arrests within the fleet to which c. Zof referred in this [Politburo]
session.

Dzerzhinsky's reply to Trotsky (document 28) is revealing. Possibly,
Dzerzhinsky was trying to deflect blame onto Stalin, not wanting a
direct confrontation with Trotsky, but this seems unlikely, since
such a tactic would have been too transparent to be effective. More
likely, Stalin was working closely with Yagoda against Trotsky,

not informing even Dzerzhinsky. In any case, the document shows how deeply Stalin was involved in operational activities of the GPU, even at an early stage—even more so than the head of the agency, Dzerzhinsky.

Stalin's supervision of the political police was logical, since he was the Party's general secretary and, although the political police was directly subordinate to the Party's Central Committee and to Sovnarkom, it was the Politburo, as the documents above show, that really determined policy and operational lines of political police activity. However, Stalin's involvement with the agency went much deeper than mere supervision. He monitored and, when he could, manipulated agency policy from the beginning. Though not as much revered or feared as Dzerzhinsky in the early and middle 1920s, Stalin was not afraid, even early on, to chide the head of the Cheka. The following document, dating from July 1922, shows Dzerzhinsky's formal relationship to Stalin, who had been elected to the new position of general secretary only in April. Like other senior revolutionaries, Dzerzhinsky saw Stalin at this time as subordinate within the Bolshevik hierarchy, and the position of general secretary as basically an administrative position. As a result, Dzerzhinsky did not address Stalin personally so much as institutionally. Still, the letter shows not only Stalin's close monitoring of GPU affairs, but the power he could wield simply by virtue of his position. Despite his revolutionary stature, Dzerzhinsky was subject to Party discipline, and therefore to the general secretary.

DOCUMENT

· 31 ·

Memorandum of F. E. Dzerzhinsky to I. V. Stalin on the reasons
for not sending a report on GPU activities for May 1922. RGASPI,
f. 76, op. 3, d. 253, l. 1.
6 July 1922

The GPU informs you that, according to the agreement with the Secretariat of the TsK RKP, our report is presented to the TsK before the 7th of each month. Dispatch of a report is usually precipitated by a reminder from the TsK Secretariat.

Not receiving this reminder at the beginning of June of this year, the GPU sent an inquiry to the TsK, [and the latter] explained that, as an exception, preparing a report for May was not necessary. As a result, the May survey was, naturally, not sent.

At present, the Information Department is compiling a report for May–June. The layout of the report is significantly improved and broader [than in previous reports]. Despite that, however, the survey will be sent to you earlier than the specified deadline (20th of July), and will arrive at the TsK no later than July 15.

Chairman OGPU Dzerzhinsky

During the early 1920s, the political police survived near elimination, reorganization, and severe financial and staff reductions. Through the aggressive leadership of Feliks Dzerzhinsky and his deputy Unshlikht, the reorganized OGPU transformed itself from a revolutionary fighting organization into a political police, and made itself useful to the leaders of the Communist Party. As general secretary of the Party, Stalin supported the OGPU, and attempted to use it to bolster his own authority, as well as the authority of the Bolsheviks against their perceived enemies. At the same time, he did not yet have the kind of control over the political police that would come later.

CHAPTER TWO

Threats from Abroad, Infiltrating the Economy
1927–1930

In the early and mid–1920s, Stalin played a moderating role within the Politburo among other and sometimes more senior members. His position as general secretary gave him influence, and he certainly saw potential in using the GPU, but he did not try to overstep the limits of his power. By the late 1920s, however, Stalin had maneuvered himself into a position of clear leadership of the Communist Party and the Soviet state. Lenin had died in 1924 and, as general secretary, Stalin used his position in an alliance with other Politburo members to isolate and then exile Trotsky. Dzerzhinsky died in 1926, and this gave Stalin a freer hand to work with Dzerzhinsky's deputy and the new OGPU head, Menzhinsky, as the most dynamic leader of that agency. Through the OGPU, Stalin kept track of Trotsky's associates still in the country, and he helped maintain adherence to the Party majority's commitment to NEP policies of state capitalism. By 1927 and 1928, however, Stalin began to fear that NEP policies were leaving the country vulnerable to hostile intervention, and defenseless in case of war.

War seemed an increasingly likely possibility in the mid- and late 1920s, as the international situation worsened for the Soviet Union. In April 1926, Dzerzhinsky, in one of his last reports to Stalin as head of the OGPU, warned of imminent invasion by Poland, especially after the coup of May 1926 brought Marshal Józef Piłsudski to power. Piłsudski had been responsible for Soviet defeats in Poland in 1920, and had long advocated a union of Baltic states against the Bolsheviks, including an independent Ukraine. Dzerzhinsky feared that, now that Piłsudski was installed as virtual dictator, nothing could stop him making an attempt to recruit Romania and even Italy into a scheme, backed by Britain, of military intervention to separate Belorussia and western Ukraine from the USSR. During the same period, Stalin received reports from Yagoda about increased Polish military intelligence activity against the USSR, also backed by the British, and carried on in collusion with intelligence services of other Versailles-created states along the Soviet border. In the same vein, Yagoda informed Stalin of increased British diplomatic and press efforts to isolate and do serious damage to Soviet international efforts.[1]

Such fears came at a time of, and reflected, deteriorating relations between Britain and the Soviet Union. British hostility toward the Soviet Union intensified for several reasons: the increasing political influence of the Conservative Party under Stanley Baldwin; perceptions of persistent revolutionary agitation by Soviet agents in Britain; and Soviet support of the Communists in China and India, which threatened British interests in the area.[2] British concerns were not unfounded, despite Soviet denial of the infamous 1924 "Zinoviev" letter, the forged missive that had supposedly been sent by Grigorii Zinoviev, encouraging the British Communists to incite an uprising. Both Communist International and OGPU disinformation campaigns had been carried out under cover of the Soviet diplomatic mission in Britain, and this led the British to take the extraordinary step of raiding the London headquarters of the Soviet trade organization, Arcos, in May 1927. The raid was one of a series of steps that led to the rupture of Soviet-British relations in 1927, and reignited fears among Soviet leaders of capitalist encirclement and war.

The break with Britain occurred just at the time that Soviet leaders faced major decisions about how to fund expanded industrialization, and gave impetus to Stalin's increasingly determined intention to bring about forced industrialization, based on autarkic policies of internal resource extraction. As if this were not enough, the British rupture came on top of the near annihilation of the Chinese Communists by Nationalist paramilitary organizations, and the collapse of Soviet intelligence activities in China.[3]

In all, then, 1927 marked a turning point for Stalin, as well as for others in the Soviet leadership, toward more aggressive plans for industrial development, and expansion of socialist sectors in agriculture. While all agreed on the necessity for a five year plan for rapid growth, questions arose about the pace of expansion, the mix of state and private growth, and whether or not to invite foreign investment. Bukharin and other moderates in the leadership argued for a continuation of policies to encourage peasants to produce for the state within the framework of a mixed private and state market, to encourage foreign involvement, and for industrial expansion within the existing framework of NEP state capitalism. On the other hand, Stalin began to move increasingly toward a more radical and isolationist interpretation of building socialism in one country. He regarded private agriculture and private trade as a dangerous threat to the Soviet state, controlled by kulaks, and market-trading middlemen, the infamous Nepmen. Stalin favored an all-out campaign to bring socialism to the countryside: to eliminate the kulak hold on rural parts of the country, and, if necessary, to bring about collectivization and state control over agriculture by force. As early as 1928, he received confirmation of his concerns in reports from the political police about the growth of kulak influence in the country, and of supposedly conscious and coordinated efforts to sabotage the state's agricultural goals.[4]

Stalin also became convinced of widespread conspiracies, involving domestic and foreign agent networks, to sabotage industrial expansion efforts. Significant increases in industrial accidents, an appalling number of train wrecks, corruption, poor construction, and delayed schedules convinced Stalin and the political police that such incidents resulted not from the reckless haste of planners, managers, and political leaders, but from the coordinated efforts of hostile governments, anti-Soviet émigré groups, and internal enemies. Some leaders, such as Sergo Ordzhonikidze, later Commissar of Heavy Industry, and Maksim Litvinov, in the Commissariat of Foreign Affairs, were not as inclined as Stalin to see the pervasive hand of conspiracy, but police reports reinforced Stalin's ingrained paranoia.

As Stalin pushed for more forceful measures of collectivization and a more intensive pace of industrial construction, moderate leaders resisted, arguing that his policies would drive the country to ruin and even civil war. Many economic and technical specialists, working in planning or administrative positions, agreed. Stalin saw conspiracy in their resistance, especially among the older technical and economic intelligentsia, trained and in prominent positions already before the revolution. He had a populist hatred of the "intellectual" intelligentsia, and believed that to question his vision of socialist construction was tantamount to questioning the revolution. Stalin saw (and created) conspiracy everywhere around him. He successfully marginalized moderate leaders by branding them as part of a "Right Deviation" within the Party, and he discredited moderate approaches to modernization by connecting them to efforts, domestically and abroad, to destroy the Soviet Union. In the late 1920s, Stalin did not attempt to arrest moderate Party leaders such as Bukharin, Mikhail Tomsky, Aleksei Rykov, Lev Kamenev, and Grigorii Zinoviev, among others. That came later, in the 1930s, but he managed to remove many long-time Bolsheviks from their positions in the Politburo, and to demote them to lesser positions within the Central Committee and state apparatus. By 1929 and 1930, Stalin and his close entourage dominated the Politburo and Party policy.

Infiltrating the Economy

The later years of the 1920s also saw an expanded role for the political police. Police reports and investigations reinforced Stalin's fears of conspiracies, and furthered his political vendetta against Party moderates. In turn, the OGPU benefited by Stalin's increasing use of it to find or create conspiracies and intrigues against him. Beginning in 1927, the role of the political police in the economy began to expand dramatically, especially in connection with Stalin's campaign to prove widespread and conscious "wrecking" (*vreditel'stvo*) among moderate specialists and economic managers, and to tie that conspiracy to the so-called Right Deviation within the Party. This was easy enough to do, since the regime's policies of forcing the pace of production and industrial construction led to an inevitable increase in accidents, material shortages, breakdowns, and worker discontent. Stalin, as well as others in the leadership, ascribed these dysfunctional aspects of industrialization to the work of saboteurs and spies. The campaign to root out these counterrevolutionary elements centered on the network of specialists, as well as the growing number of foreign workers in Soviet enterprises. By the late 1920s, several tens of thousands of foreigners were employed in key sectors, even in defense enterprises. Stalin called on the political police to combat these "subversive forces." Inevitably, this brought the OGPU into the direct management of the economy since, in order to root out saboteurs, agents had to become involved in overseeing actual work and management practices. Their involvement in economic affairs also led to a physical and permanent presence in work places, on trains, and on other forms of transport. As the following documents reveal, political police officials soon found themselves deeply involved in the forced mobilization of the populace to achieve the regime's economic goals.

DOCUMENT

· 32 ·

From the decision of the Politburo of TsK VKP(b)⁵ on security of factories
of the military industry. RGASPI, f. 17, op. 162, d. 4, l. 70.

3 March 1927

No. 89. Point 3—OGPU report.

[...]

3. In view of the lack of security in major factories of the military industry, as well as the largest factories that are directly or indirectly important for defense of the country, to create a commission consisting of cc.
Menzhinsky (c. Yagoda as substitute), Kuibyshev [...] and Rudzutak [...].
To charge said commission with the task of assessing the security situation of factories in terms of possible explosions, arson, etc. and also to
investigate reasons preventing normal work of factories. To present a
draft of practical actions for improvement of factories' security to the
Politburo.

By the end of March, Menzhinsky's commission proposed a number of measures, adopted by the Politburo, that militarized many
factories under OGPU control, and essentially criminalized accidents
as subversive counterrevolutionary activity. As the following document shows, the commission also gave broad powers to the political
police to punish individuals administratively, outside of the judicial
system.

DOCUMENT

· 33 ·

Decision of the Politburo of TsK VKP(b). On measures of struggle against
subversive actions. RGASPI, f. 17, op. 162, d. 4, ll. 89, 94–96.

31 March 1927

No. 93. Point 3—Question of the OGPU. (PB [Politburo] from 24.III.27,
protocol No. 92, Point 27). (c. Yagoda).

To confirm suggestions of the meeting of the board of the OGPU,
plenipotentiaries and heads of [OGPU] administrations, about measures
of struggle against subversive actions, fires, explosions, and other acts of
wrecking.

[...]

Section 1

1) To enact measures of firefighting, and struggle against explosions and other subversive activities, that are the result of either sabotage or administrative negligence, and also for continuing supervision and control over security, fire prevention equipment, and safety installations in warehouses, factories, and enterprises of state significance, create a permanent Commission within the OGPU: [to consist of] representatives from Voenved [Military Affairs Commissariat], the OGPU, VSNKh [Supreme Economic Council], NKPS [People's Commissariat of Transportation], and the VTsSPS [All-Union Central Council of Trade Unions], under the chairmanship of the OGPU representative, and in localities to establish corresponding commissions under the PP OGPU [local GPU plenipotentiaries].

2) To recommend that the Central Committee of the VKP(b), by special circular letter to Party organizations and by mounting a press campaign to explain to workers the dangers threatening socialist construction from fires, explosions, and damage of machine installations as a result of both sabotage by foreign states and negligent attitudes of workers and administration to the business of protecting the enterprise, and to require workers themselves to attend to the protection of their enterprise.

3) In all enterprises of state significance, to hold the director personally responsible for introducing measures to protect the enterprise and its parts, and to require the same of authoritative personnel in different parts of the enterprise (shops, etc.).

4) To consider it necessary to abolish civilian protection at enterprises of state significance, and toward this end, to recommend that the OGPU and VSNKh once again consider the list of factories and enterprises, separating those of state significance, in order to establish militarized security in the latter [...].
   To recognize as necessary the transfer of protection of military-industrial enterprises, strategically important points, and railroad infrastructure, as well as especially important state objects and enterprises—to Voenved or OGPU forces.
   [...]

6) To issue, through Soviet institutions, a decree to expel all extraneous residents [not associated with enterprises] from premises of enterprises of state significance.
   [...]

Section 2

1) To strengthen repression, through both OGPU and Party measures, for negligence, for nonimplementation of fire protection measures.

2) To raise [such] negligence […] in enterprises of state significance to the level of a state crime.

3) To give authority to the OGPU to adjudicate extra judicially, even up to the application of VMN [capital punishment], and to publicize in the press cases of subversive activity, fires, explosions, damage to machine installations, and any other cases specified in sections 1 and 2.

Section 3

1) To prohibit employment of political refugees [*perebezhchiki*] in factories of the defense industry, in military warehouses, and on railroads […]

2) To establish exclusion zones in which political refugees are prohibited from living, including in this, Ukraine, ZVO [Western Military District], LVO [Leningrad Military District] (not including the northern provinces [*severnykh gubernii*]), MVO [Moscow Military District], SKK [Northern Caucasus Territory], Transcaucasia, railroad lines, and industrial centers in other areas. Exceptions to this [order] are allowed only with OGPU permission.

3) To close borders to refugees, and to accept them only in exceptional cases, through organs of the OGPU.

4) To charge NKPS to complete within 6 months cleansing of the unreliable element [*neblagonadezhnogo elementa*] from border area rail lines in Belorussia, Ukraine, and LVO, in accordance with lists drawn up by the special railway commissions (DOK, TsOK).[6]

Foreign Spies, Industrial Wrecking, and the Antimonarchist Campaign

The murder of a Soviet special envoy, Petr Voikov, in Warsaw on 7 June 1927, gave Stalin further grounds to suspect foreign intrigues, and to expand political police activity. The Soviet foreign minister, Georgii Chicherin, regarded the murder as a personal act of revenge, with no wider implications, and the British, French, and German governments "went out of their way" to dissociate themselves from it. Still, Stalin decided that it had been initiated by the British to provoke war between Poland and the Soviet Union, and was part of an overall strategy to isolate the USSR internationally and disrupt Soviet development.[7] Whether Stalin really believed this, or found the murder a convenient excuse, is difficult to know, but the following documents show that he decided to use the murder to enact a campaign of "mass repression" against "monarchists" and "White Guardists," the name applied to those who had fought or sympathized with anti-Bolshevik military forces during the Civil War. Stalin orchestrated this campaign while on vacation in Sochi, on the Black Sea, and communicated with others through coded telegrams. In his wire to Molotov on the matter one day after the murder (document 34), as well as to Menzhinsky, Stalin hinted at but provided no firm evidence of British involvement. Nonetheless, his missives laid out a detailed and multipronged plan of police operations combined with public and international propaganda. Stalin enumerated the number of "enemies" to be tried and executed, and based on his recommendations, the campaigns also led to an unspecified increase in police personnel, and to an "improvement" in the "material conditions" of police officials. Stalin's injunction to use extrajudicial forms of sentencing led, as well, to a systematization of police administrative sentencing boards.

Significantly, the police campaigns were the first after the Civil War in which Stalin orchestrated the use of mass repression. In this case, police were given the authority to search, detain, or arrest any number of people suspected of being or having been sympathetic to monarchist or anti-Soviet political groupings. Those subject to police attention need not have committed any specific crime. Stalin initiated the campaigns and gave specific instructions when they should end. The highly publicized execution of twenty individuals precipitated strong negative reaction outside the Soviet Union, even from social democratic and communist workers' organizations, but the police campaigns and executions served the purpose that Stalin intended—to heighten domestic fears of hostile capitalist encirclement, of enemies diligently at work, and of an imminent war. These campaigns also gave the political police a sense of prestige, as well as of Stalin's public support for methods of mass repression.

DOCUMENT

· 34 ·

Coded telegram from I. V. Stalin to V. M. Molotov on hardening punitive measures in relation to the murder of the plenipotentiary of the USSR to Poland P. L. Voikov. RGASPI, f. 558, op. 11, d. 71, ll. 2–3.
8 June 1927

———

I have received [information] about Voikov's murder by an [émigré] monarchist. One senses England's hand [here]. They want to provoke a conflict with Poland. They want to repeat Sarajevo or, at least, the Switzerland incident related to the murder of Vorovsky.[8]

This requires maximum circumspection on our part. We cannot demand control over the Polish court during the trial. Poland will not agree. Poland must express regret and must issue an official statement that it will take the strictest measures to protect our people and to punish those guilty of the murder. It is necessary to publish an official notice or to make a statement to the population from an appropriate organ or person, indicating that public opinion in the USSR considers the English Conservative Party to have inspired the murder, and that it is trying to create a new Sarajevo.

We must immediately declare as hostages all known monarchists who are sitting in our prisons and concentration camps. It is necessary, now, to shoot five or ten monarchists, declaring that new groups of monarchists will be shot for each attempted murder. It is necessary to give the OGPU a directive to make mass searches and arrests of monarchists and of all kinds of White Guardists all over the USSR for the purpose of their complete liquidation by all measures.

Voikov's murder gives us the grounds for the complete destruction of monarchist and White Guard cells in all parts of the USSR by all revolutionary means. The goal of strengthening our [defensive] rear requires this from us.

The same day, the Politburo codified Stalin's suggestions to Molotov, point by point, but increased the number of people to be shot to twenty from the five or ten suggested by Stalin. Those executed became known as "The Twenty," and as documents below reveal, their execution became a focal point for a number of events.

DOCUMENT

· 35 ·

Decision of the Politburo of the TsK VKP(b). On measures in connection with White Guardist actions. RGASPI, f. 17, op. 162, d. 5, l. 35.
8 June 1927

---

1) To publish a government statement about the recent facts of White Guard actions, with an appeal to workers, and all laboring people, to maintain intense vigilance, and to commission the OGPU to take decisive measures in relation to White Guardists.
2) Also, to publish a special appeal by TsK VKP(b) on this issue.
3) To commission the OGPU to carry out mass searches and arrests of White Guardists.
4) After publishing the government statement, to publish an OGPU communiqué about the execution of 20 well-known White Guardists, who were guilty of crimes against Soviet power.

5) To agree that the OGPU can, by itself, decide to authorize PP to pass extrajudicial sentences on White Guardists guilty of a crime, up to execution by shooting.

6) To recognize as necessary strengthening the OGPU both by [an increase in] staff and by material means.

[...]

8) To organize a commission consisting of cc. Voroshilov, Menzhinsky, and Yagoda for strengthening measures of security of central [state] institutions as well as for some leaders. C. Voroshilov is charged to call the commission.

9) To create a commission consisting of cc. Rykov, Bukharin, and Molotov for working out additional political and economic actions in connection with the intensification of White Guardist activities, and the role that foreign governments play [in those activities]. To charge the commissions to present proposals at tomorrow's session of the Politburo. To assign the same commission to edit the government statement and the TsK statement. C. Rykov is charged with convoking the commission.

Two weeks later, Stalin elaborated on his suspicions about foreign intervention, sabotage, and spying to Menzhinsky. The latter had written to Stalin to inquire about the operations, which precipitated the following telegram. The document highlights Stalin's attention to OGPU activities abroad and to counterespionage matters inside the country, since these were intertwined with foreign policy. His direction of these activities reveals the extent to which Stalin immersed himself in the details of foreign policy and the political police, and his micromanagement of information to be made public. These documents also reveal his deep-seated suspicion of constant conspiracy and danger. In the following telegram, Stalin refers to Sidney Reilly, the famous British adventurer and spy, who was caught, interrogated, and executed by the OGPU in 1925.[9]

DOCUMENT

· 36 ·

Coded telegram from I. V. Stalin to V. R. Menzhinsky on tasks of the OGPU. RGASPI, f. 558, op. 11, d. 71, l. 29.[10]

23 June 1927

Thank your for your communication. Contact the TsK for instructions. My personal opinion: 1) London's agents are deeper among us than it seems, and their safe houses will remain. 2) We should use mass arrests to destroy English spy networks [and] for recruitment among those arrested through Artuzov's department and to develop a system of voluntarism among the youth in favor of OGPU and its organs.[11] 3) One or two show trials of English spies would be good in order to have official material to use in England and Europe. 4) Publication of El'vengren's interrogation loses its persuasiveness in light of the anonymity of the author of the article.[12] 5) Publication of such interrogations have a huge significance, if it can be arranged skillfully, and the authors of such articles should be well known judicial officials, lawyers, professors. 6) Pay special attention to spying in military commands, aviation, and in the fleet.

When do you think you can publish Reilly's interrogation? That *must* be arranged skilfully.[13]

Greetings, Stalin

It is unclear from Stalin's telegram whether he was justifying to Menzhinsky the value of mass arrests already completed, or making an argument for their continuation. A week after Stalin's telegram to Menzhinsky, however, the Politburo decided to end the mass operation, and issued the following decision.

DOCUMENT

· 37 ·

Decision of the Politburo of TsK VKP(b) following c. M[enzhinsky]'s information. RGASPI, f. 17, op. 162, d. 5, l. 55.
30 June 1927

1) To issue a communiqué to newspapers about the liquidation of Operput and his followers.[14]
    [...]
3) Not to continue mass operations, but to concentrate attention of the OGPU on the fastest processing of mass operations already concluded.
4) To assign the OGPU to present, within a fortnight, written information, with as exact as possible data, concerning results of operations already concluded.
5) To authorize the OGPU to exile families of the executed.
6) As an exception, to allow mass operations in Georgia [to continue]. To understand that the figures presented are significantly exaggerated. To recognize as necessary to limit arrests to the most active elements and, in particular, to take into consideration areas where *gruzmeks* [Georgian Mensheviks] have the greatest influence.

7) To place c. Chicherin in charge of publishing information about actions of English counterespionage in the USSR.

The Politburo decision is interesting for several reasons, first for what it indicates about political control of the judicial system. The Politburo showed no hesitation about dictating the outcome of judicial trials, a practice that was and continued to be commonplace. Second, the decision shows to what extent OGPU operations, especially mass operations, were dictated by the Party leadership, and not the state. On Stalin's recommendation, the campaign commenced in early June and, by Politburo decision, ceased abruptly at the end of the month. The decision also reveals how closely the Party leaders dictated the numbers of those to be repressed, and the intensity of repression campaigns in different regions.

Stalin's key role in the origin of the campaign is clear, although initiatives for ending it are less clear. The Politburo decision merely a week after Stalin's telegram to Menzhinsky might indicate that he favored a continuation, while the majority of the Politburo decided to end it. There was, in fact, a strong negative reaction, from both the Ministry of Foreign Affairs and the judiciary organs, to the administrative execution of "The Twenty." On several occasions, Chicherin in particular warned of strained relations with Germany, Poland, France, and Britain over the issue. International reaction was strongly negative, including letters of protest from communist, labor union, and social democratic organizations in different countries. The operation was creating bad press for the Soviet Union, and that must have been one factor in the decision to stop it. Stalin, as well as other Politburo members, was sensitive to these considerations. Stalin may have concluded that, while the mass operations had been useful to make a point, they had lost that utility and were becoming a liability.

The *Trest* Affair

There is a certain logic to the latter explanation given the context of the decision, which was closely connected to the roll-up of the OGPU operation *Trest*, or "Trust."[15] Begun in 1922, *Trest* ran for a number of years as one of the most successful of Soviet counterespionage operations. Controlled by the OGPU, *Trest* was a front organization that posed as an anti-Soviet monarchist underground "center." OGPU agents, working under cover, developed contacts with and infiltrated a widening network of émigré groups actively working toward overthrow of the Bolshevik regime. By 1924 and 1925, the OGPU controlled nearly all information supplied to, and domestic contacts with, émigré organizations. It was through *Trest* that the Soviets lured a number of prominent figures to sneak into or back into the Soviet Union, either to be fed false information or to be captured. The capture and execution of Sidney Reilly was orchestrated by *Trest* agents, as was the capture of the notorious Socialist Revolutionary terrorist and anti-Bolshevik agent, Boris Savinkov, in 1924.[16] By 1927, however, the web of double, triple, and even quadruple agents was moving beyond the control of the OGPU. In June, the highly publicized defection of several leading *Trest* agents to Finland, including Eduard Operput, embarrassed the Soviet Union and compromised *Trest* operations. These events occurred as the mass operations against monarchists were just beginning, and the OGPU decided to terminate the *Trest* operation. Stalin paid close attention to international politics and foreign policy, and especially to the image of the Soviet Union abroad. It is likely that he concurred in, and perhaps initiated, the ending of mass operations, since they were beginning to impinge on foreign policy goals.

The mass operation against White Guardists concluded with some twenty thousand searches and nine thousand arrests, as well as with the execution of "The Twenty" and the indignant international response. The day following the Politburo's decision to stop the mass operation, Krylenko, the Russian justice commissar, wrote his memorandum (chapter 1, document 18), proposing that administrative sentencing boards be closed, and cases of espionage and counterrevolution be tried within special courts of the judicial system. The Politburo rejected this proposal, but Stalin kept a copy in his safe, and in 1934, on his initiative, the Politburo created just these courts in a decision that copied much of Krylenko's proposal word for word.[17]

Reaction to the administrative execution of "The Twenty" was strong enough that the Bolshevik leaders felt it necessary to make a public defense of such methods, and of the OGPU in general. In part, this took the form of a meeting with delegates of foreign workers' organizations. Stalin's statements, while not surprising, are nonetheless interesting, especially his comparison of the Russian Revolution to the French Revolution, and his reference to the failure of the Paris Commune of 1870–71. Stalin articulated, as well, the essential argument of the doctrine of Socialism in One Country, which stressed the internal strength of the Revolution, but the encirclement by hostile powers. Hence, the need for a "naked sword" (namely the OGPU) to protect the proletariat.

DOCUMENT

· 38 ·

Answer of I. V. Stalin to foreign worker delegates on the role
and place of the GPU in the Soviet state.[18]
5 November 1927

Question 7:

Judicial authority of the GPU [includes] trials without witnesses, without defenders, secret organs. Since the French public opinion finds it hard to accept these measures, it would be interesting to know their basis. Can this authority be expected to change or be withdrawn?

Answer:

The GPU or Cheka is a punitive organ of Soviet power. This organ is more or less similar to the Committee of Public Safety created during the Great French Revolution. It punishes mainly spies, conspirators, terrorists, bandits, speculators, counterfeiters. It represents something like the Military-political Tribunal created for the protection of revolutionary interests against the counterrevolutionary bourge[oisie] and their agents.

This organ was created the very next day after the October revolution, after all sorts of conspiratorial, terrorist, and espionage organizations were uncovered, financed by Russian and foreign capitalists. This organ has developed and become stronger [...] and has been [...] the vigilant guard of the revolution, a naked sword of the proletariat.

[...]

I understand the hatred and mistrust of the bourgeoisie for the GPU. I understand different bourgeois travelers, who come to the USSR, and their first question is whether the GPU is still alive, and whether it is time to liquidate the GPU. All this is understandable and not surprising.

But I refuse to understand some workers' delegates, who come to the USSR, and ask with concern: whether there have been many counterrevolutionaries punished by the GPU, whether the various kinds of terrorists and conspirators against proletarian power will still be punished, whether it is not time to end the existence of the GPU? Where do some workers' delegates get this concern for enemies of the proletarian revolution? In what way can this be explained? How to justify it? They preach for maximum softness, and advise to eliminate the GPU ... But, is it possible to guarantee that, after eliminating the GPU, capitalists of all countries will stop organizing and financing counterrevolutionary groups, conspirators, terrorists, instigators, bombers! Well, is this not foolishness, is it not a crime against the working class to disarm the revolution, without having any guarantees that enemies of the revolution would be disarmed! No, comrades, we don't want to repeat errors of the Parisian Communards.

The Parisian Communards were too soft towards the Versaillers, for which Marx criticized them, with full justification.[19] And they paid for their softness, when Tier [Adolphe Thiers] entered Paris, and tens of thousands of workers were shot by the Versaillers.[20] Do the comrades think that the Russian bourgeoisie and landowners are less bloodthirsty than the Versaillers in France? We know how, anyway, they dealt with workers when they occupied Siberia, Ukraine, the North Caucasus, in alliance with French, English, Japanese, and American interventionists.[21]

By this I do not want to say at all that the domestic situation in the country obliges us to have punitive organs of the revolution. The internal situation of the revolution is so strong and unshakable that it would be possible to live without the GPU. But the fact is that internal enemies are not isolated units. The fact is that they are connected by a thousand threads to the capitalists of all countries, who support them with all their forces, with all their means.

We are a country surrounded by capitalist states. Internal enemies of our revolution are the agents of the capitalists of all countries. Capitalist states serve as a base, and a rear area for internal enemies of our revolution. Being at war with the internal enemies, we, at the same time, conduct the struggle against the counterrevolutionary elements of all countries. You decide now, whether in these conditions, it is possible to manage without such punitive organs as the GPU.

No, comrades, we do not want to repeat errors of the Parisian Communards. The revolution needs the GPU, and the GPU will live with us to put fear into the enemies of the proletariat (stormy applause).

The Ever-Widening Conspiracy: The Shakhty Affair

The atmosphere of paranoia and danger created by the antimonarchist campaigns of 1927 did not abate, but intensified, setting the stage for the famous Shakhty trial of the following year. The prosecution of fifty-five engineers for sabotage in the town of Shakhty, in the Donetsk mining region, is well known, and marked the first significant show trial since that of the Mensheviks and SRs in 1922. The engineers were accused of working with former mine owners living abroad, and foreign intelligence agencies. Along with them, British engineers from the Vickers company were also implicated, as were several Germans from AEG (Allgemeine Elektricitäts-Gesellschaft), the German electrical conglomerate, employed as consultants.[22] Five of the accused were sentenced to death, while forty-three were given prison sentences, but Stalin cautioned that the OGPU should deal carefully with the foreign engineers. Both Litvinov and Chicherin warned against arrest of German specialists, given the delicate

negotiations with German industrialists over aid. The following Politburo decision reflected that caution.

DOCUMENT

· 39 ·

Decision of the Politburo of TsK VKP(b) on the Shakhty case.
On arrests of Germans. RGASPI, f. 17, op. 162, d. 6, ll. 37–38.
8 March 1928

Strictly secret
   No. 14. Point 18—cc. Molotov's and Stalin's proposal. (PB from
2.III.28, Protocol No. 14, Point 12).

1) To arrest those Germans involved, with statement to A.E.G., that this
   concerns not [the firm], but some of [the firm's] agents, co-coordinating
   this with NKID.
2) Not to touch the Englishmen without the commission's approval; to
   interrogate and to release the arrested Englishman; to conduct strong
   surveillance of Vickers's representative, etc. in the USSR.
3) To publish a statement of the USSR public prosecutor on Saturday,
   having c. Rykov to give a speech about this case at the session of the
   Mossovet [Moscow City Council] on Friday.
4) To put in charge a commission consisting of cc. Rykov, Ordzhonikidze, Tomsky, Stalin (with replacement by Molotov), Kuibyshev, c.
   Menzhinsky (with replacement by Yagoda), and Yanson for managing the OGPU and judicial organs in connection with the Shakhty
   case, and conducting practical work along Party, trade union,
   VSNKh, Rabkrin, and GPU lines.[23]
5) To distribute a document, with a TsK introduction, to all TsK and
   TsKK [Central Control Commission of the Communist Party] members, to the narkoms [people's commissars], to the main communist
   economic officials, to the best elements of the *vuzovtsy*-communists
   [higher education students].

   Much of the investigation of the Shakhty affair was conducted by
Yagoda rather than by Menzhinsky, and a week after the Politburo
decision, Yagoda sent a memorandum to Stalin outlining a conspiracy
that went beyond just the Shakhty events. Yagoda warned that the
tentacles of counterrevolutionary activity required a consequent expansion of police investigation, stretching from the Don region to
western Ukraine, and even to Moscow.

DOCUMENT

· 40 ·

Special communication from G. G. Yagoda to I. V. Stalin on the
counterrevolutionary organization in the Donugol system [The Don
Basin Coal Administration]. AP RF, f. 3, op. 58, d. 328, ll. 20–25.
12 March 1928

The OGPU's SKK plenipotentiary [special agent in charge of the North
Caucasus Krai][24] has discovered a powerful organization, which has been
operating for many years in the Donugol. In view of the fact that this
case has gone beyond the framework of the given raion, and its further
development rests in the necessity to conduct investigations in Kharkov
(Donugol Administration) and in Moscow (VSNKh USSR), instructions
were given by us to concentrate investigation of the present case in
Moscow, since it is absolutely clear, following from the case, that this
organization has its center in Moscow, [that] it leads wrecking [activity]
not only in [the] coal [industry], but in other branches of the [national]
economy.

    [...]
The activity of this organization is directed from Poland (Dvorzhan-
chik, former chief shareholder of DGRU [Donetsk Ore Mining Associa-
tion]), and from Germany (Shkaf, former Chairman of the DGRU Shareholders Society, [...] through Moscow (VSNKh USSR) and Kharkov
(Donugol administration). Tasks from Germany are received by Donugol
engineers when they are on business abroad, as well as by specialists of
German firms who arrive in the USSR. [...] Work is carried out with support from abroad [...], sent from Poland and Germany. The organization
has set for itself a wide array of tasks, depending on the development of
the organization. In 1919–1920, the goal was to maintain the value of the
assets and mining equipment in [expectation of the] retreat of the Reds,
but subsequently the organization's program broadened. "(...) Already
in 1925–26, the goal changed, to inflict direct damage on Soviet power
by buying and obtaining unnecessary equipment abroad, by irrational
capital investment, by delaying capital investment and its turnover, by
lowering quality, increasing production costs, increasing [the amount of]
impurities in the coal, and through this, most of all, to harm transport,
decrease the ability to compete abroad, etc. All of this was done to disrupt
the economy of not only Donugol, but the rest of the industry of the
USSR. Talk within the organization is already not about preserving the
value for the old owners, but about direct wrecking of the Soviet economy" (interrogation of engineer Berezovsky).

    [...]

Engineer Berezovsky characterized the third stage of the organization's work as follows: "(...) The third stage of our work began, I think in 1927, in that all our work was tied to intervention in the USSR. [...] We all had to think, each of us in our workplace, in what way to destroy the enterprise's activity [...] [in case of intervention]."

[...]

From evidence of several of those arrested, though not yet sufficiently proven, [it seems that] apart from transfer abroad of heavy machinery, [there were plans to] smuggle weapons into the USSR from abroad, [...] and money for organizing insurgent units in Cossack regions.

The stimulus for recruiting specialists to fulfill the orders and instructions of their former owners was both ideological and material. Engineers and technicians in the organization received almost regular monthly bonuses, usually equivalent to a month's salary, and, in addition, were paid a monthly sum from 100 to 500 rubles for completing particular tasks. Engineer Berezovsky, according to his personal evidence, distributed [to other engineers] around 200,000 rubles. Of this, Berezovsky kept 20,000 for himself.

[...]

In order fully to acquaint you with case material, we will distribute an overview of the case "Wreckers," compiled by the SKK OGPU plenipotentiary.

Deputy Head OGPU (Yagoda)

The Shakhty conspiracy was not an isolated incident, in Stalin's view, and he received confirmation of this through numerous reports and memorandums. The memorandum below from Lazar Kaganovich, one of Stalin's closest associates and in 1928 general party secretary in Ukraine, is an example. In April of that year, Kaganovich warned Stalin of the discovery of an ever-widening conspiracy.

DOCUMENT

· 41 ·

Memorandum from L. M. Kaganovich to I. V. Stalin on investigation of economic counterrevolution in the Donbass. AP RF, f. 3, op. 58, d. 329, ll. 28–31.
26 April 1928

Dear c. Stalin!

OGPU [Handwritten above the line] investigation of economic counterrevolution in the Donbass is completed. The investigation went deep

enough and [was] successful. ["and ... successful": Handwritten above
the line] [...]. Investigative evidence showed that counterrevolution went
beyond the Shakhty case, and goes far beyond the boundaries of Donugol, that the counterrevolutionary organization encompassed a number
of the biggest trusts of Ukraine—Iugostal [The Southern Steel Trust],
Khimugol [Chemical-Coal Trust], IuRT [Southern Ore Trust]. The investigation has established that this kind of organization existed on an all-
union scale in Moscow. The Moscow center was headed by Rabinovich,
the chairman of the Scientific-Technical Council of VSNKh, and others
who came into this were the Chairman of the All-Union Association of
Engineers, Pal'chinsky, as well as others [...].

We have specific evidence saying that the all-union center has its cells,
and has spread its influence, to Siberia (Kuznetsk basin), the Caucasus
(Tkvibulsk coal basin and oil fields), and the Moscow Central Raion
(machine-building factories).

Of course, this latter requires further study and investigation. So far,
the investigation is complete only for the Donugol organization.

[...]

[The investigation] has established precisely that the Donugol counterrevolutionary organization had ties to the Polish and French embassies in
Moscow. [Also] to the Polish consul general in Kharkov, the French war
ministry, the bureau of political police in Berlin, and several government
circles in Germany.

The Poles played the most immediate part in the very creation of the
organization, generously subsidizing it and using it broadly for spying
and subversive work. Head of the Ukrainian organization, engineer Ma-
tov, says with absolute openness: "The organization was a subversive
group for the Polish embassy."

[...]

The organization prepared actively for intervention and, in practice,
took completely real measures for subverting the homeland from inside.

All these materials wholly and fully support your analysis at the TsK
plenary session about new forms of counterrevolutionary work, and
about preparations for interventions on the part of world imperialism.

It seems to me, comrade Stalin, that [we] must not be limited just to the
resolution that was taken at the TsK plenary session. That resolution was
completely and absolutely correct, but now, it is necessary to study more
deeply and concretely all the conditions of work of our trusts and economic organizations, and carry out [...] reorganization not only of the
structure, but of the very work of economic enterprises, which would
secure us from a repeat of similar histories.

In particular, it seems to me that it is necessary to strengthen the role of
the GPU, for example, in a way that there would be senior officials, GPU
plenipotentiaries, in the biggest trusts, something like the GPU transport

organs. ["something ... organs": Handwritten in ink above the line] This reorganization needs to be conducted under supervision and direct leadership of leading officials of the TsK and TsKK [Central Control Commission, Communist Party Inspectorate], otherwise, I am afraid that, in the sense of structures and methods of work, everything will stay the same.

With communist greetings

Your,

L. Kaganovich

As the following document shows, even the normally cautious Krylenko succumbed, at least officially, to the theory that the Shakhty group was only one part of a widespread conspiracy that involved anti-Soviet business and political interests in Poland and other countries, and that had spread from western Ukraine to the Donbass, and still further. The document, a recommendation from a Politburo-appointed commission, also highlights the relative caution expressed in official statements about the extent of conspiracy and sabotage. The statements in the document may seem unrealistic, but they are moderate compared to allegations of foreign and domestic sabotage made during the mass purges of the late 1930s.

DOCUMENT

· 42 ·

Decision of the Politburo commission of TsK VKP(b). On the Shakhty case. AP RF, f. 3, op. 58, d. 329, ll. 10–12.
11 April 1928

Strictly secret

[...] Appendix to the protocol of the meeting of the commission on the Shakhty case from 11.IV.28,

I suggest:

1) Since there is a direct connection of the Donugol case (Kharkov) with the Shakhty case, and the latter is only an episode in relation to the Donugol case;
Since the connection with the Polish [consular] mission and former shareholders can be proven clearly and concretely only for the Donugol case, while in the Shakhty case, this kind of connection might be proven, but not without knowledge of exactly who, when, and where;
And, finally, since only in the Donugol case is it possible to establish facts that compromise Moscow (Rabinovich etc.)— to change the

previous decision of combining both cases in one trial, and to limit [the case] to the top management of Donugol and Shcherbinka Rudoupravlenie [Shcherbinka Ore Mining Administration].

2) In connection with the previous decision: to delay the trial for two weeks, i.e. until 15 May, instead of 21 April, which was decided previously by the Politburo, considering the 10 days that the accused must have to become familiar with the [case] materials, after they receive the indictment on 5 May.

3) To recommend, in this regard, that the OGPU transfer to Moscow the arrested persons and Donugol materials by April 20th.

4) In connection with completion of the investigation of the Shakhty case, to allow the Procuracy to release those arrested persons whose cases will be sent to the court, and to send cases of some for further investigation, or for deportation, etc., in an extrajudicial manner, after OGPU approval.

5) To discuss whether it is expedient to include in the case two more German engineers, Vagener and Zeebald, information about whose wrecking is available. I personally believe that they should not be involved, in order not to complicate the trial, to limit their punishment to deportation from the USSR, despite direct evidence against them given by the accused Bashkin and others.

    G. Yagoda   N. Krylenko

The Shakhty "affair" opened a period of at least two years in which leaders' attention, and Stalin's attention in particular, focused increasingly on the danger posed by widespread conspiracies of specialists, allied with foreign agencies and governments, and with former owners and White Guardists living abroad. The growing hysteria about wrecking in industry seemed to give the OGPU a green light to engage in anti-*spetsy* campaigns, as they came to be called. Likewise, many local Party officials, police, factory cell communists, and workers joined in. Such was the case in Moscow, as the document below shows, and the reaction by leaders reveals their concern that the purge campaign not get out of hand. In the document, Politburo member Ya. Rudzutak requests fellow Politburo members to suspend the decision made by the Moscow Party Committee to include workers in anti-*spetsy* activities.

DOCUMENT

· 43 ·

Memorandum from Ya. Rudzutak[25] to the Politburo of the TsK
(VKP(b) on purging specialists working in Moscow factories.
AP RF, f. 3, op. 58, d. 332, l. 27.
1 June 1928

Absolutely secret
Urgent
As is apparent from the attached communication from c. Rukhimov-ich,[26] it was decided at a meeting of managers and GPU and Procuracy officials, sponsored by the MK VKP(b) [the Moscow Committee of the Party], to carry out a purge of specialists, working in Moscow factories. I request that this decision be tabled until the issue can be discussed in the PB.

Deputy Chairman, Council of Labor and Defense, c. Rudzutak

[Rukhimovich statement]
1.VI–28
[...]
Yesterday, at a gathering sponsored by the MK of managers and Procuracy and OGPU officials, it was decided to carry out a purge of specialists in Moscow factories, no matter whether they are local, republic, or all-union enterprises.

It was decided, as well, to conduct the purge openly, informing the workers. This was communicated to me by c. Tortoriisky, a representative of [...] VSNKh. I regard it as necessary that this issue be discussed in the PB.
Rukhimovich

In order to control the purge process, not to let it get out of hand, Stalin and the Politburo were also careful to restrain the political police from overzealousness.

DOCUMENT

· 44 ·

Decision of the Politburo of the TsK VKP(b). On specialists.
RGASPI, f. 17, op. 162, d. 6, l. 118.
2 August 1928

No. 36 Point 2—On specialists (c. Molotov)
a) To give to the GPU the following directive: while conducting work on
    [...] counterrevolutionary-harmful elements in economic institutions,

which must be conducted systematically and strenuously, especially concerning the major industrial and transportation organs, to require the GPU to use repression and arrests of renowned specialists, in particular, with maximal care, more than is the case now, and to allow arrests of only truly malicious counterrevolutionaries, wreckers, and spies.

Reports about wrecking in the defense industries, transport, and other economic sectors became increasingly detailed and lengthy. The following memorandum from Stalin, concerning a report on the defense industries, reflected his sense of danger and urgency. The report to which Stalin referred was not attached to the memorandum.

DOCUMENT

· 45 ·

Memorandum from I. V. Stalin to members and candidate members of the Politburo of the TsK VKP(b) on the case of the group of specialists in military industries. AP RF, f. 45, op. 1, d. 170, l. 40.
12 May 1928

Absolutely secret

I request that members and candidate members of the Politburo give serious attention to the document being distributed from the RKI, as well as the memorandum from Yagoda on activities of one group of specialists in the military industries. This affair is very serious and urgent, and probably should be examined at the next Politburo session.

I. Stalin

The following memorandum and report detail problems in the country's railroad system. The report presents what is probably a fairly accurate picture of the chaotic state of the rail lines, but the question is still debated, was it the result of wrecking, as Stalin and the OGPU assumed? Was it, instead, a combination of mismanagement, ordinary corruption, and hasty political decisions taken by Stalin and the Politburo, that overburdened and pushed the rail system into collapse? Many have argued that Stalin created, or at least encouraged, the sabotage interpretation in order to deflect blame for poor decisions of the leadership, but it is also very likely that, given the state of the lines, and the discrepancy between managers' assessments and those of the OGPU, Stalin and those around him believed in their conspiracy theories. The report, presented by Stalin, exemplifies the often convoluted language of official communications.

DOCUMENT
· 46 ·

Memorandum from I. V. Stalin to members and candidate members of the Politburo, TsK secretaries, and members of the TsKK Presidium, with appended report by the OGPU on wrecking in railroad transport. AP RF, f. 3, op. 58, d. 372, ll. 25–41.

16 June 1928

About two months ago, the first OGPU memorandum was distributed about wrecking in railroad transport. The second memorandum [...], distributed now, is supplemented by new materials, depositions by specialists, and technical data. Given the extreme importance of the issue, from the point of view of both our economic development and especially defense of the country, [you] are requested to review the memorandum *personally*, and regard it as a *strictly secret document*.

I. Stalin

Absolutely secret

Report No. 2

On the *system* of wrecking activity by a *counterrevolutionary organization* in railroad transport, and its consequences.

Part 1

In furtherance of the previously submitted preliminary report, on the basis of supplemental investigative evidence and conclusions of technical expertise compiled by major engineers and specialists, the activity of a counterrevolutionary organization directed toward the destruction of the locomotive stock is characterized extremely clearly, and exceeds, by far, our first suppositions built on preliminary investigative evidence and agents' materials about the extent of wrecking and its consequences.

The OGPU organized a network of spot inspections on all lines, of the factual condition of the permanent (mobilized) stock of locomotives (the so-called hard, cold NKPS stock). According to current orders and instructions, the mobilized locomotive stock should be maintained in the most exemplary condition and should be ready at any minute to attach to a train. The inspection showed that 25 percent of the permanent (mobilized) stock is in damaged condition, and a part of these locomotives could not even be placed in a military convoy.

This fact alone is enough to disrupt any mobilization [of stock]. Extremely indicative, as well, is the fact that the Moscow–White Sea–Baltic railroad, the most important for moving forces according to the Military Affairs Department, showed the worst condition of its cold stock, specifically, of 65 locomotives in its mobilized stock, only 2 were operable. It is necessary, as well, to note that a week prior to our inspection, an inspector from [the department of] locomotives, NKPS, visited, and his survey of the mobilized stock showed nothing catastrophic. The situation in relation to that line is made worse by the fact that, thanks to orders from the locomotive department NKPS, a huge majority of locomotives working on that line have absolutely no spare parts, so that in case of damage to these parts, a locomotive has to be taken off line. [...] Data [of an all-union technical census of rail lines] showed that the number of malfunctioning locomotives exceeds the official statistic of the NKPS locomotive department by 1,300 units. It is apparent, as well, that with this false data, it is completely impossible to manage transport, to implement correct repair policies, to conduct proper movement of trains in an emergency. [...]

Having surveyed the condition of operational (active) stock, the OGPU went on to a survey of the reserve stock, and discovered that the reserve stock is almost completely destroyed. (In 1925, there were 6,924 [locomotives] and, as of 1 May 1928, 2,200, of these nearly 1,000 have been scheduled to be scrapped.) Also uncovered was a mass transfer of operational locomotives for scrap. [...]

[...] Remarks of the deputy head of the transport planning department, Shukov, one of the most qualified engineers in NKPS, who provided much service to the OGPU, [highlighted] the characteristic attitude of NKPS specialists. In answer to the question posed by c. Blagonravov: "What is the percent of malfunctioning locomotives on the lines at the present moment"—engineer Shukov answered "Close to 30 percent." To the question "How can it be that he gave such an answer, which coincides with OGPU data (from its factual inspection), being that the answer sharply contradicts NKPS statistical data, which showed only 18 percent"—engineer Shukov said: "The number of malfunctioning locomotives is not difficult to establish for any engineer who sorts through this."

However, not one of these literate engineers went to the NKPS Collegium and declared that the locomotive stock is near catastrophe. [...]

[A table with 76 surnames is inserted here—those who had so far been interrogated—with a note that 728 others had been interrogated and had also acknowledged wrecking activity.]

Engineer-wreckers made their goal the destruction of the locomotive stock, as already noted in the pervious report. For the successful realization of their criminal goals they created a precisely calculated system of

wrecking, and covered the results of wrecking with fraudulent statistics, which reflected complete well-being, when in fact the reality was collapse.
[...]
The consequence of the c[ounter]-revolutionary system is revealed with special clarity when we compare the fraudulent statistics with the reality. According to the false numbers, there is, on the face of it, an upward curve, but the reality is a downward curve. According to official statistics, the percent of malfunctioning locomotives in [19]28 was lower than in [19]25. In reality, the percent of malfunctioning locomotives was 7.6 percent higher than in [19]25.
Capital investment in the locomotive department for the last 3 years has not had any effect. [...] Official statistics show that healthy locomotives number 12,042, when in fact there are only 11,003. Official accounts for fuel show that matters are rather good, that fuel expenditure is equal to [19]13, when in fact expenditures continue to increase and significantly exceed 1913 levels.
[...]
The consequences of [wrecking] cannot yet be calculated, although an approximate financial estimation would comprise several hundreds of millions of rubles, but the most important consequence consists in the fact that the locomotive economy of NKPS has been brought to such a situation that it could not cope with the tasks put on it in the case of mobilization and war.
[...]
The OGPU is keeping transport commissar Rudzutak, informed of its investigation, who has agreed to the prosecution of arrests and, on the other side, has carried out personnel changes in both the communist and the noncommunist sections of the NKPS department of locomotives. [...]. [The investigation] will stretch out another several months.
   Assist. Head OGPU (Yagoda)
   Chief, TO OGPU [OGPU Transport Department] (Blagonravov).

Spying Abroad

As in other wrecking cases, the railroad engineers were supposed to have been funded by, and to be working in close collaboration with, foreign military, private, and government spying agencies. The Politburo singled out Poland, Britain, France, and Germany as the countries most involved in plans to wreck Soviet industrialization and to prepare for intervention, and instructed the foreign department of the OGPU to concentrate its attention on these countries. This involved, of course, an increase of funds and personnel to carry out the required tasks.

DOCUMENT
· 47 ·

Decision of the Politburo of TsK VKP(b). On the work of
INO OGPU [Foreign Department of the OGPU]. AP RF,
f. 3, op. 50, d. 32, l. 115.
5 February 1930

Strictly secret

No. 116. Point 38—About the INO (cc. Kaganovich, Yagoda, Messing). To approve a proposal of the commission of the Politburo, with amendments.

1. Regions of intelligence work of INO OGPU.

Since it is necessary to concentrate all our intelligence forces and means on certain main territorial areas, INO OGPU [will concentrate] its intelligence activities on the following basic regions:

1. England
2. France
3. Germany (Center)
4. Poland
5. Romania
6. Japan
7. Limitrophes [Recently created border states or areas: Latvia, Lithuania, Estonia, and parts of Poland and Finland, separated from the Russian empire after World War I]

2. Goals of INO OGPU.

1. Elucidation of and penetration into émigré wrecking centers, no matter their locations.
2. Detecting terrorist organizations in all the places where they are concentrated.
3. Penetration of interventionist plans made by the leadership circles of England, Germany, France, Poland, Romania, and Japan, and clarification when they are supposed to be implemented.
4. Elucidation and exposure of plans for financial and economic blockade by the leadership circles of the mentioned countries.
5. Extraction of documents of confidential military-political agreements and contracts between the above mentioned countries.
6. Struggle against foreign espionage in our organizations.
7. Organization of the destruction of traitors, deserters, and leaders of White Guard terrorist organizations.
8. Extraction of inventions, technical-industrial drawings, and secrets for our industry that are impossible to receive in a normal manner, and

9. Surveillance over Soviet institutions abroad, and exposure of latent traitors.

3. Staff and means.

1. To appoint to the positions of foreign work of the OGPU the five most responsible Party members who may become organizers and political leaders in the major areas of the INO activities abroad. To select these comrades in accordance with OGPU requests.
2. Within a year, to appoint to the positions of foreign work of the OGPU no fewer than fifty especially vetted and reliable Party members in order to train them theoretically and practically, according to the OGPU program.
3. To recognize as essentially necessary to transfer work of INO organs from Soviet organs to an extralegal status. To carry this out gradually within a year. Orgraspred TsK [Organization and Personnel Department of the TsK], together with the OGPU, must develop a procedure for inserting INO employees in Soviet institutions abroad, [and] how to serve these institutions while maintaining the secrecy [of their INO work].
4. To increase funding of work abroad up to 300 thousand gold rubles for accomplishing the goals of the OGPU.

The Industrial Party Trial

The spiral of suspicion and repression came to a head with the Industrial Party trial (25 November–7 December 1930). In this trial, a number of prominent engineers and economists were accused of collaboration with foreign groups, especially in France, to cripple Soviet economic and industrial planning efforts in conjunction with armed intervention to overthrow the Soviet government. The eight engineers who were tried included L. K. Ramzin, supposedly the leader, an internationally renowned technical expert, and director of the Moscow Thermal Engineering Institute. The group, labeled the Trade-Industrial Committee, Torgprom, included other prominent engineers such as Professor V. A. Larichev. The group supposedly had ties to a number of other anti-Soviet conspiratorial organizations, as the documents below show. Stalin paid close attention to the process of arrest and interrogation. He made specific recommendations for how the OGPU should conduct interrogations, and how to describe the plans and activities of the main defendants.[27]

DOCUMENT

· 48 ·

Letter from I. V. Stalin to V. R. Menzhinsky on future directions of testimony of the leaders of the TKP [Labor-Peasant Party] and of the Promparty [Industrial Party]. October 1930. TsA FSB RF, f. 2, op. 9, d. 388, ll. 270–71.[28]

C. Menzhinsky!

Letter of 2.X and material received. Ramzin's interrogation is very interesting. In my opinion, the most interesting in his testimony—the issue of intervention in general and especially the issue about the timing of intervention. It turns out that intervention was suggested for 1930, but was postponed to 1931, and even to 1932. This is very probable, and important. It is all the more important given that [this information also] came from initial sources, i.e. from the group Ryabushinsky, Gukasov, Denisov, Nobel, which seems the most powerful, both because of finances and because of ties to the French and English governments. It may seem that the TKP or the "Promparty" or Miliukov's "party" are the most powerful. But this is not correct. The main power—[is] the group Ryabushinsky—Denisov—Nobel, and so forth, i.e. "Torgprom" [Trade-Industrial Committee].[29] The TKP, "Promparty," Miliukov's "Party" are merely lackeys running after "Torgprom." Even more interesting is the timing of intervention, according to "Torgprom." The question of intervention, in general, and the timing, especially, is, as we know, our primary interest.

Given this, my suggestions:

a) For new (future) testimony of top leaders of TKP, "Promparty," and especially Ramzin, make one of the most important central points the issue of intervention and the timing of intervention. 1) Why postpone intervention from 1930? 2) Is it because Poland is not ready? 3) Maybe because Romania is not ready? 4) Maybe because the limitrophes are not yet joined with Poland? 5) Why postpone intervention until 1931? 6) [What does it mean to say] intervention "can" be postponed to 1932? And so forth and so on.

b) Bring into the case Larichev and other members of the Promparty TsK [central committee] and interrogate them rigorously about this, letting them see Ramzin's interrogation.

c) Rigorously interrogate Groman,[30] who, according to Ramzin's [interrogation], pleaded with the "Unified Center" that "intervention be postponed until 1932."

d) Run Messrs. Kondrat'ev, Yurovsky, Chayanov,[31] and so forth through the gauntlet [*propustit' skvoz' stroi*], who cleverly shirk away from a "tendency toward intervention," but who are (without argument!)

interventionists, and rigorously interrogate them about the timing of intervention. (Kondrat'ev, Iurovsky, and Chayanov should know about that, as well, as does Miliukov,[32] to whom they went running for consultation.)

If it turns out that Ramzin's testimony is confirmed and concretized by the testimony of others of the accused (Groman, Larichev, Kondrat'ev and company, and so forth), then that will be a serious success for the OGPU, because we will give the material gained in this form to the TsK sections, and to the workers of every country, and [we will] conduct the widest campaign against the interventionists, and get to the point where we will paralyze, undermine attempts at intervention for the next year or two, which is not unimportant for us.

Understood?

Greetings. I. Stalin

The Politburo established a special commission to manage the trial, which included Stalin, Krylenko, and Menzhinsky. Stalin carefully managed the course of interrogations, publicity surrounding the trial, and the trial itself. He also gave specific orders to shoot "two or three dozen wreckers," including the economists N. D. Kondrat'ev and V. G. Groman.[33]

DOCUMENT

· 49 ·

Decision of the Politburo of TsK VKP(b). On use of the wreckers' depositions about intervention. RGASPI, f. 17, op. 162, d. 9, l. 53.
25 October 1930

No. 13 Point 17—About use of the wreckers' depositions in the matter of intervention (c. Stalin).

a)   To recognize as necessary to prosecute immediately the united coun-terrevolutionary center, having wreckers' depositions about prepar-ing intervention as the central point during the trial.
b)   To create a commission consisting of cc. Litvinov, Voroshilov, Stalin, Menzhinsky, and Krylenko for reviewing quickly the wreckers' depo-sitions about intervention for publication.

C. Litvinov is charged to call the commission.

DOCUMENT

· 50 ·

Decision of the Politburo of TsK VKP(b). On the trial of the
Promparty. RGASPI, f. 17, op. 162, d. 9, l. 81.
25 November 1930

No. 16 Point 48/48—To create a commission consisting of cc. Litvinov
(with replacement by Krestinsky), Molotov, Stalin, Voroshilov, Menzhinsky, Yanson, and Krylenko to direct the case of the Promparty
    C. Molotov is charged to call [the commission].

As the trial commenced on 25 November, the Politburo approved
suggestions presented by Stalin's committee to organize public responses to the trial and accusations, and to publicize the results as
widely as possible.

DOCUMENT

· 51 ·

Proposal of the commission on the case of the Promparty.
RGASPI, f. 17, op. 162, d. 9, ll. 81–82.
25 November 1930

No. 16, Point 53/53—
    To accept the suggestion of the commission to send the following direc-
tives to TsKs of the national Communist Parties, kraikoms (obkoms) of
VKP(b) [Communist Party krai and oblast committees]:
    "In connection with the trial of wreckers and agents of foreign inter-
vention, which will begin 25.XI, TsK VKP(b) suggests to engage in explanatory work among the broad working masses and in the Red Army,
revealing the interventionist plans of imperialists, and France, in particular, of White Guardist émigrés, and of their bourgeois-wrecking agents in
the USSR. A major goal of this must be mobilization of the masses against
military intervention, and for strengthening defense of the country. During this explanatory work, the counterrevolutionary-wrecking activities
of some top elements that belong to the old bourgeois engineers' and
proprietors' [society] should be revealed. However, persecution and
sweeping charges against engineers in general should be avoided.
    In this connection TsK VKP(b) directs:

a) To start extended coverage of the trial and of the goals of the Party
    and working class in their struggle against wreckers and intervention-
    ists, and for strengthening the defense of the country.

b) To organize widespread demonstrations in all cities and factory set-
    tlements, and of collective farmers, if possible, during the first day of
    the trial.
c) Main slogans must be the following:

    1. Our response to the sorties of our class enemies, foreign interven-
        tionists, White émigrés, wreckers, and kulaks will be merciless pun-
        ishment of agents of military intervention, and a broad offensive of
        socialism on all fronts of our economic construction.
    2. Our response to the threat of intervention will be to strengthen
        the defense of the country.
    3. Broaden development of military training of the broad masses, to
        strengthen the defense of the USSR, to strengthen the Red Army.
    4. Our response to the class enemy is in creating millions of shock
        workers [*udarniki*] among the working class, and a fighting uni-
        ty of workers around the Bolshevik Party.
    5. The proletarian dictatorship of the USSR, together with the in-
        ternational revolutionary proletariat, will smash all and any
        attempts of interventionists and their internal counterrevolution-
        ary agents.
    6. Down with warmongers! Long live the Red Army, a bulwark of
        peace and the true sentry of the Soviet state!"

As a result of the trial, five of the eight defendants were sentenced to
be shot, including Ramzin, and three others to prison terms. The executions were commuted to prison sentences of ten years. In specialists'
"prisons," Ramzin and many others continued to work in their areas
of expertise, and he and others were pardoned and released in the
early 1930s. The OGPU staged related trials in many other economic
sectors, arresting in all some eight thousand specialists. Most of these
were from the liberal or conservative prerevolutionary technical elite.[34]

Historians have long wondered about Stalin's motives for setting
such a campaign in motion. Most explanations center on his attempt to
create an atmosphere of crisis to gain support for his increasingly radical and reckless industrial plans, to silence moderate critics in the Party
and state apparatus, and to displace blame for problems in the economy caused by the regime's policies. The documents above lend weight
to this view, although they do not shed light on what Stalin may or
may not have really believed. At the same time, a genuine sense of paranoia comes through in these documents. Whatever other reasons
motivated Stalin, he very likely believed the prophecies of doom that
his fears generated. Whatever the case, these campaigns solidified the
prestige and authority of the political police as Stalin's main means to

accomplish his political and economic objectives. By the end of the 1920s, Stalin's position as undisputed leader and the power and prestige of the OGPU were intertwined. Stalin needed the political police to enforce his power and his version of reality, and the political police had a willing patron. As the following chapters show, however, although Stalin needed the political police, he also remained its master.

CHAPTER THREE

Subduing the Countryside
1928–1933

By the end of 1930, Stalin's group was fully in power, having defeated, with the help of the OGPU, Trotsky and the so-called Left Opposition, and then the Party moderates of the so-called Right Deviation. Having silenced potential opposition, Stalin's group pushed industrialization and collectivization plans still further. In a period of a few short years, during the era of the first Five Year Plan, begun in 1928, Stalin's revolution from above destroyed the remnants of NEP's state capitalism, and collectivized the great majority of the country's agrarian lands. Leaders forced the pace of industrial construction at the expense of wages, housing, and other basic amenities, creating widespread scarcities and deplorable work and living conditions. For several years at the beginning of the 1930s, all nonstate trade was made illegal, which worsened conditions of scarcity and fueled a large black market. In the countryside, local Party and police officials dispossessed millions of peasants, confiscating land, livestock, equipment, even homes, for the sake of collectivization. Over two million peasants were deported to penal colonies for actively resisting collectivization or for refusing to join collective farms.

Forced industrialization and collectivization on such a scale required a commensurate amount of coercion, opening up a new era of mass repressions. And this was especially true in rural areas of the country. There, the regime waged nothing less than a war to bring agrarian lands under control of the state. The movement of police, Party officials, and political troops into the countryside, and the resistance that that provoked, led to the first of several mass waves of repression of the 1930s. This chapter explores the expansion of the political police and its authority in the late 1920s and early 1930s as a revolutionary arm of the state, violently reshaping social and economic relations.

Turning to the Countryside

The early 1930s saw a change in direction for the political police. During the years 1927 to 1930, the OGPU focused its primary activities on the problems associated with Stalin's industrialization drive: the supposed sabotage of industrial enterprises, whole economic sectors, and defense industries. The Politburo even charged the OGPU abroad with orienting their intelligence activities toward uncovering foreign intentions and attempts to wreck Soviet modernization efforts. In 1929 and 1930 this began to change, as the police's attention turned increasingly to the rural areas of the country. There, Stalin's socialist offensive was not going well. Policies of forced collectivization and grain confiscation, begun in 1929, were meeting strong resistance, and the spiral of state violence and popular reaction was escalating into a full-out social war. Stalin did not trust the army to bring order and control to the countryside, since many soldiers were from the villages, and in some cases, even officers participated in resistance efforts against the regime's policies. Given the situation, Stalin and the Politburo turned to the political police to break the hold of the "kulaks" in rural areas and carry out the destruction of the "kulak class." OGPU numbers and funding rose substantially in the first years of the 1930s, and most of those increases went to expand local GPU offices and operational centers. In addition, over five thousand officers were assigned to political departments in farm equipment centers, the machine tractor stations that serviced the new collective farms. This was in many ways a brilliant solution to the problem of rural control, a network of police spies and informants that added yet another layer of contact and surveillance in the countryside.

The escalation of state violence in rural areas led the political police to engage in large-scale operations of mass purging and deportation for the first time since the Civil War years. While the OGPU worked against purported political opposition during the 1920s, the rural dekulakization campaigns of the early 1930s returned the agency to its Civil War origins as a revolutionary arm of the Bolshevik state—altering social and economic relations through administrative violence.

The dekulakization campaigns gave a new lease on life to the political police, but that was not all. In addition to expansion in the countryside, police authority also expanded in other ways. In 1930, carceral institutions and labor camps were removed from jurisdiction of the justice commissariat, and the labor camp administration, the GULAG, was founded and placed under sole authority of the OGPU.[1] In the same year, secret reorganization of the civil police brought the civil police, the *militsiia*, under operational control of the OGPU. By the end of 1932, the *militsiia* was fully integrated, administratively, as well as operationally, into the political police.

The turning point toward mass violence in the countryside came in September and early October 1930, when the Politburo demanded that the OGPU and justice officials in the Russian and Ukrainian republics "take decisive and rapid measures of repression, up to and including execution by shooting, against kulaks who organize terroristic attacks against Soviet and Party officials, and who engage in other counterrevolutionary activities."[2] In some instances, as in the case in Nizhnee Povol'zhie, below, resistance included army officers, and was described as an insurgency.

DOCUMENT

· 52 ·

Decision of the Politburo of TsK VKP(b). On kulak terror.
RGASPI, f. 17, op. 162, d. 7, l. 158.
26 September 1929

Strictly secret

No. 99 Point 8—For cc. Sheboldaev's and Trilisser's information

a) In light of uncovering an SR [Socialist Revolutionary]-kulak insurgent organization in the Nizhnee Povol'zhie region, to charge the OGPU to take decisive measures to liquidate it, shooting up to 50 leaders of the organization, especially prominent kulaks, military officers, and repatriatees.

To publish information in the press about execution of the most prominent group of nobility-kulak-SR leaders of the organization.

b) To establish that, as a rule, cases of anti-Soviet actions in the countryside must be resolved in a judicial order, except for cases of individual acts of terrorism against representatives of local Soviet and Communist Party organizations and against active supporters of Soviet power.

Uprisings in the Povol'zhie (the Volga region) were not an isolated event. Reports and telegrams from the western republics, Western

Siberia, the Black Earth region, the Caucasus, and the Central Asian republics painted a picture of widespread and open resistance. On 10 March 1930, the Politburo attempted to deflect blame by declaring, in a decision circulated to Party officials, that resistance resulted, in large part, from excesses and abuses by local authorities in their zeal to implement collectivization.[3] For a brief period, the collectivization drive was relaxed, but this led to still more mass departures from farms, and an intensification of protest. As the reports below show, local authorities and police were caught off guard and unable, initially, to quell disturbances. These reports show the kind of vacillation between repression and conciliation that was endemic in rural areas. They also show some of the first instances when mass purges were directed not just against supposed class enemies, but also against specific national groups.

DOCUMENT

· 53 ·

Note telegraphed from Tiflis, from S. F. Redens to G. G. Yagoda, with TsK cover letter to members and candidate members of the Politburo of TsK VKP(b) and of the Presidium of TsKK. AP RF, f. 3, op. 30, d. 146, ll. 74–77.

11 March 1930

Strictly secret

On c. Stalin's instruction, herewith c. Redens's note, telegraphed 11.III.30 from Tiflis, for your information

Deputy secretary of TsK
Absolutely secret
As a result of insufficient protection of a huge number of newly created collective farms, of […] excesses, of errors inside the kolkhozes, and because of general activation of anti-Soviet and kulak' forces, [Handwritten annotations by Yagoda: "to c. Stalin. G. Yagoda. 11.III.30." "The OGPU has given an order to transfer 630 bayonets and to give 500 rifles and 500 grenades, and cartridges. G. Yagoda."] mass anti–collective farm actions, which have a political tinge, have been increasing. In Kakhetiia, and in a number of areas of the Tiflis Okrug [district], some settlements of Sevan Okrug, and all Turkic areas of Armenia have been in ferment. In the listed areas, a steady disintegration of collective farms is occurring, which in some cases has been accompanied by destruction of village soviets,

beating and exiling of *partkomsomoltsy* [members of the Communist Party and Communist Youth League], and village activists. Riots that have taken place so far were liquidated by peaceful means and negotiation and, only in rare instances, by using demonstrations and a small number of army forces; initiators and participants of violence were not arrested, except in a small number of exceptions; on occasion, attempts to arrest people encountered general resistance of a whole village; as a result the planned arrests were canceled, which the population interpreted as a sign of weakness of power, and which encouraged even further impudence of the insurgents, acting under the influence of anti-Soviet forces. *The following demands were made:*

1) to release all arrested people. 2) to remove Party members and members of the Komsomol. 3) to fire and remove a number of local Soviet officials. 4) to allow free trade. 5) to allow delivery of goods from abroad. 6) to reduce prices of goods. 7) to cancel [forced] insurance and state bond purchases. 8) to hand over all informers and 9) to return exiled people and to return property to those who were dekulakized. An especially tense situation was created in Turkic areas. In Vedibasar Raion of the Yerivan Okrug, up to 250 persons, together with families, have gone into the mountains, up to 150 of them were armed. The remaining people started widespread agitation in neighboring villages for recruitment of supporters. For liquidation of the uprising, which gained a widespread character, an army unit of up to 30 bayonets had to be sent. The subsequent negotiations have not yielded results, therefore *operational actions will begin on 11 March.* In other Turkic regions of Armenia, as well as in some Turkish border villages in Georgia, there is a strong resettlement movement, escaping to Turkey. Across Georgia and Armenia, and especially in Azerbaijan, a group of kulaks have gone underground and are hiding with weapons, and make up the core of existing gangs. In connection with the general situation in the countryside, gangs in Azerbaijan have started actions, because of which army units had to be sent *to Gandzhin Okrug, Karabakh, and Nakhkrai [Nakhichevan Krai] for military operations.* The situation is serious. If drastic measures are not taken, by spring we may have serious complications, which may turn into armed uprisings. We *have been taking all possible measures along GPU lines:*

1) The local GPU apparatus in all okrugs has been strengthened; representatives have been chosen and sent, all reserve Chekists have been used. 2) Operational groups have been organized by the okrug GPU department. 3) In the most affected areas, groups of Communards were created. 4) The *militsiia* was subordinated to the GPU organs, and has been used entirely for operational work. 5) Demobilization of Red Army troops was postponed, and all they have been used for is strengthening border protection. 6) Operational groups were formed out of GPU regiments 3 through 8 and 24, 130 personnel in Azerbaijan, and

100 personnel in Georgia. 300 bayonets out of the frontier units were allotted to Armenia.

We consider absolutely necessary: 1) to remove the initiators of demonstrations, the instigators and participants of kolkhoz closings and beatings, of propagandists and malicious kulaks, not hesitating in the resolute suppression of resistance. 2) In order to maintain planned operations to liquidate active bandit groups and anti-Soviet demonstrations, to transfer 1,000 bayonets, with corresponding number of commanding officers, equipment, and technical means to GPU command. 3) To allot 30 light machine guns, 500 rifles, 500 grenades, and 300,000 cartridges to supply the [newly] created operational groups and Communard units. We are asking for urgent instructions. Acquaint Stalin and Sergo [Ordzhonikidze] with this note.

Deputy chairman GPU, Redens
Head of SOU [Secret-Operational Department] Beria

DOCUMENT

· 54 ·

Decision of the Politburo of TsK VKP(b). On Ukraine and
Belorussia. AP RF, f. 3, op. 30, d. 193, l. 154?.

Strictly secret
15 March 1930
According to available information, there are grounds to suggest that, in case of serious kulak-peasant actions in Right Bank Ukraine [western Ukraine, on the right bank of the Dnieper river] and Belorussia, especially in connection with the forthcoming eviction of Polish-kulak counterrevolutionary and espionage elements from frontier districts, the Polish government may decide on intervention. In order to avoid this, TsK considers it necessary to send the following instructions to the TsK of KP(b)U [Communist Party of Ukraine] and the TsK of Belorussia, as well as to the respective OGPU organs:

1) to implement decisively the TsK directive from 10 March [the decision to relax collectivization] on struggling against distortions of the Party line regarding the countryside, especially in frontier raions of Ukraine and Belorussia;

2) to concentrate attention in the direction of both political work and military-Cheka preparations, in order not to allow any actions of an anti-Soviet character in frontier raions of Ukraine and Belorussia;

3) to relocate sufficient numbers of skilled Party workers to frontier raions within one week to support local organizations;

4) to strengthen the quantity and quality of the operative staff and mobile OGPU units in frontier raions within one week, by drawing on other OGPU reserves;

5) to prepare with all possible thoroughness, and to conduct with maximum speed, operations to arrest and exile kulak-Polish counterrevolutionary elements;

6) to conduct the exile operation of kulak-Polish elements with maximum orderliness and minimum disruption;

7) to [understand] the major task: to prevent any kind of mass actions in frontier raions;

8) since this directive is especially secret, to share it only with members of the Politburo of TsK KP(b)U and the Bureau of TsK of Belorussia, and PP of the OGPU Balitsky and Rappoport.

DOCUMENT

· 55 ·

Note from G. G. Yagoda and G. E. Evdokimov to I. V. Stalin on political moods in Siberia in connection with collectivization and dekulakization. AP RF, f. 3, op. 30, d. 147, ll. 117–23.
20 March 1930

Absolutely secret

According to recently received material from the Siberian PP OGPU, we consider it necessary to draw attention to the following basic events:

Negative events in the course of collectivization and dekulakization:

Mass excesses and distortions in the course of collectivization and dekulakization in many Siberian okrugs have reached threatening dimensions. Continuing distortions evoke serious vacillation in the attitudes of the middle-poor mass [of peasants], which creates a favorable ground for development of kulak c.r. [counterrevolutionary] agitation, and for the spread of kulak influence among parts of the middle and even the poor [peasants]. As a result, in Siberia, the trend toward demonstrations does not diminish but grows, led by kulak counterrevolutionaries and turning into a movement of bandit gangs.

[...]

Flight from kolkhozes is increasing [...]. For the period 10–15.III in Siberia, over 2,000 households resigned from kolkhozes, and this is according to [still] incomplete data. Altogether, data from the first 2 five-day periods of March [show that] flight from kolkhozes equals 9,394.

Anti-Soviet manifestation:

Despite widespread OGPU operational work to remove c.r. elements from the countryside (as of 13.III, 8,117 c.r. activists have been arrested in the Krai as a whole, 14 c.r. organizations with 470 members, and 350 groups with 2,779 members have been liquidated), continuing excesses and distortions in the work of low-level Soviet and Party organs, the lack of more or less satisfactory political work, tied to measures of collectivization and dekulakization, has created a favorable ground for development of kulak activism, and for the spread of kulak influence among part of the middle [peasantry], and even among the poor.

Growth in the number of mass demonstrations, which started in mid-February, deserves serious attention. [...] The recent increase in demonstrations is connected with kulak strengthening [...] and, in March, mass demonstrations have taken on the character of rebellion, along with the formation of active bandit gangs.

[...]

As of 1.III, 21 bandit gangs were active, comprising in total 473 persons. As of 15.III, 28 gangs were active (3 have been liquidated) with a total number of 2,992 persons (of those, 1,442 persons have been liquidated). As this shows, there has been an increase of 7 gangs with 2,519 members in the course of 15 days.

There has been an intensification of the political aspect of active bandit kulak formation, transforming from individual acts of assault and robbery to open gang activity, such as capturing population centers and destroying Soviet power in them, organization of peasant assemblies, with an appeal to join a broad movement of rebellion under a kulak banner.

Kulak exile:

Exile of category 2 kulaks[4] in the Krai proceeds very weakly. As of 15.III, 10,302 households have been exiled out of 30,000 registered [kulak] households, which comprises 34.3 percent. [...] As such, the plan for exile will be significantly underfulfilled by the time spring makes the roads impassable.

[...]

Given the delay in exiling, and the presence of up to 8,000 kulaks escaped from their place of [exile], banditry in the Krai will inevitably be strengthened, and cannot help but have an effect on the spring planting campaign.

Everything above speaks to the necessity of taking a series of measures by Krai organizations to overcome decisively and quickly the serious inadequacies of the work of local organizations.

Deputy Head OGPU   (Yagoda)

Head SOU (Evdokimov)

DOCUMENT
· 56 ·

Telegram from M. O. Razumov, first secretary of Tatar obkom
[oblast committee] of VKP(b) to the Secretariat of TsK VKP(b)
regarding peasant riots. AP RF, f. 3, op. 30, d. 146, ll. 124–25.
22 March 1930

Secret
During the last days, in a number of both Russian and Tatar volosts
[districts] of Arsk, and in Mamadyshsk, Chistopolsk, and Buinsk can-
tons, an extraordinarily high kulak activism has been noticed. They are
trying to use the recent Party directives about the struggle against distortions, and Party work related to this, in a provocative way in order to
destroy collective farming. Kulaks' propaganda results in abolishing collective farms in a number of cases, and in poor and middle-level peasants
leaving collective farms. In these villages, preparation for spring sowing
has stopped. In twelve volosts of Arsk canton, anti–collective farm movements encompass one hundred collectivized settlements, [and] put forward demands that are obviously counterrevolutionary:
To disband collective farms [...], to stop dekulakization and exile of
kulaks, to restore rights of all *lishentsy* [those deprived of civil rights],
[...] to remove poor peasants from kulaks' houses, to close Soviet schools,
to arrest teachers, to open religious schools. In some instances, additional demands are to reopen churches and mosques.
[...]

DOCUMENT
· 57 ·

Report from G. G. Yagoda and E. G. Evdokimov on counterrevolutionary
activity in the Didoevsk Sector of Andiisk Okrug, Dagestan. AP RF, f. 3, op. 30,
d. 147, ll. 15–17.

4 April 1930 [Handwritten note: "For c. Stalin from c. Yagoda"]
The Didoevsk Sector [*uchastok*] of Andiisky Okrug is a most inaccessible and a most backward area, with an enclosed natural economy. In
the past, this area was a base of revolts of Said Bek Shamil and Gotsinsky.[5]
As a result of the worst possible distortions, naked administrative measures, forced collectivization and tractorization, etc. [...], mass revolts

started in this area on 11 March. These were inspired and led by c-r [counterrevolutionary] Sharia elements. The organized unit that appeared dispersed local Soviet organs, and created a "Sharia council" and a "Shariat court." *The leader of this revolt is a former commander of Red partisans, Vali Doigaev [also Dolgaev]. The initial number of armed people [in Dolgaev's revolt] was about 100; according to the latest information, the number of the armed people reached, ostensibly, about 500.* This movement encompassed almost all settlements of the Didoevsk Sector.

The leader of the movement, Vali Doigaev, on behalf of insurgents, has made the following demands to the *Okrispolkom* [Executive committee of the okrug soviet]:

1) To cancel collectivization.
2) To return *waqf* land [endowed religious lands].
3) To stop prosecution of clergy.

Essentially, Doigaev's complaint is about the outrages committed by local authorities, and demands their replacement. Vali Doigaev's answer to the demand that he disband his force was: "I took the leadership intentionally, because angry, uneducated, and silly *didoevtsy* [Didoev residents] may make a lot of trouble."
[...]
The area of the revolt has been surrounded by military troops and partisan units. They have occupied all mountain passes and roads to Georgia and the northeast part of Dagestan.
[...]
We consider that the Didoevsk problem must be resolved without intervention of armed force [Sentence up to here marked with double line in margin.] if Didoevsk residents follow the conditions of their surrender.

It is absolutely clear that, given the *didoevtsy*'s attitude towards the Dagestan government, the latter won't be able to resolve the question in a peaceful way (by sending a delegation to Georgia).

We consider it necessary to send urgently either a [special] *Soviet commission from the center or some official from the Rostov SKK* [North Caucasus Krai]
Deputy chairman of the OGPU (Yagoda)
Head of SOU OGPU (Evdokimov)

DOCUMENT
· 58 ·

Coded telegram from M. M. Malinov to I. V. Stalin regarding mass peasant
demonstrations. AP RF, f. 3, op. 58, d. 200, l. 132.
1 March 1931

In the village of Zmeintsy of the Shchigrovsk Raion, expropriation for
meat procurement of two cows from two prosperous middle peasants
resulted in a mass demonstration. A trial and a prosecutor arrived, and
were driven from the village. The nearby villages of Chizhovka and Konoplianka have joined Zmeintsy. Local officials sent for mass [propa-
ganda] work were beaten. The crowd forcibly took back the instigators
[of the demonstrations]. Yesterday, an operational group of the GPU
faced gunshots in the villages of Chizhovka and Konoplianka. The operational group has retreated. Today a commission of the oblispolkom
[oblast soviet executive committee] and a group of officials was sent for
mass [agitational] work. Depending on results of their work, further measures will be taken and the demonstrations will be liquidated.
  Secretary of TsChO [Central Chernozem Oblast] Malinov.
  [Note written in text: "to members of the PB. I. Stalin."]

Responding to this wave of protest and resistance, the Politburo
substantially increased the number of operational staff for the OGPU
internal and border forces. In turn, funding for the OGPU, which had
remained relatively unchanged from the mid-1920s, rose dramatically, from 56.5 million rubles in 1925 to 57.5 million in 1930 and
88.014 million in 1931:

DOCUMENT
· 59 ·

Decision of the Politburo of TsK RKP(b). On increasing the number of OGPU
employees. RGASPI, f. 17, op. 162, d. 9, ll. 16, 20.
10 August 1930

[...]
  QUESTION concerning the OGPU:
1. To increase the scheduled number of employees of the OGPU by
    3,165 employees starting on 1 October 1930.
2. To increase the number of internal troops of the OGPU by 3,500
    employees, of the troops of the frontier protection force of the

OGPU by 2,500 employees and 3,000 horses starting 1 October 1930.

3. To confirm the 88,014,000 ruble estimate for the OGPU organs for [19]30/31.
4. In case of insufficient funding for prisoner foodstuffs and supplies for the administratively exiled, to recommend that the OGPU apply for additional funding from the reserve fund of SNK [Sovnarkom] of the USSR, after submitting a report for the 2nd half-year of 30/31.
    [...]
6. To create a 250-person reserve for the struggle against kulaks.

Dekulakization and Mass Deportations

Putting new resources into the countryside, the political police and internal border forces returned to a campaign of mass deportations of peasants identified as kulaks. From 1930 through 1932, over two million peasants were forcibly relocated to penal settlements, mostly in the Ural, Western Siberia, and Kazakh areas of the country. Most of these colonies were designed to be agricultural or forestry settlements, and police referred to the inhabitants as "special settlers," or *spetspereselentsy*. The special settlements (*spetsposelki*) were to be administered by the OGPU, but local authorities were supposed to prepare areas to receive settlers. In order to conduct these large-scale operations, the Politburo established a Kulak Commission, chaired by Central Committee member A. A. Andreev, which included Yagoda and P. P. Postyshev, a Central Committee secretary and deputy head of the Ukrainian Communist Party. As the following two documents show, the commission worked up overall plans for the eviction of kulaks, their transportation to resettlement colonies, and the construction of housing; allocation of equipment, food, and medical care; and provision for educational and recreational needs and sectors of work for kulak colonies. Kulaks were to be rounded up and deported in "contingents," or "echelons," in an orderly fashion.[6]

DOCUMENT
· 60 ·

Regarding kulaks. (PB from 11.III.31, protocol No. 29, point 2/6-c). (cc. Andreev, Yagoda, Postyshev). RGASPI, f. 17, op. 162, d. 9, ll. 174, 176–78.
25 March 1931

Accept c. Andreev commission's proposal (see appendix).
Present: committee members cc. Andreev, Yagoda.
Present: cc. Evdokimov, Zakovsky, Zaporozhets, Olshansky
Appendix

I. Heard:
About resettlement of kulak households in Western Siberia (c. Zakovsky spoke).
Decided:

1. To accept c. Zakovsky's proposal concerning resettlement of 40,000 kulak households to northern areas of the Western Siberian Krai during May–June–July 1931.
2. To move the kulak households to the following raions of the Western Siberian Krai: Kargask, Parabel, Kalpashchevo [Kolpashevo], Chainsk, Krivosheino, Baksinsky, Novo-Kuskovo, Zyrianskoe, etc.
3. To suggest to the Siberian Kraikom to begin immediate preparations for eviction of the kulaks [from current residences]. To charge c. Zakovsky, the plenipotentiary of the OGPU to the Western Siberian Krai, with managing the removal, and with the responsibility for carrying out the operation.
4. Resettled kulak households are to be used in agriculture in the black earth massif of the raions mentioned in point 2, and as a workforce for the forestry industry[…].
5. To allow kulak households to take with them a minimum of agricultural tools, haulage livestock, and other productive tools (axes, pitchforks, shovels, etc.).
6. To require exiled kulak households to take with them a necessary food reserve for travel. The size to be decided in localities.
7. To require the Western Siberian Kraikom and c. Zakovsky to create a minimum reserve of food supplies for kulaks employed in forestry work.
   […]
9. To charge SNK USSR to release to the OGPU 3,000,000 rubles for resettling kulak households in the Sibkrai.
   […]

II. Heard:

Resettlement of kulak households in Eastern Siberia.

Decided:

Request c. Yagoda to present a plan for commission review in [15] days on resettlement of kulak households to Eastern Siberia, analogous to the plan for Western Siberia.

III. Heard:

Resettlement of kulak households to the former Akmolinsk and Karkaralinsk provinces of Kazakh ASSR [Autonomous Soviet Socialist Republic] (c. Evdokimov spoke).

1. To confirm the general contingent of kulak households to be resettled to Kazakhstan in 1931 at a level of 150,000 households, distributing them in the areas of the former Akmolinsk and Karkaralinsk provinces, and on lands along the river Tokrau (south of lake Balkhash).
2. Resettled kulak households must be used in the following principal ways: a) coal mining; b) copper production; c) iron ore mining; d) building railways; and e) agriculture.
3. To charge the OGPU with sending to the resettlement areas no less than 10,000 persons (heads of families), no later than 15 April, in order to use them for preparations (house building and other preparation works)—for receiving the rest of the contingent.
4. To send to the areas of future settlements (Akmolinsk-Karaganda) a commission consisting of c. Olshansky (chairman) and members cc. Berman and Gorshkov, along with representatives of VSNKh [Supreme Council of the Economy] of the USSR, of NKZ [Commissariat of Agriculture] of the USSR, and of the Kaz[akh] kraikom of VKP(b) to make all preparations for places of resettlement, and to determine places for resetting kulak households. Work of the commission to be completed in 40 days [4 *dekady*].
5. To recommend to the OGPU to submit for the commission's consideration within one and a half months a plan for financing the resettlement operation, and development of 150,000 kulak households in Kazakhstan.

IV. Heard:

Ongoing operations for resettlement of 25,000 kulak households (cc. Yagoda and Evdokimov spoke).

Decided:

1. To confirm the OGPU plan to resettle 25,000 kulak households.
2. To recommend that SNK USSR expedite release of 6,000,000 rubles from its reserve fund for expenditures connected with resettlement.

V.

[...]

To note receipt of c. Evdokimov's communication about ongoing operations to resettle kulak households in the North Caucasus Krai, Leningrad Oblast, Western Siberia, Eastern Siberian Krai, Transcaucasia, DVK [Far East Krai] and Nizhkrai [Nizhnii Novgorod Krai]. To recommend that the OGPU require local OGPU organs to resettle future kulak households only after sanction of the TsK commission. [...]

DOCUMENT

· 61 ·

Special report from G. G. Yagoda to I. V. Stalin on completion of kulak exile operation. AP RF, f. 3, op. 30, d. 195, l. 163.

15 October 1931

Absolutely secret

Exile of kulaks from areas of full collectivization, which took place from 20 March to 25 April of this year, and from 10 May to 13 September, is finished.

During this time 162,962 households (787,341 persons) were transported.

Among them: Men–242,776

Women–223,834

Children–320,731

In 1930 in total 77,795 households (371,645 persons) were transported, among them:

Men–123,807

Women–113,653

Children–134,185

Thus, in all 240,757 households have been transported (1,158,986 persons).

During the same period there were transported:

Horses–15,355

Carts–7,488

Plows–8,958

Harrows–9,528

All transportations were done in 715 echelons, using 37,897 train cars.

In fact, the campaign was plagued from the beginning by a combination of bureaucratic mismanagement and malicious indifference. Conditions in the colonies were horrific, especially in the early years of the 1930s, and above all in the alternately swampy and densely forested tracts of the Narym region in Western Siberia. In the early 1930s, hundreds of thousands of kulak families were exiled there, and the following documents reveal, in their banal language, the tragedy that was dekulakization.

DOCUMENT

· 62 ·

Report of V. M. Burmistrov[7] to Commissar of Justice, Siberian Krai, Yanson. GANO, f. 47, op. 5, d. 104, l. 10.
7 January 1930

Absolutely secret

The issue of exile and deportation procedures still has not been resolved, despite your communication from 30 October [19]29, No. 17p120, on measures to take, according to the resolution of the Presidium of the Siberian Krai Executive Committee from 12 September 1929, on the struggle against criminal banditry. Siberia continues, as before, to receive parties of exiles, sent by Moscow, with the krai-level administration learning of them only when they arrive, often a large portion of them literally naked and barefoot.

Thus, on 3 January, a completely unexpected party of 160 exiles arrived in Novosibirsk from Leningrad literally without clothes, and the receiving detention administration was forced to transport them using cars, and a part of the [exiles] had frostbite. Such an instance is not unique. The same has happened in Omsk, where 455 exiles have accumulated, in Tomsk, 825 exiles, Novosibirsk, 200, and in other provinces of the Krai. Transporting people to their place of exile in such a manner during the Siberian frost must be out of the question, and to clothe them and give them shoes costs a colossal sum of money. As well, [winter] conditions require us to maintain them in local jails until spring, so that jails are significantly overcrowded, which, as of 1 January, this year, hold 2,774 exiles, the overwhelming majority of whom are without clothing, and who cannot be sent to places of exile until spring, and, further, cannot be released, since all are from the socially dangerous element.

[...]

All of this together requires a complete cessation of transports to Siberia of exiles until 30 May 1930. Please keep me informed of your decision.

Krai Procurator, Siberia

Burmistrov

As the above report shows, poor exile conditions were not always the fault of local authorities, but of miscommunication and callousness of officials and police in charge of transporting the exiles. A Procuracy report from 1931 blamed the OGPU for many of the problems.

DOCUMENT

· 63 ·

Extract of report of the USSR Procuracy to the Presidium of TsIK [Central Executive Committee] USSR on supervision of the OGPU for 1931. 20 December 1931. GARF, f. 8131, op. 37, d. 20, ll. 50–51.

Absolutely secret

[...]

Supervision over exiles and deportees:

Survey of exiles in the Narym Krai, conducted in 1931, has established a number of abnormal phenomena in the organization of the exiles. The most fundamental abnormality is the lack of responsibility for the proper settling of the exiles, and the lack of their use for economic work.

Exiles were settled in such remote locations, that it was impossible to organize their work, and impossible to maintain a minimum of food and clothing. As a result, exiles resorted to theft and robbery, provoking sharp dissatisfaction among the local population, which found expression in vigilante murders of exiles by locals, including participation by local village council authorities.

Administration and organization of work of kulaks, exiled with their families from raions of full collectivization (*spetspereselenie*), is the responsibility of the Chief Administration of Corrective Labor Camps of the OGPU.

In 1931, by order of the OGPU Procurator [the Procuracy official in charge of judicial oversight over the OGPU], the Chief Procurator of the Western Siberian Krai conducted a survey of conditions of special settler villages in the Narym Okrug. The survey revealed the following:

Nearly 50,000 kulak families, about 200,000 individuals, were sent to the Narym Krai from regions of full collectivization, primarily in Western Siberia; this number (50,000) also included approximately 15 percent Ukrainians and Belorussians, and up to 300 families from Oiratsk Oblast [near the Russian-Mongolian border].

[...]

As a consequence of the improper distribution of the workforce (using all available hands for grain harvesting and threshing), the late arrival of exiles in the krai, and the extreme lack of building tools—housing

construction had not started. In several villages, as a result of this, housing conditions were extremely dire, and exiles were in mud huts and
sheds, with no protection from the cold and rain. This situation was made
worse by the lack of warm clothing and boots for most of the population.

Almost all villages, standing at a distance from waterways, had no
stores of foodstuffs, after the end of navigation and the shoaling of rivers,
even though a ten-day reserve of food stores is required.

The catastrophic situation with food stores in these raions, and the lack
of transport, forced the Western Siberian Krai administration to mobilize
horse transport of food stores to northern raions, which required 1,000
horses and took one month.

[...]

Due to the serious situation regarding supply of medical aid, there is a
high death rate among the elderly and the young, especially the latter.
Thus, in the Parabel'sk penal reserve, 1,375 individuals died in the
course of 1 year, [from January] to September, of whom 1,106 were
children.

In the Sredne-Vasiugansk penal reserve 2,158 individuals have died
since the arrival of the settlers on 1 September, that is, 10.3 percent of the
entire population, of which 275 were adult men, 324 women, and 1,559
children. The elderly accounted for 75 percent of the adult deaths.

[...]

Procurator of the Supreme Court of the USSR P. Krasikov

Chief Deputy to the Procurator of the Supreme Court of the USSR,
Procurator of the OGPU, Katanyan

Special settlements were remote and isolated, as this document noted, and they were often cut off for months at a time from supply
routes. Colonists died of starvation from lack of supplies, from exposure in the winter, and from dysentery and malaria in the summer.
Penal colonies were not intended to be death camps, but they often
were, for the NKVD officers as well as the colonists. In the first years
of the 1930s, the colonies lost about 10 percent of their populations
yearly to death.[8] In the remote Aleksandrovsk penal reserve, however,
one-third of the 6,114 *spetspereselentsy* died in the first three months
of their arrival in April 1933. Through lack of police planning, the
colonists and their escorts reached their island encampment on the
Nazino River in late April, only to discover that nothing had been
prepared for their arrival. Numerous settlers had already died on the
arduous trip north by river barge from Tomsk. Armed bandit gangs
had attacked the barge encampments, killed settlers, and stolen much
of their supplies. Upon arrival at their "settlement," a spring snow-
storm isolated the settlers further from supplies and help. After two

days, the heavy snow turned to freezing rain. Without food, shelter, or adequate clothing, the settlers died at a rate of thirty-five to forty a day.[9]

Resettlement Colonies

Despite such incidents, the Politburo decided to remedy problems by placing full responsibility for the camps, for selection, and for transportation with the political police, extending its domain still further.

DOCUMENT

· 64 ·

Protocol of the Andreev Commission from 15 May 1931, on organization of a *Spetspereselenie* Administration, and on productive use of special settlers. RGASPI, f. 17, op. 162, d. 10, ll. 46, 51–54.

(cc. Andreev, Postyshev, Yagoda)

I [...] In light of the outrageous use of the special settler workforce, and the disorganized way in which they are maintained by economic organs, to transfer the whole to OGPU economic, administrative, and organizational management for special settlers, as well as all material stocks and financial funds for special settlers. To recommend that the OGPU organize a special administrative apparatus under the OGPU and at the krai level (Siberia, the Urals, the Northern Krai, and Kazakhstan).

2. For the productive use of special settlers this administration will conclude contracts, both through agreements with individual economic organization, and directly by creating various economic enterprises. [...]

4. To obligate economic organizations to pay special settlers wages no lower than seasonal labor. [...]

II. Plan for resettling kulak families in 1931.

1. In view of the technical impossibility of resettling 150,000 kulak families in raions in Kazakhstan, to acknowledge the possibility of distributing kulak families this year, first of all, 56,000 to raions in Kazakhstan and 55,000 families to the Urals.

2. To allow internal resettlement in Eastern Siberia of 12,000 kulak families northward from the southern border raions, and 12,000 families from the Urals, 7,000 of which have already been settled. [...]

4. To ensure the primary needs of industry and housing construction, transfer special settlers to the northeast areas of Kazakhstan in the following order:
   May–June, 20–25,000 individuals, with transfer of families to follow.
   July–August, the remaining 35,000 households.

5. Require all economic organs of VSNKh, NKPS [Commissariat of Transportation], and Narkomsnab [Commissariat of Supply] to release funds immediately to the OGPU designated for housing construction for the special settlers workforce.
   [Points 5 through 17 enumerated requirements for fifteen commissariats to ensure necessary equipment or supplies to the OGPU settler colonies. These ranged from the agricultural commissariat to the fish industry, health, forestry, and education and culture commissariats. In section III, similar arrangements were articulated for settling or resettling 55,000 kulak families in the Urals Oblast, and the same in Bashkiria.]

[III–V]

VI. Special Consideration.

If any given special settler fulfills all decisions of Soviet power, conducts himself as an honest worker, then after a 5-year period, from the moment of resettlement, he can receive voting rights and all other civil rights.
   [... And finally]

VIII. On careful monitoring of the rules for exiling kulaks

1. In view of existing evidence of instances of a mechanical [purely bureaucratic] approach to the issue of exiling kulaks, given that exile is restricted at times only to a rescinding of voting rights, which can lead to crude mistakes, recommend to the OGPU [...] to ensure a serious and careful monitoring, and to take measures to guarantee that such mistakes do not occur.
   Plan for settlement of kulaks:

1) To the Urals Oblast 55,000 families, of which:

1.	From Ukrainian SSR	30,000 families
2.	From SKK [Northern Caucasus]	15,000 families
3.	From IPO [Ivanovo Industrial Oblast]	5,000 families
4.	From BSSR [Belorussia]	5,000 families
	Total	55,000 families

2) To Kazakhstan   56,000 families, of which:

1.	From NVK [Lower Volga Krai]	10,000 families	
2.	From SVK [Middle Volga Krai]	10,000	"
3.	From TsChO [Central Black Earth region]	10,000	"
4.	From MO [Moscow Oblast]	6,000	"
5.	From LVO [Leningrad Military District]	4,000	"
6.	From Nizh[nii Novgorod] Krai	5,000	"
7.	From Bashkiria	6,000	"
8.	From Tataria	5,000	"
Total		56,000 families	

The recommendations of the Andreev commission were accepted by the Politburo on 20 May.

New Enemies in the Countryside

Despite mass deportations, police and local Soviet officials continued to meet popular resistance to collectivization and the state's high grain quotas. The situation was particularly bad in Ukraine, where Stalin believed, or at least claimed, that peasant intransigence was being provoked by Polish spies and insurgents. Stalin regarded the situation in Ukraine as extremely dangerous, fearing that the USSR might even "lose" the republic. One of the police's most ruthless officials, S. F. Redens, was already stationed in the republic as head of the OGPU and in November 1932, the Politburo, on Stalin's recommendation, dispatched another top-level and equally ruthless official, V. A. Balitsky, to bring Ukraine under control. In Stalin's view, it was the OGPU, in the fight against counterrevolution, that would "transform" Ukraine into a "real fortress of the USSR, a genuinely exemplary republic."[10] As the documents below show, Balitsky and Redens were given complete authority to bring what amounted to a reign of terror to the republic. In turn, the Politburo required a constant stream of reports from the OGPU in Ukraine.

DOCUMENT

· 65 ·

Regarding a special plenipotentiary representative of the OGPU
in Ukraine. RGASPI, f. 17, op. 3, d. 907, l. 20.
25 November 1932

In view of the special state importance for improving work of the OGPU organs in Ukraine, and because of the extensive experience in Ukrainian work by c. Balitsky, TsK VKP(b) decides:

To recommend that the OGPU send a deputy head of the OGPU, c. Balitsky, as a special plenipotentiary representative of the OGPU to Ukraine, for a period of 6 months. To subordinate to him the PP OGPU in Ukraine, c. Redens, and the whole apparatus of the OGPU of Ukraine. To charge c. Balitsky with the task of presenting a short report on work of the OGPU organs of Ukraine to TsK VKP(b) every 20 days.

As the following document shows, Balitsky and Redens fulfilled their obligation, providing reports of counterrevolutionary activities, lengthy interrogations, and measures taken to overcome resistance to fulfilling the state's grain collection quotas. Resistance came from collective farmers, but, as the document below shows, also from local officials. This was a new twist. By late 1932, kulaks had been supposedly removed from Ukraine, and from the countryside in general, and no longer posed a widespread threat to Soviet agriculture. Even so, the regime still met large-scale resistance to fulfilling its grain collection plans. A new enemy had to be found, and this appeared in the form of local Soviet officials, masking their sabotage behind the façade of being good Party members. The lengthy report reproduced in part below became a model that Stalin distributed to officials countrywide on how to deal with intransigent areas. The report concerns events in the Dnepropetrovsk area, which Stalin had singled out even in 1932 as one of about sixty raion-level centers where local officials had protested high grain collection quotas. His preamble made clear his attitude toward local officials who protested against, or tried to mitigate demands from, the center. Stalin's preamble comes first, then a note from Redens, who introduced the investigative materials. Finally comes the original report.

DOCUMENT

· 66 ·

Sabotage of grain collection in Orekhovo Raion of Ukraine.
AP RF, f. 3, op. 58, d. 380, ll. 94–97.
7 December 1932

Secret

To all members and candidate members of the TsK and TsKK, to all obkom, kraikom, and raikom [raion-level] secretaries, and to all Party members of Narkomzem [People's Commissariat of Agriculture] USSR:

Herewith is circulated for [your] information investigative materials on sabotage of grain collection in Orekhovo Raion of Ukraine, sent to the TsK VKP(b) by GPU representative c. Redens. Since these materials are characteristic of a significant number of regions of the Soviet Union, it is, in my opinion, worth it to give them special attention. These materials show, yet again, that the organizers of sabotage are, in the main, "communists," people who carry Party cards in their pockets, but who long ago were torn from the practices of the Party, and were regenerated [into a new form].

[...]

Since the enemy with a Party card in his pocket should be more rigorously punished than one without it, it follows that people such as Golovin (former secretary of the Orekhovo raikom), Palamarchuk (former secretary of the RIK [raion-level soviet executive committee]), Lutsenko, Ordel'ian, Prigoda, and others should be arrested immediately and honored according to their service, i.e. from 5 to 10 years in prison for each. [This was Stalin's judgment on individuals who, for the most part, had not yet been charged or arrested.]

Secretary TsK VKP(b) Stalin.

Herewith, I am sending a copy of investigative materials in the case of resistance to grain collection in the Orekhovo Raion.

In this case, the former chairman of the raikolkhozsoiuz [raion-level collective farm union], Prigoda, was arrested.

[Signed] Redens

To the General Secretary of the TsK KP(b)U, c. Kosior

In Orekhovo Raion and Dnepropetrovsk Oblast, the GPU is conducting an investigation of opposition to grain collection by the administration of several collective farms.

The investigation has established that the raion-level leadership, i.e. secretary of the RPK [raion Party committee] Golovin; chairman of the

RIK Palamarchuk; chairman of the RKS [worker-peasant council], Prigoda; head of the raizu [raion-level administration of land use] Lutsenko; chairman of the control commission, Ordel'ian; and others, gave instructions to village Party organizations and collective farms not to fulfill the raion-level grain procurement plan.

To characterize this, I am sending a copy of the protocols of depositions given by Party members Masliuk, chairman of the commune "Avangard,"[11] Party member Kostenko, chairman of the "Svoboda" commune, Party member Dikyi, head of the MTS [machine tractor station], Morozov, manager of the raion-level office of the swine collective farm union, and Budyak, planner in the RIK.

Although the raion-level leadership of the Dnepropetrovsk obkom was removed, I regard it as necessary to prosecute the guilty.

Chairman, GPU, Ukrainian SSR S. Redens.

27.XI.32
Deposition protocol:

1932, November 21, was deposed as a witness, citizen Masliuk, Gavriil Amvrosievich, born 1889, native of the village Basan', Chubarevka Raion, from poor peasant [background], citizen of Ukrainian SSR, with elementary education, Ukrainian, married, registered on military list as middle political staff, grain farmer by profession, chairman of the "Avangard" commune, Novo-Karlovka village soviet, Orekhovo Raion, never under investigation or tried, Party member since 1925, Party card No. 0787758, living in the "Avangard" commune, Novo-Karlovka village soviet, Orekhovo Raion—reported the following:

"... In the 'Avangard' commune in mid-August this year, the raion-level commission gave a plan [grain procurement quota] in the amount of 10,981 quintals [1,098,100 kg]. On receiving the plan, the Party bureau passed a resolution that, while the plan was large for the commune, it had to be fulfilled. After several days, the then raion-level Party secretary Golovin arrived in the commune [...] and raised the issue of the grain quota plan, taking the position: 'You must realize your mistake in declaring the plan unrealistic, the plan should be accepted, in whatever amount, and then fulfill it 30 percent. We [the raion-level leaders] will protest the plan as unrealistic. We raion-level officials know that the plan is unrealistic, but right now, we have to state that the plan has to be accepted.' With that, the meeting ended. In my opinion, the RPK Secretary could have taken such a position only with the idea of informing the oblast Party committee that the plan was unanimously adopted, and that all is well in the Raion. After a while, the head of the RIK, Palamarchuk, arrived in the commune. I addressed a request to him to reduce the plan, to which he suggested the following:

' "… To take out as much as possible for the sowing material for collective farms of the Orekhovo Raion, so that that same amount can be counted as if the commune fulfilled the grain collections plan, rather than to count the same amount of set-aside grain twice: once by counting the grain taken out as sowing material, and the second time as a shortfall in plan fulfillment by the same quantity.'

"I rejected this statement since I considered it wrong.

"At the end of October of this year, when I was with Kostenko, the head of the commune 'Svoboda'—at the office of the head of the raikolkhozsoiuz, Prigoda, we got to talking about grain collections. I expressed an opinion that the plan is high and difficult to fulfill, to which Prigoda gave both me and Kostenko the following statement:

' "It is necessary for you to supply yourselves in full—to secure all [reserve] stocks, for sowing as well as for backup, and for a number of other [needs]. If you do not supply yourselves, we will prosecute you. Fulfilling the plan may wait, because Golovin, Palamarchuk, and Lutsenko (former head of the raizu) went to the oblast committee with a petition from the Raion to decrease the plan, and probably it will be decreased." '

Such situations deenergized and discouraged communes and artels [an early name for kolkhoz] from implementing the plan of grain procurement …

Deposition protocol:

1932, November 23, deposed as witness, citizen Kostenko, Semen Gur'evich, 37 years old, reported the following:

[This and other depositions follow]

For reference:

Golovin—(former secretary RPK) awaiting assignment from the Dnepropetrovsk obkom (still in Orekhovo)

Ordel'ian—(former chairman KK) works now as an inspector [*kontroler*] in a state farm in Sinel'nikovo

Palamarchuk—(former chairman of the KK) now director of the MTS in V. Lepetikha

Prigoda—(former chairman of a collective farm) now deputy director of a state farm in Krivorozh'e

I have communicated this information to the head of the Party cadre sector, Dnepropetrovsk Obkom, c. Vaisberg.

Dekulakization and Border Cleansing

Using police to put pressure on local officials proved but one tactic that the Politburo used to enforce its demands, and to apportion blame for failure to fulfill plans. At the same time, police also began a second wave of mass roundups, following the initial waves of deku-lakization in 1929–30 and 1931–32. These new mass arrests targeted similar peasant communities in border regions, and especially Soviet citizens with transnational ties or ethnic connections. These ties sup-posedly provided proof of sabotage organized by foreign powers—Poland, Finland, and the Baltic states.

DOCUMENT

· 67 ·

Special communication from G. G. Yagoda to I. V. Stalin on
operations to cleanse areas along the western border of the USSR.
AP RF, f. 3, op. 58, d. 201, ll. 75–87.
26 March 1933

Absolutely secret

Beginning on 16 March this year, operations to cleanse border areas along parts of the Polish border with Ukraine and Belorussia, along the Polish and Latvian borders in the Western Oblast, and along parts of the Latvian and Finnish borders with the LVO [Leningrad Military District], revealed, according to information from 20 March this year, the existence along the whole length of the borders of c-r insurgent and subversive organizations, created and led directly by the Polish and Finnish Military General Staffs, or that became connected to them as they gained strength.

These organizations were planted in the most strategic directions around railroad junctions, fortified raions, and defense installations.

Almost all of the organizations that were uncovered had established one and the same date for an uprising, sometime in the spring of this year.

Along with the rout of the insurgent organizations and centers, also liquidated were residents [local controlling agents], border crossing points, and numerous spy networks of the PGSh [Polish General Staff] and Finnish Intelligence, which, in some cases, managed to penetrate into elite units of the RKKA [Red Army], the *militsiia*, and military schools and installations.

In addition to building themselves up, and preparing and coordinating an insurgency underground, these organizations also carried out system-atic work to destroy collective farms, disrupt the spring sowing cam-paign, make the food difficulties worse (through arson, theft, and spoilage of fodder and foodstuffs), and create dissatisfaction and tense conditions all along the border areas.

In Ukrainian SSR

Liquidated a major c-r Petliuraite organization[12] in several populated areas […], tied to Polish-Petliuraite intelligence organs, preparing for an uprising in spring of this year, and led by the Polish spy Soroka, Anastasii (arrested).

The organization was designated to carry out mass terror against Soviet-Party and collective farm activists. Participants of the organization have been identified in the Kharkov tractor factory and the Moscow factory "Elektrostal," where they were sent for subversive work by their leaders.

Liquidated an insurgent spying organization in […] raions of Vinnitsa and Kiev oblasts, created by the Polish-Petliuraite agent, Kuchera, sent from across the border, and who headed a bandit gang in 1930. A cell of the organization has been identified in the Staro-Konstantinovka military installation.

[…]

In the Slavutsk border forces unit, an insurgent c-r organization was uncovered, working toward an uprising in the spring of this year, and led by agents of the Polish-Petliuraite spies Khomich and Melenchuk. The organization distributed a proclamation of the "Ukrainian Revolutionary Committee," and conducted work to disrupt the spring planting campaign and the work of collective farms.

Liquidated a c-r Petliuraite insurgency organization in the Potievka and Malin raions of Kiev Oblast, working toward an uprising in the spring of this year. Their assignment was to seize an armory in Radomysl, and then move on the town of Zhitomir.

[…]

Uncovered an insurgency organization in Korsun' Raion, Kiev Oblast, made up mainly of teachers and students. It has been established that this organization had ties to Kiev higher educational institutions.

[…]

Of insurgents formed from national minorities, special mention needs to be made of the c-r organization of German colonists in the Zel'ts Raion of Odessa Oblast, created by the SR Roteker, and building their insurgency plans on the hope of Hitler's arrival in Ukraine. A major insurgent organization of Germans, in Karllibknekht Raion of Odessa Oblast, is tied to Romania. The organization's timing for uprising was scheduled for spring of this year. The German colonist Shtekler (arrested) led the organization. Ties of the organization to Kiev and the Donbass have been identified.

[…]

Overall, 9,514 persons have been detained to date, of whom 2,311 are spies or connected with spying, 6,074 belong to insurgency organizations and groups, 1,119 acknowledged ties to those who fled across the border, have been repressed, etc. Seized 2,011 weapons, of which 1,780 are rifles, and 213 smoothbores.

In BSSR

A fundamental blow has been delivered to the subversive-insurgent organizations, planted by the second department of the Polish General Staff, in strategic directions along roads, railroad junctions, around fortified raions, and military installations.

In the Polotsk fortified raion

[report follows]

In the 110th Rifle Regiment, liquidated c-r group of officers, headed by brigade commander Slizkovsky, who attempted to manipulate others in the command staff to fulfill tasks that coincided with those [given by] the kulak-insurgent organization operating in the Krichev Raion. Slizkovsky supplied leaders of Shmatkov's organization [presumably the same kulak-insurgent organization] with cartridges and ammunition, and informed the organization about storage locations of the regiment's weapons. Arrests have been made of members of the officers' organization.

At the same time, a number of Polish resident agents and couriers have been uncovered and crushed in areas [under jurisdiction] of the 12th and 17th border guard units, and in the towns of Bobruisk, Gomel, and Borisov.

[...]

Overall, 3,492 arrests have been made to date, of which there are 445 individuals in 13 c-r organizations, 203 individuals in 16 resident agent networks, and 2,844 as spies and insurgents.

In LVO

Liquidated a widely developed network of insurgent cells, created by the Finnish General Staff and encompassing Karelia, the Karelian Isthmus, and separate national raions of LVO. Investigation has revealed information about the presence of a secret store of weapons in Karelia, created by White-Karelian insurgent gangs. An operational unit has been dispatched to discover its whereabouts.

[...]

It has been determined that wrecking work on collective farms and in the forest industry, and organization of the insurgency, has been carried out on direct orders from Finnish intelligence.

A resident agent has been uncovered, and various connections of Finnish intelligence to a skirmish-reconnaissance brigade [of the Soviet border or army forces] and Osoviakhim [voluntary association for assistance to defense, aviation, and chemical construction].

It has been established that Finnish intelligence introduced its agents into the Leningrad International Military School, and conducted c-r nationalist work there. Command staff in the overwhelming majority of brigades are comprised of those educated at the intermilitary school.

[...]

As it turns out, a significant part of the intelligence work of the 4th Department of the LVO headquarters is controlled by the Finnish defense-intelligence [ministry].

[...]

In all, 2,074 arrests [Handwritten note by Stalin: "And what fate for the arrested?"] have been made. Weapons seized: 875 rifles, 875 sawed-off [shot guns], and 2,425 revolvers.

Deputy Head OGPU G. Yagoda

OGPU Expansion

As political police functions broadened, so did police numbers. The following document shows an increase in political police and state security personnel of 8,275, from 17,298 to 25,573, during the first half of the 1930s, or 47 percent in a matter of four years. Most of the personnel growth occurred at local levels, particularly in rural areas, where some 5,000 officers took up positions as deputy directors in political departments of rural machine tractor stations. This surveillance network provided a system of monitoring rural areas through direct contact in villages, and was a crucial part of the regime's attempts to control the rural population. Police expansion also occurred in strategic border regions (especially in the Far East Krai), in the departments responsible for economic and industrial construction and, to a lesser extent, in military surveillance departments. At the same time, and despite these increases, Yagoda noted a continuing deficit in numbers of operational staff needed to support the expanding number of tasks given the political police. This was especially true, he noted, in local and border regions. Yagoda's report included valuable information on Party composition, purging within the political police, sources of recruitment, especially from demobilized army soldiers, and social origins, with a special emphasis on those of "working-class" background. Released in 1935, the report refers to the NKVD and the GUGB as well as to the OGPU, since the political police underwent reorganization in 1934. This reorganization had important consequences, and will be discussed in the following chapter.

DOCUMENT

· 68 ·

Memorandum from G. G. Yagoda on cadre conditions of the
GUGB NKVD and cadre dynamics for the period 1.VII.31 to 1.I.35.
GARF, f. 9401, op. 8, d. 41, ll. 11–37.

Absolutely secret
  1. Overall numbers.
  As a result of:
—strengthening the rural apparatus;
—strengthening of the Chekist apparatus in the Far East;
—introduction of the position ZNPO [Deputy heads, political department] for NKVD work;
—creation of a Chekist apparatus in new construction areas;
—creation of an NKVD apparatus in new krai, oblasts, provinces, and raions,
  numbers in organs of the GUGB NKVD for the period 1/VII–31 to 1/I–35 increased by 8,275 individuals, or 47.3 percent:

On 1/VII–31	On 1/I–33	On 1/I–35
17,298	20,898	25,573

In some krai and oblasts, this growth was uneven. Growth was especially intense in border raions, the strengthening of which deserves special attention:

krai or oblast	As of 1.7–31	percent	As of 1.1–33	percent	As of 1.1–35	percent
M.O.	699	100	835	120.9	1,020	145.9
Belorussia	460	100	559	121.5	803	174.5
Z.S.K.	669	100	755	112.8	1,097	163.9
D.V.K.	406	100	745	183.5	1,185	286.9
Kazakhstan	403	100	637	158.1	889	220.6

[M.O. = Moscow Oblast; Z.S.K. = Western Siberia Territory; D.V.K. = Far East Territory]

  Changes in numbers of the organs SPO [Secret Political Departments], EKO, OO [Special Departments charged with military oversight], and TO GUGB [Transport Departments] are characterized by the following dynamics:

	As of	*1.1–31*	As of	*1.1–33*	As of	*1.1–35*
	Number	*percent*	*Number*	*percent*	*Number*	*percent*
SPO	4,252	100	5,601	131.7	4.831	113.6
EKO	1,387	100	2,471	178.2	2,388	172.2
OO	2,680	100	3,645	136.0	3,769	140.6
TO	4,598	100	5,152	112.1	5,383	117.1
Total	12,917	100	16,869	130.5	16,371	126.7

[SPO = Secret Political Departments; EKO = Economic [Crimes] Departments; OO = Special Departments [military oversight]; TO = Transport Department]

The slight decline in numbers for the SPO GUGB for 1/1–35 is explained by the transfer, from 1.1–33 to 1.1–35, of 2,900 individuals to serve as deputy heads of the political departments of MTS, most of whom were drawn from SPO.

The significant increase in numbers for the EKO to 1/1–33 resulted from the development in that period of the largest industrial complexes, and from the formation of a whole series of powerful economic centers (Magnitogorsk, Kuzbas, Berezniki, etc.).

At the same time, staffing in the last two years of 1,662 state farm political departments, which was done mainly by transfer of EKO officers, somewhat lowered the overal number for the EKO by 1/1–35.

Systematic growth in the numbers of special departments is explained by strengthening of the special apparatus in connection with the strained situation in the Far East, and the necessity to service new formations of the RKKA.

With growth of overal numbers in the last 3.5 years at 47.3 percent, numbers in the organs of SPO, EKO, OO, and TO GUGB increased on average only 26.7 percent.

This testifies to the fact that basic growth in numbers of the GUGB organs occurred as a result of strengthening the lower raion-level chain of NKVD organs.

[...]

Conclusions:

1. For the period 1.VII–31 to 1.1–35, in connection with various organizational measures, numbers in the organs of the GUGB increased by 8,275 individuals, or 47.3 percent, most of the increase occurring as a result of strengthening the lower raion-level chain and the NKVD special organs.

2. On the basis of Party and government decisions, up to 4,500 positions were staffed by deputy heads of political departments of MTS and state farms, as a result of cadre regrouping, training of new cadre, and increasing the qualifications of existing [cadre].

3. The Party-Komsomol stratum among operational staff was increased up to 92.4 percent (an increase of 3.9 percent). Independent of the steady increase in Party membership in OGPU/NKVD organs, at the present time, exclusionary measures are being taken to transfer all non-Party [employees] to work outside the GUGB.

4. The workers' stratum in krai-level special departments has increased to 43.5 percent (an increase of 8.3 percent). In some border raions, as a result of special work to strengthen them, the workers' stratum has risen significantly higher (DVK–51.9 percent, Belorussia–46.1 percent). Even so, it cannot be claimed that the proportion of workers in GUGB organs is satisfactory, and this requires us [to take] decisive measures, which will secure a still more intense growth of the workers' stratum, and to do this through organizational recruitment of new cadres, primarily through the instructional network of the NKVD.

5. Leadership staff of the Chekist apparatus consists, to a person, of Party members having a long Party tenure and rich experience in operational-Chekist work. Thus, among UNKVD heads [political police heads below the republic or krai-level], GUGB NKVD administrative heads, heads of republic and oblast NKVD administrations, and heads of krai and oblast NKVD administrations, as well as their deputies, only 6.2 percent have Party tenure of less than 8 years, and only 1.8 percent of officials working in the OGPU/NKVD have less than 6 years.

6. With the goal of increasing qualifications of operational staff of GUGB organs, during the period 1.VII–31 to 1.1–35 a large [amount] of work was carried out in training new cadres, and in supplemental training of the existing operational staff of GUGB organs. In all, during this period, in the whole of the instructional network of GUGB NKVD organs, 3,913 operatives were trained, and 4,724 officials were sent through qualification improvement courses.

7. As a result of a great [amount] of work in training and requalification of operational staff and, as well, a deepening of study of the professional and moral qualities of all active operational staff of GUGB organs and their effective use, [there has been] obviously a vigorous and widespread promotion of officials in service. In just 1934 and 1935, 7,453 were promoted, or 29.1 percent of the whole staff, and among leadership staff there was even more widespread promotion.

8. With the goal of cleansing GUGB NKVD organs of alien, ideologically unworthy, and morally bankrupt people, a large [amount] of work was carried out in the last 3.5 years, and especially in 1934, to study and review the operational staff. As a result of this, in 1934, among GUGB NKVD organs, 454 people were fired for drunkeness and discrediting the organs, and 236 as a result of special review. In addition to this, as a result of a series of measures for improving the

material-daily situation of officials, we have a significant reduction in turnover due to health conditions or personal decisions.

9. As of 1.1–35, the number of vacant staff positions in GUGB NKVD organs amounts to 1,826, or 6.8 percent of the staff roster. The lack of staff is especially high in newly organized krai and oblasts (Orenburg obl.–17.7 percent, Omsk obl.–13.6 percent), and somewhat less so in the most important border areas (DVK–5.7 percent, Belorussia–5.0 percent, Ukraine–3.9 percent). In addition to the usual recruitment to vacant positions through local Party organizations of trusted, active, and literate Party members, a number of students of technicums and VUZs [higher educational institutions] are sent to NKVD [schools] to cover the lack of staff. Besides this, a number of staff vacancies will be covered by: a return to work in the NKVD of operational reserve Chekists, the best elements of demobilized Red Army soldiers, border forces, and NKVD guard units, and trusted officials promoted to operational work from administrative and technical workers of NKVD organs.

In general, the operational-Chekist core of the GUGB NKVD organs, in their professional and moral character, is healthy, and should successfully cope with and fulfill the tasks put before them by organs of the Party and government.

10 July 1935

During the era of the first Five Year Plan, from 1928 through 1932, the political police played a crucial role in pushing through and enforcing Stalin's policies of rapid industrialization and subordinating the countryside. By 1933, the political police were well ensconced in rural areas of the country, in border regions, and in economic and industrial enterprises. The police controlled a sizable and growing population of forced labor, which was employed in the OGPU's expanding economic empire in agriculture, timber, construction, and mining. Budgets were expanding, as were personnel rolls. OGPU officers regarded themselves and their organization as the fighting revolutionary arm of the Communist Party and the socialist state.

As the regime's policies led increasingly to social disaster and dislocation, however, the role of the political police evolved yet again. Starting in 1933, and throughout the 1930s, the Politburo turned increasingly to the police, not as a revolutionary organ, but to protect the state's interests and to enforce the Stalinist version of socialism. Social order policing and surveillance characterized police activities, in the main, throughout the 1930s. Merged with the civil police, this newly formed organization became a kind of social policing force, a Soviet gendarmerie.

CHAPTER FOUR

Ordering Society
1933–1937

Consolidation of Soviet power in the countryside, and the end of the first Five Year Plan, marked the high point of Stalin's revolution, which the dictator noted in his famous declaration, in January 1933, about the final victory of socialism. Addressing the plenary session, or plenum, of the Party's Central Committee, Stalin declared to the jubilant attendees that despite hardships and skepticism from many, the Party and the Soviet people had accomplished the "historic" tasks of the plan. Great factories had been erected and vast socialist farms had been organized. Soviet power ruled indisputably across the Soviet Union. Organized class resistance had been routed, and in that lay a powerful victory. The first Five Year Plan, Stalin pronounced, was a triumph for socialism and the Party.[1]

In spite of Stalin's declaration of victory, the social cost was devastating. The regime's agrarian and industrial revolution created near universal social crisis, uprooting millions of people, either through forced deportation or out of sheer necessity for survival. The dramatic shift in resources to build up industry precipitated a scarcity of basic goods, food, services, and even shelter during this period, and these scarcities led, in turn, to an appalling degradation in living standards. To make a bad situation worse, the initial years of the collective farm system proved a disaster. By the end of 1932, famine conditions were beginning to spread. A series of factors—the regime's brutally extractive policies in the countryside, the administrative chaos of the new collective farm system, peasant resistance to collectivization, and poor weather—combined to create one of the great tragedies of the twentieth century, the great Soviet famine of 1933 and 1934. In large

122

areas of Ukraine, Western Siberia, central Russia, and the North Caucasus, famine during these years killed some five million people, and forced millions of others to try to migrate out of stricken areas.[2]

Widespread confiscation of property, wholesale deportations, and forced population migration characterized the early years of the 1930s. Dispossessed and often starving, hundreds of thousands of peasants and other rural inhabitants, as well as people from former professional classes, streamed into and through the cities and industrial sites. They took to the rail lines and roads—to escape hunger, to find goods, to seek a better life, even just to survive. This unorganized movement of people drained economic resources and threatened to overwhelm the underdeveloped infrastructure of the cities and the social stability of the country. Large numbers of indigents and itinerants, criminals, unemployed youth, gypsies, the disenfranchised, and a range of other groups added to these mass migrations.[3]

Local authorities could not cope with the influx of masses of people and the shantytowns that sprang up in cities and industrial sites.[4] Social agencies could not cope with the growing numbers of homeless, and the hundreds of thousands of orphaned and unsupervised children that filled the streets and traveled the roads and rail lines. Civil police could not cope with the rising waves of criminality, whether the illegal trade in scarce goods or the mass pilfering and theft of state resources such as coal, bread, and grain.

Social displacement on such a scale not only heightened criminality and social disorder, but posed an imminent danger to the state and to the regime's ability to carry out its economic plans. The latter, especially, incensed Soviet leaders. Stalin, of course, cast the problem of social breakdown in the language of class war. He and other leaders equated even petty criminality with anti-Soviet intentions. He declared that with the victory of socialism, the only possible explanation for criminality could be counterrevolutionary sabotage. Social disorder could be explained as nothing else but class hostility toward the new Soviet order, and as sabotage of the grand project to build socialism.

In his remarks to the January 1933 Party plenum, Stalin identified the struggle against criminality and social disorder as the newest phase of class war, after the defeat of organized class resistance. While he lauded the feats of socialist construction, he also warned that this new type of class war would be even more difficult to overcome than open class resistance, since the enemy would be hidden, merging with and incorporating the "criminal element" in a subtle kind of underground war. Stalin laid out the dangers and made it clear that at the current stage of socialist construction, criminality and social disorder posed greater dangers to the state than direct political opposition.[5]

Stalin's remarks placed the problem of criminality and social disorder at the center of his address on building socialism in the country after the revolutionary upheaval of the previous three years. More than that, by linking class war and criminality, Stalin defined the latter not only as the central problem of social order, but social order as the central problem of state security. The conflation of social order with state security was new, and turned the fight against crime and social deviancy—indeed, any kind of social disorder—from a matter of social control into a political priority in defense of the state. Stalin's remarks politicized or, more accurately, statized, criminality and social disorder, and deeply influenced political police policies in the mid-1930s. In the conditions of social breakdown and weak civil government, Stalin turned to the political police, not just to repress resistance to the regime's policies, but to reimpose order in the country, and to defend the assets and infrastructure of the state. This chapter traces the transformation of the political police during the 1930s from a revolutionary fighting organization into a kind of social gendarmerie.

Hooligans and Railroads

One of the most significant aspects of that transformation involved the merging of the political and civil police. In December 1930, the Politburo gave sanction to this process. On the fifteenth, the Politburo and Sovnarkom officially abolished the republic-level commissariats of the interior that had administered the civil police, the *militsiia*. According to the reorganization, the *militsiia* now came under jurisdiction of local government councils, or soviets. In fact, a secret protocol of the reorganization placed the *militsiia* under operational control of the OGPU and its local organs, the GPU administrations. The *militsiia* operated this way for two years, and the secret nature of its subordination indicated some concern by leaders that an open relationship would look bad to the public. Whatever the case, leaders already understood that the social dislocation caused by collectivization and dekulakization, and by the negative effects of forced industrialization, would require the use of social force on a scale beyond the capabilities of the political police or the civil police separately. The idea behind the merger, then, was to create a civil police that could act as an auxiliary arm of the political police.[6]

One of the first social order operations of the combined OGPU and *militsiia* came in 1932, to keep order on passenger trains and to stop thefts and intimidation by gangs on the country's railroads. Incensed by the mounting numbers of incidents, Stalin wrote in August 1932 to Lazar Kaganovich, a Politburo member and one of Stalin's close subordinates, demanding that the political police take action.

DOCUMENT

· 69 ·

Letter of I. V. Stalin to L. Kaganovich. RGASPI, f. 17, op. 3, d. 896, l. 260.[7]
4 August 1932

———————

[...]

5. Outrages are happening on the railroads. State employees on the routes are raped and terrorized by hooligans and homeless children. Organs of the TO GPU [transport police of the OGPU] are asleep. (That's a fact!) This outrage can no longer be tolerated. Call the TO GPU to order. Force them to keep order on the lines. Issue a directive to the TO GPU to place armed personnel on the lines and to shoot hooligans on the spot. Where is the TO GPU? What is it doing? How can c. Blagonravov [chief of the TO GPU and deputy head of the Commissariat of Transport] tolerate such anarchy and outrage?

Regards, Stalin

As a result of Stalin's outburst, political police embarked on a campaign of regular sweeps of train yards, stations, and trains, even to the extent of checking freight manifests and passenger tickets. As the documents below portray, guarding the country's railroads became a routine duty for the political police, and the head of the OGPU, Menzhinsky, made a point to send regular reports to Stalin and to the Politburo.

DOCUMENT

· 70 ·

V. R. Menzhinsky's report to I. V. Stalin on the struggle against
hooliganism, homeless children, and theft on transportation.
TsA FSB RF, f. 2, op. 10, d. 145, ll. 3–7.
31 August 1932

I. Concerning the struggle against hooliganism and homeless children on
transportation, the OGPU has done the following:

1. On the railways and waterways, mobile and stationary brigades were
   organized, consisting of riflemen-guards, workers, and employees
   who are Party and Komsomol members. These are operating under
   the direction of OGPU officers at a number of stations, in trains, on
   bridge spans, piers; 873 brigades of 3–5 people each.
2. At points contaminated the most with hooliganism, permanent out-
   posts were created—243 [in number].
3. Armed units of NKPS [transportation commissariat] and OGPU rifle-
   men accompany passenger, courier, and express trains in areas contaminated the most with hooliganism.
4. In the process of fighting against hooliganism, there were detained,
   of the hooligan element, on transportation—during the period
   April–August—49,045 persons, i.e.: April—10,047, May—7,287,
   June—7,565, July—9,379, August—14,777.
5. Homeless children detained—13,122 persons.
   Of these: April—1,303,
   May—1,271,
   June—1,771,
   July—1,092,
   August—7,685
6. Investigations initiated—2,573, i.e.:
   April—444,
   May—449,
   June—418,
   July—466,
   August—796
7. Hooligans detained at a crime scene and charged—3,558 people.
   Of them:
   April—567,
   May—620,
   June—498,
   July—618,
   August—1,255

These numbers include: 640 persons arrested in August, of whom: 67 persons for breaking windows and throwing stones at trains, 11 persons for setting up obstacles on railways, 16 persons for using the emergency brake and stopping running trains, 181 persons for assaulting train crews, 340 persons for disturbing the peace at stations, 640 people for other forms of malfeasance.

8. Concluded and transferred to courts were 2,184 investigations, with a total number of 3,111 persons indicted. Of these, 407 cases were finished in August, with 706 indicted. Of those cases transferred to courts in August, only 115 cases went to trial. The rest are still under court review. Sentences were passed for cases that went to trial (mainly hard labor from three months to one year and internment in a concentration camp up to three years).

9. Fined for violation of the NKPS standing regulations (minor hooliganism offenses)—118,085 persons. Of these:
    April—10,972 persons in the amount of 59,039 rub.
    May—15,652 persons for 78,291 rub.
    June—18,078 persons for 117,862 rub.
    July—20,957 persons for 84,756 rub.
    August—52,426 persons for 128,318 rub.

10. Fined for stowaway journeys on railways and waterways—129,054 persons. Of these:
    April—17,860 persons in the amount of 109,365 rub.
    May—29,274 persons for 250,269 rub.
    June—23,541 persons for 142,362 rub.
    July—26,147 persons for 225,091 rub.
    August—32,232 persons for 289,712 rub.

A characteristic result of the whole complex of actions by the OGPU in the struggle against hooliganism and the criminal element on transportation is the sharp decrease in the number of cases of theft of passengers' luggage, and pickpocket thefts in August. Thus, in April 1,096 cases of theft from passengers were registered, in May—998, in June—1.014, in July—1.073, in August—548.

[...]

In the last months, organs of the OGPU uncovered and liquidated a network of large theft organizations on the [rail]roads, which were systematically engaged in theft of luggage and freight from train cars, station warehouses, and freight yards.

Arrested for theft:

May	2,438 persons
June	1,950
July	1,792

August	2,108
Total	8,288

Cases investigated:

May	1,130
June	1,241
July	1,357
August	892
Total	4,620

Convictions:

May	671
June	963
July	765
August	433
Total	2,832

In August, of the number of convicted, 43 persons were sentenced to the highest measure of social protection—to execution, 86 persons to 10 years, 17—to 8 years, 61—to 5 years, the others to 3 years and less.

Theft on transport in August in comparison to the previous months was reduced. If in May there were 3,596 cases of theft registered, in June 3,688, and in July 4,202, in 29 days of August, 2,469 cases were registered, which is only 58 percent of those [registered] in July.

In August, also, the percentage of solved cases of theft also improved, which reached 44.4 percent, whereas during the period of May–June it was on the average 29 percent.

In conclusion, it is necessary to note that punitive actions by the OGPU will not give definitive results in terms of eliminating thefts on transport, unless NKPS and railroad administrations accomplish completely all the necessary preventive actions developed by the OGPU and included in the above orders and circulars. To the same degree, there needs to be a real and broad mobilization of the transport workers in the struggle against theft. At the same time, there has even been some backsliding in cases where trade union organizations decline active participation in the struggle against theft.

Head of the OGPU (Menzhinsky)

Protecting Socialist Property

The problem of petty theft became so widespread that single operations by police were not enough to stem the rising tide of criminality against the state. As early as July 1932, Stalin outlined in a letter to Kaganovich from the leader's dacha in the Crimea a special law that would allow systematic police action and would entail harsh penalties. Stalin envisioned the law as having three major aspects—theft on transport, in farms and cooperatives, and "antisocial elements" in general. He emphasized to Kaganovich that such a law was needed not just to stop crime, but to enable the political police.

DOCUMENT

· 71 ·

Extract of letter from I. V. Stalin to L Kaganovich, 15 July 1932.[8]

[...]

I think that on all three of these points, we must act on the basis of a law ("the peasant loves legality"), and not just on the basis of OGPU practice, although it is clear that the role of the OGPU here will not only not be reduced, but, on the contrary, will become stronger and "ennobled" ("on a legal basis" and not just by "high handedness").

The government enacted the law on 7 August 1932, and in September the Politburo approved and sent explicit instructions to prosecutorial and judicial commissariat officials, and to the political police, on how to implement the new law.

DOCUMENT

· 72 ·

Instructions on implementing the law on protection of socialist property (PB from 8.IX.32, pr[otocol]. No. 115, p[oint]. 5). AP RF, f. 3, op. 57, d. 60, ll. 13–19.
16 September 1932

Strictly secret
Section I [...]:
The law of August 7 is to be applied to the theft of state and public property:

a) in industry (theft of factory or enterprise property)
b) in sovkhozes [state farms]
c) in state trade organizations
d) in kolkhozes [collective farms]
e) Goods on railroad, water, and local transport

Section II:
Categories of thieves, and measures of social defense to be applied to them:

1. In cases of organizations and groupings that systematically destroy state, public, and cooperative property by arson, explosives, and mass spoilage—apply the highest measure of social defense—shooting, without mitigation.

2. In relation to kulaks, former traders, and other socially dangerous elements working in state (industrial and agricultural—sovkhozes) enterprises or offices, caught in theft of property or embezzlement of large sums of money of these enterprises, and likewise in state institutions and enterprises, apply the highest measure of punishment, [and] given mitigating circumstances of guilt (in cases of single action or small thefts) reduce the highest measure of punishment to 10 years' loss of freedom.
   [...]

3. In relation to kulaks, former traders, and other socially dangerous elements, who have infiltrated organs of supply, trade, and cooperatives, as well as officials of the trade network caught in theft of goods or selling them privately and in embezzling large sums of money— apply the highest measure of punishment, and only under mitigating circumstances, in cases of insignificant amounts, change the highest measure of punishment to 10 years' loss of freedom.
   Apply the same measure to profiteers, who, although they do not engage directly in theft, [engage in] speculation of goods and products they know to have been stolen from state enterprises and cooperatives.

4. In relation to persons caught in theft of goods on transport, apply the highest measure of punishment, or, in cases of mitigating circumstances (theft of a single item or a small theft), a 10-year loss of freedom may be applied.
   [...]

5. In relation to kulaks who have infiltrated into kolkhozes, as well as those who remain outside kolkhozes, who organize or participate in theft of kolkhoz property or grain, apply the highest measure of punishment, without mitigation.

6. In relation to independent farmers and collective farmers caught in theft of kolkhoz property and grain, 10 years' loss of freedom should be applied.
   In aggravated criminal circumstances, in particular: systematic theft of kolkhoz grain, beets, and other agricultural products, and livestock, stolen in large numbers, by organized groups, theft aggravated by violence, terrorist acts, by arson, etc., and in relation to collective and independent farmers—apply the highest measure of punishment.

7. In relation to collective farm chairmen and members of the farm management who participate in theft of state and public property, it is necessary to apply the highest measure of punishment, and only under mitigating circumstances—apply a 10-year loss of freedom.

[...]
Chairman of the Supreme Court—A. Vinokurov
Deputy head, OGPU—I. Akulov

Police acted on the law quickly. By March 1933, they had arrested 127,318 persons under the August 1932 law, and had executed 2,052. The following report detailed for the Politburo the measures that police took to implement the law. As the note at the end makes clear, Stalin kept this report for his personal archive.

DOCUMENT

· 73 ·

Memorandum of G. E. Prokof'ev and L. G. Mironov to I. V. Stalin on the number of those prosecuted by the OGPU for theft of public property. AP RF, f. 45, op. 1, d. 171, ll. 87–89.

[Handwritten note by Stalin on the first page: "My archive"]
20 March 1933

The *total number prosecuted by the OGPU for theft of state and public property up to 15 March of this year is 127,318 persons.* 55,166 persons were prosecuted for thefts from shops and from warehouses of goods-manufacturing networks and from industrial enterprises, and 72,152 persons—for thefts from sovkhozes and kolkhozes [collective farms].

From the total number of those prosecuted for theft, courts and OGPU organs (OGPU Collegium [administrative sentencing board] and OGPU troikas under PP OGPU [nonjudicial sentencing boards under OGPU plenipotentiaries]) convicted 73,743 persons.

OGPU organs convicted 14,056 persons (for the largest cases of organized thefts). According to measures of punishment, the number of the convicted may be subdivided by type of punishment, as follows:

VMN [capital punishment]	2,052 persons
5–10 years of camp	7,661 persons
Less than 5 years	4,343
Total	14,056 persons

According to social composition, the number of those convicted by the OGPU organs is as follows:

Former traders, speculators, kulaks	4,467 persons
Employees, collective farmers, *edinolichniki* [independent farmers], and other workers	8,209
Others	1,080
Total	14,056 persons

From cases of thefts being investigated by the OGPU during the reported two weeks, large thefts of grain that took place in Rostov-on-Don drew attention. Thefts embraced the whole system of the Rostprokhlebokombinat [Rostov bread production combine]: the bread-baking factory, two mills, two bakeries, and 33 shops, from which bread has been sold to the population. Over six thousand puds [96,000 kg; 1 pud = 16.38 kg] of bread were plundered, along with one thousand puds of sugar, 500 puds of bran, and other products. Thefts were made possible because of the absence of a clearly established system of reporting and control, and also because of criminal nepotism and the solidarity of employees. The Public Workers Inspectorate, which was supervising the grain distribution network, failed to live up to its purpose. In all cases of proven thefts, the inspectors were accomplices who signed the obviously fictitious papers on underdelivery of bread, on write-off of shrinkage, and on spillage, etc. 54 persons involved in this case were arrested, five of whom are members of the VKP(b).

Large thefts were uncovered in the peat section of MOSPO [Moscow Oblast Union of Consumers' Societies], which was responsible for supplying peat to workers. The head of the department of trade of the peat section, Nikitin, a former officer, led the group of thieves. He selected former [prerevolutionary] traders, landowners, and others of the alien element, who had already been prosecuted, as employees for the warehouses.

The organization had its agents in local torfrabkops [peat workers' cooperatives], in particular in Orekhovo-Zuyevo and Shaturstroi.

The organization did not limit itself to direct thefts. Using money of the peat section, it bought train cars of food supply and marketed them on the side, misappropriating the obtained money. 10 persons involved in this case were arrested. The investigation continues.

[...]

In total during the period from 1 March to 15 March of this year, the OGPU organs arrested 2,829 persons for theft.

Deputy head of the OGPU, Prokof'ev

Head of EKO OGPU, Mironov

Famine and the OGPU

Along with harsh enforcement of the 7 August law, the regime's leaders continued to apply relentless pressure on the peasantry for extraction of grain, especially to meet export quotas to pay for industrialization. Largely as a result of harsh extraction policies, many of the country's grain growing areas plunged into deep and prolonged famine in the winter of 1932–33. By spring and summer 1934, when grain reserves were finally stabilized, an estimated five to seven million people were dead from the hunger. Ukraine was hit especially hard, and the famine there came to be known as the Holodomor (the Killing by Hunger). The regime's leaders were slow to react to the famine, believing that peasants were simply hoarding grain and refusing to work, prompted by foreign agents and anti-Soviet "elements." By late 1932 and January 1933, tens of thousands of people were attempting to flee stricken areas, and the Politburo ordered political and civil police to coordinate efforts to stop the out migration. The following pages document the response of the country's leaders to this mass movement and the actions by police to patrol roads, trains, and other forms of transport and to return illegally fleeing peasants to their home villages and regions. The matter-of-factness of the documents belies the implications of police actions, which, by rounding up and returning peasants to their home villages, surely condemned many of them to certain death.

DOCUMENT

· 74 ·

TsK VKP(b) and SNK USSR directive on prevention of mass departure of starving peasants. RGASPI, f. 558, op. 11, d. 45, ll. 109–1090b.[9]
22 January 1933

TsK VKP(b) and SNK USSR have been receiving information that in Kuban and Ukraine, mass departure of peasants "for bread" has started in the direction of TsChO [Central Black Earth Oblast], to the Volga, Moscow Oblast, the Western Oblast, to Belorussia. TsK VKP(b) and SNK USSR have no doubt that this departure of peasants, as well as departure from Ukraine last year, was organized by enemies of Soviet power, SRs, and agents of Poland, for the purpose of propaganda agitation "through peasants" in the northern regions of the USSR against collective farms and, in general, against Soviet power. Last year, Party, Soviet, and Cheka organs of Ukraine missed this counterrevolutionary ploy by enemies of Soviet power. This year, a repetition of last year's mistake cannot be allowed.

First. TsK VKP(b) and SNK USSR order the kraikom, kraiispolkom [executive committee of the krai soviet], and the PP OGPU of the North Caucasus not to allow mass departure of peasants from the North Caucasus to other regions, nor their entry into the Krai from Ukraine.

Second. TsK VKP(b) and SNK USSR order the TsK KP(b)U, Ukrsovnarkom [SNK of Ukraine], Balitsky, and Redens not to allow mass departure of peasants from Ukraine to other krai, nor their entry into Ukraine from the North Caucasus.

Third. TsK VKP(b) and SNK USSR order the PP OGPU of Moscow Oblast, TsChO, the Western Oblast, Belorussia, the Lower Volga, and the Middle Volga to arrest "peasants" who have made their way to the north of Ukraine and the North Caucasus and, after sorting out counterrevolutionary elements, to return others to their places of residence.

Fourth. TsK VKP(b) and SNK USSR order [head of] TO GPU Prokhorov to send the corresponding order through the TO GPU system.

Chairman of SNK USSR V. M. Molotov

Secretary of TsK VKP(b) I. Stalin

DOCUMENT

· 75 ·

Report of G. E. Prokof'ev to I. V. Stalin on measures taken in the struggle against mass departures from Ukraine and SKK [North Caucasus], with attached notes by V. A. Balitsky and E. G. Evdokimov. AP RF, f. 3, op. 30, d. 189, ll. 3–10.

[Handwritten note on the first page: "To Molotov, Kaganovich, Postyshev. I. Stalin"]

23 January 1933

Absolutely secret.

Herewith are attached the first reports of cc. Balitsky, Evdokimov on struggle against mass departures from Ukraine and SKK. [...]

Deputy head of the OGPU, Prokof'ev

Appendix: Memorandum of cc. Balitsky and Evdokimov [telegraphed] on a direct line.

Absolutely secret

Memorandum on a direct line from Rostov:

No. 141256

The issue of struggle against flight [of peasants] was raised as soon as [my] arrival in SKK, based on materials from a number of raions, which showed intense flight, which, in some places, was taking on a mass character. *At the end of November and later, categorical orders were given repeatedly by me to opersektors [operational sectors], to oblast administrations, to gorraiotdelenie [raion-level departments in cities and towns], to DTO [GPU road transport departments], to the militsiia of the Krai, on taking diverse and decisive measures for blocking flight.* Generally, at this time, actions in localities are being carried out along the following lines: 1) agent networks have been mobilized for struggle against mass flight, especially against the fugitive kulak–White Guardist element, especially for the identification of organizers and propagandists provoking flight. Explanatory work has been carried out: explanatory campaigns, summons [to interviews or interrogations], etc. 2) In localities, measures were taken and attention has been brought continuously to the issue of strengthening mass explanatory work for the purpose of organizing public counteraction to the flight. This issue was raised in the kraikom, which has given special instructions to localities. 3) Along the line of DTO, besides agitation-operational work on transportation, mobile groups were created, operational road blocks were set up at points—raions of the greatest congestion of movement of fugitives, especially in the direction of Ukraine, Transcaucasia, even checking travelers and ticket buyers. 4) *Militsiia* forces, with the assistance of partsovaktiv [Party and soviet activists], have organized check points along the main paths of movement of runaways [bezhashchie], especially in the direction of the Black Sea area, Transcaucasia, the Black Sea coast, along the border with Abkhazia, and also to Dagestan at the border with Azerbaijan, in the main passes to Transcaucasia. *Detained kulaks, c-r [counterrevolutionary] elements were arrested, the others were filtered, some after processing were returned to their place [of residence] for explanatory work.* Departures without the permission of soviets, collective farm boards, are forbidden, however these actions do not have any effect, [peasants] flee without permission.

5) In cities, agent networks have been mobilized for identification of runaways, and for suppression of possible c-r active subversive work of runaways settled in cities, in enterprises, at new contracting sites. Measures were taken along agent line[s] of work and physical protection of the most important strategic points, state constructions, and large enterprises, the first priority given to those of military importance. A number of operations were conducted [against] runaways in cities.

6) *Major efforts were directed toward organized insurgent c-r[s], and their agitational, organizing role in the flight[s].* As you know, in the Kuban a large insurgent organization was uncovered in Kurganensk

and other raions of SKK—the affair of colonel Popov and others. In this case, work on organizing flight for the purpose of sabotage was uncovered, forming insurgent groups from the runaways (in the areas of the Black Sea coast). Along with this, from other liquidated cases, counterrevolutionary work was found, of concentrating runaways in deep wooded mountain areas, and also in cities. As a result of the actions undertaken in the Krai (and also the operations carried out in Shakhty, Taganrog, Rostov, and elsewhere), our organs detained 7,534 people of the runaway element. Of them: in the Black Sea opersektor up to 5,000 escapees from the Kuban raions, from which 1,216 people of c-r elements. In the Shakhty opersektor, 349 people were removed of the kulak–White Guardist element in the coal industry; among them, 104 White Guardists, 18 repatriatees. By transport organs along lines of the sevkavkazsky [North Caucusus] [rail] roads, 11,774 runaways were detained, among them 659 kulaks. In Dagestan 1,074 people. It is necessary to consider that in connection with the lack of forces, concentration of our main forces in the countryside [and] the rapid spread of sabotage, purging work in cities, naturally, has not yet been completed. For November–December, flight in some places, in some stanitsas [Kazakh villages], showed an increase. In particular, in villages where the strongest pressure in connection with grain collections took place. As of now: 1) *in January, flight showed a decrease, in comparison with November–December.* However in some areas, stanitsas, flight continues. We found a concentration of runaways in the Azov Sea reed beds. *We are preparing an operation.* We are preparing an operation in Rostov. At the same time, in a number of places, the fact of returning runaways has been noticed. 2) Now, in connection with the completion of grain collections in the majority of raions of the Krai, [we are conducting] preparatory work for the spring sowing, together with expanding our measures, along with mass explanatory work. Certainly, flight may show a further decrease. It is necessary to point out: mass explanatory work in localities is weak. 3) I repeatedly send orders to localities to organize a review of [measures] to strengthen actions along all lines. I am asking to take into consideration that, given the real conditions in raions, stanitsas, given the number of our workers, of army and *militsiia* resources, naturally, there is no physical possibility to organize total, guaranteed interdiction, covering all roads. 4) According to our information, questions of flight were continuously elucidated since my first telegram from Kuban, and also in reports along the line of SPO, in information on black villages [designated] for exile.

0170064 Evdokimov

[Telegram 2]
To the Secretary, SPO OGPU[10]
22 January 1933.
Secret
Mass departure of peasants from villages, which began at the end of December 1932, mainly in Kharkov, Odessa, Kiev, and partially in Chernigov oblasts, is expressed in the following form:

In Kharkov oblast, departure was registered in 19 raions, 39 villages. In all, 20,129 individuals left; of these 20,129 were collective farmers, 12,698 were independent farmers, 8 activists.

[...]

In total, in these oblasts, departure was registered in 74 raions, 721 villages, 228 collective farms, totally 31,693 individuals departed, 2,789 families, among them collective farmers—10,539 and families—1,262. Single independent farmers—19,203, families 1,131, *tverdosdatchiki* 823 [individual farmers with fixed grain quota paid to the state], families 396, activists 126.

[...]

In most cases, those leaving villages go to the Donbass and large industrial centers. Flight of collective farmers [occurs] on a significantly smaller scale than flight of independent farmers. Also, unwarranted departure of heads of soviets and collective farms, including "communists," takes place. The latter flee from villages because they are afraid of repressions for sabotage of grain collections and failure to fulfill Party assignments. A check of the junction stations of Lozovaia and Sumy in Kharkov Oblast, where flight from villages is especially widespread, shows a large sale of train tickets for long-distance trains in January of this year. Thus, in January at the station of Lozovaia, 16,500 tickets were sold, and at the station of Sumy, 15,000. The increase in sale of tickets has been noted also at the junction station of Pomoshchnaya in the Odessa Oblast. Thus, if in the month of November 879 tickets were sold for long-distance trains, in December 3,614, and in the first half of January—1,617. The rest of the junction stations in other oblasts do not show a sharp increase of ticket sales for long distance. For the purpose of a decisive suppression of flight from the countryside, in the beginning of January, the GPU of Ukraine started to remove organizers and instigators of flight, and to strength agent-informant work in the places contaminated with mass departure. Over 500 malicious instigators of departures were arrested.

The GPU of Ukraine gave information to the KP[b]U and SPO OGPU on mass departures since 25 December, 1932. I am giving additional directives based on your instructions.—V. Balitsky

DOCUMENT
· 76 ·

Memorandum from G. G. Yagoda to I. V. Stalin on results of
operational measures to curb mass flight of peasants. AP RF,
f. 3, op. 30, d. 189, ll. 36–37.

[Note on the first page: "To Molotov. I. Stalin"]
   17 February 1933
   Absolutely secret
   As an addendum to the memorandum from 13.II of this year on the
results of operational measures by local OGPU organs to curb mass flight
of peasants from SSR Ukraine, CKK, and others, I report:
   In Ukraine SSR—for the period from 11–13 February, this year, 2,377
of the fleeing element were arrested and filtered; of these 2,354 were
returned to their place of residence, and 23 were arrested.
   In TsChO for the period 10 to 12 February, this year, 118 individuals
were detained. Together with those already detained, 297 were returned
to their place of residence, and 96 are scheduled to be returned to Ukraine.
   In NVK [Lower Volga Krai] for the period 7–14 February this year, 227
individuals were detained. Together with those already detained, 1,209
individuals were returned to their place of residence.
   For the period 11–14 February this year, in railroad stations, 2,450
individuals were detained, of whom 2,392 were returned, 9 have been
arrested, and the rest are still undergoing filtration.
   *In the past days, there has been a significant reduction in the flow of
those in transit along railroads.*
   Here is a table of data as of 14 February:
   Numbers detained of the fleeing element from the beginning of the
operation to 14.II.33.

From	Total detained	Returned to residence	To be indicted	Sent to concentration camp	Exiled to Kazakhstan
UkSSR	31,783	28,351	3,434	—	579
TsChO	27,368	26,578	694	—	—
SKK	29,116	8,663	10,528	192	—
NVK	2,261	1,653	—	—	99
ZSFSR	7,302	2,037	1,148	2,490	—
Western Oblast	5,115	4,087	432	—	—
SVK	27	29	—	—	—

ODTO	47,417	43,411	2,825	11	—
TOTAL	150,391	114,759	19,059	2,693	678

[UkSSR: Ukrainian Soviet Socialist Republic; TsChO: Central Black Earth Oblast; SKK: Northern Caucasus District; NVK: Lower Volga District; ZSFSR: Trans-Caucasus Socialist Federated Soviet Republic; SVK: Middle Volga District; ODTO: OGPU Transport Department.]

Secretary SPO

One of the last reports sent to Stalin about the above operations, from March 1933, listed a total of 219,460 people picked up since the start of the operations, and 185,588 returned to their place of residence.[11]

Yagoda's Proposal for New Settlements

In anticipation of further policing activities, Yagoda and his deputy M. D. Berman proposed a significant expansion of the system of special settlements. In the following memorandum to Stalin, from February 1933, the two police officials estimated an additional two million people to be deported and settled in areas of Kazakhstan and Western Siberia. These would not be kulaks, primarily, but other "anti-Soviet elements," largely from cities and industrial areas. If approved, the population of special settlements would reach some four million people by 1934. As the memorandum shows, the plan was ambitious, representing an attempt at social engineering on a large scale. As such, real people were rarely mentioned, but were categorized into "elements"—socially harmful, socially dangerous, anti-Soviet, etc. Social "elements" were to be moved about in "contingents" and "echelons," and assigned privileges or, more often, restrictions, accordingly. Based on the number and types of restriction, it is clear that Yagoda regarded those of the socially harmful element as more of a threat to the state than those of the kulak element.

DOCUMENT

· 77 ·

Memorandum from G. G. Yagoda and M. D. Berman to I. V. Stalin on the organization of special settlements. AP RF, f. 3, op. 30, d. 196, ll. 127–38.

[Notes on the first page: "To archive. I. Stalin. Besides everything else, need to tie this business to the population *reduction* in prisons."

"Expenditures (1,394 m. rub.) grossly exaggerated. Costs need to be covered by exiles themselves. Molotov"]

13 February 1933

*In connection with instruction from the TsK VKP(b) the OGPU is developing a resettlement plan for 1933 and 1934 for anti-Soviet ele-*ments exiled from rural and urban areas, and for organizing them into labor settlements.

A preliminary idea for resettlement of *2,000,000 persons in raions of Western Siberia and Kazakhstan* is laid out below.

Kazakhstan:

In Kazakhstan, resettlement is to be carried out mainly in the following raions: Naurzumsky, Akhmolinsky, Atbasarsky, Evropeisky, Leninsky, *Revoliutsionny*, Sotsialistichesky, Kurgol'dzhimsky, Aryk-Balyksky, Uritsky, and Ubagansky.

According to Narkomzem [Commissariat of Agriculture], the total area of open land comprises 2,244,000 hectares, of which 1,100,000 hectares is arable land. Distance from the railroad of these land funds is 280 klm at the maximum. (Naurzumsky Raion) and 35–40 klm at the minimum (Akhmolinsk and Evropeisky raions).

A significant number of these raions are located in Central Kazakhstan, thinly populated and underdeveloped. The soil in these raions is mostly loamy, interspersed partially with black earth and saline soil. Several regions are distinguished by periodic aridity (Atbasarsky and Sotsialistichesky). Water supply comes from existing rivers and lakes and ground water lying at a depth of 8 to 10 meters.

These tracts [*fondy*] are good for agriculture, with grain crops being cultivated by natural irrigation (*bagara*), and gardens and [...] potatoes by watering.

Based on a calculation of one family per 3.5–4 hectares of land, it is possible to settle up to a million people on 1,100,000 hectares of land.

Western Siberia:

In Western Siberia, resettlement will be carried out in the open lands of the following northern raions: Narymsky, Krivosheinsky, Biriliussky, Narabel'sky, Kargassky, Rybinsky, Kozhevnikovsky, Ishimsky, Tarsky, Suslovsky, and Novokuskovsky, as well as in the southern [raions]: Kurgansky, Ongudaisky, Ust'-Abakansky (see map).

These regions are located at a distance of 50 to 500 klm from railroad stations. There are 1,600,000 hectares of land in these areas, of which 418,000 are arable, 237,000 are for haying, 407,000 for pasture. Water saturation of these areas is fully adequate, the soil is good for agriculture. At the present time, through the PP OGPU in Western Siberia, we are calculating more precisely the amount of land and the possibilities for exploiting it.

[...]

[The report goes on at length, detailing the kinds of economic activities to be carried out by settlements: agriculture, commercial grain crops, animal husbandry, fishing, forest work, and even the kinds of artisan industries that could be established for "second and third members of families, those not fully capable of work, or invalids." Yagoda and Berman estimated the number of special settlers to be roughly equal to the number exiled in the three years 1930–32, about two million, but these new settlers would be of slightly different social makeup.]

The following contingents should be sent to the special settlements: a) Kulaks exiled from raions of total collectivization, b) Those exiled for disrupting and sabotaging grain collection and other campaigns, c) The urban element, unwilling to leave cities as a result of passportization [the system of residence registration designed to limit urban in migration [See below.], d) Kulaks who have fled the countryside and who are [found in and] removed from industrial production sites, e) Exiles removed in the course of border cleansing (Western [Oblast] and Ukraine), f) Exiles sentenced by OGPU organs and courts for periods up to 5 years, except for the socially dangerous.

[The exiles are to have the same legal status as current special settlers, that is, loss of voting rights and the right of free movement for 5 years, with the possibility for restoration of rights,] if they prove their devotion to Soviet power through hard work. [This part of sentence marked with two bold lines in margin next to Stalin's handwritten note: "Resettled for how long? 10 years"]

[...]

The new special settlements will be organized from a calculated distribution in each of 500 to 1,000 [Written in pencil above this figure: "300 to 500"] households. [...] The special settlements will be headed by commandant-Chekists. Groups of villages numbering 7,500 families will be united into raion-level police reservations [*kommandatury*], headed by a raion-level commandant. Protection of villages will be carried out by civil police, subordinated in all matters to the raion-level and village commandants.

[Yagoda and Berman further detail plans for preparing settlement areas before the arrival of exiles, and the amounts of money and supplies that would be necessary to transfer administration from other commissariats to the OGPU. These include everything from tons of nails (6,929) to amounts of boarding, numbers of tractors and horses (2,640 and 90,000 respectively), to numbers of train cars needed, to tons of tea (fourteen) and other food staples, to medical, educational, propaganda, and other support personnel. Given the amount of preparation time required, Yagoda estimated that the OGPU could start moving exiles in April of the year, 1933. In a last section, Yagoda notes the especially dangerous category of the anticipated exiles, and what that would entail.]

[...]

The composition of those being resettled is more serious in its social danger than the special settlers of 1930–31. In [the former] contingent is the declassed urban element and so the command and guard staff of entire resettlement will have to be administratively strengthened for a short period.

According to preliminary estimates, there will be needed:

Commandants and deputies: 3,250 individuals
Policemen   5,700
[...]

Rough calculations show that the cost of development for a 2 million contingent is as follows:

1. Agricultural development, including agricultural construction and organization of 66 MTS. 325,593 t. r. [thousand rubles, i.e. 325,593,000 rubles]
2. Housing and cultural—sanitary structures. 571,396 t. r.
3. Food commodities for one year. 218,000 t. r.
4. Economic appliances and commercial goods. 63,000 t. r.
5. Livestock fodder. 10,000 t. r.
6. Instruments. 8,000 t. r.
7. Medical services. 34,000 t. r.
8. Transfer from rail stations: to place of resettlement. 165,000 t. r.

Total. *1,394,989 t. r.*
[...] in the course of [the first] year, the settlers will have to be supplied with foodstuffs free of charge.

As a result of the general expenditure to develop the new contingent, 657,000 t. r. will not be returned, and 737,153 t. r. will be reimbursed.

[...]
Deputy head OGPU (Yagoda)
Head of GULAG (Berman)

Yagoda's proposal was based on the assumption that mass social cleansing would continue at the pace of the previous two years, but Stalin's comment on the first page, that such a proposal had to be tied to the problem of prison overcrowding, referred to a decision already taken to curtail mass repression operations, reduce the prison population due to overcrowding, and regulate arrest procedures under judicial supervision.

Depopulating Prisons and the 8 May 1933 Reform

By the spring of 1933, the problem of overcrowded prisons was serious. Nearly twice as many people were incarcerated than the facilities were supposed to accommodate. At the same time, as Stalin's July

1932 letter to Kaganovich indicated (document 71 above), the Soviet leader was concerned about the appearance of arbitrary actions by the political police, and he made it clear to their leaders that they had to start acting within judicial procedures. By this time, as well, and as his note on the February 1933 memorandum from Yagoda and Berman shows (document 77), Stalin was disinclined to increase the number of special settlements by the number they suggested.

On 8 May 1933, the Politburo issued a decision that tied these concerns together. The directive was a curious document. Its main point emphasized the need to depopulate the country's overburdened prisons. In order to alleviate this overcrowding, some prisoners, convicted of minor violations, were to be released. Most, however, close to half a million, were to be transferred to a scaled-down version of Yagoda's proposed special settlements and penal colonies. Restrictions on and regulation of OGPU activities seemed almost an afterthought, motivated by concern not for legality, but for reducing the number of people in confinement. Moreover, the document called for an end to mass administrative deportation, but then called for at least 12,000 "households" to be evicted and exiled.

DOCUMENT

· 78 ·

Directive-instructions of the TsK VKP(b) and SNK USSR on cessation of mass exile of peasants, regulating arrests, and reducing prison populations. AP RF, f. 3, op. 30, d. 196, ll. 163–1630b.[12]

8 May 1933*

Strictly secret
[...]
Not for publication
To all Party and Soviet workers and all organs of the OGPU, courts, and Procuracy
The desperate resistance of the kulak class to the collective farm movement of the working peasants, which developed at the end of 1929, and took the form of arson and acts of terrorism against collective farm figures, has created the need for Soviet power to carry out mass arrests and extreme kinds of repression in the form of mass exile of kulaks and kulak spongers to northern and remote areas. Further resistance by kulak elements, wrecking on collective and state farms, uncovered in 1932, and widely spread mass thefts of collective and state farm property have

demanded the further strengthening of repressive measures against kulak elements, thieves, and any saboteurs.

Thus, the three last years of our work in the countryside were years of struggle for the liquidation of the kulak class and for the victory of collective farms.

In this way, these three years of struggle led to the defeat of forces of our class enemies in the countryside, to the final strengthening of our Soviet socialist positions in the countryside.

Summing up, we may now say that the position of the independent farmers economy has already been overcome in all main regions of the USSR, collective farms have become the universal and dominating form of economy in the countryside, the collective farm movement has been strengthened firmly, the full victory of the collective farm system in the countryside is ensured.

Now the goal is no longer to defend the collective farm form of economy in its struggle against private forms of economy, for this task was already resolved successfully. Now the task is to meet the growing thirst of individual working peasants for collective farms, and to help them to enter collective farms, the only place where they can save themselves from the threat of impoverishment and hunger.

TsK and SNK USSR consider that all these circumstances create a new favorable situation in the countryside, which gives the chance to stop, as a rule, the application of mass exile and extreme forms of repressions in the countryside.

[...]

However, demands for mass exile from the countryside and for application of extreme forms of repressions continue to arrive from a number of oblasts. TsK and SNK have received demands from oblasts and krai for immediate exile of about one hundred thousand families.

TsK and SNK have information showing clearly that our officials continue the practice of mass chaotic arrests in the countryside. Heads of collective farms and members of boards of collective farms arrest. Heads of village soviets and secretaries of [Communist Party] cells arrest. Raion-level and krai-level plenipotentiaries arrest. Anybody who is not too lazy, and who, as a matter of fact, has no right to arrest, arrests. It is not surprising that in such a rampage of arrests, the organs having the right to arrest, including the OGPU organs, and especially the *militsiia*, lose their sense of proportion, and often make arrests without any reason, operating by the rule: arrest first, and then think.

So, what does all this mean?

All this says that in oblasts and krai there are more than a few comrades who do not understand the new situation, and who continue to live in the past.

All this means that despite the existence of new conditions, which require a shift in the center of gravity to mass political and organizing work, these comrades cling to increasingly obsolete forms of work, which no longer fit the new situation, and create a threat of weakening the authority of Soviet power in the countryside.

[...]

It would be wrong to think that the existence of new conditions and the necessity to move to new methods of work means liquidating or even easing the class struggle in the countryside. On the contrary, class struggle in the countryside will inevitably become aggravated, since the class enemy sees that collective farms have won; he sees that the last days of his existence have come, and in his despair, he cannot but engage in the most extreme forms of struggle against Soviet power. Therefore, there must be no talk about easing our struggle against the class enemy. On the contrary, our struggle must be in every possible way strengthened; our vigilance must be in every possible way sharpened. So, we are talking of strengthening our struggle against the class enemy.

But the problem is that it is impossible in the current new conditions to strengthen the struggle against the class enemy and to liquidate it using the old methods of work for they, these methods, have become obsolete. So, we are talking of improving the old ways of struggle, of rationalizing them and of making our strike more targeted and organized. So, we are saying, finally, that each of our strikes must be prepared politically in advance, that each of our strikes must be supported by actions of the broad masses of peasantry. For only using these ways of improved methods of our work will we be able to liquidate completely the class enemy in the countryside.

TsK and SNK do not doubt that all our Party-Soviet and Cheka-judicial organizations will take into consideration the new situation resulting from our victories, and respectively, will reconstruct their work according to the new conditions of struggle.

TsK VKP(b) and SNK USSR decide:

I. Regarding termination of mass deportation of peasants:

To stop immediately any mass deportations of peasants. To allow deportation only individually and on a small-scale order, and only in relation to those households the heads of which conduct active struggle against collective farms and organize nonparticipation in sowing and grain collecting.

To allow exile only from the following oblasts and in the following limited numbers:

Ukraine	2,000 households
North Caucasus	1,000 households
Lower Volga	1,000 households
Middle Volga	1,000 households

TsChO	1,000 households
Urals	1,000 households
Gorky Krai	500 households
Western Siberia	1,000 households
Eastern Siberia	1,000 households
Belorussia	500 households
Western oblast	500 households
Bashkiria	500 households
Transcaucasia	500 households
Central Asia	500 households
Total	12,000 households

II. Regarding regulation of arrests:

1) To prohibit making arrests by persons who are not given this power by law: heads of RIKs, plenipotentiaries of raions and krai, heads of soviets of villages, heads of collective farms and of collective farm associations, secretaries of cells, and so forth. Arrests may be made only by organs of the Procuracy, the OGPU, or heads of the *militsiia*. Investigators may make arrests only after preliminary sanction of a prosecutor has been given. Arrests made by heads of *militsiia* must be confirmed or canceled by OGPU plenipotentiaries or by the Procuracy [...] no later than 48 hours after the arrest.

2) To forbid Procuracy, OGPU, and *militsiia* organs to use imprisonment before trial ["before trial" written in by Stalin] as a measure of restraint, for unimportant crimes. Taking into custody before trial [again written in by Stalin] as a measure of restraint may be used only in relation to people who are accused of: counterrevolution, acts of terrorism, wrecking, banditry and robbery, espionage, crossing borders and smuggling, murder and infliction of severe wounds ["murder ... wounds" written in by Stalin], large-scale theft, professional speculation, speculation in foreign currency, counterfeiters, malicious hooliganism, and professional recidivists.

3) To establish preliminary consent of a prosecutor for making arrests by the OGPU organs for all cases, except for cases involving acts of terrorism, explosions, arsons, espionage and deserters, political banditry, and counterrevolutionary antiparty groupings.

[...]

III. Regarding reduction in the prison population:

1) To establish that the maximum number of people to be held in custody in jails of NKIust [Commissariat of Justice], OGPU, and the *militsiia*, except for camps and colonies, should not exceed 400 thousand people for the entire USSR. To oblige the Procurator of the

USSR and the OGPU to define limits on numbers of prisoners in individual republics and oblasts (krai), based on the total number specified above ["based ... above" written in by Stalin], within twenty days.

To oblige the OGPU, NKIust of republics, and the Procuracy of the USSR to start immediately reducing prison numbers and to decrease the total number of those deprived of freedom from 800,000 imprisoned now, to 400,000 within a two-month ["within ... two-month" written in by Stalin] term.

To give the Procuracy of the USSR responsibility for fulfillment of this decision.

2) To establish for each jail a maximum number of people to be held, based on the figure of 400,000 established above.

[...]

[5]b) To transfer those convicted for a term from 3 to 5 years to labor settlements of the OGPU;

c) To transfer those convicted for a term over 5 years to the camps of the OGPU.

[...]

To oblige NKIust of republics and Narkomzdravs [Commissariats of Health] of republics to liquidate completely typhus diseases in jails within a one-month term.

Head of the Council of National Commissars of the USSR V. Molotov (Skryabin)[13]

Secretary TsK VKP(b) I. Stalin

Decision accepted by poll of members of the PB 7.V.33.

The 8 May directive supposedly curtailed all activities of the OGPU administrative sentencing boards, the so-called troikas. This directive, however, did not end the activities of these boards. Typical of the Stalinist regime was to enact laws, and then immediately to make exceptions and, in this case, exceptions that covered most of the country. As the following directives show, the Politburo no sooner prohibited troikas than it gave permission to these same troikas to operate in crucial grain areas of the country, or in areas where many deportees had been relocated. The first of these permissions, granted in March 1933, continued in force even after the 8 May directive.

DOCUMENT

· 79 ·

Decision of the Politburo of the TsK VKP(b). RGASPI,
f. 17, op. 162, d. 14, l. 96.
20 March 1933

To give authority to review cases of insurgency and counterrevolution in
Ukraine, with application of the highest measure of social defense, to the
troika consisting of cc. [B. A.] Balitsky, [K. M.] Karlson, and [I. M.]
Leplevsky.

Analogous permissions were given for Belorussia and, in July, for
the whole of Western and Eastern Siberia. There, the krai-level troikas
were given authority to apply the death sentence extrajudicially in
cases of banditry, especially of gangs "terrorizing" farms and populated areas.[14] The regime did not publicize these kinds of exceptions,
but they gave leaders flexibility to act within legal procedures or to
take extraordinary measures. Such a system also gave Stalin flexibility
to manipulate the tension between the judicial and police organs,
so that neither gained too much power. In the spring of 1933, for
example, deputy OGPU head Agranov issued operational orders to
arrest grain "saboteurs" and send them through the OGPU administrative sentencing boards. This order elicited a sharp response from
Nikolai Krylenko, then head of the Russian Federation Justice Commissariat. As the memo below shows, Krylenko chastised Agranov for
overstepping the legal authority of the OGPU in prosecuting cases. In
his note, Krylenko referred to violations of the recently enacted 8 May
1933 directive from the Politburo. As Krylenko's memorandum dem-
onstrates, Yagoda paid little attention to the directive.

DOCUMENT

· 80 ·

Memorandum from N. I. Krylenko to I. V. Stalin, V. M. Molotov, D. E.
Sulimov, G. G. Yagoda, and A. Ya. Vyshinsky on the illegality of OGPU
instructions. AP RF, f. 3, op. 57, d. 60, l. 55.
14 July 1933

---

*The OGPU, over the signature of c. Agranov, issued an order, No. 00237,
9 July, about cases of grain theft under the 7 August law, as well as under
statutes of the UK [criminal code].*

The text of point 10 reads as follows:

"All cases of grain theft should be processed in a two-week period by review in judicial troikas under the PP OGPU. Cases demanding the highest measure of social defense should be sent for confirmation to the OGPU Collegium."

1. *Apart from the formal illegality of this decision, given that the OGPU has no authority to determine the jurisdiction of cases [...] the order, issued without any consultation from the Procuracy or the Commissar of Justice, is completely unrealizable in practice.*
    The general number of cases under the 7 August law that pass through courts is counted in the tens of thousands. The number of cases involving the highest measure, which pass only through the RSFSR Supreme Court, is in the thousands. Given this situation, a more or less careful hearing is physically impossible in troikas of the PP. And if it is necessary to struggle against judicial excesses in [the sense of] simply rubberstamping cases, then we have a complete lack of guarantees not to make mistakes in hearings of the extrajudicial troikas. The same goes for cases involving the highest measure. If 25 members of the Supreme Court have trouble coping with cases of this category, then, given the concentration of cases in the OGPU Collegium from all over the Union, we have an even greater burden and even less of an ability for review and control.

2. *This order completely violates the TsK decision of 8 May on sanctioning arrests by the Procuracy. [...]* In this redaction, the order leaves out any possibility for control on the part of the Procuracy, since any raion-level OGPU representative can answer the demand of a procurator to sanction an arrest: "I don't need any [Procuracy] sanction, I have an OGPU order and for me it is obligatory," and from his point of view, he will be correct.
    [...]

3. Even more unintelligible is p. 4 which recommends: "Collective farmers indicted for grain theft, in those cases where they do not organize thefts, or if the theft they commit is of an insignificant character, are not subject to arrest, instead the cases should be transferred to comrades' collective farm courts."[15]

It is completely unclear: first, who decides the question of sending cases to comrades' courts—the *raiupolnomochennyi* OGPU [raion-level OPGU plenipotentiary]? the head of the *militsiia*? the [judicial] court? or the procurator?

Second, these comrades' courts, far and away, do not exist everywhere, [and] there is no law governing them. As much as I have tried to push through a law about them, TsIK USSR has tabled it as "premature," although these courts now number 25,000.

[...]

On these grounds, I suggest it as expedient to: 1) Rework the order, 2) Recommend that the OGPU together with the USSR Procurator determine a more precise designation, which cases to send through extrajudicial channels.

[...]

(N. Krylenko)

In this instance, Krylenko won his point. The issues he raised reached the level of Politburo discussion, and on 14 July, Yagoda issued an emendation of the original order, in accordance with the new statutes regarding jurisdiction and police authority. Still, this was but one case in a constant struggle over jurisdiction between police and judicial review agencies. It was a tension that Stalin adjudicated many times, but never resolved, and most likely did not wish to resolve.

To Count and to Cleanse

Yagoda's plan from February for new settlements was ambitious, but in April, the Politburo limited the number of deportees to a target figure of slightly less than 500,000 by the end of 1933, and much of this target was to be fulfilled by the transfer of hundreds of thousands of people from prisons to special settlements.[16] Still, such a reduction did not idle the police, and neither did the 8 May directive. While mass police operations tapered off in rural areas, police turned their attention to the growing problems of urban in migration. Concerned about the influx of "antisocial" and "anti-Soviet" migrants to cities from the countryside, the Politburo and then Sovnarkom inaugurated a system of residence registration and identity cards, or internal passports. These were to be issued to citizens in key cities at first, and then eventually to residents in all urban, border, and other strategic areas, in sovkhozes (farms in which farmers were salaried workers), and in some collective farm areas close to cities. The passport system was to be administered mainly by the civil police, but under supervision of the OGPU. To this end, in December 1932, a national police administration was formed, the Chief Administration of Worker's and Peasants' Police, the GURKM, and placed both operationally and administratively under control of the OGPU. In accordance with the distribution of the new passport, the combined police mounted operations to clear cities of "socially harmful elements," that is, people who did not have official residence, or engage in "productive" work, in the cities. Socially harmful elements were either sent to special

settlements, or allowed to settle in cities and areas of lesser importance than those designated as strategic or privileged "regime areas."

Regime areas included the major centers of the country, special industrial zones, and places close to borders or government and Party
resort areas. In major cities, such as Moscow and Leningrad, initial
social cleansing operations were undertaken by the political police,
and were conducted by both civil and political police on a periodic
basis throughout the middle years of the 1930s. Instituted, originally,
as a means to cleanse cities (the urban equivalent of dekulakization),
passport checks and sweep operations soon became a major instrument in the struggle against petty criminals, unwanted or undocu-
mented populations such as gypsies, suspect ethnic populations, especially those near the country's western borders, and those committing
economic crimes, especially "speculators" and thieves. As the police
geared up to issue passports, they began to make lists to pinpoint and
monitor anti-Soviet and socially dangerous "elements," and rid cities
of these groups.

DOCUMENT

· 81 ·

OGPU circular on organizational and operational measures in
connection with passportization. GARF, f. 9401, op. 12, d. 137,
document 46 (l. 200).
21 May 1933

Absolutely secret
Moscow
To all PP OGPU and head of GPU Yakutsk ASSR
By the decision of SNK from 28/IV this year, no. 861, the RK *militsiia*
has responsibility to carry out passportization. To ensure successful com-
pletion of this task, you are requested:

1. To provide aid and supervision [to the *militsiia*] in developing
   organizational-political preparations for the [passportization] campaign through information from leading Party, Soviet, and professional organizations.
2. To provide assistance to your police assistants in setting up the passport department apparatus (of the central offices) using Chekist cadres
   and special accounting staff, and in mobilizing Party forces for work at
   passport [distribution] points.

3. To prepare and process registration material for the PP of the socially alien and parasite element.
4. To provide agent and open monitoring of the work of passport points, not permitting deviations, and eliminating organizational defects.
5. If, during passportization, there is mass saturation in some enterprises and institutions by socially alien and parasite elements, to suggest to local Party and Soviet leaders to fire the socially alien elements from the enterprises and institutions (not rescinding passports and the right of residence in that population center).
6. During passportization within the 100 km strip along the western European border of the Union (according to the special regime established for Moscow and other cities) to involve the operational staff of the UPO [border forces].

Deputy head OPGU, Prokof'ev.

As early as January, OGPU offices in major cities such as Moscow and Leningrad already began plans, in conjunction with passportization, to "cleanse" (*ochistit'*) the streets and districts of undesirable "elements."

DOCUMENT

· 82 ·

OGPU Order No. 009. On Chekist measures to introduce the passport system. GARF, f. 9401, op. 12, d. 137, doc.1.
5 January 1933

In accordance with the decision of the government, 27.XII.32, "On introduction of the passport system," and with the goal to cleanse the city of Moscow of counterrevolutionary, kulak, criminal, and other anti-Soviet elements, I order:
All Moscow Oblast OGPU departments, administrations, and special plenipotentiaries to pay special attention to conducting operations for cleansing the city of Moscow of [the above] indicated elements.
Operational departments of the OGPU and PP OGPU of Moscow Oblast are to develop, verify, and centralize material on all persons subject to expulsion from Moscow. All administrations and departments of the OGPU, PP OGPU MO [Moscow Oblast], and the Moscow RKM [*militsiia*] administration are to present, in the suggested form, lists of counterrevolutionary, kulak, criminal, and other anti-Soviet elements that have been processed through operational materials (narrative reports, official

forms, agent notes, and catalog information) by 8.1.33 to the OGPU and PP MO administrations and departments, and by 13.1.33 to RKM administration.

By the same date, present to the Operational department of OGPU and PP OGPU MO special lists of persons, enumerated in p. 3 above, who are to be allowed to remain in Moscow for operational reasons (agents, persons under current operational observation, etc.). In the lists include only persons who are actually necessary for ongoing operational work, making your task the maximum liberation (and expulsion from Moscow) of [those of] little [operational] value, those who are incapable of [operational] work, and those unqualified for agent exploitation.

[...]

Realizing that, as a result of introducing passports, a number of people, who are on OGPU secret surveillance lists (former White officers, police, Party members, etc.) will leave Moscow, it is necessary to obtain their surveillance information and relay to [OGPU organs in] their new place of residence.

G. Prokof'ev, deputy head, OGPU

Kartoteki

Point three of document 81, above, is especially interesting, for it marked the first systematic attempt on a national scale to create card catalog lists, the infamous *kartoteki*, of socially and ethnically suspect populations. The passport system in general, and passport catalogs specifically, though at first inaccurate and poorly maintained, nonetheless gave police an increasingly precise source of information, a social-geographic map of the population. These catalogs told police who lived where, the social makeup of the population, where socially suspect groups were concentrated, and they provided information about migration trends, work, and other demographic patterns. The passport system, more than any other form of surveillance, transformed the OGPU from a political and revolutionary fighting organ into the state's primary organ of mass social surveillance and control.

Control over the passport system, and measures of repression associated with it, also changed the relationship of the OGPU to Soviet citizens. The task of identifying citizens and aliens was new to the police. During the 1920s, identification of aliens fell under the jurisdiction of local soviet officials, derived from the control these officials exercised over election and disenfranchisement laws.[17] During the 1920s, civil and political police enforced laws of inclusion and exclusion, but police did not decide who was a loyal citizen and who a social alien. Those decisions were made by local communities and local Party and government officials. In Stalin's militarized state, and under the 1933 passport laws, identification and adjudication of aliens and suspect populations was transferred from the jurisdiction of local civic government to the purview of the police. It was the police who wrote identities into passports, based on whatever documents people presented, and whatever information police had at hand. As a result, the assignment of citizenship and social place passed from civic into police hands. Social engineering that had involved whole communities and was centered in civil government was replaced by a bureaucratized system of police repression, administered largely under secret orders, and with little possibility of citizen interaction and redress.

The police's catalog system expanded rapidly, which also meant an exponential increase in information available to them about the population. By August of 1934, about one year after the start of passportization, over 27 million people had been registered for passports in the Russian republic alone. And police not only gathered information, they acted on it, using passportization as a mechanism to clear cities, industrial areas, and border zones of undesirables. During the two months of initial passportization, the population of Moscow, approximately 3.6 million, declined by 65,000. The population of the Magnitogorsk metallurgical complex and city dropped from 250,000 to less than 215,000. Population along the Eastern Siberian border dropped by 10 percent, and by 1–2 percent along the western border zones.[18]

In the Russian republic, about 390,000 people were refused passports, about 3.3 percent of the population that was eligible to receive them. The problem of what to do with all these people prompted Yagoda to issue the following guidelines about whom and how to punish.

DOCUMENT

· 83 ·

OGPU circular on the use of measures of extrajudicial repression in
relation to citizens violating the law on passportization of the population.
GARF, f. 9401, op. 12, d. 137, ll. 202–4.

13 August 1933

Absolutely secret
Moscow
To PP and prosecutors supervising the PP OGPU

1. In conformity with the Statute of the Special Sentencing Board
   [*Osoboe Soveshchanie*] to establish measures of extrajudicial repression in relation to the following categories of people:

   a) Those who refused to move voluntarily out of the areas where
      they are prohibited to live, because they were refused a passport;
      Those who returned, after being ejected, to the areas where they
      were prohibited to live, and
   b) Those, who, after they were refused a passport, arrived for resi-
      dence in areas in which passportization of the population was
      carried out according to the instruction of the SNK USSR from
      14/I-33 (regime areas) [...]

2. To organize for this purpose special troikas of the PP OGPU consisting of: chairman—deputy PP OGPU for *militsiia*, and members—
   chief of the passport department, and chief of Operod [Operational
   department] PP OGPU.

[...]
7. Troikas will consider cases according to lists submitted by the
departments of the RK *militsiia*. These lists are to be submitted through
passport offices of departments of the RK *militsiia* of the autonomous
republics or of krai and oblasts.

Lists are to be made according to the following form: a) number; b) last
name, first name, middle name; c) age; d) social status; e) brief characteristic of a person; f) (when necessary)—[number of the paragraph] of
the SNK [passport] directive, according to which a person was refused a
passport.

[...]
In relation to the persons mentioned in point 1, troikas are to choose
measures of extrajudicial repression according to the exemplary table
below, with variations depending on one or several conditions.

Categories of people	Measures of repression
Persons not employed in institutions and enterprises, "rolling stones," and disorganizers of production	Minus 30 [km]—prohibition to live in areas where passportization was carried out according to the instruction of SNK USSR from 14/1-33 [regime areas]. In case of a second violation—up to three years in trudpos [special labor settlements].
Lishentsy [deprived of civil rights], kulaks, and dekulakized	Transfer to special settlements for up to three years.
Served some term of imprisonment, exile, or deportation	Transfer to special settlements for up to three years; in cases of previous detentions—up to three years in camps, except for those who support family members—labor settlements for up to three years.
Criminal and other antisocial element	Transfer to camps for up to three years.

[Minus 30 = prohibition on living within 30 kilometers of a regime area]

[...]
Deputy Head of the OGPU G. Yagoda
OGPU Prosecutor Katanyan

More Social Cleansing

Despite passportization and associated operations, officials still regarded levels of criminality as unacceptably high, especially in such cities as Moscow. As a result, the regime's leaders issued even harsher measures of repression, first in the capital, and then in other selected cities. Such campaigns were also motivated by leaders' concerns, Stalin in particular, that continued illegal economic activity threatened the ability of collective farms to establish themselves against private competition. Still sensitive to the 8 May directive, however, leaders urged police not to engage in mass sweeps, but as in the case of Kharkov (document 86), to conduct operations in more discreet ways. The first order, against speculators, was initiated by Stalin.

DOCUMENT

· 84 ·

Memorandum from G. E. Prokof'ev and L. G. Mironov to I. V. Stalin on the number of those "detained" [*privod*] for speculation, as of 1 April, by OGPU organs. AP RF, f. 45, op. 1, d. 171, l. 90.

[Note in text: "My archive. I. Stalin"]

2 April 1933

Secret

The total number of those brought in for speculation, as of 1 April, by OGPU organs *comprises 54,370 persons.*

Of the total number brought in for theft, *32,340* persons were convicted by courts and OGPU organs (OGPU Collegium and PP OGPU troikas).

16,636 individuals were convicted by OGPU organs. These are subdivided according to type of punishment:

5–10 years in camps	7,124
Less than 5 years	9,512
Total	16,636

By social composition, those convicted by OGPU organs are subdivided as follows:

Former traders, speculators, kulaks	13,364
Administrative employees, collective farmers, independent farmers, and other workers	2,655
Others	617
Total	16,636

In all, from 15 March to 1 April, 1,350 individuals have been arrested by OGPU organs.

Deputy head OGPU, Prokof'ev

Head EKO, Mironov

DOCUMENT

· 85 ·

Decision of the Politburo TsK VKP(b). On the struggle against criminal and déclassé elements in the city of Moscow. RGASPI, f. 17, op. 162, d. 15, l. 161.

20 January 1934

---

1. For all participants in armed robbery, apply the highest measure of punishment.

2. For all persons who have two or more convictions in the last year for
    theft, as well as for those who have been detained[19] two or more
    times for hooliganism, exile from Moscow and [Moscow] oblast to a
    distant place, according to instructions by the OGPU Collegium.
3. In relation to the begging and declassed element, apply expulsion to
    the place of residence, to special settlements, or to a kontslager [con-
    centration camp].

DOCUMENT

· 86 ·

Decision of the Politburo TsK VKB(b). On deportation from
Kharkov Oblast of the déclassé element. RGASPI, f. 17,
op. 162, d. 15, l. 164.
20 January 1934

a) To allow the Kharkov Obkom to deport from Kharkov Oblast to
    labor colonies and camps 2,000 people of the déclassé element.
B) To carry out the deportation through the OGPU, gradually, in small
    parties of 80–100 people, during the months of January, February,
    and March.

Political police also continued social order policing on the country's
railroads.

DOCUMENT

· 87 ·

Decision of the Politburo TsK VKP(b). On measures of struggle
against hooliganism and train wrecks on railroads. RGASPI,
f. 17, op. 3, d. 946, l. 65.
9 June 1934

Due to the increasing number of train crashes, provoked by subversive
acts and hooliganism on railroads [...], SNK USSR and TsK VKP(b) have
decided:

1. To require the TO OGPU, on the basis of existing agent material, and
    in the course of ten days, to remove professional hooligans, crimi-

nals, and orphan children from all railroad lands and zones of exclusion along railroads.

2. To grant authority to the OGPU to imprison in concentration camps for a period of 6 months to 3 years malicious hooligans who interfere with orderly movement on railroads, who damage railroad property, who terrorize railroad personnel and passengers, and to imprison orphan children who hooliganize on railroads in special camps.

3. To require NKPS railroad guards to strengthen the struggle against the hooligan element and against orphan children, to establish orderly boarding of trains, not to allow riding on the train cattle guards, car platforms, and car roofs.

4. To require OGPU organs to arrest and imprison in concentration camps for a period of 6 months all persons riding on freight trains without special permission of station heads.

[...]

7. To require TO OGPU organs to organize stringent adherence to rules for living in railroad exclusion zones.

Reorganization

As police activities expanded, and as jurisdictional issues became more complicated, the Politburo initiated a discussion about the reorganization of the OGPU. In February and then March 1934, as part of that discussion, USSR Chief Prosecutor A. I. Akulov and Justice Commissar Krylenko urged an end to the administrative sentencing boards of the OGPU, especially since they dealt with cases much beyond the OGPU's jurisdiction. Krylenko recommended that this jurisdiction be returned to what it was in 1922, limited only to cases of espionage and direct political opposition. Yagoda sought to maintain as broad a jurisdiction as possible, but the Politburo, and even Stalin, intervened to limit the administrative sentencing authority of the political police to the *Osoboe soveshchanie*, the OGPU special sentencing board, as outlined in the 8 May 1933 directive. Still, the outcome of reorganization was not a disappointment for Yagoda and the police. Formation of an all-union commissariat of internal affairs, the *Narodnyi Kommissariat Vnutrennykh Del*, or NKVD, in July 1934 consolidated political police power as the chief agency in a federal-level organ that encompassed all policing and carceral functions. The *militsiia*, the labor camps and special settlements administration, and even the firefighting administration were subordinated to Yagoda and to the political police.

Along with reorganization came a new name for the political police, the *Glavnoe upravlenie gosudarstvennoi bezopasnosti*, the Chief Administration of State Security, or GUGB. The change of name denoted a subtle but important shift in function, from a political administration to a state security organization. The GUGB was, from 1934, no longer a policing force for struggle against political opposition, but an organ formally charged with the protection of the state and its interests. From this moment, the task of the security force was to preserve and protect the revolutionary gains of the state rather than to spearhead further revolutionary changes. Struggle against political opposition was still one of the main tasks of the GUGB, but that agency now defined itself not only as the "fighting arm of the Party," but as the guarantor of the Soviet state and Soviet order, at least the Stalinist version of it. The basic tasks of the new commissariat reflected this shift and were outlined in a draft statement from August 1934. The first task was the protection of revolutionary order.

DOCUMENT

· 88 ·

Memorandum from G. G. Yagoda to I. V. Stalin requesting confirmation
of the statute of the NKVD USSR and the Special Board. AP RF, f. 3,
op. 58, d. 4, ll. 60–77.
24 August 1934

Herewith, I am distributing a draft of the statute for an All Union Commissariat of the Interior.

Peoples Commissar of Internal Affairs USSR, Yagoda.
Draft [...]
The basic tasks of the Peoples Commissariat of the Interior are:

a). Securing revolutionary order and state security in all territories of the Union of SSR;
b). Protection of personal and property security of citizens;
c). Protection of the state borders of the Union of SSR;
d). Protection of social (socialist) property;
e). Registration of civil acts;
f). Fulfillment of special tasks of the government of the Union of SSR.[20]

[...]

Cleansing Borders, Again

As the guarantor of Soviet order, the OGPU and then the NKVD continued to engage in civil policing tasks. Indeed, the next two years, 1935 and 1936, brought new campaigns of social order policing. As in 1933 and 1934, many of these campaigns were associated with passportization and public order, especially with the renewal and exchange of passports originally issued in 1933. During the two middle years of the decade, police campaigns against social marginals intensified as the newly formed NKVD widened and systematized campaigns of "social defense" against indigents, displaced peasants, and illegal urban residents. The country's political leaders also applied campaigns of mass police repression against suspect ethnic populations. Leaders and police gave special attention to the western border regions, particularly the Polish-Ukrainian border. As the following documents show, Politburo leaders gave the political police full authority to cleanse these border regions of what were described as "Polish" and "German" inhabitants, and to replace them with "loyal" Ukrainian populations. One raion, Markhlevsk, proved so "saturated" with anti-Soviet elements that local authorities requested police to cleanse it twice in the course of a year.

DOCUMENT

· 89 ·

Report from St. Kosior to I. V. Stalin on strengthening border zones. AP RF, f. 3, op. 58, d. 130, ll. 162–66.

23 December 1934

In response to the directive of the TsK VKP(b) concerning Kamenets-Podolsk and strengthening all border areas of Ukraine, in the first place 11 specially selected border regions [*polosy*],—TsK KP(b)U has taken the following major measures:

[...]

2. Work has been carried out reviewing and strengthening staffs of the heads of the raion-level NKVD departments [and] inspectors. [...] Only four raion-level heads were retained, and 7 raion-level heads were replaced by stronger workers.

[...]

4. Measures have been outlined for the cleansing of border regions of the unreliable and anti-Soviet element, in the first place, in all raions and villages with Polish and German populations, namely:

    a) Cleansing by the NKVD of border regions of anti-Soviet elements, and deporting them to the North (approximately, 2,000 households).
    b) Resettling unreliable elements of independent farmers, and also some collective farmers from border regions, to the eastern districts of Ukraine, in total about 8–9 thousand households. Areas and villages will be cleansed especially carefully that are occupied by Poles and Germans, in the first place, all the villages located close to [military] points in fortified raions, and other structures of strategic importance (railroad hubs, bridges etc.).

5. Recruitment is planned of 4,000 households from among the best collective farmers and activists of the Kiev and Chernigov oblasts (where conditions are most similar to a border area) for the strengthening of the border area and for replacing those deported deeper into Ukraine. As well, we have [submitted] a request to the TsK VKP(b) to move to the frontier areas 2,000 demobilized soldiers of the Red Army in 1935.

6. For practical implementation of points 4 and 5, we have planned:

    a) to send 11 troikas, led by members of the TsK KP(b)U, consisting of representatives of the NKVD and military commanders, to 24 border raions. On the one hand, these troikas should work up numbers and lists of people to be exiled by the NKVD to the North, and, on the other hand, should draw up lists of villages and numbers of households to be resettled from border raions. Plans are to send troikas to each of the three most complicated raions: Markhlevsk and Novograd-Volynsk raions—with a dense Polish population, and to Pulin—with German and Polish populations.
    b) 20 high-ranking officers were sent to the raions of Staroselshchina and Dnepropetrovsk, to Kharkov Oblast, and to the eastern part of Odesshchina [the Odessa area], to determine the number of households that can be moved to these areas, and what measures are required in preparation for this resettlement.

Along with these main actions, we have been carrying out the following measures:

7. Since, in the past, Polish soviets were created in a number of villages where the majority of the population is non-Polish, now 18 such Polish village soviets in Vinnytsa Oblast have been reorganized into Ukrainian [soviets], and in the Kiev raion—7 Polish village soviets. Review continues for the purpose of further reorganization. Since a

number of Polish schools were artificially created in a number of villages whose native language is Ukrainian, we now have been reorganizing these schools. Across Vinnytsa Oblast, 135 out of 291 Polish schools were completely reorganized or merged with existing Ukrainian schools.

[...]

DOCUMENT
· 90 ·

Report from P. P. Postyshev to I. V. Stalin on the need to resettle counterrevolutionary elements. AP RF f. 3, op. 58, d. 131, ll. 106–7.
31 July 1935

The Markhlevsk (border) Raion of Kiev Oblast, which has been considered a national Polish area, has been an area most saturated by anti-Soviet and counterrevolutionary elements.

In the spring of 1935, according to the decision of TsK VKP(b) 1,188 households of anti-Soviet and unreliable elements were exiled to remote places in the Union, and moved to raions of Ukraine remote from the border; 745 households, made up of reliable Ukrainian collective farmers, shock workers selected from the southern districts of Kiev Oblast, were moved into the Markhlevsk Raion, for the purpose of border strengthening.

These actions yielded considerable results for the strengthening of Markhlevsk Raion. However, spring resettlement and deportations outside the borders of Ukraine did not give a complete result, since the number of households [slated] for deportation and resettlement out of Markhlevsk Raion for spring was limited. In eleven village soviets of the Markhlevsk Raion, resettlement and deportation was not done at all. In the Markhlevsk Raion, there still is a large number of former members of gangs, White armies, Polish Legionnaries, former smugglers, persons having connections with previously uncovered espionage organizations, former kulaks, and dekulakized Polish nationalist elements.

Additional study of 20 settlements by the NKVD revealed 350 households, of which 300 households must be resettled to other oblasts of Ukraine, and 50 households to be deported to the North. Among these 350 households are those with the following social and political backgrounds: former kulaks and dekulakized—129, former noblemen—14, bandits and participants of White armies and Polish Legionaries—75, former smugglers—45, suspected of espionage—37.

The Obkom and Oblispolkom are asking the TsK VKP(b):

In addition to those already resettled in the spring of this year, to allow resettlement of 300 households of hostile and unreliable elements outside of Markhlevsk Raion to other areas of Ukraine, and to deport outside the borders of Ukraine to the North 50 households of the most dangerous anti-Soviet elements.

To allow resettlement and deportation in the same order as last spring, which was established by the decision of TsK VKP(b)U from 23.1.1935, and also to allow deportation from Markhlevsk Raion, family members to [join] their heads, who earlier were convicted and exiled for active anti-Soviet and harmful activities.

Head of Kiev Oblispolkom [Executive Committee of the Kiev Oblast soviet]
Vasilenko
Secretary of Kiev Obkom KPU [Communist Party of Ukraine]
Postyshev

Order 00192

Policing agencies were not weakened by reforms and reorganization in 1934. To the contrary, through colonization of social policies, the combined police organs in the NKVD continued to grow in power and jurisdictional authority. Even the ban against use of troikas, instituted in summer 1934, lasted only a few months. As in spring and summer of 1933, the Politburo sanctioned the renewed formation of political police troikas in large areas of the country. In August 1934, despite continued debate over the activities and authority of the NKVD, Yagoda urged approval of the activities of the *Osoboe soveshchanie*, since, as he wrote, "operations to cleanse cities and transport of socially harmful elements are causing a large backlog of people who have been arrested, and of cases that need to be reviewed."[21] In early January 1935, Yagoda and Andrei Vyshinsky, by then the procurator general of the USSR, gave instructions to reestablish special troikas to handle cases of passport violations by "criminal and déclassé elements." In 1935, as in 1933, during initial passport campaigns and operations against social harmfuls, the country's underdeveloped court system could not handle the crush of cases that passed through it. The attempt to pass from administrative to judicial repression broke down. Troikas were once again necessary to handle the overwhelming number of passport violations associated with passport exchange and the continuing purge of urban areas. The January special order from Yagoda and Vyshinsky sanctioned special "police boards" (*militseiskie troiki*) similar in makeup and function to the recently disbanded OGPU passport troikas. In the letter, below, to Stalin from 20 April, Vyshinsky explained that the formation of these troikas had been necessary due to the significantly large number of passport cases of socially harmful elements. These cases had clogged the judicial system and the NKVD special sentencing board, the *Osoboe soveshchanie*. They had led to overcrowding of preliminary holding cells and the consequent violation of Soviet law for holding individuals without indictment. Vyshinsky was writing to Stalin for approval of a draft Central Committee directive that would give approval to the continuation of these troikas, as well as permission for operations that would "achieve the quickest cleansing (*bystreishaia ochistka*) of cities of criminal and déclassé elements." As the letter shows, Stalin approved the use of the troikas, but with a handwritten note not to engage in social cleansing operations with "excessive administrative enthusiasm."

DOCUMENT

· 91 ·

Note from G. G. Yagoda and A. Ya. Vyshinsky to Stalin. AP RF, f. 3, op. 58, d. 158, l. 150.[22]

20 April 1935

Absolutely secret

To the Secretary of the TsK VKP(b) c. Stalin I. V.

To the Head of SNK USSR c. Molotov V. M.

For the purpose of the most rapid purging of cities that fall under p[aragraph] 10 of the passportization law[23] from criminal and déclassé elements, and from malicious violators of the Passport Statute, on 10 December Narkomvnudel [NKVD] and the Procuracy of the USSR issued a directive about creation of special troikas in localities for resolving cases of this category.

This decision was dictated by the very significant number of those detained under these kinds of cases, and reviewing these cases in Moscow, at the Special Board [Osoboe Soveshchanie], resulted in extreme delays in reviewing these cases, and in overcrowding of preliminary detention centers.

Considering it expedient to organize such troikas in localities for preliminary review of cases of the above mentioned categories, with final confirmation by the Special Board, we request approval of the attached draft of the decision.

People's Commissar of Internal Affairs of the USSR G. Yagoda
Prosecutor of the USSR A. Vyshinsky
20 April 1935

Stalin approved the recommendation, but with a handwritten note across text: "A 'most rapid' purging is dangerous. Need to purge gradually and fundamentally, without shocks and excessive administrative enthusiasm. It would be good to define a year-long period to complete the purge. With the rest—I agree."

Having Stalin's approval, Yagoda issued NKVD Operational Order 00192 on 9 May 1935.

DOCUMENT
· 92 ·

NKVD Order 00192. Instructions to NKVD troikas for reviewing cases of criminals and déclassé elements, and on malicious violations of passport laws.
GARF, f. 8131, op. 38, d. 6, ll. 62–64.
9 May 1935

Secret

1. Troikas are to be organized for preliminary review of cases involving criminal and déclassé elements, and also persons maliciously violating passport laws, consisting of the chairman or head of the NKVD or his deputy, and members: head of the RKM and head of the corresponding department that enforces passport laws.

2. Cases to be reviewed:

    a. Individuals convicted or who have been detained [*privod*] for statutory crimes, and those who have not yet severed ties with the criminal world;

    b. Individuals who have no previous judicial convictions, but engage in no socially useful work, having no defined residence, and with ties to the criminal world;

    c. Professional beggars;

    d. Malicious violators of the passport regime, specifically: individuals who refuse willingly to leave a locality, individuals who return to localities in which they are forbidden to live [...].

3. In cases where troikas review passport violations, [said] troikas are required to confirm the correctness and basis for depriving a citizen of the right to live in a given regime locality. For this purpose, police are required to secure the following information:

a. When, by whom, and on what basis was the violator forbidden to live in a given regime locality.

b. Who obtained the signed affidavit of the violator to leave the regime zone, when [was the affidavit obtained], and an explanation of why the violator did not then leave.

4. In forwarding to troikas cases of persons under §2 above, police are to provide the following material:

    a. Statement about the reason for apprehension.
    b. Certificate of conviction or police registry.
    c. Investigative material, i.e. protocols of interrogations, witnesses, and material evidence, if available.
    d. Short statement of indictment.

5. The accused must be present at any hearing. In each case, write a protocol of who is in attendance, a short explanation of when and where apprehended, and where held. In the indictment, instruct what kind of administrative measures are recommended and for how long.

6. Troika are required to review cases within 10 days of arrest. If a longer [period is needed], [this] must be granted by the corresponding UNKVD head.

7. Decisions of troikas, if there are no protests, are to be carried out immediately. A protocol is to go to the NKVD Special Board for approval.

8. Removal of the criminal and déclassé element, and passport regime violators, should be carried out without excessive haste, so as to avoid mass operations and campaigns. In reviewing cases, troikas are to study attentively all conditions and circumstances of each case, in light of instructions of SNK and TsK from 8 May 1933.

Signed Yagoda and Vyshinsky

There was no clearer example of how the political police conflated social order policing with state security than a speech by Yagoda to civil police heads in 1935, in which he claimed that "For us, the highest honor is in the struggle against counterrevolution. But in the current situation—a hooligan, a robber, a bandit—is he not the real counterrevolutionary? In our country ... where the construction of socialism has been victorious ... any criminal act, by its nature, is nothing other than an expression of class struggle."[24] In one of his first directives as head of the newly reorganized political police, in August of 1934, Yagoda emphasized similar priorities, especially protection of state property, as the foremost concern for operational and territorial organs in the struggle against counterrevolution.[25]

Homeless Children

Yagoda maintained this emphasis in his operational administration of the political police. Throughout the mid-1930s, as the documents above show, the OGPU and then the GUGB usurped control over a number of functions that normally belonged to the state's agencies of social welfare and civil administration, and this was especially true of the system of orphan children's homes and detention centers. The sheer numbers of homeless children (*besprizorniki*) and unsupervised children (*beznadzorniki*) during the early and mid-1930s created problems of social stability, as did the threat to order that resulted from the connections between homelessness and crime. Because of the social upheavals of the early 1930s, the population of homeless and unsupervised children in the Russian republic alone jumped dramatically from a low of 129,000 in 1929 to a peak of 400,000 in the late months of 1933, and these were only the children who were counted as they passed through children's homes or temporary gathering centers. These figures excluded Kazakhstan, for example, which had a population of around 43,000 homeless children in 1933 and 68,000 in 1934, and Ukraine, where, according to a Sovnarkom report, children's homes counted about 228,000 inmates in 1933.[26] In the whole of the USSR there existed well over half a million homeless children during the middle years of the 1930s.

Originally, care for homeless children in special centers, or children's homes, fell under jurisdiction of Narkompros and Narkomzdrav (the health and education commissariats). By spring 1935, however, harsh new laws gave the NKVD control over most of the homeless centers in the country, and also the authority to round up orphaned children and send them either to special colonies or to detention centers or even to camps or special settlements, or to remand them for prosecution. Yagoda reported that territorial and railroad police detained nearly 160,000 homeless or unsupervised children in the second half of 1935 as a result of sweep campaigns. Of these, 62,000 were sent to NKVD colonies, while another 74,000 were returned to parents or relatives. Narkompros or Narkomzdrav homes received 13,700 children, and according to Yagoda, the rest—about 10,000—were arrested, charged with crimes, and given over to courts for trial.[27]

As with passport and other campaign operations, NKVD assessments of results differed considerably from figures given by other agencies. Yet, despite discrepancies, there was no doubt about the dramatically increased role played by the NKVD in dealing with the problem of street children. Various reports noted the large shift in administration of placement centers from Narkompros to the NKVD. In addition to increased police involvement in rounding up and disposing of children, Yagoda reported that by June 1935, 260 children's centers had changed hands from Health and Education administration to NKVD control. This meant that a population of 23,000 children living in these centers suddenly found themselves under police jurisdiction instead of under the administration of social welfare agencies.[28] This was in addition to 22,000 children in centers or colonies already run by the NKVD. In all, some 325,000 children were taken off the streets in the two years between spring 1935 and August 1937.[29] Given this kind of numbers, there is no doubt that social order policing was one of the major priorities of the state's security police during the mid-1930s, whether as the OGPU or as the GUGB.

Despite similarities, however, the Soviet state security organ, the GUGB, looked very different from its predecessor, the OGPU. In 1925, the OGPU operated on a shoestring budget of 45 to 50 million rubles. By 1936, the GUGB dominated an entire state commissariat, the NKVD, and ruled over an empire worth hundreds of millions of rubles. During the 1920s, the OGPU functioned as a political police, to protect the ruling Bolshevik Party from its perceived enemies. By the mid-1930s, the GUGB had expanded its jurisdiction to encompass even issues and problems that normally fell to other state social agencies. Through the passport system and its various catalog registries, the GUGB could monitor nearly the entire Soviet population, not just criminals and supposed oppositionists. The political police did not create the social identities that were written into passports, but it was the agency, along with the civil police, responsible for ascribing, or allocating, those identities to each citizen. Those identities determined where citizens could live and work, and as a result, the GUGB, more than any other single institution except the Politburo, determined the social-geographic makeup of Soviet socialism. By the mid-1930s, the OGPU had grown from being the "fighting arm of the Party" to being the oft-remarked-on state within the state.

CHAPTER FIVE

The Great Purges
1935–1939

In December 1934, Leonid Nikolaev, a disgruntled former Party
member, shot and killed Sergei Kirov, the head of the Leningrad
Party organization. Nikolaev shot Kirov inside the Party headquarters building. Remarkably, he entered the building without chal-
lenge, carrying a concealed gun. The breach in security was bad
enough, and the assassination shocked Stalin and other leaders—that
a Party official so high up, in fact, a close confidant of Stalin, could
be so vulnerable, shot dead by a single individual inside one of the
country's centers of power.

What Stalin may or may not have thought about Nikolaev's motives
is unclear, but officially, he left no doubt from the beginning that the
murder could only have happened as the result of a carefully orchestrated plot to exterminate the Party's leaders. As a result, and at Stalin's
insistence, Kirov's murder set in motion an ever-widening cycle of investigations, accusations, trials, and executions that eventually terrorized every institution and touched every corner of Soviet society. No
one was immune: not the police who conducted the investigations, not
the Party, not the military high command, not even symphony orches-
tras, educators, scientists, economic managers, not even peasants or
workers, or any of their families or acquaintances or distant relatives.
In the end, the mounting number of investigations of plots, secret organizations, and conspiracies caused leaders, and police, to see the omni-
present hand of Leon Trotsky, Stalin's exiled nemesis, numerous foreign
agents and governments, and the Old Bolshevik, and anti-Stalinist
Party leaders, Grigorii Zinoviev and Lev Kamenev. These, and their
agents and spies, supposedly had amassed and coordinated, over the

years, a series of organizational networks inside the Soviet Union dedicated to the elimination of the Stalinist leadership group, the dismemberment of the country, and the return of capitalism. Revelation of this ever-widening conspiracy culminated in massive purges of all Soviet institutions, the Party, and even the police, and then to the great show trials and the secret military tribunals of the late 1930s.

In addition to instigating the purge process and trials, Stalin's paranoia extended as well to the masses of ordinary citizens who, he believed, would rise up against Soviet power in the increasingly likely event of invasion and war. Beginning in the summer of 1937, and through the late autumn of 1938, the combined political and civil police set in motion a series of "mass operations" approved and coordinated by the Politburo. These operations targeted former kulaks and their families, criminals, other marginal groups, and then foreign nationals living in the Soviet Union, and domestic ethnic groups deemed suspicious by leaders. By 1939, over the course of two years, over two million people were affected by purges and mass operations. Close to 800,000 were murdered outright, and hundreds of thousands more were sent to harsh labor camps, where many died.

Much has now been written about this episode in Soviet history, and while there are still debates outstanding about causes and dynamics, this is not the place to try to untangle and analyze these issues.[1] This chapter traces the role of the security police during this period, and the way that the Kirov murder shifted the fundamental direction of police activities. Yagoda continued to follow Stalin's policy directives from 1933 on the importance of social order policing, but documents show the increasing burden that political conspiracy investigations placed on police resources and time. By late 1936, Stalin had become impatient with Yagoda for not exposing and bringing to light the full extent of anti-Soviet conspiracies. Replacing him with Nikolai Yezhov, a Central Committee member and an ambitious seeker of Yagoda's position, Stalin pushed the pace of political repression faster, a process that delivered even the hapless Yagoda into the maw of the Stalinist killing machine. That process plunged the country into the two years, 1937 and 1938, that came to be known, first as the Yezhovshchina, and then as the "Great Terror."

Spinning the Kirov Murder

Within two weeks of Kirov's assassination, a circular letter set the framework in which political police officials were to understand the event. The tone, accusations, and implications of the following document set the direction of police work for the next years.

DOCUMENT
· 93 ·

From a circular letter of the NKVD USSR to all local organs of the Commissariat. January 1935. AP RF, f. 3, op. 58, d. 51, ll. 15, 18, 19.

Strictly secret

Draft

Investigation of the case of the villainous murder of c. Kirov committed by Leonid Nikolaev has revealed that he was a member of "the Leningrad terrorist center," a counterrevolutionary Zinovievist organization, which has existed with impunity for a long time, and which prepared and carried out this act of terrorism according to a carefully worked out plan.

How could it happen that our organs in Leningrad overlooked, in a criminal way, a ~~multibranched Zinoviev organization~~ an existing terrorist group of Zinovievites, and could not manage to save the life of comrade Kirov, one of the strongest leaders, and one of the best people of our Party?

How could it happen that, at one of the most important sites in the fight against counterrevolution in Leningrad, where the revolutionary Chekist vigilance of our organs should have been especially sharp, the enemy dropped out of the view of Chekists, and managed thoroughly to prepare and to strike the hardest blow against the Party and the working class?

The reasons lie in the following:

a) Despite the obvious intensification of terrorist inclinations among the remnants of the enemy, not yet completely beaten, a number of leading foreign terrorist centers [attempt] to penetrate the borders of our territory to commit terrorist acts against leaders of the Party and Soviet government.

And all this at a time when Leningrad and the oblast are saturated with a large number of the remnants of the former aristocracy, imperial officials and court servants, Guard officers, and escaped kulaks who have penetrated into manufacturing, etc.

And all this at a time when, in Leningrad, in fact, there remained untouched a considerable number of former participants of the Zinoviev-Trotsky c-r [counterrevolutionary] block.

Ranking officials in the UNKVD [the local police headquarters] in the Leningrad Oblast have criminally ignored the directive of the TsK VKP(b) and SNK USSR from 8/V-1933, which reads:

"The class enemy sees ... that the last days of his existence have arrived,—and, in despair, he cannot help but grasp at the sharpest forms of struggle against Soviet power. Therefore, there can be no discussion about weakening our fight against the class enemy. On the contrary, our fight must be in every possible way strengthened, our vigilance—in every possible way must be sharpened. Thus, discussion must be about strengthening our fight against the class enemy."

But the leadership of the NKVD in Leningrad laid down arms and fell asleep at the most crucial fighting revolutionary post, which was entrusted to them by the Party.

~~Ranking officials of the Leningrad oblast UNKVD forgot the instructions of the leader of our Party, c. Stalin, at the XVII congress of the VKP(b):~~

~~"It is clear that a classless society cannot come about on its own. It must be won and constructed by efforts of all workers, by strengthening organs of the dictatorship of the proletariat, by expansion of the class struggle, by destruction of classes, by liquidation of the remnants of capitalist classes, in struggle with enemies both internal, and external.~~

~~The matter, it seems, is clear. But, meanwhile, who doesn't know that the declaration of this clear and elementary thesis of Leninism generated considerable confusion in [people's] heads, and unhealthy moods among a segment of Party members. The thesis about our movement toward the classless society, given as slogan, they understood as a spontaneous process. And they calculated, if [there will be] a classless society, then it is possible to weaken the class struggle, it is possible to weaken the dictatorship of the proletariat and, in general, to be done with the state, which all the same must die off soon. And they began to frolic like calves in anticipation that soon there will be no classes—which means it is possible to lay down arms and go to bed—to sleep in anticipation of the coming classless society."~~

But where was the Party organization of the UNKVD of the Leningrad Oblast?

Why did the Party organization not see [...] the complacency, the criminal smugness, the obstruction of class intuition and of revolutionary vigilance, bordering on opportunism, that gripped a number of communists?

Why did the Party organization not notice the moral decay in some links of the apparatus, did not notice that such unvetted people, obviously raising doubts, such as Baltsevich, were appointed to the most important positions in the struggle against terror and espionage?

Tea Gossip, Librarians, and Plots to Kill Stalin

Following Kirov's murder, Stalin insisted that the GUGB conduct a thorough review of government and Party officials. Investigators were to focus on issues of social background; any past involvement in opposition groups, or in non-Bolshevik factions or political parties; and anything else that might compromise loyalty to the Party and the state. Police understood, of course, that it was their duty to find conspiracies and plots. That was a foregone conclusion. So began the period of absurd investigations that led to fantastic charges of sabotage and intrigue by the most unlikely people. In January 1935, for example, Yagoda informed Stalin in a memorandum that the NKVD had uncovered an anti-Soviet group working inside the Kremlin. As the following documents show, this conspiratorial group amounted to two janitorial staff and a telephone operator complaining about life over a cup of tea. By March, however, the investigation had widened, now extending to plots by a "terrorist group" against Stalin and other leaders, in conjunction with the Czechoslovakian intelligence service. The conspiracy supposedly reached into the staff of the Central Executive Committee of the government (TsIK), members of which were former Mensheviks or members of other non-Bolshevik parties, and who included even Nikolai Rozenfel'd, the brother of the Bolshevik leader Lev Kamenev.

DOCUMENT
· 94 ·

Special report from G. G. Yagoda to I. V. Stalin regarding a counterrevolutionary group in the Kremlin. AP RF, f. 3, op. 58, d. 231, ll. 1, 14.
20 January 1935

Absolutely secret
I am sending to you protocols of interrogations of:

1. Zhalybina-Bykova M. S., from 20.1. of this year 2) Mishakova E. S., from 20.1. of this year 3) Avdeeva A. E. from 20.1. of this year and 4) protocol of the confrontation between Avdeeva A. E. and Mishakova E. S. from 20.1. of this year. From materials of the preliminary investigation it has been established that, besides Avdeeva A. E., whom we arrested for distribution of provocations and malicious anti-Soviet [propaganda], Konstantinova A., Katynskaya, and others

also engage in anti-Soviet expression and distribution of provocations, who will be arrested today.

People's commissar of internal affairs of the USSR, Yagoda.

Protocol of confrontation between Avdeeva, Anna Efimovna, and Mishakova, Efrosiniia Semenovna, from 20 January 1935:

Question to Mishakova: You just discussed one conversation, in which Avdeeva expressed anti-Soviet statements, lies, and provocations concerning comrade Stalin. Repeat your testimony.

Mishakova's answer: We were sitting—myself, Avdeeva, and Zhalybina-Bykova—on the 1st floor of the government building, in a small room, and were having tea. Avdeeva began to say that our life is bad, our bosses drink, eat well, and we eat very badly. And I told her that I now live better than I lived before. Then Avdeeva began to say that Stalin is not Russian, left his first wife, and, he is said to have shot the second one. I said that it is not true, we don't know. The conversation ended, and we all went to work.

Question to Avdeeva: What can you say to the interrogation on this matter?

Avdeeva's answer: I testify that I didn't say anything that Mishakova said. All this was said by Zhalybina.

Recorded from our words correctly and read to us. Mishakova, Avdeeva.
Interrogated: Molchanov
Pauker

DOCUMENT

· 95 ·

Note from Ya. S. Agranov to I. V. Stalin regarding more arrests among personnel in the Kremlin. AP RF, f. 3, op. 58, d. 231, ll. 15–17.
2 February 1935

Absolutely secret

In addition to No. 55173 from 20.1.1935, I am informing that, so far, the investigation uncovered involvement of the following persons in the spread of provocations in the Kremlin:

1. Avdeeva, A. E., 22 years old, non-Party, cleaning woman in the Kremlin; 2. Kochetova, M. D., 20 years, old member of VLKSM [All-Union Leninist Communist Youth League (Komsomol)], Kremlin telephone operator; 3. Konstantinova, A. M., 35 years old, non-Party, cleaning woman in the Kremlin; 4. Katynskaia, B. Ia., 50 years

old, non-Party, cleaning woman in the Kremlin; 5. Orlova, A. A., 22 years old, member of VLKSM, courier in the Kremlin post office; 6. Rozenfel'd, N. A., 49 years old, non-Party, from the princely family Be[i]butov, librarian of the government library; 7. Raevskaia, E. Iu., 31 years old, non-Party, born princess Urusova, librarian of the government library; 8. Sinelobova, K. I., 29 years old, non-Party, librarian of the government library.

All these persons were arrested.

Avdeeva, A. E., who at the beginning denied her participation in spreading provocations, testified that she had been passing provocative hearsay to the cleaning women Zhalybina, M. S., and Mishakova, which she had learned from the telephone operator of the Kremlin, Kochetova M. D.

Kochetova, M. D., admitted her counterrevolutionary conversations with Avdeeva, but has not given frank testimony yet.

Konstantinova, A. M., testified that Katynskaia, B. Ia., had anti-Soviet conversations with her. She still denies her participation in spreading provocations, but she has been proven guilty by testimony of Zhalybina, M. S.

Katynskaia, B. Ia., so far admitted only her participation in counterrevolutionary conversations with Konstantinova, A. M., but she has been proven guilty by testimony of Zhalybina, M. S.

Orlova, A. A., admitted that she spread provocations, which she had passed to the cleaning woman Zhalybina, M.

Rozenfel'd, N. A., still denies her guilt, but she is proved guilty by testimony of Sinelobova, K. I.

Raevskaia, E. Iu., still denies her guilt, admits her participation in conversations of anti-Soviet character. She has been proved guilty by testimony of Sinelobova, K. I.

Sinelobova, K. I., admitted spreading provocative hearsay among the staff of the government library and Kremlin janitors, and testified that she passed provocative gossip to the following persons:

Konnova, A. I., Burkova, L. E., Simak, E. O., Raevskaia, E. Iu., Gordeeva, P. I., Mukhanova, E., and to the Kremlin cleaning woman Korchagina, who were working in the library.

Sinelobova, K. I., also names a senior librarian, Rozenfel'd, N. A., as a participant in counterrevolutionary conversations.

Thus it was established that one of the sources for spreading provocations among staff of the government library and janitors was Sinelobova, K. I.

Sinelobova, K. I., in turn, received provocative hearsay from her brother Sinelobov, A. I., age 35 years, member of VKP(b) since 1930, an assistant to the commandant of the Kremlin.

Arrested Sinelobov, A. I., [who] testified that he was connected with a Trotskyist, Doroshin, V. G., age 40 years, member of VKP(b), an assistant to the commandant of the Kremlin, who had conversations with him of a counterrevolutionary character directed against the Party leadership.

I am attaching the protocol of interrogation of Sinelobova, A. I., from 31 January 1935. I consider it necessary to arrest Doroshin, V. G.

Deputy Head of the OGPU Agranov

The mention of N. A. Rozenfel'd, above, was significant. Nina Rozenfel'd was the former wife of Nikolai B. Rozenfel'd, who was the brother of Lev Kamenev. Kamenev, one of the original Politburo members with Lenin, had long been an opponent of Stalin. He was twice expelled from the Party under Stalin, and then allowed to return. He had close ties to Grigorii Zinoviev, along with Trotsky the supposed arch conspirator against Stalin. Kamenev was most likely the ultimate target of the Kremlin investigation, and it was typical of Stalin to get at his enemies in such a roundabout way. The first mention of N. A. Rozenfel'd, though seemingly part of the normal progress of investigation, was likely intended. She was arrested, which implicated her former husband, Nikolai, which then led to Lev Kamenev. Before the police got to Kamenev, however, there were at least a couple of more steps.

DOCUMENT

· 96 ·

Report from G. G. Yagoda to I. V. Stalin on the course of investigation of the Kremlin case. AP RF, f. 3, op. 58, d. 231, ll. 22–26.
5 February 1935

Absolutely secret

In addition to No. 55173 from 20/1 and 55270 from 2/P-1935, I am informing that, in addition, we arrested:

1. Doroshin, Vasily Grigor'evich, age 40, assistant to the commandant of the Kremlin, member of VKP(b) since 1918;
2. Gavrikov, Ivan Demianovich, age 35 years, head of chemical service of the 2nd Regiment of the Moscow Proletarian Infantry Division, member of VKP(b) since 1919.

Doroshin, V. G., remains very stubborn. In the first interrogation he admitted only systematic spreading of slander concerning Party leaders, and testified that, for purposes of slander, he distorted Lenin's so-called testament[2] in a Trotskyist way.

I am attaching Doroshin's testimony.

Gavrikov has not confessed so far.

Lukianov, Ivan Petrovich, age 37 years, manager of the Grand Kremlin palace, member of VKP(b) since 1920, and

Kozyrev, Vasily Ivanovich, age 36 years, 4th-year student of the Military-Chemical Academy, member of VKP(b) since 1919—we are arresting [these individuals].

[interrogation protocol follows]

People's Commissar of Internal Affairs

(G. Yagoda)

DOCUMENT

· 97 ·

Letter of Ya. S. Agranov to I. V. Stalin with appended protocol of
interrogation of L. B. Kamenev (Kremlin case). AP RF, f. 3,
op. 58, d. 234, l. 1.
21 March 1935

Absolutely secret

I am sending you protocols of interrogations of:

1. Kamenev, Lev Borisovich, from 20/III-1935,
2. Burkova, Liudmila Emelianovna, from 20/III-1935,
3. Kochetova, Maria Dmitrievna, from 20/III-1935,
4. Mukhanov, Konstantin Konstantinovich, from 20/III-1935,
5. Sosinatrov, Aleksei Maksimovich, from 19/III-1935,
6. Gusev, Avram Makarovich, from 20/III-1935.

On March 20 of this year we arrested Ignatiev, Vladimir Ivanovich, born 1887, originally from Leningrad, former member of the TsK of the "Laboring People's Socialist Party"; was a member of Tchaikovsky's government in Arkhangelsk;[3] former active participant of the counterrevolutionary movement in Siberia in 1918–1920, former consultant to the Secretariat of the Presidium of TsIK USSR, now—member of the Bar of Advocates.

We have been investigating and will arrest Gogua, Irina Kalistratovna, born 1904, daughter of the well-known Menshevik Gogua, who works as a technical secretary of the Budgetary Commission of TsIK USSR.

Named in Kochetova, M. D.'s testimony, Smoltsova has been located and will be arrested.

Named in Kochetova, M. D.'s testimony, the kulaks, Diachkovs and the Kasatkins, hiding in Moscow, have been located and will be arrested.

Deputy people's commissar of internal affairs of the Union of SSR

(Agranov)

The implication of Nikolai Rozenfel'd in the plot led, consequently, to the interrogation of his brother, Lev Kamenev.

DOCUMENT

· 98 ·

Protocol of interrogation of Kamenev, Lev Borisovich,
from 20 March 1935. AP RF, f. 3, op. 58, d. 234, ll. 1–6.

[Handwritten note by Stalin on the first page: "A stupid interrogation of Kamenev." Typewritten note: "Send to: c. Molotov, c. Kaganovich, c. Voroshilov, c. Yezhov."]

Question: What do you know about the political attitudes of your brother, N. B. Rozenfel'd?

Answer: I have not considered him as a person having principled views about political issues. On his part, I saw only personal sympathy for me, which I explained not as any kind of considered political opinion, but as ordinary familial feelings.

Question: Your brother testified that he shared your political views, which you have defended in the fight against the Party.

Answer: I was not interested in his political views specifically, but I assume that my personal authority could have influenced the formation of his political views similar to mine.

Question: What do you know about the counterrevolutionary activity in which your brother N. B. Rozenfel'd engaged?

Answer: I know only that during the era of our open fight against the Party, he drew several drawings—lampoons of the Party leadership, and, in particular, of Stalin.

Question: Do you know that he was spreading these lampoon drawings around the city, and to whom?

Answer: From his words in 1934, I know that he gave these lampoon drawings to his acquaintance, an artist, Etinger. He also gave me these drawings. Whether he gave these to someone else I do not know.

Question: We arrested your brother N. B. Rozenfel'd for terrorist activity. During the interrogation he admitted that he participated in preparation for the murder of comrade Stalin, and testified that his terrorist intentions were formed under your influence. What can you say about this matter?

Answer: I was not aware that N. B. Rozenfel'd participated in preparations for the murder of Stalin. Rozenfel'd visited me from time to time, I was helping him financially. When visiting, he was present at conversations, which were conducted in my apartment and in the dacha in Il'inskoe. These conversations, mainly, were conducted with Zinoviev. In these conversations with Zinoviev we criticized activities of the Party, of the Central Committee, and allowed attacks against Stalin. At different times, with more or less sharpness, we talked with Zinoviev about our situation. We expressed the belief that we would not be allowed to conduct an active political life. At times, we reacted to the hopelessness of our situation by spiteful attacks against Stalin.

Counterrevolutionary conversations, which we conducted with Zinoviev in N. B. Rozenfel'd's presence, influenced him as an enemy of Soviet power and the Party, and kindled in him animosity in relation to Stalin. I imagine that N. B. Rozenfel'd, who was embittered by my exile to Minusinsk, and reacted to it extremely painfully, was fed up with the counterrevolutionary conversations that I conducted with Zinoviev later, about Stalin in particular, and [that this could have] driven him to terrorist intentions.

Question: What kind of conversations have you conducted with Zinoviev in connection to the counterrevolutionary documents issued by Trotsky abroad?

Answer: Zinoviev became acquainted with the so-called opposition bulletins at the Lenin Institute. He kept me informed about the contents of Trotsky's counterrevolutionary documents, stating his positive attitude toward some of Trotsky's assessment of the situation in the Party and in the USSR. I didn't object to Zinoviev, and before my arrest did not report to anybody higher about his counterrevolutionary views on this matter.

Question: Meaning, you agreed with his counterrevolutionary views?

Answer: I have not read these documents myself, I did not offer him my assessments, but I did not object to his counterrevolutionary views.

Question: what kind of conversations did you conduct with Zinoviev in connection with the arrests made after the murder of comrade Kirov?

Answer: After the arrests of Bakaev and Evdokimov, Zinoviev came to me, extremely nervous, and told me about these arrests. I calmed him in every possible way. He nevertheless was extremely agitated, and tossed out the phrase that he was afraid that the case of Kirov's murder may turn into the same picture as in Germany on 30 June, when Röhm was eliminated, and Schleicher was destroyed along with him.[4]

This parallel had an inadmissible counterrevolutionary character. I attributed it exclusively to Zinoviev's nervous condition, and was calming him down.

This protocol was transcribed from my words correctly and was read to me.

L. Kamenev

Head of the Secret Political department GUGB (G. Molchanov)

Interrogated:

Deputy head of the SPO GUGB (Liushkov)
Head of Department 2 of the SPO GUGB (Kagan)

As Stalin's comments show, he was unsatisfied with the interrogation of Kamenev, but it was enough to seek the removal of A. Enukidze, a high Party member and the longtime secretary of TsIK. Enukidze had supposedly turned a blind eye to the background of the employees under him, and had thereby allowed this dangerous organization to grow inside the Kremlin walls. The nerve center of this terror organization was located in the Kremlin library, and had ties to another counterrevolutionary group within the Kremlin guard. As the following censure shows, no blame as yet fell on Enukidze though he was removed from his position. But, as with many others, he was revisited within a couple of years by the police and eventually "shown" to be a Trotskyist conspirator. Like so many others, he was eventually executed.

DOCUMENT

· 99 ·

Decision of the Politburo of TsK VKP(b). On the apparatus of
TsIK USSR and c. Enukidze. AP RF, f. 3, op. 58, d. 234, ll. 47–53.
(Cyrillic alphabetical listing of items is retained.)
3 April 1935

To approve the draft of the information of the Politburo TsK elaborated by cc. Stalin, Molotov, Kaganovich, Yezhov On the apparatus of TsIK USSR and c. Enukidze.

Secret

[...]

Information of the Politburo TsK VKP(b) to members and candidates of the TsK VKP(b) and of commissions of Party and Soviet control.

C. Enukidze, A. S. was removed from the position of secretary of the TsIK USSR, to which he was appointed for many years, and was transferred to a lesser position as one of the deputy chairmen of the TsIk of Transcaucasia [Transcaucasian Socialist Federated Soviet Republic]. C. Musabekov, also a deputy chairman [from Transcaucasia] will retain his position as representative of the Transcaucasian Federation to the TsIK USSR.

The real motives for this transfer cannot be disclosed officially in the press as their publication might discredit the supreme organ of Soviet power—the Central Executive Committee of the Union of the SSR. However, TsK VKP(b) considers it necessary to communicate all the facts that served as the reason for removal of c. Enukidze from the position of secretary of TsIK USSR, and of his transfer to a lesser position.

At the beginning of the current year, it became known that among employees of the government library and the staff of the commandant's office, there was a systematic counterrevolutionary hounding of the leadership of the Party and the government, particularly of c. Stalin, that occurred for the purpose of discrediting them. A close investigation by NKVD organs of the sources of this hounding revealed several connected counterrevolutionary groups, whose purpose was the organization of acts of terrorism concerning leaders of Soviet power and Party, first of all concerning comrade Stalin.

The NKVD organs uncovered: a) *a terrorist group in the government library.* Employees of the government library, N. A. Rosenfel'd—born princess Beibutova, former wife of L. B. Kamenev's brother; and active White Guardist Mukhanova—former noblewoman, daughter of an officer under Kolchak, who served in the Czech counterintelligence, created a terrorist group, worming their way into the Kremlin library, along with former noblewomen Davydova, Burago, Raevskaia, and others.

According to the testimony of Kamenev's brother, N. B. Rosenfel'd, and his former wife N. A. Rosenfel'd, their terrorist attitudes were inspired by L. B. Kamenev, who declared to them multiple times that elimination from the leadership and destruction of comrade Stalin is the only means to change Party policy and to bring to power the Kamenev-Zinoviev group.

Nina Rosenfel'd and Nikolai Rosenfel'd took L. B. Kamenev's instructions as a direct order to commit an act of terrorism against comrade Stalin.

For the purpose of a more successful organization of the attempt upon comrade Stalin, the Rosenfel'd-Mukhanova group involved a former Kremlin librarian, Barut, who created a terrorist group inside the Armory Museum of the Kremlin.

As a member of this terrorist group, Mukhanova was connected with a female employee of a foreign embassy in Moscow, from whom she, in turn, received instructions for preparing the murder of comrade Stalin.

б) *The terrorist Trotskyist group in the commandant's office of the Kremlin.*

This group was organized by, and consisted of, employees of the Kremlin commandant's office: assistants to the commandant Doroshin, Poliakov, Lavrov, and officers Sinelobov, Lukianov, and others. The leader of the group, Doroshin, was organizationally connected with the Trotskyist terrorist group outside the Kremlin, consisting of several commanders of the RKKA [Red Army], and led by a student of the Military-chemical Academy—Kozyrev.

The investigation established that Trotskyist groups of military officers set as their purpose the organization of an act of terrorism against comrade Stalin. The terrorist group of Rosenfel'd-Mukhanova was connected with Doroshin's terrorist group through Sinelobov, who was one of the persons directly responsible for security of the room where the Politburo usually meets.

B) *Terrorist group of Trotskyist youth.*

Acting on instructions from N. A. Rosenfel'd, her son, B. Rozenfel'd, a Trotskyist, created an independent counterrevolutionary group of Trotskyist youth outside the Kremlin, which the Trotskyists Nekhamkin, Sedov (Trotsky's son), Asbel, Belov, and others joined. This group conducted preparations for the murder of comrade Stalin outside the Kremlin.

All counterrevolutionary groups were trying to achieve their objective in different ways, considering, however, the most convenient plan to get inside comrade Stalin's apartment.

Toward this end, Mukhanova and Rosenfel'd tried to get into comrade Stalin's apartment as librarians, using Minervina, comrade Enukidze's secretary. Only because comrade Stalin refused categorically the services of librarians whom the Kameneva-Rozenfel'd-Mukhanova group tried to send through Minervina was it possible to prevent terrorists from implementing their villainous plan.

All these groups apparently represented the counterrevolutionary block of Zinovievists, Trotskyists, agents of foreign states, united by the overall objective of terror against leaders of the Party and the government.

Penetration and settling of these counterrevolutionary elements in TsIK USSR (secretariat of TsIK USSR, commandant's office of the Kremlin, Government library, the Armory Museum) was facilitated by a peculiar system of selecting workers in the secretariat of TsIK USSR, having nothing to do with the principles of Soviet power. Male and female employees of TsIK USSR were hired not because of their administrative qualifications, but by acquaintance, personal connections, and often because of the readiness of female employees to cohabit with this or that ranking official of the secretariat of the TsIK.

The direct result of such a system of selection of workers was that the apparatus of TsIK USSR became extremely saturated with elements alien and hostile to the Soviet state, who conducted their subversive work under cover as employees of the secretariat of TsIK USSR. Along with low qualifications, picked up arbitrarily, and because of personal connections, declassed elements, remnants of the nobility—former princesses, noblewomen, etc.—infiltrated into the secretariat of TsIK USSR.

The degree of contamination of this apparatus is confirmed by the fact that during the vetting of employees of the secretariat of TsIK USSR by the commission especially appointed by TsK VKP(b), it turned out that it was possible to keep at work in the Kremlin only 9 people out of 107;

the rest were either subject to firing or transferred to work outside the Kremlin.

It is necessary to say that many members and, in particular, female participants of the Kremlin terrorist groups (Nina Rosenfel'd, Nikitinskaia, Raevskaia, etc.) had the direct support and high protection of comrade Enukidze. Comrade Enukidze personally employed many of these female assistants, with some of whom he cohabited.

Needless to say, comrade Enukidze knew nothing about preparations for an attempt on comrade Stalin, but he was used by the class enemy, a person who lost political vigilance and who has shown an unnatural attraction, for a communist, to former people [members of dispossessed middle and upper classes].

However, c. Enukidze bears political responsibility for all this, since, when selecting workers, he was guided by reasons not connected to the interests of business, thereby he promoted infiltration by terrorist elements hostile to Soviet power into the Kremlin. C. Enukidze's guilt is aggravated by the trust he placed in his personal secretary, Minervina, non-Party, and now arrested, to send female employees of the government library, among whom happened to be terrorists, to the apartments of Politburo members, to their private libraries.

In discussing the question of transferring c. Enukidze, information about the activity of the terrorist groups provided here was still unknown, thus a comparatively mild decision concerning c. Enukidze was made by TsK VKP(b). Since these new materials were revealed, TsK VKP(b) considers it necessary to discuss at the next Plenum of the TsK the question whether to retain c. Enukidze as member of the TsK VKP(b).

As a result of his deposition, Lev Kamenev was sentenced to ten years, and in August was tried in the first major Moscow show trial. He, along with Zinoviev, were the key defendants in what became known as the Trial of Sixteen. He and Zinoviev were convicted, and became the first of the well-known revolutionary Bolshevik leaders to be executed.

The NKVD Goes After the Party

The investigations and interrogations continued, as did the review of Party members in general. As a result, tens of thousands of people were expelled from the Party, and these came to be of special concern to Stalin and other leaders. As the following memorandum shows, police kept the Politburo informed of the numbers of former Party members, where they were located, and the reasons for their expulsion.

DOCUMENT
· 100 ·

Report of L. G. Mironov to I. V. Stalin and N. I. Yezhov about results
of operational actions of the Tatar Republic UNKVD in connection
with verification of Party documents [membership cards].
TsA FSB RF, f. 3, op. 3, d. 62, ll. 144–76.
15 February 1936

Absolutely secret

I am sending you a copy of the report of the Tatar Republic NKVD
administration about results of operational actions in connection with
verification of Party documents.

Head of the Secret Political Department of the GUGB

PP [Plenipotentiary] Commissar of State Security of 2nd Rank

(G. Molchanov)

Absolutely secret

To the Head of the Secret Political Department of the GUGB

PP Commissar of State Security of 2nd Rank c. Molchanov

[...]

Verification of Party documents of members and candidates of the
Party in the Tatar Party organization is generally finished.

As a result, in the course of verification, 4,875 persons, or 19.2 percent
of a total number of 25,395 communists, were expelled from the Party.

Of 4,875 people expelled from the Party, expelled:

1. For c-r propaganda and activity ...... 91 persons, or 1.92 percent
2. Spies and those suspected of espionage .... 6, or 0.12
   percent
3. Trotskyist-Zinovievists .... 42, or 0.9
   percent
4. White Guardists who served in the White Army and gendarmes
   .... 252, or 4.2 percent
5. Kulaks, traders, speculators .... 150, or 3.1 percent
6. Great power chauvinists and local nationalists .... 28, or
   0.5 percent
7. Hiding their social background .... 702, or 14.4
   percent
8. For communication with class-alien and hostile elements 470,
   or 9.4 percent
9. Swindlers and criminals .... 269, or 5.5 percent
10. Deserters from the Red Army .... 29, or 0.6 percent
11. For moral behavior decay .... 1,029, or 21.1 percent
12. Other offenses .... 1,807, or 38.26 percent

In addition to close ties to Party organs regarding realization of materials, which the UGB organs [local departments of state security] possessed concerning certain communists; along with review of a number of communists according to the special assignments of the Communist Party organization, the counterrevolutionary kulak–White Guard element that was revealed in the course of the review was placed immediately under active agent-operational study by us. As a result, as of today, we have placed 451 persons expelled from the Party under operational investigative surveillance, which makes 9.2 percent in relation to the total number of [those] expelled during the overall course of verification of Party documents.

[...]

From the 451 expelled, 93 persons are subject to operational investigative processing by the Transport Department of UGB UNKVD TASSR [Tatar Autonomous Republic]. A major contingent from among this number consists of those accused of damaging railway and water transport, of embezzlement, theft, and professional malfeasance.

[...]

In addition, in the city of Kazan and raions of the Tatar ASSR, persons who have evaded Party document review and disappeared from workplaces consist of 45 people.

Concerning these persons, we took and have been taking search measures.

Of the 1,997 persons working in the Party apparatus, expelled from the Party, 16 persons were brought to trial, 32 persons are the objects of agent investigations.

1. Group counterrevolutionary activity of people exposed and expelled during the Party document review.

The prevailing form of group counterrevolutionary activity of the hostile element that infiltrated into the Party is identified as theft [of socialist property], embezzlement, economic mismanagement, and professional malfeasance. Revealed, as well, was the bloc-making activity of this element with other c-r cadres: White Guardists, bandits, and others of the c-r element.

[...]

Yagoda's Replacement

Despite the efforts of Yagoda and the police under his command, Stalin grew dissatisfied, believing that Yagoda was drawing out important investigations and not getting at the real enemies of the regime, the so-called United Trotsky-Zinoviev Bloc. A final "break" in this investigation came only in June 1936, when a key defendant, E. A. Dreitser, admitted, under torture, that he was a key figure in the central organizing group of the bloc, and that he had received direct instructions from Trotsky. Still, it took Yagoda another two months to prepare the evidence and witnesses necessary to stage the trial of the supposed leaders of the bloc, which took place in August. During that period, Yagoda sent Stalin sixty-four memorandums with accompanying protocols of witness interrogations.[5]

It was not just Yagoda's slowness that turned Stalin against him, but also intrigues by another Central Committee secretary, N. I. Yezhov. Stalin began to rely on Yezhov for outside evaluations of the NKVD as early as 1934 and 1935. In early 1935, following Kirov's murder, and acting on Stalin's instructions, Yezhov delivered to Stalin a damning report on the overall dysfunctional state of the GUGB. In Yezhov's telling, the state security service was not just incompetent, but was a major vehicle for spies, saboteurs, and anti-Soviet agents to infiltrate to the very heart of the regime.[6] In September 1936, Stalin was ready to replace Yagoda, and he wrote to other Politburo members from his dacha in Sochi.

DOCUMENT

· 101 ·

Coded telegram from I. V. Stalin to members of the Politburo of TsK of VKP(b) on appointment of N. Yezhov as Commissar of Internal Affairs.[7]
25 September 1936

First. We consider it absolutely necessary and urgent to appoint comrade Yezhov to the position of Narkomvnudel [People's Commissar of Internal Affairs]. Yagoda clearly is not keeping on top of the task of uncovering the Trotsky-Zinoviev Bloc. The OGPU was four years late in this business. All *partrabotniki* [Party workers] and the majority of oblast representatives of Narkomvnudel talk about this. It is possible to keep Agranov as Yezhov's deputy at Nakorkomvnudel.
      [...]

The Show Trials, and Yezhov's Purge of the NKVD

On 11 October 1936, the Politburo officially relieved Yagoda of his duties as head of the NKVD, replacing him with Yezhov. Yagoda was given a position as head of the communications commissariat. Yezhov moved quickly to push investigations and trials to a conclusion. In

January 1937, already, the second major show trial took place, against the so-called Anti-Soviet Trotskyist Bloc. This trial exposed the supposed second, or reserve, Trotskyist center, and included the prominent revolutionary figures Karl Radek, Yurii Pyatakov, and Grigorii Sokol'nikov among the seventeen defendants. Based on confessions extracted from these individuals, especially from Radek, further trials followed. One of the most infamous of these involved the trial and execution of major military commanders, including General Mikhail Tukhachevsky. This trial, in June 1937, was closed to the public, the results being made known only after the execution of the major defendants. It set off a major purge of the military high command that removed three of five marshals, thirteen of fifteen army commanders, eight of nine admirals, and somewhere between 5 and 8 percent of the general officer corps.[8]

The final major show trial took place in March 1938, for which the NKVD collected evidence to condemn the remaining major revolutionary figures who had opposed Stalin. These included Nikolai Bukharin, Aleksei Rykov, Christian Rakovsky, and Mikhail Tomsky, who committed suicide in anticipation of his arrest. In this third trial, Yagoda also found himself in the dock, accused as a co-conspirator with the very "enemies" he had been charged to expose. Neither was Yagoda the only one of the political police to be purged. As the following document shows, Yezhov made a clean sweep of the commanding group that had surrounded Yagoda. Those removed for treason and counterrevolutionary activities were, of course, stripped of their many medals and honors.

DOCUMENT
· 102 ·

Decision of the Politburo of Tsk VKP(b). On deprivation of decorations of former executives of the Narkomat of Internal Affairs of the USSR. RGASPI, f. 17, op. 3, d. 987, ll. 100–101.
1 June 1937

No. 49, p. 406—To approve the following draft of the decision of TsIK of the USSR:

For treachery and counterrevolutionary activity to deprive of decorations of the USSR:

1.   Molchanov G. A.—Order of the Red Banner

2. Volovich Z. I.—″ ″ ″ Red Star
3. Loganovsky M. A.—″ ″ ″ Red Banner
4. Margolin S. L.—″ ″ ″ Red Banner, Lenin, and the Red Star
5. Ukhanov K. V.—the Order of Lenin
6. Yagoda G. G.—″ ″ ″ Lenin, 2 Orders of the Red Banner
7. Pivovarov I. N.—the Order of Lenin
8. Kabakov I. D.—″ ″ ″ Lenin
9. Gvakhariya G. V.—″ ″ ″ ″ Lenin
10. Prokof'ev G. E.—″ ″ ″ the Red Banner
11. Pauker K. V.—2 Orders of the Red Banner and the Red Star
12. Enukidze A. S.—[Order of] Lenin
13. Gorbachev B. S.—3 Orders of the Red Banner
14. Peterson R. A.—Orders of the Red Banner and Lenin
15. Garkavy I. N.—[Order of] the Red Banner
16. Kork A. I.—2 Orders of the Red Banner, Honorary Revolutionary Weapon
17. Eydeman R. P.—2 Orders of the Red Banner and the Red Star
18. Pogrebinsky M. S.—Orders of the Red Banner and the Red Star
19. Gai M. I.—Order of the Red Banner
20. Bokiya G. I.—″ ″ ″ the Red Banner
21. Bulanov P. P.—Order of Lenin
22. Golov G. V.—″ ″ the Red Banner
23. Puzitsky S. V.—2 Orders of the Red Banner
24. Firin-Pupko S. G.—Order of the Red Banner and the Lenin order
25. Chertok L. I.—the Token of Honor
26. Rykov A. I.—Order of the Red Banner

One of the most senior police officials from Yagoda's circle to be arrested was V. A. Balitsky, the ruthless operational officer and head of the political police in Ukraine throughout the 1930s, also a member of the Party's Central Committee. Balitsky oversaw some of the most brutal operations of the dekulakization campaigns of the early 1930s. He had headed the OGPU/GUGB in Ukraine during the great famine of 1933 and 1934, and had overseen the mass purge of Ukrainian social and intellectual leaders during the middle part of the decade. In July 1937, Balitsky was arrested in the course of Yezhov's purge of Yagoda's police, as a pivotal figure supposedly linking the anti-Soviet conspiracy inside the Ukrainian security service with the alleged anti-Soviet military conspiracy, the so-called Trotskyist Anti-Soviet Military Organization. Initially, of course, Balitsky protested his innocence as a spy and counterrevolutionary. But, he, too, fell into the same ritual dance of confession and denunciation, as did so many others. His appeal to Stalin, below, was typical.

DOCUMENT

· 103 ·

Memorandum of M. P. Frinovsky to I. V. Stalin on V. A.
Balitsky's statement. AP RF, f. 3, op. 24, d. 316, ll. 8–12.

[On the first page, handwritten note by Stalin: "To discuss with Yezhov"]
21 July 1937
To the secretary of the TsK VKP(b) c. Stalin
I am sending you the statement of the arrested, Balitsky V. from
17 July of this year.
Deputy People's Commissar of Internal Affairs of the USSR
Frinovsky
To People's Commissar of Internal Affairs of the USSR, General Commissar of State Security N. I. Yezhov
From arrested Balitsky V. A.
Statement
On 14 July 1937, I submitted a statement to you. Now, I must retract completely this statement, not of course because I took too much guilt upon myself, but because, in this statement, I basely deceived you. In this note, I maliciously, and in a double-dealing way, tried to present myself to you as a person who is guilty only in an objective sense, in that I unconsciously facilitated the anti-Soviet activity of enemies of the people.
After much thought, I came to the conclusion that, in any case, I will be inevitably exposed by interrogation and, therefore, I decided to tell how I deceived in the most base way the Party and the government, which entrusted to me a high state position.
My crimes before the country are huge. After long-term honest work, I fell into the camp of the worst enemies of the Party and the people.
I will testify in detail to the interrogation the kind of hostile work I carried out.
In this note I will try to outline the main elements of my criminal activities.
1. *First of all I directly declare—I am a participant in the anti-Soviet Trotskyist-fascist military conspiracy.* I was recruited into this plot by Yakir,[9] after the well-known operations at the end of 1935.
2. *The Ukrainian center of the military plot consisted of the following persons: Yakir, Popov, N. N., Shelekhes, Veger, Demchenko, and myself, Balitsky.*
   We joined our maturing Ukrainian plot to the all-Union anti-Soviet military conspiracy, which was directed by Gamarnik and Tukhachevsky, *and the leading role in the all-Union military-fascist plot belonged not to Tukhachevsky, but to Gamarnik.*[10]

Gamarnik was in turn connected with leading centers of Trotskyists and of the rightists.

Within the rank-and-file apparatus in all oblasts of Ukraine there were participants in the conspiracy among leading Party and Soviet workers, mainly from people who were former Trotskyists and rightists.

3. Speaking of the political orientation of the conspiracy, given those tasks that we set for ourselves, I should declare that the political direction and organizational communications of our conspiracy were right-Trotskyist-fascist. Our conspiracy was military in the sense that the leadership in the center and in Ukraine was military (Gamarnik–Yakir). In essence, however, it was connected to a number of civilian Trotskyists and rightists.

4. Parallel to our plot and in close coordination with it, an anti-Soviet Ukrainian nationalist organization was active, led by Khvylya, Trilissky, and Lisovik [all three names circled in pencil].

   The Ukrainian nationalist organization was connected with the Ukrainian anti-Soviet centers in Germany and Poland.

5. The main objectives of the conspiracy were: *overthrow of the central leadership of the Party and the country by armed force*. If it would not be possible to accomplish this prior to the beginning of war, the task of the conspiracy was to create all necessary conditions for defeat of the Soviet Union in a war with Germany, Japan, and Poland. Toward these ends, a broad harmful work was conducted for weakening the power of the Red Army along the main strategic lines (Novograd–Volynsk–Zhitomir), the Korosten' line, the Letichev militarized Raion.

   The main operative lines of the People's Commissariat of Internal Affairs of UkSSR, directed by myself, were also placed in the service of these tasks of the conspiracy.

6. Participants in the conspiracy:

   a) military: head of the headquarters [staff] of the KVO [Kiev Military District] Division Commander *Butyrsky*, deputy commander of the KhVO [Kharkov Military District] Corps Commander *Turovsky*, head of the Political Administration of the KVO—*Amelin*, his deputy *Orlov*, Division Commander *Grigoriev*, Division Commander *Demichev*, Corps Commander *Germonius*, Brigadier Commander *Ziukaa*, Corps Commander *Sablin*;

   b) Chekists: my former deputy Ivanov Vasily, my former deputy for the *militsiia* Bachinsky, former head of the Special Department Aleksandrovsky, head of the transportation department Pismenny, head of the Kharkov Oblast Administrations Mazo, head of the Odessa Oblast Administration Rozanov [All personal names in this paragraph circled in pencil].

According to my instruction, Bachinsky was supposed to engage in conversation and enlist in the conspiracy the head of the Kiev Oblast Administration Sharov [Circled in pencil]. Whether Bachinsky enlisted Sharov or not, I did not have time to ask Bachinsky.

In this statement I only briefly touched on the main elements of criminal activity and the conspiracy.

I undoubtedly do not remember, and therefore also did not name, all the participants I know in the conspiracy.

During the investigation, I will put all my diligence toward the task of uncovering all our criminal activity and all conspirators.

17 July 1937 V. Balitsky

Balitsky was executed in November 1937, neither the first nor the last to fall victim to the system that he helped create.

CHAPTER SIX

Social and Ethnic Cleansing: The Mass Operations, 1937–1938

The show trials were the most famous and most publicized of the purges conducted by the security police, but they were not the only purges to take place and, as important as they were, they did not match the "mass operations" of 1937 and 1938 for scale and social impact. These differed considerably from the political purges of Party, military, and state institutions, inasmuch as they did not target individuals so much as whole social and ethnic categories of the population. Leaders suspected these groups of potential disloyalty, and as a basis for insurgency in case of war and invasion. People swept up in the mass operations were generally arrested not on the basis of individual case files, but because their names were listed in police catalogs or rosters as part of criminal or otherwise suspect groups. In many cases, arrests were simply arbitrary. People were arrested not for specific acts of political opposition, but because of their ethnic or social background. They were generally not interrogated or tortured for information. They did not undergo lengthy court trials. Most victims were convicted en masse, by administrative sentencing boards, and shot or imprisoned fairly soon afterward.

Politburo resolutions initiated these mass purges of the population, but each was carried out under specific police operational orders. Arrest quotas were established for the different provinces and territories of the country, and time limits were specified, although these usually were extended, with Politburo approval. According to Operational Order 00439 of 25 July 1937, for example, Soviet citizens of German background, and German immigrants and refugees, were to be rounded up. Some 42,000 were shot, while another 13,000 were deported to guarded colonies in Western Siberia. Similarly, 140,000 Poles or those of Polish background were swept up under Order 00485 from 11 August 1937. Some 111,000 were shot. Latvian, Finnish and Karelian, Romanian, and Greek populations also suffered. Some 174,000 Koreans living in Eastern Siberian border regions were also deported from their homes and resettled in Kazakhstan and Uzbekistan. While the Koreans were not regarded as an "enemy nation," they were nonetheless relocated from the coastal regions and Japanese-occupied Chinese border areas.[1]

An interesting feature of the so-called nationality operations was that neither the police nor the Politburo seemed too interested in distinguishing the ethnicity of individuals arrested. Many people of Russian and other ethnic backgrounds, for example, were arrested as part of the "German" and "Polish" operations. Although called "nationality" operations, these purges targeted people not so much because of their ethnic origins, but because they supposedly had connections to counterrevolutionary organizations, or anti-Soviet activities, associated with foreign governments related to the national minorities concerned. The largest German-speaking population in the country, along the Volga river, was not targeted in these operations, but was targeted several years later, when mass operations were carried out specifically against ethnic groups. During the 1937 and 1938 period, a total of about 335,000 people were arrested and shot or imprisoned in the course of the nationality operations.

Social Conspiracies and NKVD Order 00447

The largest single mass operation lasted from late summer 1937 until November 1938 under the infamous order 00447 of 30 July 1937. This operation, in fact, involved a number of ongoing efforts by both political and civil police over the course of sixteen months either to exterminate or to place in penal colonies all those who fell under the category of "anti-Soviet elements." These elements included those who had been branded as kulaks, even and especially former kulaks, and other socially marginal groups, especially petty criminals and those with records of hooliganism. As the order indicates (document 109), leaders feared that these groups formed a large base for anti-Soviet insurgency movements, to be organized by foreign agents and Trotskyist sympathizers. As Yezhov described in his instructions, these groups had infiltrated back into Soviet society throughout the 1930s, in rural as well as industrial and urban areas, and now stood poised to wreak havoc once the signal was given for uprising. The threat from these groups needed to be resolved "once and for all time," as Yezhov wrote. Through a series of operational meetings, telegrammed instructions, and correspondence, quotas were set and sentencing boards were named. Over the course of the operation, close to 800,000 people were executed in this Soviet version of a final solution. Several hundred thousand others were imprisoned in labor camps or sent to special settlements or colonies.

The specific motivations behind this social cleansing operation remain obscure, but the first official indication of such a massive social purge came on 2 July 1937, with the following Politburo resolution.

DOCUMENT

· 104 ·

Decision of the Politburo of the TsK VKP(b). On anti-Soviet elements. AP RF, f. 3, op. 58, d. 212, l. 32.
2 July 1937

To send the following telegram to all obkom, kraikom secretaries, and all TsK of national parties.

"It has been noticed that a large proportion of former kulaks and criminals exiled at one time from various oblasts to the northern and Siberian raions—but then returned to their former oblasts after their exile term ended—are the main instigators of all sorts of anti-Soviet and subversive crimes, in both state and collective farms, and in transport and various branches of industry.

The TsK VKP(b) recommends that all secretaries of oblast and krai organizations and oblast, krai, and republic NKVD representatives register all kulaks and criminals who have returned to their homes, so that the most dangerous of them can be arrested and shot, through administrative processing of their cases by troikas, and the remainder, less active but still hostile elements, can be listed and exiled to raions designated by the NKVD.

The TsK VKP(b) recommends that the makeup of troikas be transmitted to the TsK, as well as the number to be shot, and the number subject to exile."

After this initial political resolution, the machinery of repression moved rapidly. Already, within days, the Politburo began approving lists of sentencing boards and numbers to be shot or imprisoned.

DOCUMENT
· 105 ·

Decision of the Politburo of the TsK VKP(b). On anti-Soviet
elements. AP RF, f. 3, op. 58, d. 212, l. 33.
5 July 1937

Confirm troikas for processing anti-Soviet elements:

a) For the Crimea: cc. Pavlov—NKVD (Chairman) and members
   Monatov—Procurator, Crimea ASSR, and Trupcha—Obkom Second
   Secretary.
b) For Udmurtia ASSR: cc. Baryshnikov, Shlenov—NKVD; Shevel'kov—
   Deputy Procurator Republic.
c) For Tatar ASSR: cc. Lep, Mukhametzianov and El'shin (Deputy NKVD).

Permit Tatar ASSR to provide information about numbers to be shot
in a month instead of in five days.

DOCUMENT
· 106 ·

Decision of the Politburo of the TsK VKP(b). On anti-Soviet
elements. AP RF, f. 3, op. 58, d. 212, l. 34.
9 July 1937

Confirm troikas for processing anti-Soviet elements:

1) For North Ossetia ASSR: cc. Maurer, Togoev, and Ivanov. Confirm
   169 individuals designated for shooting and 200 for exile.
2) For Bashkir ASSR: cc. Isanchurin, Bak, and Tsipnyatov.
3) For Omsk Oblast: cc. Salyn', Nelip, and Fomin. Confirm 479
   individuals designated for shooting and 1,959 for exile.
4) For Chernigov Oblast: cc. Markitan, Samovsky, and Sklyavsky.
   Confirm 244 individuals designated for shooting and 1,379 for exile.
5) For Chuvash ASSR: cc. Petrov, Rozanov, and Elifanov. Confirm 86
   kulaks and 57 criminals for shooting, and 676 kulaks and 201 criminals for exile.
6) For Western Siberia: cc. Mironov (Chairman), Eikhe, and Barkov.
   Confirm 6,600 kulaks and 4,200 criminals for shooting.
7) For Krasnoyarsk Krai: cc. Leoniuk (Chairman), Gorchaev, and Rabinovich. Permit northern raions of Krasnoyarsk Krai to provide information about numbers to be shot and exiled by 1 August.

8) For Turkmen SSR: Mukhamedov, Zverev, and Tashli-Anna-Muradov. Confirm 400 kulaks and 100 criminals for shooting, and 1,200 kulaks and 275 criminals for exile. Agree with recommendation by the TsK Turkmenistan to include for repression and exile members of the nationalist c-r organization "Turkmen-Azatlygi," Muslim clergy, and others who have been released from prison; recommend that the NKVD determine the number subject to arrest and exile.

As justification for such operations, police organizations suddenly reported the presence of "insurgency" groups in their regions. The following reports were typical, from Western Siberia and Yaroslavl.

DOCUMENT
· 107 ·

Report of S. N. Mironov, Head of the UNKVD [local NKVD administration] of the West Siberian Krai to the kraikom VKP(b), On the case of an S-R [Socialist-Revolutionary]-monarchist plot in Western Siberia. GANO, f. R-4, op. 34, d. 26, ll. 1–3.[2]
17 June 1937

UGB [local Department of State Security] of the UNKVD uncovered a Kadet [Constitutional Democrat]-monarchist, and an S-R organization in the Krai of West Siberia. They were preparing an armed overthrow and seizure of power on orders of the Japanese intelligence service, and of the "Russian All-Military Union" [ROVS]. A Kadet-monarchist organization calling itself "Union for the Rescue of Russia" was created by former princes Volkonsky and Dolgorukov, former White generals—Mikhaylov, Eskin, Sheremetev, and Efanov, on orders from active figures of ROVS abroad—Obolensky, Golitsyn, and Avralov. The counterrevolutionary organization created large branches in the cities: Novosibirsk, Tomsk, Biisk, and in Narym. White officers and Kadet-monarchist elements from among the former people, and from a reactionary part of the professorate and scientists, joined them.

The counterrevolutionary organization was guided by instructions of the ROVS branches in Harbin and Prague, and by official Japanese representatives to the USSR. The counterrevolutionary organization conducted communication with those abroad by illegal border crossings.

The S-R organization was headed by the so-called "Sibbiuro PSR" [Siberian Bureau of the Party of Socialist Revolutionaries], which consisted of Petelin, Osipov, Zanozin, Yevstigneyev, and Gorokh. On orders of the "Central Bureau of the PSR" and of the Japanese intelligence service, the organization spread its recruiting work widely, and also created a number of terrorist and espionage-subversive formations in Novosibirsk, Tomsk, Barnaul, Toguchin, Oyashino, and other raions. The S-R organization, as well as the organization "Union for the Rescue of Russia," was preparing insurgent staffing for the armed struggle against Soviet power. On this basis, in 1935 a bloc was created between "Sibbiuro PSR" and the headquarters of the "Union for the Rescue of Russia." Eskin, under the agreement with Petelin, took leadership of the whole of the struggle and insurgency work of the S-Rs. Kulaks—special resettlers located in the Narym Krai and in towns of the Kuzbass—served as a basis for formation of the insurgent staff for the headquarters of the "Union for the Rescue of Russia" and "Sibbiuro PSR." Commanders for the insurgent formations were appointed from among White officers. If [one] considers that 208,400 ex-kulaks, 5,350 former White officers, active bandits, and convicts in administrative exile are located in the Narym Krai and the Kuzbass, it becomes clear how broad a social basis there is on which to build an insurgent rebellion.

Insurgent formations were created on the principle of military units (divisions, regiments, battalions). As a result of testimonies of Captain Eskin, Dolgorukov, and a former Staff Captain Pirotsky, 26 such military units that they created in the raions of the Narym Krai and the Kuzbass were already unmasked. The headquarters developed a plan of revolt scheduled for the beginning of war. Commanders from among the participants—former White officers—were appointed for all these insurgent formations. The headquarters planned to arm the insurgent formations by capturing military depots of SibVO [the Siberian Military District]. One of the accused in the case, Berzin, a former head of the department of military communications of the SibVO headquarters, a longtime Japanese agent and an active participant in the S-R organization, testified about measures he took, and about the plan for taking over the military depots of the SibVO.

In the case of the "Union for Rescue of Russia" and "Sibbiuro PSR," 382 people were arrested. 1,317 members of the organization were unmasked by agent-investigative measures.

Head of the UNKVD of the West Siberian Krai, Mironov

DOCUMENT
· 108 ·

Coded telegram from A. S. Zimin to I. V. Stalin on "insurgency" groups
in Yaroslavl Oblast. RGASPI, f. 558, op. 11, d. 65, l. 53.
16 July 1937

Yaroslavl
Investigation of a counterrevolutionary organization of rightists in
Yaroslavl Oblast has established that rightists, together with SRs, in a
whole number of raions of the oblast and in particular factories, have
organized insurgency groups. In these insurgency groups, rightists, SRs,
monarchists, and criminal elements have united. Leadership of these
organizations has been achieved by Zheltov, [Notes: "C. Yezhov. Zheltov
absolutely need to *arrest*. St[alin]." "Done. P[oskrebyshev]."] head of
the oblast administration of communications, who received instructions
directly from Rykov,[3] and the former chairman of the Oblispolkom, Zar-
zhitsky. We are conducting [operations to] remove these groups.
Secretary Yaroslavl Obkom VKP(b)
Zimin

On 30 July, Yezhov's deputy, M. N. Frinovsky, sent NKVD Operational Order 00447 for approval to the Politburo. It presented a
detailed, dispassionate, and calculated account of state planning for
the killing of hundreds of thousands of its citizens. Order 00447 is one
of the most remarkable documents to survive the twentieth century. It
came to light only in 1992.[4]

DOCUMENT
· 109 ·

Memorandum from M. I. Frinovsky to the Politburo TsK VKP(b)
with appended Operational Order NKVD USSR No. 00447. AP RF,
f. 3, op. 58, d. 212, ll, 55, 59–78.
30 July 1937

To C. Poskrebyshev
I am sending Operational Order No. 00447 on repression of former
kulaks, criminals, and anti-Soviet elements, and a [draft of Politburo]
decision. I request to send the decision to members of the Politburo for
voting, and send an extract to c. Yezhov.

Operational Order of the People's Commissar of Internal Affairs of the Union of SSR

No. 00447

On operations to repress former kulaks, criminals, and other anti-Soviet elements.

30 July 1937

Moscow

Investigative materials in cases of anti-Soviet formations have established that a significant number of former kulaks have settled in the countryside who were earlier repressed, who have evaded repression, who have escaped from camps, exile, and labor settlements. Settled [also] are many church officials and sectarians, previously repressed, former active participants of anti-Soviet armed campaigns. Significant cadres of anti-Soviet political parties (SRs, Georgian Mensheviks, Dashnaks, Mussavatists, Ittihadists,⁵ etc.), as well as cadres of former active members of bandit uprisings, Whites, members of punitive expeditions, repatriatees, and so on, remain nearly untouched in the countryside.

Some of the above-mentioned elements, leaving the countryside for the cities, have infiltrated enterprises of industry, transport, and construction.

Besides this, significant cadres of criminals are still nested in both countryside and city. These include horse and cattle thieves, recidivist thieves, robbers, and others who were serving sentences and escaped, and are now in hiding. Inadequate struggle against these criminal contingents has created conditions of impunity for them, promoting their criminal activities.

As has been established, all of these anti-Soviet elements constitute the chief instigators of every sort of anti-Soviet crime and subversion in kolkhozes and sovkhozes, as well as in transport and in certain branches of industry.

Before the organs of state security stands the task—of crushing in the most merciless way this entire gang of anti-Soviet elements, of defending the laboring Soviet people from their counterrevolutionary intrigues, and, finally, of putting an end, once and for all, to their vile undermining of the foundations of the Soviet state.

Accordingly, I order that, as of 5 August 1937, all republics, krai, and oblasts launch a repressive campaign against former kulaks, active anti-Soviet elements, and criminals.

[...]

The organization and execution of this campaign should be guided by the following:

I. Contingents subject to repression.

1. Former kulaks who have returned home after having served their sentences and who continue to carry out active anti-Soviet sabotage.

2. Former kulaks who have escaped from camps or from labor settlements, as well as kulaks who have been in hiding from dekulakization, who carry out anti-Soviet activities.

3. Former kulaks and socially dangerous elements who were members of insurgent, fascist, terrorist, and bandit formations, who have served their sentences, who have been in hiding from repression, or who have escaped from places of confinement and renewed their anti-Soviet criminal activities.

4. Members of anti-Soviet parties (SRs, Georgian Mensheviks, Mussavatists, Ittihadists, and Dashnaks), former Whites, gendarmes, bureaucrats, members of punitive expeditions, bandits, gang abettors, émigré abettors, reemigrants, who are in hiding from repression, who have escaped from places of confinement, and who continue to carry out active anti-Soviet activities.

5. [Persons] unmasked by investigators, against whom evidence is verified by materials obtained by investigative agents, and who are the most hostile and active members of Cossack–White Guard insurgency organizations slated for liquidation, and fascist, terrorist, and espionage-saboteur counterrevolutionary formations. Elements of this category who are at present kept under guard, whose cases have been fully investigated but not yet considered by the judicial organs, are subject to repression, as well.

6. The most active anti-Soviet elements from former kulaks, members of punitive expeditions, bandits, Whites, sectarian activists, church officials, and others, who are presently held in prisons, camps, labor settlements, and colonies and who continue to carry out in those places their active anti-Soviet sabotage.

7. Criminals (bandits, robbers, recidivist thieves, professional contraband smugglers, recidivist swindlers, cattle and horse thieves) who are carrying out criminal activities and who are associated with the criminal underworld. In addition, repressive measures are to be taken against elements of this category who are kept at the present under guard, whose cases have been fully investigated but not yet considered by the judicial organs.

8. Criminal elements in camps and labor settlements who are carrying out criminal activities in them.

9. All of the groups enumerated above, to be found at present in the countryside—i.e., in kolkhozes, sovkhozes, in agricultural enterprises—as well as in the city—i.e., in industrial and trade enterprises, in transport, in Soviet institutions, and in construction—are subject to repression.

II. Measures of punishment and numbers of those subject to repression.

1. All repressed kulaks, criminals, and other anti-Soviet elements are broken down into two categories:

    a) To the first category belong all the most active of the above-mentioned elements. They are subject to immediate arrest and, after consideration of their case by the troikas, to be shot.

    b) To the second category belong all the remaining, less active but nonetheless hostile, elements. They are subject to arrest and to confinement in concentration camps for a term ranging from 8 to 10 years, while the most vicious and socially dangerous among them are subject to confinement for similar terms in prisons, as determined by the troikas.

2. In accordance with the registration data presented by the people's commissars of the republic NKVDs and by the heads of krai and oblast administrations of the NKVD, the following numbers of persons are subject to repression:
[Chart of quotas, by category, and by republic and oblast or krai]

3. The approved figures are for orientation. However, republic NKVD commissars and heads of krai and oblast NKVD administrations do not have the authority independently to raise them. No independent increase in figures is permitted.

    In cases where the situation warrants an increase in approved figures, republic NKVD commissars and heads of krai and oblast NKVD administrations are required to present me with a corresponding petition of justification.

    Reducing figures, and equally, transferring persons slated for first category repression to the second category, and vice versa, is permitted.

4. The families of those sentenced in accordance with the first or second category are not, as a rule, to be repressed. Exceptions to this include:

    a) Families, members of which are capable of active anti-Soviet actions. By special decision of the troikas, members of such families are subject to transfer to camps or labor settlements.

    b) The families of persons repressed in accordance with the first category who live in border areas are subject to expulsion beyond the border area within the republics, krai, or oblasts.

    c) The families of those repressed in accordance with the first category who live in Moscow, Leningrad, Kiev, Tbilisi, Baku, Rostov-on-the-Don, Taganrog, and in the raions of Sochi, Gagry, and Sukhumi, are subject to expulsion from these centers to other oblasts of their choice, except for border raions.

5. All families of persons repressed in accordance with the first and second categories are to be registered and placed under systematic observation.

III. Order of the operation.

1. The operation is to begin 5 August 1937 and end in a four-month period.

   In the Turkmen, Tadzhik, Uzbek, and Kirgiz SSR to begin operation 10 August this year, and in the Eastern Siberian Oblast, and Krasnoyarsk and Far East krai—15 August this year.

2. Contingents assigned to the first category are subject to repression, first of all.

   Contingents assigned to the second category will not be subject to repression until special instructions [are given].

   In cases where the republic NKVD commissar or the NKVD administrative head or head of the oblast department, having completed the operation against contingents of the first category, deems it possible to begin the operation against contingents of the second category, he is obligated to request my sanction before beginning the actual operation, and only after receiving [my sanction] to begin the operation.

   In relation to those arrested and sentenced to confinement in camps or prisons for various periods [...] advise me how many persons, for what time period to be sentenced to prison or camp. After receiving this information, I will give instructions about the order in which to send the convicts and to which camps.

3. Divide republic, krai, and oblast territories into operational sectors, in accordance with the situation and local conditions.

   For organizing and conducting the operation, form an operational group for each sector, headed by a ranking official of the republic-, krai-, or oblast-level NKVD administration who is capable of coping successfully with the serious operational tasks to be laid upon him.

   In some cases, highly experienced and capable heads of raion or city offices may be appointed heads of operational groups.

4. Staff operational groups with the necessary number of operational officers and provide them with means of transport and communication. In accordance with operational requirements, supplement groups with militarized or civil police units.

5. Heads of operational groups have responsibility for registering and identifying those subject to repression, for leading the investigation, for formulating indictments, and for carrying out sentences of the troikas.

   The head of the operational groups is responsible for the organization and conduct of the operation in his operational sector.

6. For each person repressed, collect detailed information and compromising material. On the basis of the latter, make up arrest lists, signed by the head of the operational group, with two copies to be sent for review and confirmation to the commissar of internal affairs, or to

the head of the [NKVD] administration, or the NKVD oblast administration.

The commissar of internal affairs, or the head of the NKVD administration, or the NKVD oblast administration will review the list and
give sanction for arrest [...].

7. On the basis of the approved list, the operational group head will
    carry out the arrest. Each arrest is to be formulated as an order. Dur-
    ing arrest, conduct a thorough search. Confiscate: weapons, ammuni-
    tion, military equipment, explosive materials, poisonous materials,
    counterrevolutionary literature, precious metals in the form of mon-
    ey, bullion, jewelry, foreign currency, print reproduction equipment,
    and correspondence.

    Everything confiscated is to be registered in the search protocol.

8. Those arrested are to be collected at points designated by the com-
    missar of internal affairs, or the head of the NKVD administration or
    oblast department. Collection points for arrestees are to have struc-
    tures suitable for holding those arrested.

9. Arrestees are to be closely guarded. All measures must be organized
    to prevent escapes or any kind of excesses.

IV. Order for conducting the investigation.

1. Investigation shall be conducted into the case of each person or group
    of persons arrested. The investigation shall be carried out in a swift
    and simplified manner. During the course of the investigation, all crim-
    inal connections of persons arrested are to be exposed.

2. At the conclusion of the investigation, the case is to be submitted for
    consideration to the troika.

[...]

VI. Order for carrying out sentences.

1. Sentences are to be carried out by persons in accordance with instruc-
    tions by chairmen of the troikas—i.e., by commissars of the republic
    NKVDs, heads of [NKVD] administrations, or by the raion-level
    departments of the NKVD.

    Implementation of the sentence shall be based on the certified extract
    from the minutes of the troika session containing an account of the
    sentence regarding each convicted person and a special directive
    bearing the signature of the chairman of the troika, which are to be
    handed to the person who executes the sentence.

2. Sentences included under the first category are to be carried out in
    places and in the order as instructed by the commissars of internal
    affairs, by the heads of [NKVD] administrations, or by the raion-
    level departments of the NKVD, under complete secrecy of time and
    place [...].

Documents concerning the implementation of the sentence are attached in a separate envelope to the investigative dossier of each convicted person.

3. Assignment to camps of persons convicted under the second category is to be carried out on the basis of warrants communicated by the GULAG of the NKVD of the USSR.

VII. Organizing the operational leadership and maintenance of records.

1. I place [responsibility for] general direction of the operations on my deputy, comrade Frinovsky, Corps Commander, head of the Chief Administration of State Security. A special group is to be formed under him in order to implement the tasks associated with the direction of these operations.
    [...]
3. Reports on the conduct and results of the operation are to be sent every 5 days, on the 1st, 5th, 10th, 15th, and 25th of each month by telegram and in detail by post.
4. Inform immediately by telegram of any counterrevolutionary formations newly uncovered in the process of the operation, any excesses that arise, escapes across the border, formation of groups of bandits and thieves, and other emergencies.

Thoroughgoing measures are to be taken during the organization and implementation of the operations in order to prevent persons subject to repression from going underground, in order to prevent their escape from their places of residence and especially beyond the border, in order to prevent their forming groups of bandits and thieves, and to prevent any excesses. Any attempts to commit some counterrevolutionary actions are to be exposed promptly, and quickly stopped.

People's Commissar of Internal Affairs of the USSR and General Commissar of State Security,
[N. Yezhov]
Confirmed: M. Frinovsky

The following day, the Politburo approved the order, and issued instructions about how to deal with the huge influx of new prisoners, those who were lucky enough not to be executed outright. The document below gives specific meaning to the oft-used description of the NKVD as a state within the state. Repression was a huge enterprise in the Soviet Union, and the demands of the state's security organization extended into nearly every other state institution, and cost tens of millions of rubles.

DOCUMENT

· 110 ·

Decision of the Politburo of the TsK (VKPb). On the question
of the NKVD. AP RF, f. 3, op. 58, d. 212, ll. 52–54.
31 July 1937

1. To confirm the draft presented by the NKVD of an operational order concerning repression of former kulaks, criminals, and other anti-Soviet elements.

2. To commence operations in all oblasts of the USSR on 5 August 1937; in the Far East Krai, in the Eastern Siberia Oblast, and in Krasnoyarsk Krai as of 15 August 1937; in the Turkmen, Uzbek, Tadzhik, and Kirghiz republics as of 10 August 1937. The entire operation is to be completed within a period of 4 months.
[...]

5. To issue to the NKVD 75 million rubles from the reserve fund of the SNK [Council of People's Commissars] to cover operational expenses associated with the implementation of the operation, of which 25 million rubles is for payment of rail transport fees.

6. To require the NKPS [Commissariat of Transport and Communications] to grant the NKVD rolling stock in accordance with its demands for the purpose of transporting the convicted within oblasts and to camps.

7. To utilize, as follows, all kulaks, criminals, and other anti-Soviet elements convicted under the second category to confinement in camps for periods of time:

   a) on construction projects currently under way in the GULAG of the NKVD of the USSR;
   b) on constructing new camps in the remote areas of Kazakhstan;
   c) on the construction of new camps especially organized for timber works undertaken by convict labor.

8. To propose to the People's Commissariat of Forestry that it forthwith transfer to the GULAG of the NKVD the following forest tracts for the purpose of organizing camps for forest works. [List follows.]

9. To propose to the People's Commissariat of Forestry and to the GULAG of the NKVD of the USSR to determine within a period of ten days which additional forest tracts, other than those listed above, should be transferred to the GULAG for the purpose of organizing new camps.

10. To commission the State Planning Commission (Gosplan) of the USSR, the GULAG of the NKVD, and the People's Commissariat of

Forestry to work out within a period of 20 days and to present for confirmation to SNK USSR:

a) plans for the organization of timber cuttings, the labor force needed for this purpose, the necessary material resources, the funds, and the cadres of specialists;

b) to define the program of timber cuttings of these camps for the year 1938.

11. To issue to the GULAG NKVD a 10 million ruble advance from the reserve fund of SNK to organize camps and to conduct preparatory work.

[...]

12. To propose to the oblast and krai committees of the VKP(b) and of the All-Union Leninist Communist Youth League (VLKSM) [Komsomol] in oblasts where camps are being organized, to assign to the NKVD the necessary number of communists and Komsomol members in order to bring the administrative and camp security apparatus to full strength (as demanded by the NKVD).

13. To require the People's Commissariat of Defense to call up from the RKKA [Red Army] reserves 210 commanding officers and political workers in order to bring to full strength the cadres of supervisory personnel of the military security forces of newly organized camps.

14. To require the People's Commissariat of Health to assign to the GULAG of the NKVD 150 physicians and 400 medical attendants for service in the newly organized camps.

15. To require the People's Commissariat of Forestry to assign to the GULAG 10 eminent specialists in forestry and to transfer 50 graduates of the Leningrad Academy of Forest Technology to the GULAG.

Other Mass Operations

As operations got under way, arrest quotas began to rise. Some of the pressure for this came from local officials, either out of a desire to show the requisite zeal, or as a way to settle accounts with a number of troubling populations in their regions. On the other hand, Stalin and Yezhov used a coterie of selected killers whom they sent to specific regions to step up the pace of repression. One of Stalin's most ruthless killers during the mass operations was G. F. Gorbach, a career NKVD officer who was assigned and reassigned several times, before his own arrest, to push sluggish fulfillment of mass operations. As soon as he arrived in a new oblast, such as Omsk, he immediately requested, and always received, permission to raise arrest quotas.

DOCUMENT

· 111 ·

Coded telegram from G. F. Gorbach to N. I. Yezhov on increasing the limit for
the "kulak" operation in Omsk Oblast. AP RF, f. 3, op. 58, d. 212, l. 87b.
15 August 1937

As of 13 August 5,444 individuals of the first category have been arrested
in Omsk Oblast, 1,000 weapons confiscated. I request instructions
regarding my letter, No. 365, concerning a limit for first category up to
8,000 individuals.

13.VIII. No. 1962 Gorbach

Stalin's handwritten note on the telegram approved the increase to
eight thousand.

Even as the political police were conducting arrests according to
the various national and anti-Soviet operational orders, the Politburo
approved yet another mass operation, the so-called Harbin operation.
This involved the arrest of some twenty-five thousand people who had
worked in China along the rail line owned by the Soviet Union from
the Soviet border to the Chinese city of Harbin. As with the "nationality" operations, leaders feared that all individuals who had been
abroad or worked for the rail line, or who had fled as refugees from
China, were potential or actual traitors, working for the Japanese,
whose troops occupied Manchuria, where Harbin was located. As a
result, the Politburo approved the following instructions.

DOCUMENT

· 112 ·

Decision of the Politburo of the TsK VKP(b). On the NKVD, with appended
draft for Operational Order No. 00593. AP RF, f. 3, op. 58, d. 254, ll. 223–28.
19 September 1937

To confirm the closed letter [for limited circulation] of the NKVD USSR
and the order for measures in connection with terrorist, subversive, and
spying activities of Japanese agents among the so-called *Kharbintsy*
[Harbin people].

Operational order of the USSR Commissar of Internal Affairs.

NKVD organs have registered up to 25,000 so-called *Kharbintsy* (former employees of the Chinese Eastern Railroad, and reimmigrants from

Manchukuo [Japanese occupied Manchuria]) [who] have settled into the railroad transport and industries of the [Soviet] Union.

Reliable agent-operational materials show that the great majority of the *Kharbintsy* entering the USSR consist of former White officers, policemen, gendarmes, members of various immigrant spy-fascist organizations, and so forth. For the most part, they are agents of Japanese intelligence, which has sent [these agents] into the Soviet Union for terrorist, subversive, and spying activities.

Investigative materials serve, as well, to prove this. For example, in the railroad and industries, up to 4,500 *Kharbintsy* have been repressed in the last year for active terrorist and subversive intelligence activities. Investigation of their cases reveals carefully prepared and executed work by Japanese intelligence [organs] to organize subversive spy bases among the *Kharbintsy* on the territory of the Soviet Union.

[...] with the goal of crushing the cadres of spies among the *Kharbintsy* planted in the transport and in industries of the USSR
I order:

1. Beginning 1 October 1937, launch a broad operation of liquidation of subversive spying and terrorist cadre of *Kharbintsy* in transport and in industries.

2. All *Kharbintsy* are subject to arrest:

    a) Those who have already been discovered and [those] suspected of terrorist, subversive, spying, and wrecking activities;

    b) Former Whites, reimmigrants, those who either emigrated during the Civil War, or military personnel of various White formations;

    c) Former members of anti-Soviet political parties (SRs, Mensheviks);

    d) Members of Trotskyist and right formations, as well as *Kharbintsy* having connections with the activities of these anti-Soviet formations;

    e) Members of various immigrant fascist organizations ("Russian United Military Union," "Union of Cossack Villages," "Union of Musketeers," "Yellow Union," "Black Ring," "Christian Union of Young People," "Russian Student Society," "Brotherhood of Russian Truth," "Working Peasants Party," and so forth);

    f) Employees of the Chinese police and army, both from before Japanese occupation of Manchuria, and after the formation of Manchukuo;

    g) Employees of foreign firms, Japanese, first of all, but White Guardist as well (the Churin firm, and others);

    h) Graduates of known Harbin courses "Internationale," "Slavia," "Prague";

    i) Owners and co-owners of various enterprises in Harbin (restaurants, hotels, garages, etc.);

    j)   Illegal arrivals in the USSR without legal Soviet documents;
    k)   Those who took Chinese citizenship, and then Soviet citizenship again;
    l)   Former smugglers, criminals, opium and morphine traffickers, etc.;
    m) Members of counterrevolutionary sectarian groups.

    [...]

5. Investigation of cases of arrested *Kharbintsy* should be developed in such a way as to expose, in the shortest possible time, all members of subversive-spying and terrorist organizations and groups.
Arrest immediately any new networks of spies, wreckers, and subversives that are uncovered in the process of investigating the *Kharbintsy*.
    [...]

7. Every ten days make an album of arrested *Kharbintsy* [...] with concrete depiction of investigative and agent materials, which determines the degree of guilt of the arrested. Send the album to the NKVD USSR for confirmation.
    [...]

11. Complete the operation by 25 December 1937.
    [...]

13. Inform me about the progress of the operation every five days by telegram [...].

Commissar of Internal Affairs, USSR, General Commissar of State Security,
Yezhov

According to data collected by the Russian organization Memorial, 46,317 *Kharbintsy* were repressed, of whom 30,992 were shot.

The Messiness of Mass Repression

As the documents above show, operational orders were specific about arrest and processing procedures, especially about documenting investigative materials, confessions, convictions, and sentences. In practice, however, local police officials came under such pressure to fulfill arrest quotas that they were forced to streamline the process of repression, dispensing with any kind of procedure and creating a kind of conveyor system of terror. In January 1938, a special procurator on the Kirov railroad line described in a report how this mass-production system worked. In the context of this report, "conveyor" refers not to the oft-cited practice of continuous interrogations, but to the bureaucratic assembly-line character of the purge machine. The procurator, a certain Vorob'ev, submitted his report in the form of a rare complaint to his superiors about investigative methods used by local political police officials and operational groups.

DOCUMENT
· 113 ·

Report of 26 January 1938 from Procuracy transport investigator of the 5th Kirov railroad, Vorob'ev, to Deputy Procurator of the Kirov railroad, Shapiro. GARF, f. 8131, op. 37, d. 69, ll 8–10.

———————

In January of 1938, a plenipotentiary of the Petrozavodsk DTO GUGB [transport department, GUGB], Pukhov, M. V., was assigned to us to conduct several case investigations (arrests, interrogations, witnesses, etc.). Since we had no special room for him, I gave him my office. During our conversation, he told me he had much work, serious work, and a fixed deadline, and that, alone, he could not do it. He asked me to give him help. I didn't have any pressing cases (only 1) and so I said yes. I agreed to give him five people.

What did our work consist of? It consisted of gathering eyewitness accounts. They were very easy to gather.

Pukhov invited several of his acquaintances, [list follows of eight names, including two railroad dispatchers and a local medical clinic administrator] and others, and before briefing them, said to each, "I need eyewitness accounts for such and such, and such and such people (he had a list), they have been shot, you will not be called into court, evidence is needed only to formulate the case. We will write the protocol, then you stop by and sign it." I repeat, he said this to each of the "witnesses."

After such conversations, Pukov and I got down to business. He made up a rough draft of an [arrest and indictment] protocol and said: "(...) Write the protocol for these people." He gave me 3–4 names, first and last, and the last place they worked, so that I could answer the first question, "Do you know so and so?" There were three questions: "Do you know this person?" "What do you know about anti-Soviet activities of this person?" and "Tell about your connections to this person." That was all.

I took a blank form, filled out the biographical data, answered that I understood the penalty for giving false evidence, according to statute 95 of the criminal code, and began my conversation with the absent witness—gave them the required questions and answered them myself. [Except for the biographical information], the rest all depended on my own fantasy. And, I won't be modest, since I don't lack imagination, the result came out smoothly.

Pukhov said that such and such a machinist conducted c-r agitation, sabotaged all measures of the Party and government, slandered the great leaders, carried out wrecking activities in production. He invited me to fill in the protocol in such a fashion. And I wrote it just so. I wrote that the machinist, his name was Iul', I think, is dangerously disposed against the Party and Soviet power in his counterrevolutionary soul; that he systematically slandered all measures of the Party and government; called socialist competition [production competition campaigns] as exploitative of workers as in any capitalist country; that the right to vacation is given only to Party and government leaders; that in the resorts and sanatoriums communists lay about and don't do a stroke of work, and only squander the money of workers; that the Stalinist constitution is a fiction, a deceit, blatant cheating on the part of communists, who systematically betray the working class in their own interests; that the elections to the Supreme Soviet were also a fiction; that only those whom the communists wanted became deputies, and the workers were pushed aside. Etc. I wrote a lot. Protocols for the others I changed somewhat, so as not simply to repeat myself. And the "work" went on, without interruption.

During the day we scribbled away, completing eight such protocols. In the evening, the "witnesses." Several were completely indifferent, signing my creation without even reading it; others gave a surprised look, read with trepidation, and adamantly refused to sign. But Pukhov calmed them, said that these citizens had been shot, that you will not be called into court, etc. Their resistance was broken and they signed the protocol. Clearly, the witnesses did not know the people whose protocols they signed [...] had never looked them in the face.

[...]

In one of the conversations I had with Pukhov afterward, he said, "I will send you 200 rubles to settle accounts," and this surprised me. Something else he said, "I had to give a bit to Lashmanovoi, because not everybody would agree to sign this kind of a protocol or a blank form." I understood from this that Pukhov had paid Lashmanovoi to give an eyewitness account.

This was our work. Pukhov signed all the protocols. Certainly, our actions were illegal and criminally liable. In plain Russian, they were falsifications, deceits. Given such investigative methods and actions, personal freedom in our country cannot be guaranteed. Such methods are alien to our Soviet intelligence service, alien to the work of our glorious Chekists. From my work with Pukhov I learned nothing except that, in the end, I was fed up with creating fantasies and such disgusting fictions. Was Pukhov correct? Do we allow such investigative methods? I ask you to clarify this.

By the way, I ask you, Comrade Shapiro, to answer the following: We now have people working here from the NKVD opergruppa [operational group]. Two operatives. They have arrested a number of people. They can't interrogate them all themselves. So, they have mobilized others from Party-Komsomol activists such as Borshov, deputy head of the political department, [...], and Kudriatseva, another Komsomol member, head of a fire brigade. Is this proper? I don't think so.

In perusing the above document, the reader wonders if Vorob'ev experienced a certain vicarious thrill in being able to enumerate with impunity such a long list of unmentionable truths about the Soviet system. Vorob'ev certainly did not attempt to abbreviate the list of "slanderous lies" that he put into the mouths of the condemned victims.

The Wizard Behind the Curtain

By early 1938, political police cadres were working under tremendous pressure, attempting to fulfill quotas for a number of mass operations, as well as for the ongoing purges of regional Party organizations, the military, and state institutions. Despite the burden of work, Stalin continued to press Yezhov for results. There are not many documents to show Stalin's close control of events, since much was communicated through oral instruction, but the following memorandum and resolution shows the extent to which the general secretary followed and directed various purging operations closely.

DOCUMENT

· 114 ·

Memorandum from I. V. Stalin to N. I. Yezhov concerning SRs. AP RF, f. 3, op. 24, d. 330, l. 18.
17 January 1938

C. Yezhov,

1. The line on SRs (left and right together) has not been completely unraveled. Fishman and Paskutsky are leading the NKVD by the nose. If Belov himself had not unraveled the line on the SRs, the NKVD would be sitting in the dark. Belov said some things, but did not say everything. Paskutsky, Uritsky, and Fishman must supplement Belov. It must be kept in mind that there are not a few SRs in our army and outside the army. Does the NKVD have a registry of SRs ("former") in the army? I would like to have it, and soon. Does the NKVD have a registry of SRs outside the army (in civilian institutions)? I would like to have this, as well, within 2–3 weeks.

2. What has been done to identify the SRs on the basis of the known evidence from Ryskulov?
3. What has been done to identify and arrest all Iranians in Baku and Azerbaijan?
4. I can tell you from my own experience that at that time SRs were very strong in Saratov, in Tambov, in Ukraine, in the army (command staff), in Tashkent, and in general, in Central Asia, in the Bakinsk power-generating stations where they still sit and still engage in wrecking in the oil industry. You must act livelier and push harder.
5. A very important task: strengthen the oblasts of the DVK [Far East Krai] with new Chekists, from outside. This is far more important than strengthening the Kazakhstan oblasts, which may be given a lower priority.

Still Higher Limits

The original order 00447 placed a time limit on operations of the end of 1937, but in January, the Politburo approved an extension of the operations in a number of areas with even higher quotas.

DOCUMENT

· 115 ·

Decision of the Politburo of the TsK VKP(b). On anti-Soviet elements.
AP RF, f. 3, op. 58, d. 212, ll. 155–56.
31 January 1938

[...]

a) Adopt the recommendation by the NKVD USSR to confirm additional numbers subject to repression of former kulaks, criminals, and active anti-Soviet elements, in the following krai, oblasts, and republics:

1.	Armenia SSR:	1000 in cat[egory] 1 and 1,000 in cat. 2			
2.	Belorussia SSR:	1,500	-"-		
3.	Ukraine SSR:	6,000	-"-		
4.	Georgia SSR:	1,500	-"-		
5.	Azerbaijan SSR:	2,000	-"-		
6.	Turkmenistan SSR:	1,000	-"-		
7.	Kirgiz SSR:	500	-"-		
8.	Tadzhik SSR:	1,000	-"-	and 500	-"-
9.	Uzbek SSR:	2,000	-"-	and 500	-"-
10.	LVK:	8,000	-"-	and 2,000	-"-

11. Chita Oblast:	1,500	-"-	and 500	-"-
12. Buryat-Mongolia:	500	-"-		
13. Irkutsk Oblast:	3,000	-"-	and 500	-"-
14. Krasnoyarsk Krai:	1,500	-"-	and 500	-"-
15. Novosibirsk Oblast:	1,000	-"-		
16. Omsk Oblast:	3,000	-"-	and 2,000	-"-
17. Altai Krai:	2,000	-"-	and 1,000	-"-
18. Leningrad Obl.:	3,000	-"-		
19. Karelia SSR:	500	-"-	and 200	-"-
20. Kalinin Oblast:	1,500	-"-	and 500	-"-
21. Moscow Oblast:	4,000	-"-		
22. Sverdlovsk Oblast:	2,000	-"-		

b) Recommend that the NKVD USSR complete all operations in the above-designated oblasts, krai, and republics no later than 15 March 1938, and in DVK no later than 1 April 1938.

c) In accordance with this decision, extend the work of troikas for reviewing cases of former kulaks, criminals, and anti-Soviet elements in the oblasts, krai, and republics listed under point "a."

In all other oblasts, krai, and republics, complete troikas' work no later than 15 February 1938, so that, by that date, all cases will be finished and reviewed within the given limits [quotas] established for those krai, oblasts, and republics.

The Politburo also extended the nationality operations, and in 1938, NKVD officials began to insist that local officials arrest people according to genuinely ethnic rather than associational criteria.

DOCUMENT

· 116 ·

Decision of the Politburo of the TsK VKP(b). On continuing repression among populations according to their nationality. AP RF, f. 3, op. 58, d. 254a, l. 90.
31 January 1938

1. To allow Narkomvnudel [the NKVD] to continue until 15 April 1938 the operation to crush spying-subversive contingents of Poles, Latvians, Germans, Estonians, Finns, Greeks, Iranians, *Kharbintsy*, Chinese, and Romanians, either foreign or Soviet citizens, under existing NKVD orders.

2. Continue until 15 April the existing extrajudicial review of cases of those arrested under this operation, regardless of their citizenship.

3. Recommend that the NKVD conduct an analogous operation until
    15 April to crush cadres of Bulgarians and Macedonians, both for-
    eign and Soviet citizens.

In addition to purging potentially hostile ethnic minority populations, leaders also attempted to seal the borders of the country against
"contamination." The following document attests to the level of paranoia of leaders who instructed the police to arrest and either shoot or
imprison all refugees coming into the country, and to strengthen
police control of border regions in eastern Siberia. What is interesting
is that refugees were to be "punished" by imprisonment even if police
interrogation determined that their motives for seeking asylum were
genuine, and that they had no intention of conducting anti-Soviet
activities. Such an instruction shows how much the repressive nature
of the purges, especially the mass operations, was intended as prophy-
lactic, regardless of a person's actions or intentions.

DOCUMENT

· 117 ·

Decision of the Politburo of the TsK VKP(b). On refugees. AP RF, f. 3,
op. 58, d. 6, l. 53.
31 January 1938

It has been established that foreign intelligence services insert into the
USSR their massive network of spies and subversive intelligence agents
mainly in the guise of refugees: those purportedly seeking political asylum
in the USSR; better material conditions, as a result of unemployment;
deserters from military units and border guards; reimmigrants; and
immigrants.

The TsK VKP(b) decides:

1) To recommend that the NKVD USSR apprehend, immediately arrest,
    and carefully interrogate all refugees at the border, regardless of their
    motives for crossing into the territory of the USSR.
2) All refugees—if it is established directly or indirectly that they crossed
    into the territory of the USSR with spying, subversive, or other anti-
    Soviet intentions—remand to the military tribunal court with a man-
    datory application of shooting.
3) Cases of all refugees, for whom it is established that they crossed into
    territory of the USSR without malicious intent, remand for review by

the Special Board [*Osoboe soveshchanie*] of the NKVD USSR, with application of punishment measures of 10 years of prison confinement.

[...].

And, still, the requests for higher and higher limits continued.

DOCUMENT

· 118 ·

Coded telegram from Ia. A. Popok to I. V. Stalin regarding an additional limit for review of cases of anti-Soviet elements. RGASPI, f. 558, op. 11, d. 65, l. 108.
2 February 1938

From Engels
Strictly secret
To: Moscow, TsK VKP(b) c. Stalin
The troika reviewing cases of former kulaks, criminals, anti-Soviet elements has reached its limit, and not succeeded yet in completing its work to crush active elements.

I request an additional limit of one thousand persons by February 15. Secretary of Nemobkom [German Oblast Party committee] VKP(b), Popok

DOCUMENT

· 119 ·

Coded telegram from Iu. M. Kaganovich to I. V. Stalin and N. I. Yezhov on increasing the limit for Gorky Oblast. AP RF, f. 3, op. 58, d. 212, l. 158.
4 February 1938

Gorky
Absolutely secret
Work of the troikas is finished. In accordance with the oblast limit 9,600 kulak, SR, insurgent and other anti-Soviet elements have been repressed. Additionally, kulak–White Guardist elements conducting subversive work have been discovered. In all up to 9,000 of the anti-Soviet element are calculated.

The Obkom requests establishment of an additional limit of 3 thousand in the first category and two thousand in the second. Continue the period of operation until 20 March.

Secretary of the Obkom VKP(b),
Iu. Kaganovich

DOCUMENT

· 120 ·

Decision of the Politburo of the TsK VKP(b). On the question of the NKVD. AP
RF, f. 3, op. 58, d. 212, l. 161.
17 February 1938

To allow the NKVD Ukraine to conduct additional arrests of kulak and others of the anti-Soviet element and review cases in troikas, increasing the limit for the NKVD SSR Ukraine by 30,000.

As Stalin pressed Yezhov, so Yezhov pressed his subordinates, who were required to provide regular reports on the progress of operations. This meant, of course, that local police officials had to keep all the various operations straight, and to make sure that they were complying with the varying deadlines for different operations. As a result, the lists of those arrested, shot, imprisoned, or deported became meaningless; they became bureaucratic numbers to be manipulated to satisfy bureaucratic demands. Nonetheless, numbers were important, all important. Yezhov passed on the numbers to Stalin that local commanders passed to him and, as the following document shows, Stalin read numbers carefully.

DOCUMENT

· 121 ·

Special communication from N. I. Yezhov to I. V. Stalin with appended copy of telegram by S. I. Lebedev on progress of the foreign nationalities operations. AP RF, f. 3, op. 58, d. 254, ll. 200–205.

[On the first page, handwritten note by Stalin: "Important"]
24 March 1938
Absolutely secret
To the Secretary of the TsK VKP(b) c. Stalin

I am sending a copy of telegram No. 3/1909 by the Head of the NKVD administration of Tula Oblast, c. Lebedev, on the progress of operations against Germans, Estonians, and others.

Commissar of Internal Affairs USSR

General Commissar of State Security (Yezhov)

Absolutely secret

To the Commissar of Internal Affairs USSR

General Commissar of state security, c. Yezhov, N. I.

Post-telegram

On progress of operations under NKVD orders 00485, 00439, and 00593

In accordance with your directive No. 233, from 1 October 1937 through 20 March 1938, 1,646 persons were arrested by us, of which: 824 along the Polish line [of operation], 299 along the German line, 230 along the Latvian line, 21 along the Estonian line, 13 along the Romanian line, 7 along the Finnish line, 136 along the Kharbin line, 35 along the Chinese line, 48 along the Iranian line, 33 along the Greek line.

These include 127 persons arrested by us in the five-day period from 15 through 20 March, this year, of which: 91 along the Polish line, 12 along the German line, 17 along the Latvian line, 1 along the Kharbin line, 5 along the Chinese line, 1 along the Romanian line.

During the same five-day period the following counterrevolutionary formations were uncovered and liquidated:

[...]

The operation continues, according to your directive.

Head of UNKVD for the Tula Oblast

Major of state security,

Lebedev

In May 1938, not satisfied with the pace of the nationality operations, the Politburo once again extended the deadline for their completion.

DOCUMENT

· 122 ·

Decision of the Politburo of the TsK VKP(b). On the question of the NKVD. AP RF, f. 3, op. 58, d. 212, l. 177.

26 May 1938

To continue until 1 August 1938 the simplified procedure for reviewing cases of persons of Polish, German, Latvian, Estonian, Finnish, Bulgarian, Macedonian, Greek, Romanian, Iranian, Afghan, Chinese Nationalists, and *Kharbintsy* discovered in spying, terrorist, and other anti-Soviet activities.

Ending the Operations and Ending Yezhov

The mass operations under order 00447 also extended into the summer of 1938, although the peak of arrests passed already in February and March. Individual areas continued to request higher quotas, and there was a last spasm of violent repression in Eastern Siberia, spurred by the flight, in June, into China and then to Japan, of the NKVD chief for the krai, G. S. Liushkov. By late summer, all the mass operations were beginning to wind down, and Stalin began to maneuver in order to bring the purges to a close and to reassert Party control over the NKVD. To what extent Liushkov's betrayal contributed to Stalin's decision to get rid of Yezhov is not clear, although Yezhov believed that the defection to the enemy of one of the highest-ranking security officers would be blamed on him. In any case, a clear sign came in August with the reassignment of Yezhov's deputy, M. P. Frinovsky, to head the navy. Frinovsky was not only a deputy head of the NKVD, but Yezhov's top aide in perpetrating the mass operations. At the same time, the Politburo endorsed the appointment of Lavrentii Beria to replace Frinovsky. Although Beria had worked previously in the OGPU, from 1931, he had been Party head in the Caucasus Krai. His appointment as first deputy was essentially a first step in isolating Yezhov and in bringing Party control back to the security organs. Throughout the early autumn, other of Yezhov's deputies were reassigned and replaced with people recommended by Beria.

As Stalin and Beria maneuvered to weaken Yezhov, the Politburo began to move toward ending the mass operations. In early October, the Politburo established a commission to review arrest procedures and Procuracy supervision of the NKVD. Yezhov was appointed as a nominal head, but the commission included Beria as well as Andrei Vyshinsky, the USSR chief procurator and a longtime rival of the NKVD. On 17 November, the Politburo issued a decision that effectively brought the mass operation purges to a close, reestablished dormant legal procedures for arrest and investigation, and reasserted Procuracy supervision of investigations and arrests. The document described accurately the way in which the purges were conducted, only now it condemned them as illegal and anti-Soviet.

DOCUMENT
· 123 ·

Decision of the Politburo of the TsK VKP(b). On arrests, procuratorial supervision, and the conduct of investigations. RGASPI, f. 17, op. 3, d. 1003, ll. 85–87.[6]
17 November 1938

[...]

Absolutely secret

To the people's commissars of internal affairs of the Union and autonomous republics, to the heads of krai and oblast administrations of the NKVD, to the heads of the military district, city, and raion-level departments of the NKVD;

To procurators of the Union and autonomous republics, to procurators of krai and oblasts, military districts, cities, and raions;

To secretaries of the TsK of national communist parties, krai committees, oblast committees, the military district, city, and raion-level committees of the VKP(b)

On arrests, supervision by the Procuracy, and the conduct of investigations.

Decision of the Council of People's Commissars of the USSR and the Central Committee of the VKP(b).

SNK USSR and the TsK of the VKP(b) recognize that the NKVD organs, under the leadership of the Party, have accomplished much during 1937–38 in inflicting a crushing defeat on enemies of the people and in purging the USSR of numerous espionage, terrorist, subversive, and wrecking cadres consisting of Trotskyists, Bukharinists, SRs, Mensheviks, bourgeois nationalists, White Guardists, fugitive kulaks, and criminal elements—all providing crucial support to foreign intelligence agencies in the USSR and, in particular, to the intelligence agencies of Japan, Germany, Poland, England, and France.

At the same time, the NKVD has also accomplished much in inflicting a crushing defeat on espionage-subversive agents of foreign intelligence services transferred to the USSR in great numbers from abroad under the guise of so-called political émigrés and deserters: Poles, Romanians, Finns, Germans, Latvians, Estonians, *Kharbintsy*, and others.

The purging of the country of subversive, insurrectionary, and espionage cadres has played a positive role in securing the further success of socialist construction.

Nonetheless, one cannot think that the purging of the USSR of spies, wreckers, terrorists, and saboteurs is at an end.

In continuing to wage a merciless campaign against all enemies of the USSR, our task now consists of organizing this campaign by making use of more precise and reliable methods.

This is all the more necessary insofar as the mass operations engaged in crushing and eradicating hostile elements, carried out by organs of the NKVD during 1937–38 and involving a simplified procedure of conducting investigations and trials, could not help but lead to a number of major deficiencies and distortions in the work of the NKVD and the Procuracy. Moreover, enemies of the people and spies employed by foreign intelligence agencies, having wormed their way into both the central and local organs of the NKVD and continuing their subversive activities, sought in every way possible to confuse investigative and agent work. They sought consciously to violate Soviet laws by carrying out mass, unjustified arrests while at the same time saving their confederates (especially those who had joined the NKVD) from destruction.

The chief deficiencies, recently revealed in the work of the NKVD and the Procuracy, are as follows:

First of all, officials of the NKVD completely abandoned work with agents and informers in favor of the much simpler method of making mass arrests without concerning themselves with the completeness or high quality of the investigation.

Officials of the NKVD became so much unaccustomed to meticulous, systematic work with agents and informers and so much developed a taste for a simplified method of conducting the investigation of cases, to such an extent that up until very recently they were raising questions concerning the so-called limits imposed on the conduct of mass arrests.

This has led to a situation where work with agents, weak as it was, has regressed even further, and worst of all, many officials of the NKVD have lost the taste for agent procedures that plays an exceptionally important role in the work of a Chekist.

This has finally led to a situation where, in the absence of properly organized work, the investigative [organs] have, as a rule, been unsuccessful in fully unmasking the spies and saboteurs under arrest who were in the employ of foreign intelligence agencies, and in fully exposing all of their criminal ties.

[...]

Second, a major deficiency in the work of the NKVD organs has been the deeply entrenched simplified procedures of investigation, during which, as a rule, the investigator is satisfied with obtaining from the accused a confession of guilt and totally fails to concern himself with corroborating this confession with the necessary documents (testimonies of witnesses, the testimony of experts, material evidence, etc.).

[...]

Investigative documents are formulated carelessly; drafts of testimonies being written in pencil, and corrected and crossed out by who knows whom, are entered into the record; protocols of testimonies, unsigned by the person under interrogation and uncertified by the investigator, are entered into the record, along with unsigned and unconfirmed indictments by the prosecution, etc.

The Procuracy organs, for their part, have not taken the measures necessary for the removal of these deficiencies, as a rule, reducing their participation in the investigation to a simple registration and stamping of investigative materials. The organs of the Procuracy not only have not removed these violations of revolutionary legality but have in fact legitimized them.

Such an irresponsible and arbitrary attitude to investigative work, and such a crude violation of procedural rules established by law, have not infrequently been cleverly utilized by enemies of the people, who have wormed their way into the organs of the NKVD and Procuracy, both in the center and in localities. They have consciously subverted Soviet laws, committed forgeries, falsified investigatory documents, instituted criminal proceedings, and subjected people to arrest on trivial grounds and even without any grounds whatsoever, instituted "cases" against innocent people, while at the same time taking every possible measure to conceal and save their confederates—involved with them in criminal anti-Soviet activities—from destruction. Such instances took place both in the central and in the local apparatus of the NKVD.

All of these intolerable deficiencies observed in the work of the organs of the NKVD and Procuracy were possible only because enemies of the people, who had penetrated into the organs of the NKVD and Procuracy, attempted with every means possible to cut off the work of the organs of the NKVD and Procuracy from Party organs, to evade the Party's control and leadership, and thereby to make it easier for themselves and their confederates to continue their anti-Soviet, subversive activities.

With the aim of decisively eliminating the deficiencies listed above, and of organizing properly the investigative work of the organs of the NKVD and of the Procuracy, the SNK USSR and the TsK of the VKP(b) hereby decide:

1. To prohibit the NKVD and Procuracy organs from carrying out any mass arrests or mass deportations.
   In accordance with Article 127 of the Constitution of the USSR, arrests are to be carried out only by court order or with the sanction of the procurator.
   [...]
2. To abolish the judicial troikas created by the special decrees of the NKVD USSR, along with the judicial troikas attached to raion, krai, and republic boards of the RK *militsiia* [civil police].

From now on, all cases must be directed for review by courts or the Special Board of the NKVD USSR, in strict accordance with existing laws on judicial competence.

3. In making arrests, the NKVD and Procuracy organs are to be guided by the following:
    [...]
4. In conducting investigations, the organs of the NKVD are obligated to observe precisely all the requirements of the Criminal Procedure Code.
    [...]
5. The Procuracy organs are obligated to observe precisely the demands of the Criminal Procedure Code in their supervision over investigations conducted by the NKVD organs.
    [...]
8. The NKVD USSR and the Procurator of the USSR are obligated to give their local organs instructions for the precise implementation of the present decision.

The SNK USSR and the TsK of the VKP(b) call the attention of all officials of the NKVD and the Procuracy to the need for a resolute elimination of the aforementioned deficiencies in the work of the organs of the NKVD and the Procuracy, and to the extraordinary significance attached to the organization of investigative and procuratorial work in a new way.

The SNK USSR and the TsK of the VKP(b) warn all officials of the NKVD and the Procuracy that the slightest infraction of Soviet laws and of the directives of the Party and the government by any official of the NKVD and the Procuracy, regardless of who the person is, shall be met with severe judicial penalties.

V. Molotov,
Chairman of the Council of People's Commissars
I. Stalin,
Secretary of the Central Committee of the VKP(b)
17 November 1938

In the meantime, Beria intrigued against Yezhov in the same manner that Yezhov had connived against his predecessor Yagoda. As a TsK member, Beria was part of a commission to oversee NKVD affairs, even as he was Yezhov's deputy. Beria accused Yezhov of concealing compromising materials about his deputies who, it was alleged, had ties to Trotskyite, counterrevolutionary groups. In his 23 November letter of resignation, below, Yezhov admitted to this charge, and to negligence resulting in the defection of Liushkov, and the disappearance of another official, A. I. Uspensky, the NKVD chief in Ukraine (later captured).

DOCUMENT
· 124 ·

Letter from N. I. Yezhov to the Politburo TsK VKP(b) [and to] I. V. Stalin.
RGASPI, f. 17, op. 3, d. 1003, ll. 82–84.[7]
23 November 1938

Absolutely secret

I request that the TsK VKP(b) relieve me of work as Commissar of Internal Affairs USSR for the following reasons:

1. Discussion in the Politburo, 19 November 1938, of the statement by the head of the Ivanovo Oblast UNKVD, c. Zhuravlev, fully confirmed the facts contained in the statement. Primarily, I accept responsibility—that c. Zhuravlev, as apparent from his statement, signaled me about the suspicious behavior of Litvin, Radzivilovsky, and other ranking NKVD officials, who attempted to hush up cases of various enemies of the people, being themselves linked to them in conspiratorial anti-Soviet activities. In particular, especially serious was the note from c. Zhuravlev about the suspicious behavior of Litvin, who tried everything to hinder the discovery of Postyshev, with whom he himself was linked in conspiratorial work. Clearly, if I had given the required Bolshevik attention to the seriousness of Zhuravlev's signals, that enemy of the people, Litvin, and other scoundrels, would have been uncovered long ago, and would not have been appointed to responsible positions in the NKVD.

[...]

Fifthly, my fault lies in that, doubting the political honesty of such people as the former UNKVD DVK traitor, Liushkov, and more recently, the Narkomvnudel Ukrainian SSR traitor, Uspensky, I did not take sufficient Chekist precautionary measures, and thereby allowed the possibility for Liushkov to escape to Japan, and for Uspensky to hide somewhere still unknown, while they still look for him. All of this together makes it impossible for me to continue work in the NKVD.

I request, again, to be relieved of work as Commissar of Internal Affairs of the USSR. Despite all these great drawbacks and lapses in my work, I may still say that under the constant leadership of the TsK, the NKVD has given the enemy a real beating. I give my Bolshevik word, and I pledge before the TsK VKP(b), and before c. Stalin, to learn all these lessons in my future work, to learn from my mistakes, correct them, and in whatever capacity the TsK deems necessary to use me—to justify the trust of the TsK.

Yezhov

Change of Command

On 25 November, the Politburo approved the appointment of Beria to head the NKVD. Simultaneously, Stalin issued a telegram to Party organs laying the blame for "excesses" of the mass operations on the "criminal band" that had infiltrated the NKVD under Yezhov, immediately following the defeat of the "criminal band" that had supposedly controlled the police under Yezhov's predecessor, Yagoda. The telegram, reproduced below, referred to a declaration from a certain V. P. Zhuravlev, head of the Ivanovo NKVD, alerting leaders to untoward and suspicious activities among senior NKVD officials. Certainly, Zhuravlev was prompted to write such a letter, since the activities to which he referred were well known. Still, the letter provided Stalin with the pretext he needed to establish a "script" for ending the purges setting in motion the machinery of recrimination, but without affecting the stability of the regime or his own personal power and responsibility.[8]

DOCUMENT

· 125 ·

Coded telegram from I. V. Stalin to Party organ leaders on the unsatisfactory situation in the NKVD. RGASPI, f. 558, op. 11, d. 58, l. 61.
25 November 1938

In mid-November of this year, the TsK received a statement from Ivanovo Oblast, from c. Zhuravlev (head of the UNKVD) about shortcomings in the NKVD apparatus, about mistakes in the work of the NKVD, about inattention to local signals, about warnings of the treachery of Litvin, Kamensky, Radzivilovsky, Tsesarsky, Shapiro, and other ranking officials of the NKVD, about the fact that Commissar c. Yezhov did not respond to these warnings, etc.

Simultaneously, information has been received by the TsK that after the crushing defeat of the Yagoda gang in the NKVD organs, a different gang of traitors appeared in the persons of Nikolaev, Zhukovsky, Liushkov, Uspensky, Passov, Fedorov, who consciously distort investigative cases, shield notorious enemies of the people, all the while these people not meeting sufficient counteractions on the part of c. Yezhov.

Placing the situation of the NKVD under discussion, the TsK VKP(b) demanded an explanation from c. Yezhov. C. Yezhov submitted a declaration in which he acknowledged the above-mentioned mistakes, acknowledged in addition that he carries responsibility for not taking measures to stop Liushkov's defection (UNKVD of the Far East), the flight of Uspensky (commissar of the Ukraine NKVD), acknowledged that he was far from able to cope with his duties in the NKVD, and requested to be relieved of his duties as NKVD commissar, retaining the post of water transport commissar and continuing his work in organs of the TsK VKP(b).

The TsK VKP(b) fulfilled c. Yezhov's request, relieving him of his work in the NKVD, and confirmed c. Beria, L. P., as commissar of the NKVD, by unanimous consent of the TsK members.

You will receive the text of c. Yezhov's declaration by post.

[Handwritten note by Stalin:] Immediately acquaint with this communication all NKVD commissars and heads of NKVD administrations.

The day after his appointment, Beria issued an internal order annulling all the operational orders connected with the mass operations. The order reproduced much of the procedural detail contained in the 17 November Sovnarkom and Central Committee decision. One interesting difference, however, was the section that focused on cessation of mass operations of arrest and deportation. In one of the few documents of the 1930s to spell out what, exactly was meant by "mass operation," he defined it as "group arrests or deportations without a differentiated approach to each of those arrested or deported, and [without] a thorough review of all incriminating materials for each person." He reiterated that "all arrests must be made on a strictly individual basis ..." Beria also listed all of the special NKVD mass repression orders that were to be annulled, eighteen of them in all.[9]

Beria wasted little time in purging the top ranks of the NKVD. Even before the end of the year, nearly all of the heads of administrations and their deputies had been replaced, many of them arrested, and nearly all of the republic-, krai-, and oblast-level leadership had been swept away. In all, 332 officials were arrested, 140 from the central apparatus and 192 from peripheral organs. Beria also arrested and replaced 18 republic and autonomous krai commissars.[10] Purging and arrests continued into 1939, but Beria, supported by Stalin and the Politburo, acted quickly to lay blame on and silence Yezhov and the leading cadres of the mass purges. As the following chapter shows, Beria spent the next several years attempting to consolidate a new cadre of Chekists, and to fulfill the new tasks given to the political police by the Politburo.

CHAPTER SEVEN

The Security Organs at War
1939–1944

Back to "Normalcy": A Delicate Balancing Act

The Politburo decision of 17 November 1938 and the NKVD order that followed stopped the various mass operations. Beria's purge of Yezhov's leadership circle also went a long way to send the signal that the cycle of violence was to change. To repair the damage to the Party, state, and military institutions took longer and was more complicated. Stalin had to bring the political police once again under Party control, and this was difficult, given the power of the police during the previous two years, and the culture of fear that pervaded the political apparatus. The Politburo also had to find a way to normalize relations within state institutions, with the military, and with enterprises, factories, and other workplaces. Stalin and those around him had to convince officials that they could fulfill their responsibilities without constant fear of arrest. These were difficult tasks and required some adroit maneuvering.

One key problem for Stalin was to decide how to place blame on the NKVD for what were clearly policies initiated and approved by him. Blaming and eliminating Yezhov and his command, of course, was an obvious answer, but many police officials had been arrested, and Vyshinsky pressed Stalin about whether to try NKVD officials in open courts. At first, Stalin approved, as the following terse memorandum shows.

DOCUMENT

· 126 ·

I. V. Stalin's note to A. Ya. Vyshinsky on organizing public trials of
NKVD officials. AP RF, f. 3, op. 57, d. 96, l. 110.
3 January 1939

To c. Vyshinsky
Public trials of the guilty are necessary. I. Stalin
In the end, however, most officials were tried in closed courts of the
state's military tribunal, to which the police were legally subject as a
militarized force.

As part of the Politburo's attempt to place controls on the police
and to reinvigorate regional Party structures, the 17 November 1938
order specifically instructed local Party officials to take a leading role
in vetting and approving NKVD heads. Regional leaders, however,
were reluctant to take such an initiative, and as a result, the Politburo
made an example of several Party organizations in order to get the
message across. The next document also shows how the Politburo
attempted to deflect blame onto local Party organs both for excesses
of the security organs, and for the consequent damage to the economic functioning of the country.

DOCUMENT

· 127 ·

From the decision of Politburo TsK VKP(b) on the work of the Bashkir Obkom
[Oblast Committee] of the VKP(b). RGASPI, f. 17, op. 3, d. 1005, ll. 12–13.
9 January 1939

Having heard the report of the first secretary of the Bashkir Obkom of
the VKP(b) c. Zalikin, the Tsk VKP(b) considers work of the Bashkir
Obkom of the Party unsatisfactory.

Knowing about the unsatisfactory work of the NKVD of the Bashkir
Republic, about contamination of the NKVD organs with obviously
doubtful elements, c. Zalikin not only did not take any measures for
checking and eliminating shortcomings in work of the NKVD, and for
purging its apparatus of these doubtful people, which was the clear duty
of the Obkom of VKP(b), but also hid signals and facts he received from
the Obkom; by doing so, he covered up significant problems and outrages at the NKVD organs.

Weak leadership of industry by the Bashkir Obkom of VKP(b) resulted
in the failure of the largest enterprises (The Ufa motor plant, Beloretsky
plants, the enterprises of "Bashzoloto" [Bashkir Gold] trust, etc.) to fulfill
their production program.

[...]

Regional leaders in Dagestan, the Altai, Irkutsk, and other areas
received similar reprimands.

Stalin had to walk a fine line when it came to the issue of torture,
which had been used freely during the great purges. Use of physical
coercion was illegal, but had been sanctioned officially by the Politburo during the purges. Stalin now had to justify its use while not
seeming to violate the law. In January 1939, he sent the following
memorandum to regional Party heads.

DOCUMENT

· 128 ·

Coded telegram from I. V. Stalin to secretaries of obkoms, kraikoms, and to the
leadership of the NKVD-UNKVD [local NKVD administrations] on using
measures of physical coercion in relation to "enemies of the people." AP RF, f.
3, op. 58, d. 6, ll. 145–46.

10 January 1939

Coded from TsK VKP(b) [...]

It has become known to TsK VKP(b) that secretaries of obkoms–
kraikoms, when reviewing UNKVD officials, blame them for using physical coercion against arrested persons as something criminal. The TsK
VKP(b) clarifies that using physical coercion in the practice of the NKVD
was permitted in and after 1937 with the sanction of the TsK VKP(b). It
was specified that physical coercion is allowed as an exception, and only
in relation to obvious enemies of the people who, by undergoing a humane method of interrogation, impudently refuse to name conspirators,
refuse for months to testify, try to prevent exposure of the conspirators
remaining at liberty—in this way, they continue in prison their struggle
against Soviet power. Experience has shown that this method yielded results, considerably accelerating the business of exposing enemies of the
people. It is true that later, in practice, the method of physical coercion
was dirtied by such scoundrels as Zakovsky, Litvin, Uspensky, and others,
for they turned it from an exception into a rule and began to use it for
randomly arrested, honest people. For this they incurred a deserved penalty. But this does not discredit the method itself at all, since it has been
correctly put into practice. It is known that all bourgeois investigations

use physical coercion in relation to representatives of the socialist proletariat and, besides, they use it in its ugliest forms. It may be asked, why
should socialist investigation be more humane in relation to the inveterate
agents of the bourgeoisie, sworn ["inveterate" and "sworn" handwritten
by Stalin] enemies of the working class and collective farmers. The TsK
VKP(b) considers the method of physical coercion an absolutely correct
and expedient method to be used compulsorily from now on, as an exception, in relation to obvious and diehard enemies of the people. The TsK
VKP(b) requires secretaries of obkoms, kraikoms, the TsKs of national
Communist Parties to be guided by this clarification when they review
NKVD officials.

Secretary of TsK VKP(b) I. Stalin

At Vyshinsky's request, the Politburo instructed local Party heads to
distribute the memorandum both to prosecutorial and to judicial
officials.

In early 1939, Vyshinsky also returned to a recommendation that
he had made in the mid-1930s, to no avail then, to remove the conviction records and thereby lift the residence restrictions on individuals
who had been sentenced by troikas and who had served their sentences. With the backing of Beria, he presented the following draft
proposal, which was finally approved in April. The most interesting
aspect of this proposal is the figure given at the beginning of over two
million people sentenced extrajudicially since 1927. It is not clear
which categories Beria had in mind, since over two million peasants
had been deported as kulaks already by 1933. Either Beria's figure did
not count them, or he had other kinds of "contingents" in mind.

DOCUMENT

· 129 ·

Special communication from L. P. Beria and A. Ya. Vyshinsky to I. V. Stalin on
removal of criminal records of those people who had been convicted by
extrajudicial organs of the NKVD USSR, with appended draft of the decree of
the Supreme Council of the USSR. AP RF, f. 3, op. 58, d. 212, ll. 207–9.

5 February 1939

Absolutely secret
TsK VKP(b), to c. Stalin
During the period from 1927, the Special Board of the NKVD, former
OGPU Collegium, and local troikas convicted with various measures of

punishment (up to and including imprisonment in camps, expulsion, and exile)—2,100,000 people.

Organs of the OGPU and NKVD have not been removing criminal records in relation to cases in which punishment was set for no more than three years of imprisonment, in particular, since, according to article 55 of the RSFSR Criminal Code, these criminal records must be removed automatically after a certain period, and judicial offices are required to provide papers confirming this to the formerly convicted. Likewise, the Special [Sentencing] Board [of the NKVD] never once reviewed the issue of criminal record review in any other manner. All these people are considered convicted, and according to the passport regime law (Decree of the Sovnarkom of the USSR No. 1441 from 8 August 1936) the majority of them, even after serving their punishment, cannot live in a number of cities of the country.

Narkomvnudel [the Commissariat of Internal Affairs] and the Procuracy of the USSR consider it expedient to clarify this issue, and present the following suggestions for your consideration.

1. To remove criminal records and related restrictions from all those— the socially dangerous, as well as those convicted under all statutes of the criminal code (except for 58-1-14)[1]—convicted by the former OGPU Collegium, the Special Board of the NKVD, and troikas of the OGPU-NKVD, after three years following the end of their term of punishment, if these persons do not commit new crimes.

2. To grant authority to the Special Board of the NKVD USSR to remove criminal records of those convicted by the former OGPU Collegium, the Special Board of the NKVD USSR, and by the OGPU-NKVD troikas under all subsections of article 58 of the Criminal Code of the RSFSR (and corresponding articles of Criminal Codes of federal republics), in accordance with appeals [of the convicted], if these persons did not commit new crimes during a period of no less than three years after their release from punishment, and if, during this whole period, they were engaged in socially useful work.

Formulation of this decision should be carried out under point "3" of Article 49 of the Constitution of the USSR, by a decree of the Presidium of the Supreme Council of the USSR.

People's Commissar of Internal Affairs of the Union of SSR (L. Beria)
Procurator of the Union of SSR (A. Vyshinsky)
[...]

The institutional culture of the NKVD proved difficult to change, despite Politburo orders, operational instructions from Beria, and even purges of those who had been part of Yezhov's police machinery. As the following report shows, old habits died hard within the security forces. The report also shows the extent to which the purges decimated and made dysfunctional the judicial and prosecutorial system.

DOCUMENT

· 130 ·

Special communication from L. P. Beria, A. Ya. Vyshinsky, and N. M. Rychkov
[Commissar of Justice] to I. V. Stalin, with a draft order appended about
implementation of the decision of SNK USSR and TsK VKP(b) of 17 November
1938 on arrests, procuratorial supervision, and conducting investigations. AP
RF, f. 3, op. 58, d. 6, ll. 172–75.
21 February 1939

TsK VKP(b), to comrade Stalin

For the purpose of verifying fulfillment of the Decision of SNK USSR and TsK VKP(b) of 17 November 1938 "About arrests, procuratorial supervision, and conducting investigations" by the organs of the NKVD and the Procuracy, in the organization of investigative work and implementation of the procurator's supervision of investigation, on 19 February of this year a meeting was called, in which 26 heads of oblasts, krai UNKVD heads, and commissars of internal affairs of union and autonomous republics, and a number of high officials from both the center and the periphery participated.

At the meeting it was established that at present there are large numbers of incomplete investigative cases in the NKVD organs, which negatively influences the quality of investigative work, which still lags behind the requirements of the Decision of SNK USSR and TsK VKP(b) of 17 November 1938.

The meeting revealed a very weak exercise of the public procurator's supervision over investigations, both at the center, and, especially, in the periphery.

The weakness of public procurators' supervision is explained by the inappropriateness of a number of the public prosecution officials from both the political and the professional aspect, and also by a large gap between the required number of workers and the actual staff available.

The SNK of the USSR and TsK VKP(b)'s decision has not been fulfilled in the aspect concerning verification and presenting for approval of the TsK VKP(b) the candidates for all procurators who are to carry out supervision of investigations by the NKVD organs, although the deadline for this has passed.

In particular, it is necessary to emphasize the weak participation of procurators in the investigative work carried out by NKVD organs, the inadmissible delay of case reviews arriving from the NKVD organs, and red tape in transferring cases according their jurisdiction, which is in direct relationship to the lack of staff, and to the self-protection that has been practiced by a number of procurators.

The TsK VKP(b) and SNK of the USSR's Decision from 17 November 1938, in connection with elimination of the judicial troikas that were created under special orders of the NKVD USSR, and also of troikas of oblast, krai, and republic [NKVD] administrations, required the Narkomiust [Commissariat of Justice] and judicial authorities (military tribunals, oblast and supreme courts, railway and water transportation courts) to prepare for reception of these cases, in order to provide a correct and timely hearing of cases arriving from the NKVD organs. For this purpose it was necessary to reconsider and to strengthen judicial authorities with verified and qualified personnel; such preparations were not made on the part of Narkomiust.

In many judicial instances, court examinations are carried out extremely slowly, examination of cases backs up for months, examination itself is unsatisfactory, there are many cases of unreasonable return of cases for supplementary examination.

For the purpose of ensuring implementation of the TsK VKP(b) and SNK USSR Decision of 17 November 1938, we are asking TsK VKP(b):

1. To increase the number of procurators who carry out the supervision of the NKVD organs by 1,100 people.
2. To assign comrade Vyshinsky, together with obkoms, kraikoms, and TsKs of national communist parties to check the staff of procurators carrying out supervision of investigations, and to remove doubtful and bad workers. To report to TsK VKP(b) on the results in one month.
3. To require obkoms, kraikoms, and TsKs of national communist parties to render full assistance to c. Vyshinsky in reviewing the staff of procurators.
4. To oblige obkoms, kraikoms, and TsKs of national Communist Parties, under personal responsibility of the first secretaries, to fill out the staff of the local Procuracy organs supervising investigations by the NKVD organs with vetted and qualified workers within one month. To present a report of accomplished work to TsK VKP(b).
5. To require c. Malenkov and c. Vyshinsky to select 100 people for the Procuracy of the USSR, mainly from among graduates of higher educational institutions.
6. To require Narkomiust USSR, c. Rychkov, and the head of the Supreme Court of the USSR, c. Golyakov, to take measures for court examination of backlogged cases transferred from the organs of the NKVD and the Procuracy, and to establish a process that would guarantee, in the future, timely and correct examination of cases transferred to courts.

7. To assign c. Rychkov, together with the relevant Party organizations, to verify and complete staffing of the judicial organs of Leningrad, Saratov, Ukraine (Sumy, Kirovograd, and Zaporozhye oblasts), Rostov, Chelyabinsk, Perm, and others, and to report the results to TsK VKP(b).

We are attaching a copy of the order of the NKVD USSR and of the Procurator of the USSR regarding actions for ensuring implementation of the SNK USSR and TsK VKP(b) Decision of 17 November 1938.

Narkomvnudel USSR (Beria)
Procurator of the USSR (Vyshinsky)
Narkomiust of the USSR (Rychkov)

Enemies Still Abound

The attempt to return to some kind of legal normalcy was hindered not just by the previous years of purging and violence, but also by the continuation of purges. Although Soviet leaders stopped mass repression operations, the Politburo pursued the "struggle" against counterrevolutionary sabotage and Trotskyist plots. As a result, officials in the security organs received mixed signals. They were now told to adhere to legal norms, and were well aware of the fate of those who had participated in the purges by falsifying evidence and fabricating cases. At the same time, they were under pressure to "root out" enemies in the very same manner. In the course of 1939, more than forty-four thousand people were arrested as counterrevolutionary Trotskyist saboteurs. This was a number some fifteen times lower than the number arrested in 1938, but it showed that Stalin was not done purging.[2]

DOCUMENT

· 131 ·

Decision of the Politburo of the TsK VKP(b). On bringing to trial members of the Right-Trotskyist organization. AP RF, f. 3, op. 24, d. 373, l. 1.
16 February 1939

Absolutely secret
    To bring to trial before the Military Board of the Supreme Court of the USSR cases of the most active enemies of the Party and Soviet power—

those in the leadership of the counterrevolutionary Right-Trotskyist conspiratorial espionage organization—in number 469 people, under the law of 1 December 1934.[3]

DOCUMENT
· 132 ·

Decision of the Politburo of the TsK VKP(b). On conviction of counterrevolutionary elements. RGASPI, f. 17, op. 162, d. 25, l. 7.
8 April 1939

Strictly secret
To transfer cases of active participants of the counterrevolutionary Right-Trotskyist conspiratorial and espionage organizations, in number 931 persons, to the Military Board of the Supreme Court of the USSR for trial under the law of 1 December 1934. And for 198 leading participants of these organizations—to apply the highest measure of criminal punishment—execution, and to sentence the other 733 accused to imprisonment in camps for a term not less than 15 years each.

In the early months of 1939, both Yezhov and his deputy M. P. Frinovsky were arrested as part of the same circus that they had helped create—as spies and saboteurs. They were interrogated in the same manner that they had helped perfect. And, as the following fragments show, they played their appropriate roles in the familiar ritual of required self-destruction.

DOCUMENT
· 133 ·

Special communication of L. P. Beria to I. V. Stalin with appended statement by L. S. Frinovsky. RGASPI, f. 17, op. 3, d. 1009, l. 34.
13 April 1939

TsK VKP(b) to comrade I. V. Stalin
With this I am sending the statement of the arrested Frinovsky from 11.III.39.
[...]
People's Commissar of Internal Affairs of the USSR Beria

To the People's Commissar of Internal Affairs of the Union of Soviet Socialist Republics—Commissar of State Security of the 1st rank: Beria L. P.

From arrested Frinovsky L. S.

Statement

The investigation charged me with anti-Soviet conspiratorial work. During the period when I was free, I struggled long inside myself with the thought that I must confess my criminal activity, but the wretched condition of the coward got the better of me. I had the possibility to tell you honestly about everything, as well as the leaders of the Party of which I was an unworthy member for the last years, even as I was deceiving the Party, but I did not do it. Only after arrest, after the accusation was brought, and after the conversation with you personally, I stepped on the path of repentance, and I promise to tell the investigation the whole truth to the end, both about my criminal-enemy work, and about persons who have been accomplices and leaders of this criminal-enemy work [...].

DOCUMENT

· 134 ·

Memorandum from L. P. Beria to I. V. Stalin regarding N. I. Yezhov, with appended protocol of interrogation. AP RF, f. 3, op. 24, d. 375, ll. 122–64.

27 April 1939

Absolutely secret

Comrade Stalin

With this I send you the protocol of Yezhov's interrogation from 26 April 1939.

Interrogation continues.

People's Commissar of Internal Affairs of the USSR L. Beria

Protocol of the interrogation of arrested Yezhov, Nikolai Ivanovich, from 26 April 1939

Yezhov N. I., born 1895,

Native of city of Leningrad, former member of the VKP(b) from 1917.

Before arrest—People's Commissar of Water Transport.

Question: In the previous interrogation, you testified that you conducted espionage work in favor of Poland for ten years. However, you have hidden a number of your espionage connections. The interrogation demands from you a truthful and full testimony on this matter.

Answer: I must admit that, while giving truthful evidence about my espionage work in favor of Poland, I, in fact, hid from the investigation my espionage connections to the Germans.

Question: For what purposes did you try to lead the investigation away from your espionage connections with the Germans?

Answer: I did not want to testify to the investigation about my direct espionage connection with the Germans, since my cooperation with the German intelligence service was not limited just to espionage work assigned to me by the German intelligence service; I organized an anti-Soviet plot and was preparing a revolt by way of terrorist acts against leaders of the Party and government.

Question: Talk about all the espionage connections that you tried to hide from the investigation, and the circumstances of your recruitment.

Answer: I was recruited as an agent of German intelligence in 1934, under the following circumstances: in summer of 1934 I was sent for treatment abroad to Vienna to Professor Norden [...].

Throughout 1939, Vyshinsky attempted to press his advantage against the NKVD, as the following complaints show, to limit the arrest and sentencing jurisdiction of the NKVD, and to strengthen the authority of the Procuracy.

DOCUMENT

· 135 ·

Note from A. Ya. Vyshinsky to I. V. Stalin on violations of arrest procedures.
AP RF, f. 3, op. 58, d. 6, l. 185.
31 May 1939

To comrade Stalin
To comrade Molotov
According to the SNK USSR and TsK VKP(b) Decision of 17 November 1938, organs of the NKVD are forbidden to make arrests without preliminary sanction from the Procuracy.

This Decision fully meets the requirements of article 127 of the Constitution of the USSR.

Meanwhile, instances continue to take place in the practice of the NKVD of making arrests without obtaining preliminary sanction of the Procuracy of the Union. So, for example, Frinovsky, M., Belen'ky, Z., Kedrov, and others were arrested without obtaining preliminary sanction of the Procuracy USSR.

Reporting this, I ask that the NKVD USSR be given instructions to follow strictly the procedure of making arrests established by article 127 of the Constitution of the USSR and by the Decision of TsK VKP(b) of 17 November 1937.

Vyshinsky

DOCUMENT
· 136 ·

Note of A. Ya. Vyshinsky to I. V. Stalin regarding the Special Board of the NKVD USSR. RGANI, f. 89, op. 18, d. 2, l. 1.

31 May 1939

Absolutely secret

To TsK VKP(b)—to comrade Stalin

To SNK USSR—to comrade Molotov

Recently, large numbers of cases have passed through the Special Board of the People's Commissar of Internal Affairs of the USSR, and at each session of the Special Board, from 200 to 300 cases are reviewed.

In such a situation, the possibility of making erroneous decisions cannot be excluded.

I presented my thoughts about this to c. Beria, along with a suggestion to establish an operating procedure of work of the Special Board in which its meetings are scheduled more often, and with fewer numbers of cases to be reviewed at each session.

I would consider it expedient if the Commissariat of Internal Affairs received special instructions from the TsK VKP(b) and the SNK USSR about this matter.

A. Vyshinsky

Beria, for his part, held his own against Vyshinsky, and was able to protect the interests of the security organs to the extent that Stalin and the Politburo allowed. The latter, for example, agreed with the NKVD to end the Procuracy's practice of permitting early release of prisoners for good behavior. Beria insisted, and the Politburo agreed, that prisoners should serve their full term, or be released early only under extraordinary circumstances, and that the decision should be made by the NKVD, not the Procuracy. Further, and most important, Beria secured the right of the NKVD to have exclusive use of prison labor for economic activities, not having to share with other commissariats.

DOCUMENT

· 137 ·

Decision of the Politburo of the TsK VKP(b). On camps of the NKVD USSR.
RGASPI, f. 17, op. 162, d. 25, ll. 54–55.
10 June 1939

Strictly secret [...]

To approve the proposal of the NKVD on carrying out the following measures:

1. To reject the system of conditional early release of camp contingents. A convict must serve the full term in a camp established by the court. To instruct the Procuracy of the USSR and courts to cease hearing cases of conditional early release from camps, and Narkomvnudel to cease the practice of offsetting one working day for two days of a term of punishment.
2. To establish as the main incentive for increase of labor productivity in camps—improved supply and food rations for good workers who have high rates of labor productivity, a monetary award for this category of prisoners, and a lighter camp regime, with a general improvement in their living conditions.

In relation to certain individual prisoners—excellent workers, who show consistently high rates of work productivity—to allow their conditional early release through a decision made by the Collegium of the NKVD or the Special Board of the NKVD, supported by a special petition of the camp commander and the chief of the Political Department of the camp.
[...]

DOCUMENT

· 138 ·

Decision of the Politburo of the TsK VKP(b). On securing a labor
force for work carried out by the NKVD USSR in 1939. RGASPI,
f. 17, op. 3, d. 1011, l. 4.
16 June 1939

To approve the following decision of the SNK USSR:
In order to ensure fulfillment of the capital construction plan at the major construction sites of the GULAG [camp administration]

of the NKVD USSR in 1939, the Council of People's Commissars of the USSR decides:

1. To allow the NKVD USSR to cease the allocation of GULAG labor to other commissariats and administrations.
2. In order to provide labor for construction undertaken by the Narkomvnudel USSR in the Far East, to allow the Narkomvnudel USSR to transfer to the Far East 120 thousand people during June and July 1939 by means of:
   a) removal of 60 thousand persons-prisoners from work in the other commissariats [...];
   b) transferring convicts for a term of up to two years from correctional labor colonies to camps.
3. To suggest that the NKPS [Commissariat of Transport] provide transportation of 120 thousand people to the Far East according to requirements of the Narkomvnudel USSR, under authority of p. 2 of this decision.
4. In order to carry out the recommended measures, to suggest to Narkomfin [Commissariat of Finance] USSR, together with Narkomvnudel USSR, to revise the plan for financing the GULAG of the NKVD USSR for 1939, and to submit it for approval of Ekonomsovet [Council of the Economy] of SNK USSR within a 10-day period.
5. To allow Narkomvnudel USSR to remove all labor of the GULAG NKVD USSR from other commissariats, administrations, and organizations, starting 1 January 1940.

Despite repeated attempts to regularize investigative and arrest procedures, jurisdictional conflicts continued and, more important, tens of thousands of people were being arrested yearly, subjected to harsh treatment by police, their lives often ruined, and still half of them being released for lack of evidence or improper procedures of investigation. The following circular letter, from July 1939, gives remarkable figures for the number of people arrested and then released. The letter also reflects the attempt by the security and justice commissariats, along with the Procuracy, now headed by M. I. Pankrat'ev, to define more precisely arrest and investigation jurisdictions. As the letter shows, the three officials involved, Beria, Pankrat'ev, and N. M. Rychkov, then the justice commissar, came to something of a truce, each willing to take criticism and to make tradeoffs. At first glance, the document appears to be overly critical of the NKVD, but it also lays blame for the high number of quashed cases on the inactivity of the Procuracy during investigations, leaving that to the security organs, and then complaining about illegal procedures. The following excerpt summarizes the problems. It was followed by an order, which is not included here since it reiterates procedures codified in the 17 November 1938 Sovnarkom decision.

DOCUMENT

· 139 ·

Circular of NKVD USSR, the Procuracy of the USSR, and Narkomiust USSR on investigative work. AP RF, f. 3, op. 58, d. 7, ll. 18–19.

25 July 1939

Absolutely secret

To people's commissars of internal affairs of union and autonomous republics, heads of krai and oblast administrations of the NKVD, procurators of union and autonomous republics, krai, and oblasts, heads of supreme courts of union and autonomous republics, heads of courts of krai and oblasts, heads of military tribunals.

Despite a number of instructions and directives of the NKVD USSR, the USSR procurator, and Narkomiust about procedures for fulfilling the decision of the SNK USSR and TsK VKP(b) of 17 November 1938, there are serious shortcomings in the investigative work of organs of the NKVD, in supervisory work of the Procuracy of the USSR, and in the work of supreme, krai, oblast, okrug courts, and military tribunals in hearing cases of counterrevolutionary crimes. Some NKVD and UNKVD still have not completed investigations of old backlogged investigation cases. In the course of investigations, organs of the NKVD do not always take all necessary measures to complete full investigations of cases, which results, not infrequently, in having them returned by the Procuracy and courts for supplementary investigation. In turn, Procuracy and court organs return cases for supplementary investigation to the organs of the NKVD, either without sufficient reason or for unimportant reasons, at times making impracticable demands (interrogation of persons sentenced to capital punishment, or who have left the USSR, or who are under active surveillance, etc.). From 1 January until 15 June 1939, the Procuracy and courts returned to the organs of the NKVD for supplementary investigation over 50 percent of cases. In some krai and oblasts, the percentage of returned cases is even higher. So, in Chelyabinsk Oblast, out of 1,559 cases transferred to the organs of the court and the Procuracy during the same period of time, 1,599 cases were returned. The UNKVD of the Altai Krai sent to the court and Procuracy cases of 661 persons, but received returned cases of 787 people (the surplus of the returned cases is those sent to the Procuracy and judicial authorities before 1 January 1939).

A similar pattern of returning cases for supplementary investigation occurs in the Ordzhonikidze Krai, Moscow, Leningrad, Tula, and other oblasts.

Organs of the Procuracy would be able to considerably decrease the return of cases for supplementary investigation if they took active part in the investigations, and if they pointed out, in time, the circumstances that may be a subject of supplementary investigation to those conducting an investigation.

Courts often return cases for supplementary investigation for reasons that might be resolved during an actual court hearing.

Along with all this, long delays occur in examination of investigative cases by Procuracy and court organs, which results in a significant backlog of those under arrest.

[...]

People's Commissar of Internal Affairs L. Beria

USSR Procurator Pankrat'ev

People's Commissar of Justice Rychkov

Stalin was careful to manipulate the balance between the legal and security organs of the dictatorship. If orders such as the one above seemed to give too much authority to the Procuracy, Stalin redressed that balance by sanctioning the appointment, in August 1940, of V. M. Bochkov to be the Chief Procurator of the Soviet Union. Bochkov was a career NKVD military officer. During the 1930s, he had been head of the NKVD prison administration, head of the border forces training school, and immediately prior to his appointment as chief procurator, he had served as head of the NKVD Special Department, the department with political and security oversight over the military.

Purging New Territories

Institutional infighting was the least of the NKVD's activities during 1939 and 1940. The advent of war brought new problems and tasks. After the German annexation of the Sudeten areas of Czechoslovakia in late 1938, Stalin abandoned hope of drawing the French and British democracies into a "United Front" alliance against Germany under Adolf Hitler and the National Socialists. Convinced that war was inevitable, Stalin decided to strike a deal with the German dictator directly. As the Commissar of Foreign Affairs, Litvinov, continued allied negotiations, Molotov, Stalin's trusted associate and chairman of Sovnarkom, began the secret talks with German Foreign Minister Joachim von Ribbentrop, that led to the Soviet-German agreement of August 1939. The Molotov-Ribbentrop Pact, as it became known, was publicly a nonaggression agreement, but it included secret protocols that carved up eastern Europe between Germany and the Soviet Union. When German troops invaded Poland on 1 September 1939, the Soviets "responded" by annexing the three Baltic states and parts of the border areas in eastern Poland and Romania.⁴ At the same time, the Soviets pressured Finland to concede territory in Karelia that was close to Leningrad. When the Finnish government refused, the Soviets invaded Finland, precipitating the short and inglorious "Winter War" from November 1939 until March 1940. The Soviets failed to secure a complete victory, but did force the annexation of about 10 percent of Finnish territory along the two countries' mutual border.⁵

Assimilation of these new territories presented the Soviet government, and the security organs in particular, with serious challenges, and at first, Soviet leaders refrained from large-scale purges and repressions. This policy did not last, however, as local resistance persisted. Soon, Party, state, and security forces launched large-scale programs of sovietization: arrests, confiscation of property, deportation. Along with other policies, Sovietization included social purging of "anti-Soviet elements," similar to policies carried out during the mid-1930s.⁶ As the following documents show, these purges received high priority, especially cleansing border areas of Polish settlers called *osadniki*, who had been granted land by the Polish government for military or other valuable service during World War I and the conflicts that followed. Beria reported to Stalin in early December 1939 on how many *osadniki* there were, and in the following document, on the operation to deport them. The document is particularly revealing of the enormous scale such mass removals had reached already in 1939.

DOCUMENT

· 140 ·

Special communication from L. P. Beria to I. V. Stalin on results of the operation to remove *osadniki* and forest guards from the western oblasts of Ukraine and Belorussia. AP RF, f. 3, op. 30, d. 199, ll. 50–51.
12 February 1940

TsK VKP(b) to comrade Stalin
I am informing you about preliminary data on results of the operation to remove *osadniki* and forest guards from the western oblasts of Ukraine and Belorussia conducted by the NKVD SSSR.

Preparatory work was performed with the intention to complete the operation within the course of one day, in order to exclude the possibility of escapes and concealment of persons who were subject to eviction.

Fifty-two thousand NKVD and *militsiia* officers, NKVD troops, and raion and village activists participated in the operation.

The operation started at sunrise on 10 February. By the beginning of 11 February the eviction of *osadniki*, forest guards, and their families was completed.

According to statistics:

In total:	UkSSR:	BSSR:
27,356 families	17,753	9,603
Subject to removal:		
146,375 people	95,065	51,310
Evicted by noon:		
26,776 families	17,227	9,549
By 11 February:		
137,501 people	88,262	49,239
Loaded in echelons:		
24,133 families	16,388	7,745
By 11 February:		
124,247 people	85,362	38,885

Withdrawal continues of people who escaped from the eviction or were unavailable at their permanent residences.

No incidents worthy of attention occurred during the conduct of the operation. In some villages there were attempts by *osadniki* to flee or resist the eviction. In the village of Kovynichi, Dragobych Oblast, a group of locals tried to stop eviction of *osadniki*. However, the NKVD operational group took measures and evicted 27 families subject to eviction. In the village of Kuklintsy of Tarnopol Oblast, a group of women, in number 60, appealed not to remove an *osadnik*. After corresponding explanations, the group dispersed.

On 10 February, at night, in the station of Voropaevo, Vileika Oblast, the corpse of the chief of the station, c. Kiselev E. I., was found. After examination of the corpse it was established that Kiselev's death was caused by a blow to the back of the neck with a blunt instrument. An investigation is being conducted.

In the Belorussian SSR, in connection with hard frosts, reaching −30° C, some cases of light finger frostbite were noted among Red Army soldiers participating in the operation.

The population of the western oblasts of the Ukrainian SSR and Belorussian SSR have reacted positively to the eviction of *osadniki* and forest guards. In some cases, locals assisted operational groups of the NKVD to capture escaped *osadniki*.

Echelons of the evicted *osadniki* and forest guards are on the way to their places of resettlement.

As the security organs cleansed new territories, the Politburo also became worried about the number of foreigners slipping into and settling in areas of the country adjacent to the territories. Murmansk, on the White Sea and close to Finland, was a favored destination for refugees and others fleeing the new border areas. In 1940, the Politburo ordered the NKVD to purge the city of "foreigners," and other "suspicious" or anti-Soviet populations, but to do so without "overly disturbing" the local population.

DOCUMENT

· 141 ·

From the decision of the Politburo of TsK VKP(b) on resettlement of citizens of foreign nationalities from the city of Murmansk and the Murmansk Oblast.
RGASPI, f. 17, op. 162, d. 27, ll. 166–67.
23 June 1940

[...]
To approve the following draft of a decree of the SNK USSR:
The Council of People's Commissars of the USSR decides:
To approve the following proposals of the People's Commissariat of Internal Affairs of the USSR:

1. To charge the NKVD USSR with carrying out resettlement of all citizens of foreign nationalities, in the number of 3,215 families—8,617 persons, from the city of Murmansk and Murmansk Oblast.
2. To place the resettled:

    a) 2,540 families, consisting of 6,973 persons: Finns, Estonians, Latvians, Norwegians, Lithuanians, and Swedes in the Karelian-Finnish SSR, in the following raions:
        Zaonezhsky Raion   —600 households,
        Pudozhsky   -"-   —700 -"-
        Medvezh'egorsky   -"   —340 -"-
        Sheltozersky   -"-   —900 -"-
    b) to the Altai Krai—675 families, consisting of 1,743 persons: Germans, Poles, Chinese, Greeks, and Koreans, in the following areas:

[...],

6. To suggest to Narkomzdrav USSR [Commissariat of Health] to provide those resettled with medical care, necessary medicines, and sanitary supplies for their trip, per request of the NKVD USSR. The requests must be submitted to Narkomzdrav USSR no later than three days prior to the departure of echelons.

7. To require Narkomtorg USSR [Commissariat of Trade] to organize food supplies for the resettlers on their way at points to be determined by the NKVD USSR.

8. To set the deadline of completion of resettlement as 10.7.1940.

Katyn

The NKVD conducted cleansing operations in all of the new territories, affecting over 400,000 people in western Ukraine and Belorussia alone between 1939 and 1941.[7] Most of these operations involved deportation and exile, but some, especially in the Baltic areas, and in the new western regions of Ukraine, also involved purging similar to the deadly mass operations of 1937 and 1938. The most infamous of these operations involved the murder of some twenty-two thousand Polish military officers and other Poles who had been captured and interned in the Soviet Union as a result of the annexation of Polish territory. In trying to decide what to do with them, NKVD officials interviewed many of the internees. Based on these interviews, Beria concluded that the Polish "contingents" were predisposed against Soviet power and represented the core of an army of resistance. As the documents below show, he recommended to Stalin that all of the groups listed be executed. On 3 March, the Politburo agreed and issued the order. Nearly all the executions took place over the course of April 1940, and the bodies were buried in mass graves in several locations near the various internment camps in Belorussia and western Ukraine. After the German invasion of the Soviet Union, Hitler's government publicized the discovery of grave sites in the forest of Katyn. The Soviets blamed the executions on the Germans, and the issue remained officially contested until the late 1980s, when the Soviet government finally released the following documents.[8]

DOCUMENT
· 142 ·

Report of L. P. Beria to I. V. Stalin on imprisoned Polish military and police
personnel. RGASPI, f. 17, op. 166, d. 621, ll. 130–33.

TsK VKPB(b), to c. Stalin
   5 March 1940
   Absolutely secret
   [Handwritten above the text: "C. Stalin, K. Voroshilov, V. Molotov, A.
Mikoyan," and in the margins: "c. Kalinin—in favor, c. Kaganovich—in
favor"]
   At the present time, in NKVD prisoner of war camps, and in prisons of
the western oblasts of Ukraine and Belorussia, there are being held a large
number of former Polish army officers, former officials of Polish police
and intelligence organs, members of Polish nationalist c-r [counterrevolu-
tionary] parties, members of exposed insurgent organizations, deserters
from the enemy, and others. They all are sworn enemies of Soviet power,
full of hatred toward the Soviet System.
   Prisoners of war—officers and policemen—are trying to continue
counterrevolutionary work in camps, conduct anti-Soviet propaganda.
Each of them is just waiting for the moment of his release in order to have
a chance to become actively involved in the struggle against Soviet power.
   NKVD organs in the western oblasts of Ukraine and Belorussia have
uncovered a number of counterrevolutionary insurgent organizations.
Former officers of the former Polish army, former policemen, and gendarmes played active leading roles in all these c-r organizations.
   A considerable number of people who are members of c-r espionage
and insurgent organizations were exposed among the detained deserters
and border violators.
   In all (and not counting soldiers and noncommissioned officers), 14,736
former officers, officials, landowners, policemen, gendarmes, prison guards,
osadniki, and intelligence officers are being held in camps for prisoners of
war. Over 97 percent of them are Polish.
   Of these:

Generals, colonels, and lieutenant colonels	295
Majors and captains	2,080
Poruchiki, podporuchiki, and *khorungie* [low-ranking officers]	6,049
Officers and junior commanders of police, border security, and gendarmes	1,030
Policemen, gendarmes, prison guards, and intelligence officials	5,138
Officials, landowners, priests, and *osadniki*	144

In prisons of the western oblasts of Ukraine and Belorussia, 18,632 arrestees (10,685 of them are Polish) are being held. These include:

Former officers	1,207
Former police agents and gendarmes	5,141
Spies and subversives	347
Former landowners, factory owners, and officials	165
Members of different c-r and insurgent organizations and various c-r elements	5,345
Deserters from the enemy	6,127

[Handwritten in margin: "O.P. Re: NKVD USSR." O.P. stands for *Osobaia papka*, "Special Folder," the name given to materials involving especially sensitive state secrets, and controlled by Stalin.] Since they all are inveterate and incorrigible enemies of Soviet power, the NKVD USSR considers it necessary:

I. *To suggest to the NKVD USSR:* to consider under special order, with implementation of the highest measure of punishment—shooting—in:

1) cases of those held in prisoner of war camps—14,700 people, being former Polish officers, officials, landowners, policemen, intelligence agents, gendarmes, *osadniki*, and prison guards,
2) and also cases of arrestees held in prisons in the western oblasts of Ukraine and Belorussia, in number 11,000, members of various c-r espionage and subversive organizations, former landowners, factory owners, former Polish officers, officials, and deserters from the enemy.

II. To conduct hearings of the cases without calling the arrestees to court, without bringing charges, and without issuing court decisions and sentences—in the following order:

persons held in prisoner of war camps—according to indictments issued by the Administration of Affairs of Prisoners of War of the NKVD USSR.

Persons under arrest—according to indictments in cases of the NKVD UkSSR and NKVD BSSR [Belorussia].

III. To assign a troika consisting of Kobulov [This name handwritten above a crossed-out word], Merkulov, and Bashtakov (head of the 1st Special Department of the NKVD USSR) for examination and making decisions on cases.[9]

People's Commissar of Internal Affairs of the Union SSR L. Beria

The Katyn massacre remains the most notorious of the mass murders conducted by the NKVD, but it was by no means unusual, given the background of the mass repression operations of 1937 and 1938, and the purge of the new territories in general after 1939. Indeed, the

NKVD had conducted a similar purge of urban, political, and rural elites in Ukraine in 1934 and 1935.[10]

The Politburo and the NKVD paid special attention to exterminating armed resistance groups in the new territories of western Ukraine, which were coordinated under the name of OUN, the Organization of Ukrainian Nationalists. The document below is a typical example of the orders that were given to deal with the OUN. This document also refers to the organizational division, briefly implemented in 1941, that separated the NKVD into two commissariats, with the state security organ, the GUGB, forming its own Commissariat of State Security, or NKGB.

DOCUMENT

· 143 ·

Decision of the Politburo of the TsK VKP(b). On removal of counterrevolutionary organizations in the western oblasts of the UkSSR. RGASPI, f. 17, op. 162, d. 34, l. 156.

14 May 1941

Strictly secret

[...] Decision of the TsK VKP(b) and the SNK USSR

Due to the strengthening of the activities of the counterrevolutionary "Organization of Ukrainian Nationalists (OUN)" in western oblasts of the UkSSR, which has been expressed in armed raids of the *ounovtsy* [members of the OUN] on village soviets, collective farms, in murders of village activists, and for the purpose of a resolute suppression of criminal activities of the *ounovtsy*, who destroy the peaceful work of collective farmers in the western oblasts of the UkSSR, TsK VKP(b), and the SNK USSR USSR decide:

1. To require organs of the NKGB and NKVD of Ukraine to continue removal of participants of the counterrevolutionary OUN organizations.

2. To arrest and send to exile in settlements in the remote areas of the Soviet Union for a period of 20 years, with confiscation of properties:

    a) members of families of participants of counterrevolutionary Ukrainian and Polish nationalist organizations, the heads of which went into underground and into hiding from authorities;

    b) members of families of mentioned participants of counterrevolutionary nationalist organizations, heads of which were sentenced to VMN [capital punishment].

3. Organs of the NKGB and NKVD [must] strengthen their agent-operational work, securing good organization and execution of operational measures.
4. The NKGB and NKVD of Ukraine must send operational officials to help local organs in the western oblasts, for rapid identification, pursuit, and removal of members of bandit groups. To station several troop units of the NKVD Ukraine in the raions of the western oblasts of the UkSSR most contaminated by banditry, for use in the struggle against bandit groups.
5. TsK KP(b)U [Communist Party of Ukraine] and SNK UkSSR [must] strengthen the Party and Soviet staff in raions of the western oblasts contaminated by banditry.
6. To apply with all severity the order of the NKVD USSR on prohibition of possessing and carrying firearms without special permission; to arrest and bring to criminal justice persons who are found having weapons without permission.
7. To designate the deputy NKGB USSR, c. Serov, to organize the struggle against bandit groups in the western oblasts of Ukraine, based on this decision.
8. To charge the NKVD and NKGB USSR and the secretary of TsK of Belorussia c. Ponomarenko to discuss the possibility of carrying out similar measures in western Belorussia.

The security police conducted similar operations throughout May 1941, and right up to the day of the German invasion, 22 June 1941.

DOCUMENT
· 144 ·

Special communication from V. N. Merkulov (then head of the NKGB) to I. V. Stalin regarding the results of the operation to arrest and remove "anti-Soviet" elements from the western oblasts of Belorussia. RGANI, f. 89, op. 18, d. 7, ll. 1–3.
21 June 1941

TsK VKP(b)—to comrade Stalin
Total results of the operation to arrest and remove anti-Soviet and the socially alien element from the western oblasts of the Belorussian SSR are summarized.
I. In Belostok Oblast:

arrested .... 500 persons
removed .... 11,405 persons
repressed in all .... 11,905 persons

In Brest Oblast:
arrested .... 300 persons
removed .... 3,039 persons
repressed in all .... 3,339 persons

In Baranovichi Oblast:
arrested .... 476 persons
removed .... 2,723 persons
repressed in all............. 3,199 persons

In Pinsk Oblast:
arrested .... 363 persons
removed .... 2,299 persons
repressed in all .... 2,662 persons

In Vileika Oblast:
arrested .... 420 persons
removed .... 2,887 persons
repressed in all .... 3,307 persons

II. In all western oblasts of Belorussian SSR:
arrested .... 2,059 persons
removed .... 22,363 persons
repressed in all .... 24,412 persons

This includes:
a) Leaders and active members of various Polish, Belorussian, Ukrainian, Russian, and Jewish c-r nationalist organizations, officials of the former Polish state, and other c-r element, arrested.................................... 2,059 persons,
Their family members removed .... 6,655 persons,
b) Family members removed of those sentenced to VMN .... 1,293 persons,
c) Family members removed of those who have gone underground .... 3,652 persons,
d) Family members removed of those escaped abroad .... 7,105 persons,
e) Family members removed of those previously arrested, who are currently under investigation as leaders and active members of various c-r organizations ...... 2,093 persons,
f) Family members removed of previously repressed landowners ....47 persons,
g) Family members removed of previously repressed gendarmes and policemen ....231 persons,

h) Merchants, manufacturers, dealers, and their family
members removed. . . . . .708 persons,
i) Family members removed of previously high-ranking
officials and officers of the former Polish army. . . . . . .469 persons.

People's Commissar of State Security of the USSR V. Merkulov

As the documents above show, Beria was no longer Commissar of State Security by the time of the German invasion. In January 1941, Beria sent to Stalin an outline for reorganization of the NKVD, writing that he was acting in accordance with Stalin's instructions. In fact, Beria had been pressing for reorganization, and for good reason. By 1941, the Commissariat of the Interior had become unwieldy, responsible for an increasing number of disparate functions. The organization was responsible for both foreign intelligence work and domestic order and counterintelligence. It ran a huge economic-industrial empire, administering a prisoner labor force of hundreds of thousands of people. It was responsible for the security of state and Party leaders, and for guarding the country's borders and strategic points and enterprises. It controlled the civil police and firefighting administration, as well as passport and all civil registration processes.

Beria proposed a separation of operational sectors involved in espionage and counterespionage into a separate Commissariat of State Security (*Narodnyi Kommissariat Gosudarstvennoi Bezopasnosti*, NKGB), and in February, the Politburo approved the reorganization. V. N. Merkulov became head of the NKGB, while Beria remained head of the NKVD.

DOCUMENT

· 145 ·

Draft of a decision of TsK VKP(b) on reorganization of the Commissariat of Internal Affairs of the USSR. January 1941. RGASPI, f. 17, op. 163, d. 1295, ll. 103–6, 109.

Draft
Absolutely secret
Decision of TsK VKP(b)
January " " 1941 Moscow
Due to the need for maximum improvement of agent-operational work of the organs of state security, and the increased volume of work carried out by the People's Commissariat of Internal Affairs of the USSR, and its

disparate functions (protection of state security, protection of public order, protection of state borders, militarized security of especially important industrial enterprises and railway buildings, management of places of confinement, fire prevention/protection, local antiaircraft defense, management of highways, guarding camps and organizing use of convict labor, carrying out very large-scale economic activity, development of new areas in the remote northern areas of the USSR, the management of archives and civil registration, etc.), TsK VKP (b) decides:

1. To divide the People's Commissariat of Internal Affairs of the USSR into two narkomats [People's Commissariats]:

   a) People's Commissariat of Internal Affairs of the USSR (NKVD);
   b) People's Commissariat of State Security of the USSR (NKGB).

2. To assign to the People's Commissariat of Internal Affairs of the USSR the following tasks:

   a) protection of public (socialist) property, protection of citizens' personal security and property, and protection of public order;
   b) protection of state borders of the USSR;
   c) organizing local antiaircraft defense;
   d) guarding convicts in prisons, correctional labor camps, correctional labor colonies, labor and special settlements, and organizing use of their labor and reeducation;
   e) struggle against children's homelessness and neglect;
   f) reception, convoying, guarding, and maintenance and use of labor of prisoners of war and of those interned;
   g) state supervision of fire prevention and management of fire prevention actions;
   h) registration of reservists;
   i) construction, repair, and maintenance of roads of federal importance;
   j) registration, protection, scientific and operative development of the state archival holdings of the USSR;
   k) civil registration.

3. To approve the following structure of the People's Commissariat of Internal Affairs of the USSR (see appendix No. 1).

4. To assign to the People's Commissariat of State Security of the USSR the tasks of ensuring state security of the USSR:

   a) conducting intelligence work abroad;
   b) struggle against subversive, espionage, diversionary, terrorist activities of foreign intelligence services in the USSR;
   c) operational development and elimination of the remnants of any anti-Soviet parties and counterrevolutionary formations among

various segments of the population of the USSR, in the system of industry, transportation, communication, agriculture, and so on;
d) guarding leaders of the Party and the government.

5. To affirm that the NKGB is released from carrying out any other work that is not connected directly with the tasks listed in point 4 of the present decision.
6. To approve the following structure of the People's Commissariat of State Security of the USSR (see appendix No. 2).
7. To organize republic People's Commissariats of State Security and Internal Affairs in the Union and autonomous republics, and administrations of the NKGB and of the NKVD in krai and oblasts respectively. To conduct the organizing of republic, krai, oblast, and raion-level organs of the NKGB and of the NKVD on the basis of dividing existing offices of the NKVD, having them structured in accordance with the structures of the NKGB and of the NKVD USSR, approved by this decision.
8. To accomplish division of the NKVD USSR into two narkomats within one month.
To submit for approval of TsK VKP and SNK USSR the provision on People's Commissariats of State Security and Internal Affairs in one month.
9. To approve a draft of the decree of the Presidium of the Supreme Council of the USSR about division of the People's Commissariat of Internal Affairs of the USSR.

Transition to War

The German invasion of the Soviet Union on 22 June 1941 delayed any further moves, and in July the Politburo approved a reunification of the two organs. Throughout the first years of war, the NKVD remained one organization, but it was divided again in April 1943, when the security organs were once again separated from the NKVD and organized as a separate commissariat, the NKGB. Beria remained head of the NKVD and V. N. Merkulov once again became the head of the NKGB, a position he retained until 1946. In a further reorganization, in February 1941 the NKVD special departments in charge of military control were transferred from the NKVD and subordinated to the Commissariat of Defense. In April 1943 the special departments were reorganized again, forming a counterespionage organization within the military. This organization came to be known as *Smersh*, "Death to Spies," and was responsible not only for counterespionage, but also for monitoring anti-Soviet activity and sentiment in the military.

DOCUMENT
· 146 ·

Resolution of the GKO [State Committee of Defense] approving the
operational and administrative charter of the GUKR [Main Administration
of Counterintelligence] "Smersh" of the NKO [People's Commissariat
of Defense] USSR.[11]
21 April 1943

Absolutely secret

Of special importance

To approve the provisions of the Main Administration of Counterintelligence "SMERSH"—(Death to Spies) and its local organs (see appendix).

Head of the State Committee of Defense, I. Stalin

Appendix to the resolution of the GKO

[...] from 21.04.43.

"Approve"

Head of the State Committee of Defense I. Stalin

I. General provisions

1. The Main Administration of Counterintelligence, "Smersh," created
on the basis of the former Administration of Special Departments of the
NKVD USSR, is a part of the People's Commissariat of Defense.

The chief of the Main Administration of Counterintelligence of the NKO
("Smersh") is a Deputy People's Commissar of Defense, subordinated
directly to the People's Commissar of Defense, and obeys only his orders.

Organs of "Smersh" are a centralized organization: organs of "Smersh"
at the front and in military districts [...] obey only their higher organs [...]

II. Tasks of the organs of "Smersh"

1. The following tasks are assigned to the organs of "Smersh":

    a) struggle against espionage, sabotage, terrorist, and other subver-
        sive activities of foreign intelligence services directed against
        units and offices of the Red Army;

    b) struggle against anti-Soviet elements who have infiltrated into
        units and offices of the Red Army;

    c) taking necessary agent-operational and other measures (through
        headquarters) to create conditions at the fronts that exclude the
        possibility of undetected enemy agents infiltrating through the
        front line, with the goal of making the front line secure against
        espionage and anti-Soviet elements;

    d) struggle against treachery and betrayal of the Motherland in
        units and offices of the Red Army (deserting to the enemy's side,
        concealment of spies, and in general, assistance to the latter);

e) struggle against desertion and self-inflicted wounding at the fronts;

f) verification of military personnel and other persons who have been in captivity and encircled by the enemy;

g) accomplishing special tasks of the People's Commissar of Defense.

2. Organs of "Smersh" are released from carrying out any other work that is not connected directly to the tasks listed in the above section [...].

As this document suggests, Smersh became a new and important center for espionage work and thereby also a potential rival of espionage and counterespionage organs of the NKGB.

The document also reflects another significant change brought about by the war. When war broke out, Stalin and the Politburo reorganized the Party and government structure to deal with the crisis. They did not dismantle existing structures, but created an emergency war cabinet called the State Committee of Defense (*Gosudarstvennyi Komitet Oborony*, GKO, or sometimes GOKO). Stalin, of course, headed this body of several dozen people, which included the highest-ranking members of the Politburo, key members of Sovnarkom, and members of the General Staff. With creation of the GKO, power, both political and governmental, shifted from the Central Committee and from Sovnarkom to the GKO. All important decisions were issued by the GKO rather than by the Central Committee. This situation lasted throughout the war, until Stalin dissolved the GKO in 1946.

With the onset of war, the state security organs focused increasingly on espionage and operations connected with the war, but they continued to engage in mass forms of repression. These operations were either punitive in nature or directed against populations that leaders considered potentially dangerous. In October 1941, for example, NKVD commander M. S. Mil'shtein reported to Beria on security police operations to arrest and shoot "military personnel separated from their units or who deserted" from the front. As the report below describes, this included over 600,000 individuals who were labeled as deserters or who refused to serve at the front. Some 10,200 were shot, and of these, over 3,000 were executed in front of their units.

DOCUMENT

· 147 ·

Report of S. R. Mil'shtein to L. P. Beria on the number of arrested and
executed military personnel who were separated from their units and fled
from the front. October 1941. RGANI, f. 89, op. 18, d. 8, ll. 1–3.

Absolutely secret
  To the People's Commissar of Internal Affairs of the USSR
  To the General Commissar of State Security
  Comrade Beria
  Report
From the beginning of the war until 10 October of this year, 657,364
military personnel who deserted their units and escaped from the front
were detained by special departments of the NKVD, NKVD guard units,
and NKVD guard units for protection of the rear.
Operative guard units of the special departments detained 249,969
persons, and NKVD guard units for protection of the rear [detained]
407,395 military personnel.
From among detainees, special departments arrested 25,878 people,
another 632,486 people were formed into units and were sent to the front
again.
  Among those arrested by special departments:
  spies—1,505
  subversives—308
  traitors—2,621
  cowards and alarmists—2,643
  deserters—8,772
  spreaders of provocative rumors—3,987
  those committing self-inflicted wounds—1,671
  others—4,371
  In total—25,878
By decisions of special departments and sentences of military tribunals
10,201 persons were shot. Of them, 3,321 persons were shot in front of
military formations. [...]
  Deputy head of the Administration of the OO [special departments] of
the NKVD USSR
  Commissar of state security of the 3d rank (Mil'shtein)
  "   " October, 1941.

Ethnic Deportations

In late summer of 1941, the NKVD launched the first of a series of ethnic deportations that marked the war years. In August, Beria reported to Stalin on preparations for the deportation of German populations from the Volga region and nearby oblasts. As the document below shows, these deportations targeted the whole of the population, as with the Koreans in 1939. Beria's terse and neutral language shows careful calculation. He did not refer to the Germans in negative terms as proven enemies, or even as potential collaborationists with the invading German army, although the fear of collaboration was what prompted the Politburo decision. Beria was also careful to state that he was fulfilling Stalin's orders. Also of interest to note, is the specific reference to Communist Party members who were also to be removed.

DOCUMENT

· 148 ·

Special communication of L. P. Beria to I. V. Stalin with appended draft of a decision of the SNK USSR and TsK VKP(b) about procedures for resettlement of Germans from the Volga German Republic and from Saratov Oblast and Stalingrad Oblast. AP RF, f. 3, op. 58, d. 178, ll. 6–9.

25 August 1941

TsK VKP(b)—to comrade Stalin

With this, and according to your instructions, I am submitting the draft of a decision of SNK USSR and TsK VKP(b) on procedures for resettling [of Germans] from the Volga German Republic, and from Saratov and Stalingrad Oblasts.

In all, 479,841 people must be removed from the specified areas, including 401,746 people from the Volga German Republic, 54,389 people from the Saratov Oblast, and 23,756 people from the Stalingrad Oblast. It is planned to resettle them in the northeastern oblasts of the Kazakh SSR, Krasnoyarsk and Altai krai, and the Omsk and Novosibirsk oblasts.

First secretaries of the obkoms of VKP(b), c. Vlasov (Saratov), c. Chuyanov (Stalingrad), c. Malov, (Volga Germans), are acquainted with the draft of the decision.

I request your instructions.

People's Commissar of Internal Affairs of the Union of SSR L. Beria

Copy
Absolutely secret
Decision of the Council of People's Commissars of the Union of SSR
"   " August 1941
Moscow, Kremlin
The Council of People's Commissars of the USSR and TsK VKP(b) decide:
1. To move all Germans from the Volga German Republic and from the Saratov and Stalingrad oblasts, in total number 479,841 persons, to the following krai and oblasts:

Krasnoyarsk Krai—75,000 people
Altai Krai—95,000   "
Omsk Oblast—84,000   "
Novosibirsk Oblast—100,000   "
Kazakh SSR—125,000   "
including:
Semipalatinsk Oblast—18,000   "
Akmolinsk Oblast—25,000   "
North Kazakhstan Oblast—25,000   "
Kustanai Oblast—20,000   "
Pavlodar Oblast—20,000   "
East Kazakhstan Oblast—17,000   "

All Germans without exception, both urban and rural residents, are subject to resettlement, including members of VKP(b) and VLKSM [All-Union Leninist Communist Youth League (Komsomol)].

In 1944, similar operations were conducted to deport Kalmyk, Chechen, and Ingush populations. These operations followed in the wake of the Soviet reconquest of the Caucasus area, and were likely intended as punishment for what the GKO and Politburo considered collaboration with the enemy.

DOCUMENT

· 149 ·

Special communication of L. P. Beria to I. V. Stalin and V. M. Molotov on conducting the resettlement operation of people of the Kalmyk nationality.
GARF, f. 9401 s/ch [secret section], op. 2, d. 64, l. 1.
3 January 1944

Absolutely secret
State Committee of Defense
to comrade Stalin I. V.

to comrade Molotov V. M.

According to the instruction of the Presidium of the Supreme Council and the decision of SNK USSR from 28 December 1943, the NKVD USSR carried out the operation of resettlement of people of the Kalmyk nationality to eastern areas.

To ensure completion of the operation and prevention of cases of resistance or escape, the NKVD took prior and necessary operational-military actions, organized protection [encirclement] of settlements, collected those being resettled, escorted them to the places where they were loaded in echelons [on trains].

At the beginning of the operation, 750 Kalmyks—bandit gang members, gang helpers, collaborators of the German occupiers, and others of the anti-Soviet element—were arrested.

In all, in 46 echelons there were loaded 26,359 families, or 93,139 people, resettlers who were sent to resettlement places in the Altai and Krasnoyarsk krai, Omsk and Novosibirsk oblasts.

During the conduct of the operation there were no incidents or excesses.

Echelons of those moved were accompanied by NKVD officers.

The NKVD USSR together with the local organizations took necessary measures for reception, providing shelter and employment for those being resettled in the place of their resettlement.

People's Commissar of Internal Affairs of the Union of SSR, L. Beria

In the case of the Chechen deportations, Beria described in some detail measures taken by the NKVD to isolate mountain villages and to prepare for expected resistance.

DOCUMENT

· 150 ·

Telegram of L. P. Beria to I. V. Stalin regarding preparations for the eviction of Chechens and Ingush. GARF, f. 9401 s/ch, op. 2, d. 64, l. 167.
17 February 1944

Absolutely secret
17. II-44
To comrade Stalin

Preparations for the operation of eviction of Chechens and Ingush are coming to an end. After verification, 459,486 people were registered who are subject to resettlement, including those living in the raions of Dagestan bordering on Checheno-Ingushetia, and in the city of Vladikavkaz. I have reviewed conditions and preparations in the localities of resettlement, and the necessary measures have been taken.

Considering the scale of the operation and peculiarities of the mountain areas, it was decided to carry out the removal (including boarding people in echelons) within 8 days. Within [this period], the operation in all lowland and foothill areas and in some mountain settlements will be completed during the first three days, encompassing more than 300 thousand people. During the next four days, removal in all mountain areas will be carried out, encompassing the remaining 150 thousand people.

During the conduct of the operation in lowland areas, i.e. during the first three days, all settlements of mountain areas where removal will start three days later will be blockaded by military forces under the command of Chekists, which will be stationed there beforehand.

Among Chechens and Ingush, there has been much said, in particular in connection with the appearance of troops. Part of the population reacts to the appearance of troops in accordance with the official version, according to which Red Army units are allegedly conducting training maneuvers in mountain conditions. Another part of the population assumes [that the troops are there for the] deportation of the Chechens and Ingush. Some think that bandits, German collaborators, and other anti-Soviet elements will be removed.

There was much talk about the need to put up resistance to the removal. We considered all this when planning our operational-Chekist actions.

All necessary measures are being taken in order to conduct the removal in an orderly manner, within the planned period, and without serious incidents. In particular, involved in the removal will be 6–7 thousand Dagestanis and 3 thousand Ossetians from collective farm and rural regions of Dagestan and North Ossetia, adjacent to Checheno-Ingushetia, and also rural activists from among Russians, in those areas where there is a Russian population. Russians, Dagestanis, and Ossetians also will be used in part for protection of cattle, housing, and the households of those who will be moved. Within the next few days, preparations for carrying out the operation will be completely finished, and the removal is planned to begin on 22 or 23 February.

Considering the importance of the operation, I request permission to stay in place until completion of the operation, at least in general, i.e. until 26 or 27 February.

NKVD USSR Beria

The reality of the Chechen deportations belied the confident bureaucratic orderliness reflected in Beria's memorandum. In fact, the relocation of the Chechen population in 1944 constituted one of the greatest tragedies of social cleansing of the twentieth century. In all, somewhere between 350,000 and 400,000 Chechens were deported from their mountain villages to arid areas of Kazakhstan. Thousands died resisting the deportation; invalids and others unable to travel were murdered, often brutally, in their villages. An unknown number of deportees died in transit due to poor conditions, lack of food and water, and diseases such as typhus. Somewhere between 14 and 23 percent died in the hard first years of resettlement, 1944 to 1948. In all, researchers estimate that as much as 30 percent of the Chechen population died between 1944 and 1952. Demographic estimates suggest that the deficit of births in the same period may have raised the population loss to over 50 percent. The difference between the horror of such an event and the banal hubris of its planning and execution has been much discussed in the literature, but even in direct confrontation with the documents, this kind of event remains almost unfathomable. As well, the cost in time, money, effort, and people required to carry out such an operation is staggering in and of itself. Somewhere between 50,000 and 100,000 people and military personnel participated in the roundups and deportations. Yet the Chechen deportation was neither the first nor the last such operation by Stalin's security police.[12]

In May 1944, deportation of Tatar and Muslim populations from the Crimea was connected with operations to "secure" the area from anti-Soviet, pro-German, and pro-Turkish "elements," collaborators, and spies. Though the operation did not target ethnic or religious populations specifically, Tatars and Muslims suffered inordinately.

DOCUMENT

· 151 ·

Special communication of L. P. Beria to I. V. Stalin, V. M. Molotov, and
G. M. Malenkov regarding work of operational-Chekist groups in cleansing
the Crimean ASSR [Autonomous Soviet Socialist Republic]. GARF,
f. 9401 s/ch, op. 2, d. 64, ll. 385–89.
1 May 1944

Absolutely secret
State Committee of Defense—
to comrade Stalin I. V.
to comrade Molotov V. M.
TsK VKP(b) to comrade Malenkov G. M.
In addition to our communication of 25 April of this year, the NKVD USSR reports on the work of operational-Chekist groups in cleansing the Crimean ASSR from the anti-Soviet element.

Organs of the NKVD-NKGB and "Smersh" NKO arrested 4,206 people of the anti-Soviet element, out of whom 430 spies were discovered.

In addition, from 10 to 27 April, NKVD troops for protection of the rear detained 5,115 persons. Among them were arrested 55 agents of German intelligence and counterintelligence organs, 266 turncoats and traitors to the Motherland, 363 collaborators [*posobnikov*] and henchmen [*stavlennikov*] of the enemy, and also participants of punishment units.

Arrested were 49 members of Muslim committees, including Izmailov Apas, head of the Karasubazar raion-level Muslim committee; Batalov Batal, head of the Muslim committee of the Balaklava Raion; Ableizov Beliai, head of the Muslim committee of the Simeiz raion; Aliev Musa, head of the Muslim committee of the Zuya Raion.

Muslim committees carried out recruitment of Tatar youth into voluntary units to fight against partisans and the Red Army, selected appropriate personnel to penetrate to the rear of the Red Army, and conducted active profascist propaganda among the Tatar population in Crimea on the instructions of German intelligence organs.

Members of Muslim committees were subsidized by Germans and, in addition, had an extensive network of "trading" and "cultural enlightenment" organizations, which they used simultaneously for espionage work.

After the defeat of Paulus's 6th German army at Stalingrad,[13] the Feodosia Muslim committee collected from Tatars one million rubles for aid to the German army.

Members of Muslim committees in their work were guided by the slogan "Crimea for Tatars only," and were spreading rumors about joining Crimea to Turkey.

In 1943, Turkish emissary Amil Pasha came to Feodosia. He called on the Tatar population to support actions of the German command.

In Berlin, the Germans created a Tatar national center, whose representatives came to Crimea in June 1943 to learn about the work of the Muslim committees.

A significant number of people from the enemy's agents, henchmen, and collaborators with German-fascist occupiers were discovered and arrested.

According to our agent's information, an organization, the NTSNP [People's Labor Union of Russian Solidarism], created in 1943 in Simferopol by the German intelligence service, was engaged in anti-Soviet propaganda among the Russian population of the Crimea, in the recruitment of anti-Soviet intellectuals for these purposes, and also in the recruitment of espionage personnel for the enemy's intelligence service among Soviet prisoners of war.

Our agent communicated a large amount of valuable data on the activities of this organization, the authenticity of which has been verified.

A Russian fascist organization, "The Party of Truly Russian people," created by the German command in the Crimea, was headed by count Keller, chief of Romanian counterintelligence in the Crimea, who lived in Sevastopol before the occupation of the Crimea. Participants of the Crimean center of this organization were Fedov, also Gavrilidi, A. P., an employee of the military department of the Gestapo, arriving in the Crimea from Bulgaria, and Buldeev, an activist traitor, the editor of a fascist newspaper "Voice of the Crimea."

[...]

The organization also engaged in recruiting youth between the ages of 15 and 19 for sabotage work against the USSR, by organizing them under cover of all sorts of sport teams, theatrical and musical, and other societies.

Measures were taken for identification of participants of this organization. In winter 1942, the German intelligence service created in the Crimea the "Ukrainian National Committee," headed by a certain Shopar. A trade enterprise, Konsum, was the headquarters of the "Ukrainian National Committee." All Konsum's personnel were Committee members.

People's Commissar of Internal Affairs of the Union of SSR (L. Beria)

Still plagued by fears of anti-Soviet activities, Beria proposed further deportations from the Crimea of Greek, Armenian, and Bulgarian populations. As the recommendation below describes, Beria justified the deportations on the ground that these populations had been predisposed to cooperate with German occupation forces.

DOCUMENT

· 152 ·

Special communication from L. P. Beria to I. V. Stalin on the expediency of removing Bulgarians, Greeks, and Armenians from the territory of Crimea.
GARF, f. 9401s, op. 2, d. 65, ll. 161–63.
29 May 1944

Absolutely secret
State Committee of Defense
to comrade Stalin I. V.

After removal of Crimean Tatars, work continues in the Crimea by organs of the NKVD-NKGB to identify and remove the anti-Soviet element, checking and combing through settlements and forest areas to capture

Crimean Tatars who might have hidden from the expulsion, and deserters and the bandit element.

Now living in the Crimean Krai are 12,075 persons, registered Bulgarians, 1,300 Greeks, and 9,919 Armenians.

The Bulgarian population lives mostly in settlements between Simferopol and Feodosia, and also near Dzhankoi. There are up to 10 village soviets with a population from 80 to 100 Bulgarian inhabitants in each. Also, Bulgarians live in small groups in Russian and Ukrainian villages.

During the German occupation, a considerable part of the Bulgarian population actively participated in actions carried out by the Germans: stockpiling bread and food for the German army, assisting German military authorities to identify and detain military personnel of the Red Army and Soviet partisans.

For their help rendered to German occupiers, Bulgarians received so-called "protection licenses" that specified that the German command [would] protect both the persons and properties of such Bulgarians, and threatened execution for violation of the protection licenses.

Germans organized police units from among Bulgarians, and also recruited Bulgarians for work in Germany, and for military service in the German army.

The Greek population is scattered throughout the majority of Crimean raions. A considerable proportion of the Greeks, especially in the seaside cities, became engaged in trade and small-scale production after the arrival of the occupiers. German authorities assisted Greeks in trade, transportation of goods, etc.

The Armenian population is scattered throughout the majority of Crimean raions. There are no large settlements with an Armenian population.

The "Armenian Committee," organized by the Germans, actively assisted the Germans and carried out large-scale anti-Soviet work.

The German intelligence organization, "Dromedar," existed in the city of Simferopol, headed by the former Dashnak [member of the Armenian Revolutionary Federation Dashnaktsutyun] general Dro, who directed intelligence work against the Red Army, and for this purpose created several Armenian committees for espionage and guerrilla operations in the rear of the Red Army, and for assistance in organizing Armenian voluntary legions.

Armenian national committees, with the active participation of immigrants arrived from Berlin and Istanbul, conducted propaganda work for "Independent Armenia."

So-called "Armenian religious communities" engaged in organizing trade and small-scale production among Armenians, in addition to their religious and political affairs. These organizations helped Germans, especially by fund raising for the military needs of Germany.

Armenian organizations created the so-called "Armenian Legion," which existed through support of Armenian communities.

The People's Commissariat of Internal Affairs of the USSR considers it expedient to remove all Bulgarians, Greeks, and Armenians from the territory of the Crimea.

People's Commissar of Internal Affairs of the Union of SSR (L. Beria)

In July 1944, Beria reported to Stalin the results of the Crimean operations.

DOCUMENT

· 153 ·

Special communication of L. P. Beria to I. V. Stalin on removal of *spetspereselentsy* [special resettlers] from the Crimea. GARF, f. 9401s, op. 2, d. 65, l. 275.

4 July 1944

Absolutely secret

State Committee of Defense to comrade Stalin I. V.

The NKVD USSR reports that removal of special resettlers—Tatars, Bulgarians, Greeks, and Armenians from Crimea—is completed.

In all, 225,009 people were removed, including:

Tatars	183,155	persons
Bulgarians	12,422	"
Greeks	15,040	"
Armenian	9,621	"
Germans	1,119	"
Also foreign citizens	3,652	"

All Tatars arrived in their places of resettlement and were resettled:

In oblasts of the Uzbek SSR—151,604 people.

In oblasts of the RSFSR, in accordance with the resolution of the GKO from 21 May 1944—31,551 people.

Bulgarians, Greeks, Armenians, and Germans, in number 38,202 persons, are on their way to the Bashkir ASSR, Mari ASSR, to the Kemerovo, Molotov, Sverdlovsk, Kirov oblasts of the RSFSR, and to the Guryev Oblast, Kazakh SSR.

3,652 foreign citizens were sent for resettlement in the Fergana Oblast, Uzbek SSR.

All special resettlers were placed in satisfactory living conditions.

A considerable proportion of the able-bodied Tatar special resettlers were put to agricultural work—in collective farms and state farms, at timber cuttings, at enterprises and construction sites.

There were no incidents during the conduct of the removal operation, neither in the localities nor in transit.

People's Commissar of Internal Affairs of the Union of SSR (L. Beria)

Deportation of national groups from the Crimea was one of the last of the ethnic operations during the war, but these operations did not achieve the goal of securing Soviet borders. As the next chapter shows, Soviet security and political chiefs faced serious insurgency movements along the length of the country's borders as the war drew to an end. The history of these insurgencies is still little known, but, together, they amounted to a war within the war, one that continued even after the fall of Berlin.

CHAPTER EIGHT

Border Wars, Plots, and Spy Mania
1945–1953

As Soviet armies pushed west, driving German forces out of the USSR, Stalin's regime faced new challenges. These, in turn, created new tasks for the security organs. One of the most dangerous threats arose from a new kind of war that erupted in recently liberated or reoccupied territories, especially in the areas incorporated into the Soviet Union after 1939. In many of these areas, armed resistance groups formed to fight Soviet occupation, from the Baltic states through Belorussia into Ukraine, and as far south as the former Bessarabian territories that had belonged to Romania. The effort to subdue and "sovietize" the "rear" of the advancing Soviet armies involved more than disarming a few scattered bands of fighters. The Soviet regime found itself engaged in borderland wars that involved significant numbers of organized resistance groups, and that resulted in large numbers of casualties on all sides. At the same time, Stalin employed the security apparatus in an ongoing round of campaigns to root out internal enemies, supposedly associated with the country's new international opponents. The victory in the war routed the fascist threat but presented the Soviet Union with a new and even more menacing danger from its wartime ally, the United States, and the coalition of western European countries that came to make up the North Atlantic Treaty Organization. Stalin relied heavily on the security organs, and on increasingly sophisticated techniques, to provide information about, and to carry out operations against, the NATO alliance, but he continued to employ the security organs to root out perceived enemies and conspiracies inside the USSR. These functions—sovietizing new territories, international spying, and traditional domestic purging—dominated the work of the postwar "Cheka" until Stalin's death in March 1953.

These functions were carried out by a reorganized security apparatus. In 1946, the Politburo reconfirmed the separation of the NKVD and NKGB, which had occurred in 1943, and renamed all commissariats as ministries. As a result, the Commissariat of the Interior, the NKVD, became the Ministry of Interior, the MVD. Analogously, the Commissariat of State Security, the NKGB, became the MGB. S. N. Kruglov, Beria's deputy in the NKVD, replaced him as interior minister, a post Kruglov held until Stalin's death in March 1953. V. S. Abakumov, the head of the counterintelligence organization Smersh, moved to head the newly formed MGB. The labor camp system remained under control of the MVD, except camps for especially dangerous political criminals under the MGB. Although Beria was head of neither the MVD nor the MGB, he retained an important oversight role as part of his brief as a Politburo member.

The Borderland Wars

The campaigns to subdue border areas and border states engaged Soviet security forces in one of their largest and most costly operations since the Civil War era. On the Soviet side, this war was waged by the combined forces of the state security apparatus, the NKGB, and forces of the NKVD, especially the border forces and the Chief Administration for the Struggle against Banditry (*Glavnoe upravlenie bor'by s banditizma*, GUBB), an administration that had been created in 1938. Together, these organs fielded units, spies, and informants to destroy centers of resistance to Soviet authority. As the following documents show, much of the activity of the security organs focused on Ukraine, against the so-called Organization of Ukrainian Nationalists, the OUN, whose collective members were called *ounovtsy*, and against the Ukrainian Insurgent Army, the UPA. Soviet leaders regarded these kinds of resistance organizations as fascist remnants. Others, especially many locals, saw them as nationalist heroes fighting against foreign domination. Either way, the newly occupied territories became zones of ruthless fighting.

DOCUMENT
· 154 ·

Special communication of L. P. Beria to I. V. Stalin, V. M. Molotov, and G. M. Malenkov on the conduct of Chekist-military operations to liquidate armed groups of the OUN. GARF, f. 9401 s/ch, op. 2, d. 66, ll. 130–31.

5 August 1944

Absolutely secret
GOKO—to comrade Stalin I. V.
SNK USSR—to comrade Molotov V. M.
TsK VKP(b)—to comrade Malenkov G. M.
According to information of the NKVD-NKGB of the Ukrainian SSR, the OUN underground, and gangs of the UPA have become active again recently, in connection with the advance of the Red Army to the west, and with the departure of several units of NKVD troops, relocated in raions from the Rovno Oblast.

OUN gangs from Poland and Lvov Oblast were noticed moving to raions of the Volynsk, Tarnopol, and Rovno oblasts.

Several gangs crossed the Western Bug River to raions of Volynsk Oblast, a number up to 1,000 persons.

During the last two weeks, cases of murders have increased of Soviet and Party activists, family members of Red Army soldiers, and of former bandits, who gave themselves up to the organs of the NKVD. Cases of violent capture by OUN gangs have occurred of persons called up for military service, at the call-up stations, and on the way [to their points of service].

On 28–30 July, gangs of the UPA operating in raions of the Volynskaya Oblast captured and took into the forest several teams of recruits, totaling 1,130 persons.

Deputy commissar of internal affairs of the USSR comrade Kruglov was sent to the area to take measures to suppress actions of the OUN gangs.

NKVD troops have been transferred to the contaminated raions.

For suppression of infiltration of the OUN gangs from Polish territory to raions of Lvov, Volynsk, and Rovno oblasts, measures have been taken for establishment of frontier groups along the border line between the USSR and Poland.

During Chekist-military operations to liquidate OUN gangs (February–July) 17,550 were killed, and 17,480 bandits captured alive.

3,795 persons surrendered to NKVD organs.

4,743 active members of the OUN and the UPA were arrested.

Weapons and ammunition captured: guns—14, mortars—85, large-caliber and tripod and submachine guns—600, revolvers—436, grenades—6,567, cartridges—600,000, mines—6,060, shells—6,110; 20 radio stations were removed. 158 food supply depots were captured.

As a result of the detention of persons evading draft and mobilization in the Red Army, 270,600 persons were sent to raivoenkomats [raion-level military draft boards].

During operations, 700 operational workers, officers, and soldiers of the NKVD and Red Army troops were killed, and 562 were wounded.

People's Commissar of Internal Affairs of the Union of SSR (L. Beria)

DOCUMENT

· 155 ·

Special communication from L. P. Beria to I. V. Stalin, V. M. Molotov, and
G. M. Malenkov on the struggle against the anti-Soviet underground in the
Belorussian SSR. GARF, f. 9401 s/ch, op. 2, d. 68, ll. 103–7.
12 December 1944

Absolutely secret
GOKO—to comrade Stalin I. V.
SNK USSR—to comrade Molotov V. M.
TsK VKP(b)—to comrade Malenkov G. M.
Comrade Kobulov, who was sent to the western oblasts of Belorussia, together with the NKVD and the NKGB of Belorussia c.c. Belchenko and Tsanava, reports on the work done by the NKVD-NKGB of the Belorussian SSR in the struggle against the anti-Soviet underground and armed gangs in the western oblasts of Belorussia, and on further actions of cleansing these oblasts of the anti-Soviet element.

As of 1 December of this year, 288 anti-Soviet Polish and Belorussian organizations were uncovered and liquidated. 5,069 participants of these organizations and 700 agents of the organs of the intelligence service were arrested. Thirteen spy residencies of the German intelligence service were liquidated.

There were 22 removed and 11 killed who were emissaries of the Polish government in exile in London, and also of the Warsaw and Vil'na centers of the "Armiia Kraiova" [Home Army], who were sent to the western oblasts of the BSSR to organize the armed struggle of Poles against Soviet power.

During the Chekist-military operations of liquidation of bandit groups, 800 bandits were killed; 1,543 deserters and 48,900 draft evaders were detained.

As well, in the Brest, Pinsk, and Polesie oblasts adjoining Ukraine, 11 OUN bandit groups were liquidated, which had moved from the Rovno and Volynsk oblasts of the UkSSR. During liquidation of these gangs, 385 were killed, and 160 OUN bandits were captured alive.

Eight operating radio stations of the Polish nationalist underground and 6 illegal printing houses issuing anti-Soviet literature were discovered and removed.

We provide brief data on the most characteristic insurgent organizations liquidated in the territory of the western oblasts of the BSSR.

[...]

In July 1943, German counterintelligence organs created "Ragner," a large bandit-insurgent organization, which was called "Forces South" [Soedinenie Iug]. The organization was receiving arms and ammunition from German counterintelligence and conducted active struggle against Soviet partisans in the territory of the Baranovichi and Grodno oblasts.

After leaving the western oblasts of the BSSR, the Ragner organization, consisting of 120 persons, joined the "Armiia Kraiova" and conducted armed struggle against Soviet power, carried out subversive and terrorist acts, spread anti-Soviet flyers, incited the Polish population to engage in sabotage actions against Soviet power. The organization was headed by a lieutenant of the Polish army, Zainchkovsky, Cheslav, under the code-name "Ragner," who was directly connected with the Polish government in exile in London and received instruction for subversive activities from the latter on a handheld transceiver.

As a result of Chekist-military operations over a period of time, 80 members of the "Ragner" gang were killed or arrested.

On 3 December, as a result of another operation in pursuit of this gang, the latter was crushed—"Ragner" was killed, and his headquarters liquidated.

In the Baranovichi Oblast a multibranched White Polish insurgent organization "Polish Union Underground" was liquidated.

[...]

Despite NKVD-NKGB measures to liquidate the anti-Soviet underground, active enemy operations of the Polish anti-Soviet organizations and gangs continue in the western oblasts of the BSSR, in particular in the Grodno, Baranovichi, and Molodechno oblasts where the Polish population prevails.

According to available intelligence and investigation materials, and also from captured documents, it was established that the Polish nationalist underground in the western oblasts of Belorussia is a part of the "Armiia Kraiova," and receives instructions for its anti-Soviet work from the Polish government in exile in London, through the Warsaw and Vil'na centers.

A number of the organizations of the anti-Soviet Polish and Belorussian underground were created by the German intelligence organs during the occupation of Belorussia, and were left for subversive work against the USSR.

With a view to liquidation of White Polish and other anti-Soviet organizations and armed gangs in the western oblasts of the BSSR, and to cleansing these areas of anti-Soviet elements, the NKVD-NKGB of the BSSR is conducting [further operations].

People's Commissar of Internal Affairs of the Union of SSR (L. Beria)

The Polish-Ukrainian borders were not the only contested areas. In March 1945, Beria reported to Stalin on efforts to subdue "bandit" activity in Central Asia. To what extent this activity was simple lawlessness or organized political activity is not clear, but to the Soviet state security forces there was no distinction.

DOCUMENT

· 156 ·

Special communication from L. P. Beria to I. V. Stalin, V. M. Molotov, and G. M. Malenkov on results of work to liquidate bandit formations in 1944.
GARF, f. 9401 s/ch, op. 2, d. 94, ll. 39–40.
14 March 1945

Absolutely secret
GOKO—to comrade Stalin I. V.
SNK USSR—to comrade Molotov, V. M.
TsK VKP(b)—to comrade Malenkov, G. M.
[...] In 1944 in the RSFSR, the republics of Central Asia, the Northern Caucasus, and Transcaucasia 2,709 gangs were uncovered and liquidated, with a total number of 16,469 bandits and their helpers.

In 1943, in the same republics and oblasts, 3,790 gangs were uncovered and liquidated, with a total number of 29,913 bandits and their collaborators.

	1943		1944	
	Liquidated			
	Bandit groups	Bandits and helpers	Bandit groups	Bandits and helpers
Areas of the RSFSR freed from German occupation	1,117	9,242	902	4,511
Central areas of the RSFSR	834	5,265	885	4,330

Central Asia and Kazakhstan	772	5,193	328	1,818
North Caucasus	255	4,889	95	2,910
Transcaucasia	324	2,016	80	703
Siberia and the Urals	358	2,250	304	1,702
Far East	130	1,058	115	495

In addition, in the course of work to liquidate banditry in the territories of the above-noted republics, removed were: deserters and draft evaders—206,118 persons; parachutists dropped in by Germans for subversive and bandit work—264 persons; German agents—242 persons; traitors, betrayers, German henchmen and collaborators—7,001 persons.

In 1944, 4,356 bandit strikes occurred, including: attacks on officers and soldiers of the Red Army and of troops and organs of the NKVD-NKGB—264 persons; attacks on Soviet officials—165; attacks on state and collective farm offices—885; robberies of citizens—3,402.

NKVD organs solved 4,233 cases of banditry, or 97.2 percent. Confiscated from bandits, deserters, enemy agents, and the population: machine guns 411, automatic rifles 2,223, PTR [antitank rifles] 58, mortars 345, rifles 25,498, revolvers and other handguns 7,993, grenades 7,793, cartridges 1,960,000, mines 16,310, other weapons 11,668, explosives about 1,000 kilos.

According to information of the NKVD USSR, by 1 January of this year, in the territories of the specified republics and oblasts, 204 bandit groups numbering 745 persons, and 320 single bandits, remained at large.

[...]

People's Commissar of Internal Affairs of the Union of SSR (L. Beria)

As the Red Army moved into Germany, the NKVD continued operations to cleanse the areas behind the Soviet lines. At the same time, officers set up special "filtration" points to vet Soviet citizens repatriated from prisoner of war camps or otherwise the returning to the Soviet Union. The following documents give an idea of the activities of the filtration units.

DOCUMENT

· 157 ·

Special communication from L. P. Beria to I. V. Stalin on cleansing the rear area of Red Army operations. RGANI, f. 89, op. 75, d. 5, ll. 1–3.

17 April 1945

Absolutely secret
State Committee of Defense
To comrade Stalin, I. V.

In response to your instruction, from January to April 15 of this year, the NKVD USSR removed 215,540 persons—enemy elements—from the rear areas of Red Army operations.

These include:

agents and official staff of the intelligence and counterintelligence organs of the enemy, terrorists and subversives—8,470 persons, participants of fascist organizations—123,166 persons, command and regular staff of armies fighting against the USSR— 31,190 persons, command and operational staff of police organs, prisons, concentration camps, employees of the public prosecutor's office, and judicial authorities—3,319 persons, heads of large economic and administrative organizations, and workers of journals and newspapers—2,272 persons, traitors to the Motherland, betrayers, henchmen, and collaborators, who escaped along with the fascist troops—17,495 persons, others of the enemy element—29,628 persons.

Out of the total number of those removed, Germans make up 138,200 persons, Poles—38,660 persons, Hungarians—3,200 persons, Slovaks—1,130 persons, Italians—390 persons, and citizens of the Soviet Union (Russians, Ukrainians, Belorussians, Lithuanians, Latvians, Kazakhs, etc.)—27,880 persons.

Out of the total number of those removed, 215,540 persons: 148,540 persons were sent to NKVD camps; 62,000 persons are in front line NKVD prison camps; 5,000 persons died on their way to the camps.

NKVD USSR investigative and verifying work established that among those arrested, there is a significant proportion of ordinary members of various fascist organizations (professional, labor, youth).

Removal of persons in these categories was dictated by the need for *the fastest cleansing of enemy elements from behind the front lines.*

It is necessary to note that from among those arrested and sent to NKVD camps, no more than half may be used for physical work, while the rest consist of old men and persons unsuitable for physical work.

At present, only up to 25,000 persons are used for work in coal, light metal industry, in peat production for power plants, and in construction.

The NKVD USSR considers it necessary to instruct plenipotentiaries of the NKVD at the fronts:

1. From now on, in the course of the advance of the Red Army into the territory of Germany, when cleansing rear operational areas of the Red Army, to limit removal of persons to the following categories:

    a) espionage and subversive, and terrorist agents of German intelligence organs;

b) members of all organizations and groups left by the German command and by the intelligence organs of the enemy for sabotage work in the rear of the Red Army;
c) holders of illegal radio stations, armories, underground printing houses, and to confiscate material equipment intended for enemy work;
d) active members of the National Socialist Party;
e) oblast, city, and raion-level heads of fascist youth organizations;
f) employees of the Gestapo, "SD" [security service], and other German retaliatory organs;
g) heads of oblast, city, and raion-level administrative organs, as well as editors of newspapers, journals, and authors of anti-Soviet publications.

2. To cease removal to the USSR of persons arrested during cleansing operations behind operating units of the Red Army, organizing on the spot the necessary number of prisons and camps. To transfer to the USSR only those arrested who present some operational interest.
3. To review materials of all those arrested in all categories specified above, and to release and to return to their places of residence, in an organized manner, as far as possible, those people not suitable for physical work, about whom there is no evidence of working for the enemy. *I request your approval of this draft of the order of NKVD.*

People's Commissar of Internal Affairs of the Union of SSR (L. Beria)
On the first page there is a note by Beria: "Personal report approved by comrade Stalin. 17/IV-45. L. Beria."

DOCUMENT
· 158 ·

Special communication from L. P. Beria to I. V. Stalin, V. M. Molotov, and G. M. Malenkov on the work of filtration points for Soviet citizens. GARF, f. 9401 s/ch, op. 2, d. 92, ll. 6–8.
2 January 1945

Absolutely secret
GOKO—to comrade Stalin
SNK USSR—to comrade Molotov
TsK VKP(b)—to comrade Malenkov
The NKVD USSR reports that during the period of work in filtration points for processing of Soviet citizens returning to the Motherland, as of 30 December 1944, 96,956 persons were received and vetted.

This includes points in:

Ukrainian SSR—13,960
Belorussian SSR—7,228
Moldavian SSR—9,688
Estonian SSR—18,459
Leningrad Oblast—45,011
Murmansk Oblast—2,610

From this number, 38,428 persons were given permission documents and sent to places of permanent residence; 5,827 persons of draft age were transferred to the voenkomats [military draft boards]; 43,693 persons were sent to NKVD special camps for further vetting.

From those vetted, 153 persons—collaborators, betrayers, and traitors to the Motherland—were discovered and arrested.

[...]

People's Commissar of Internal Affairs of the Union of SSR (L. Beria)

As the war with Germany came to a close in May 1945, the war along the Soviet Union's western borders intensified. Stalin, along with other Politburo members, followed events in these areas closely and, as the following documents show, received monthly reports from Beria and other security officials.

DOCUMENT

· 159 ·

Special communication from L. P. Beria to I. V. Stalin, V. M. Molotov, and G. M. Malenkov on the course of struggle against an armed underground in the western oblasts of Belorussia. GARF, f. 9401 s/ch, op. 2, d. 99, ll. 167–69.
17 September 1945

Absolutely secret
SNK USSR—to comrade Stalin, I. V.
SNK USSR—to comrade Molotov, V. M.
TsK VKP(b)—to comrade Malenkov, G. M.
[...]
From 1 August to 1 September of this year, as a result of agent-operational actions and Chekist-military operations, 6,146 people were arrested and detained, including:

bandits .... —219
bandit helpers .... —60
members of anti-Soviet organizations .... —57
German henchmen, collaborators, and other
anti-Soviet elements... —69

deserters and draft evaders .... —5,741
Also:
bandits killed.. —79
voluntarily surrendering to the NKVD organs......................... —243

In all, during the operations from July 1944 to 1 September 1945, the Belorussian SSR NKVD arrested and detained 97,094 persons, including:

bandits .... —6,514
bandit helpers .... —1,036
members of anti-Soviet organizations .... —651
German henchmen, collaborators, and others of the
anti-Soviet element.. —6,141
deserters and draft evaders .... —82,752

3,282 bandits, deserters, and others of the anti-Soviet element were killed.

Also, 698 bandits, 44 members of anti-Soviet organizations, and 8,188 deserters and draft evaders gave themselves up.

Confiscated, as a result of the operations: mortars 62, PTR 30, machine guns 657, automatic rifles 1,359, rifles 10,485, revolvers 771, grenades 1,435, mines 1,164, cartridges 94,845, explosives 893, handheld transceivers 12, radio receivers 51.

On 4 August a gang headed by "Grechko" in the Logishchin Raion of Pinsk Oblast was liquidated. Killed were 3 bandits, and 7 were detained. Confiscated: automatic rifles 2, rifles 7, cartridges 390.

On 12 August, "Shumsky's" gang was liquidated in the Domachevo Raion of the Brest Oblast. Killed were 29 bandits, and captured 16. Confiscated from the bandits: machine guns 2, automatic rifles 4, rifles 16, guns 2, grenades 50, cartridges 3,000.

On 24 August, in the Oshmiany Raion, Molodechno Oblast, "Matsulevich's" gang was liquidated. [...]

During the reporting period the following most characteristic bandit instances took place:

On 13 August 1945, in the Mironychi village of the Radoshkovichi Raion, Molodechno Oblast, an armed gang of 8 people murdered Dvornikov, head of the planning department of the Radoshkovichi raional [soviet] executive committee, and robbed a shop.

[...]

People's Commissar of Internal Affairs of the Union of SSR (L. Beria)

The following summary report gives an idea of the scale of the borderland wars in the several years following the cessation of military activities against Germany and its allied powers.

DOCUMENT

· 160 ·

Liquidation of anti-Soviet nationalist organizations and gangs linked
to them, as well as of others of the anti-Soviet element, on the territory
of the Western Oblast of Ukraine SSR, 1944–47. February or March
1947. GARF, f. 9478, op. 1, d. 764, ll. 1–15.

Anti-Soviet and nationalist bands liquidated:

1944 .... 0.
1945 .... 928.
1946 .... 415.
1947, January .... 19.

Liquidated bands linked to anti-Soviet underground:

1944 .... 0.
1945 .... 890.
1946 .... 337.
Jan 1947 .... 21.

During the same period, the numbers of people killed or arrested:

	1944	1945	1946	Jan 1947
Members of anti-Soviet organizations:	6,233		246	
Members of gangs tied to above:	124,366	115,784	710	
Totals	130,008	129,016	29,503	1,189

Of 130,008 people above, 57,414 were killed, 56,655 arrested.
Victims of bandit activities, Western Ukraine. Killed:

	1944	1945	1946	Jan 1947
MVD MGB officials	142	279	46-	
Police officials	-	144	5	
MVD internal forces officers	40	14	-	
Other ranks of the internal forces	752	313	77-	
Red Army officers	-	21	1	
Other ranks, Red Army	65	1		
Fighers in *istreb.*[1] and other local formations	113	344	6	
Party activists	901	785	335	35
Other citizens	2,953	4,249	1,677	132
Totals	4,748	5,779	2,723	180

[...]

The document above also gave information for Belorussia and Lithuania. In the former, close to 10,000 people were either captured, arrested, or killed in 1944, 8,237 in 1945, and 1,507 in 1946. In Lithuania, for the period covering 1944 through January 1947, some 14,000 people were killed by MVD, NKGB, and military forces, or by local extermination units. Some 43,276 were arrested or detained in some manner. As other documents show, this underground war continued sporadically even into the early 1950s.

Security organs paid special attention to illegal religious groupings, which they monitored carefully, regardless of denomination. These included Uniate, Roman Catholic, Greek and Russian Orthodox, and Jewish groups, as well as Jehovah's Witnesses.

DOCUMENT

· 161 ·

From a special communication of V. S. Abakumov to I. V. Stalin
on the work of state security organs of the UkSSR to liquidate
anti-Soviet church-sectarian groups. TsA FSB RF, f. 4os
(especially secret), op. 8, d. 11, ll. 354–62.
30 November 1950

Absolutely secret
To comrade Stalin, I. V.
I report that according to information from the minister of state security of the Ukrainian SSR, c. Kovalchuk, in 1950, organs of the MGB uncovered and liquidated 85 anti-Soviet church and sectarian groups in the territory of Ukraine; 809 persons from among the leadership and activists of the church-sectarian underground were arrested.

During the same time, 5 illegal centers of clergy and sectarians were liquidated.

Investigation of the cases of the arrested established that they were giving sermons at illegal gatherings, in which they urged sectarians to sabotage actions of the Party and government, not to participate in public and political life, to refuse service in the Soviet Army.

Along with this, active participants of the church-sectarian formations carried out anti-Soviet propaganda among the population, slandered the leadership of the Party and government, spread provocative rumors about Soviet reality, predicting the death in the near future of the Soviet system.

Heads of the church-sectarian underground also tried to arrange a unification of separate groups, to subordinate them to a centralized leadership, and discussed actions of strengthening the underground for struggle against Soviet power.

Along with this, I present comrade Kovalchuk's report with more detailed data on this specific question.

Abakumov

[...]

The Security Organs Abroad

The Soviet security organs also became involved in the internal affairs of the newly formed Soviet bloc countries in Eastern Europe. In Poland, security organs engaged in the same kind of purging operations as across the border in the newly occupied territories of the Soviet Union. In Poland and other countries including China, the NKGB also lent its expertise to the new governments.

DOCUMENT

· 162 ·

Decision of Politburo TsK VKP(b). On organizing trials of American and English agents. RGASPI, f. 17, op. 162, d. 44, l. 132.
23 October 1950

[...].

1. To accept a proposal by the MGB USSR (c. Abakumov) and the Soviet Control Commission in Germany (c. Chuikov) about organizing three trials of American and English agents who were carrying out espionage and subversive work against Soviet occupation troops in Germany and the German Democratic Republic.

2. To try cases of the American and English spies at closed court sessions of the military tribunal of Soviet occupation troops in Germany. To try the first case at the beginning of November, the second at the end of November, and the third—in the first half of December of this year.

3. To oblige the Soviet Control Commission in Germany (c. Chuikov) to publish short press releases about sentences of the convicted Anglo-American spies in the German press.

4. To assign preparation of cases to the MGB USSR.

DOCUMENT

· 163 ·

Decision of the Politburo of the TsK VKP(b). On assistance to organs
of state security of the People's Republic of China. RGASPI, f. 17,
op. 162, d. 44, l. 138.

6 November 1950

1. To oblige the Ministry of State Security of the USSR (comrade Abakumov) to send c.c. Kuleshov V. I. and Evdokimov A. I., experts on
   identification of enemy underground radio stations, with necessary
   technical equipment; c. Arefyev D. A., specialist on border security;
   and c. Fatyanov Z. A., [specialist] on work of *militsiia* organs, to the
   People's Republic of China for assistance to the [Chinese] organs of
   state security.
2. To approve the following draft of a telegram from comrade Filippov
   to comrade Mao Zedong:

To comrade Mao Zedong.

In connection with your request to send to China experts on organizing
the struggle against enemy underground radio stations, and officials of
border troops and the *militsiia*, two experts on radio stations, with the
necessary technical equipment, and also one specialist in border security,
and another, a *militsiia* specialist, will go. They will arrive in Beijing within the next several days.

Filippov

DOCUMENT

· 164 ·

Decision of the Politburo of the TsK VKP(b). On sending MGB advisers
to Czechoslovakia. RGASPI, f. 17, op. 162, d. 45, l. 16.

21 December 1950

Politburo TsK VKP(b) decides:

1. In response to comrade Slánský's² request regarding sending additional advisers of the MGB USSR to Czechoslovakia, to oblige the
   Ministry of State Security of the USSR (c. Abakumov) to send to
   Czechoslovakia four advisers on questions of organizing counterintelligence in the army, on the struggle against espionage, subversions and
   sabotage in industry, and also on *militsiia* work, and on organizing

operational record keeping in the Ministry of State Security of Czecho-slovakia.
2. To charge MID USSR [Ministry of Foreign Affairs of the USSR] (c. Gromyko) to inform c. Slánský through c. Silin, ambassador of the USSR to Czechoslovakia, that advisers of the MGB USSR on these specific questions will be sent to Czechoslovakia soon.

The very next year, The MGB sent more agents to Czechoslovakia to advise in the interrogation and trial of Slánský, then accused, along with other leaders, in a Stalinist-initiated purge of the Czech leadership.[3]

Stalin Cleans House, Again

As the war drew to a close, Stalin, now an aging dictator, distanced himself from many of the daily affairs of government, leaving these to his deputies. At the same time, he retained control over foreign policy, and over the security organs. He continued to use the latter as he had since the 1920s, to neutralize, and even to destroy physically, those he regarded as political threats. In the postwar years, such purges did not reach the level of the mid- and late 1930s, but Stalin, through the MGB, used the same tactics as before—falsified conspiracies by groups supposedly working against the Party. The so-called Leningrad Affair in 1949 and the early 1950s was the largest of these purges, involving the arrest or removal of a couple of thousand Party and Soviet officials from Leningrad, or officials elsewhere closely associated with the Leningrad apparatus. Stalin feared the prestige and esprit of the Leningrad Party organization, which had organized the successful nine-hundred-day defense of the city during the war, and he feared what he perceived as the growing independence of the organization, possibly as a rival power center in the country.[4]

According to later depositions by V. Abakumov, who was still MGB chief in 1949 and 1950, he received specific instructions from the highest "directive level" (presumably, Stalin, or Molotov or Georgii Malenkov, acting for Stalin), about whom to arrest and what lines to pursue in interrogations of those arrested.[5] In secret trials in October of 1950, six high-ranking officials were convicted of embezzlement of government funds, and of creating an anti-Party group. They were all executed. Among these were two of the most powerful younger leaders in the Party: Nikolai Voznesensky, chairman of the state planning agency, Gosplan, and Mikhail Rodionov, chairman of the Russian Republic Council of Ministers.

Stalin did not limit the purge to top leaders, but "cleansed" Leningrad in a deep purge. As the following documents show, the purge affected public figures in all walks of life, branding them as unreliable or hostile, as foreign agents, and even as Trotskyists. Some five hundred were arrested and fifteen hundred were exiled from the city with their families.

DOCUMENT
· 165 ·

Special communication from V. S. Abakumov to I. V. Stalin on arrests in the city of Leningrad and the Leningrad Oblast. TsA FSB RF, f. 40s, op. 8, d. 1, l. 124.
14 January 1950

Council of Ministers of the USSR
To comrade Stalin, I. V. [...]
I report that, during 1949, in the city of Leningrad and in the oblast, 1,145 persons in all were arrested as a result of Chekist actions carried out by the administration of the Leningrad Oblast of the MGB.
Among those arrested:
agents of foreign intelligence services 164
Trotskyists, Zinovievists, Rightists, SRs [Socialist Revolutionaries], Mensheviks, and anarchists 279
members of anti-Soviet organizations and groups 194
other persons conducting hostile activity ... 508
Abakumov

DOCUMENT
· 166 ·

Special communication from V. S. Abakumov to I. V. Stalin on the need for expulsion of the unreliable element from the city of Leningrad and the Leningrad Oblast. TsA FSB RF, f. 40s, op. 8, d. 1. 125–27.
14 January 1950

TsK VKP(b)
To comrade Stalin, I. V.
Regarding the need for expulsion of 1,500 persons from the city of Leningrad and the Leningrad Oblast who compromised themselves by their links to Trotskyists, Zinovievists, Rightists, Mensheviks, SRs, Germans, and Finns.

The MGB USSR considered necessary to report to you, again, that during investigation and arrests of Trotskyists, Zinovievists, Rightists, and other criminals in the city of Leningrad and the Leningrad Oblast, the MGB Leningrad Oblast administration uncovered 400 people, compromised to some extent by their links with Trotskyists, Zinovievists, Rightists, Mensheviks, SRs, and members of other anti-Soviet organizations and groups, as well as with "former" people of bourgeois class origins and privileged estates.

In addition, in Leningrad and the Leningrad Oblast, 1,100 people were compromised by links to Germans and Finns during the Patriotic War.

Considering that there is insufficient evidence to arrest such people, [and] with a view to purging Leningrad and the Leningrad Oblast from the politically unreliable element, the MGB USSR considers it necessary to expel 1,500 persons of the above-mentioned categories together with their family members from the city and the oblast for permanent residence in raions of Kazakhstan, the Krasnoyarsk Krai, and Novosibirsk Oblast.

If a positive decision is made, it is expedient to conduct the deportation in small groups, according to the decisions of the Special Board of the MGB USSR.

Work on identification of Trotskyists, Zinovievists, Rightists, and other enemy elements continues, and arrests of this category of criminals occur regularly.

With this, I present a draft of a decision of the TsK VKP(b) on this specific question.

I request your decision.

Abakumov

The purge even affected the security organs in the city.

DOCUMENT

· 167 ·

From special communication from V. S. Abakumov to I. V. Stalin
on replacement of UMGB officials of the Leningrad Oblast.
TsA FSB RF, f. 40s, op. 8, d. 1, ll. 61–62.
10 January 1950

TsK VKP(b)
To comrade Stalin I. V.
We report that during the last 8 months, in total 102 persons—ranking and operational officials—were either fired or transferred from the Leningrad Oblast MGB administration to the organs of the MGB of other oblasts. Out of these, 38 people were transferred on account of working

at the UMGB, Leningrad Oblast, for a long time, and 64 people were fired in connection with the existence of compromising materials affecting their work reliability.

[...]

Now, following your instructions, we are preparing a second group of 50 leading and operational officials to be sent to work in the Leningrad Oblast MGB administration.

First, we are planning to replace ranking officials (heads of departments, deputy heads of departments) and operational workers who already have been working at the UMGB of the Leningrad Oblast for a long time, and also those who had lived in Leningrad before they started working at the MGB.

We will be reporting on the course of this work.

Abakumov   Ogol'tsov

Historians have speculated that Both Beria and Malenkov intrigued against the Leningraders—Beria, in particular, fearing that the newly promoted elites were a threat to him and his patronage networks. If so, the purge of the Leningrad organization did not secure his position for long. In late 1951, the MGB "uncovered" an anti-Party group within the Georgian Party organization, specifically of Mingrelian Party functionaries under the former second secretary of the Georgian Party, M. I. Baramiia, a protégé of Beria. Baramiia was charged with taking bribes and, more seriously, with creating an underground separatist movement with ties to Iran, Turkey, and Georgian émigré circles in Paris. As a result of the following police investigation and purge, over six thousand people, connected in some way with Baramiia, were deported permanently to Kazakhstan and other areas. Beria retained his position in the Politburo. Stalin, for whatever reason, did not feel the need to kill or remove him, but Beria's power base in the Georgian Party, and in the central Party apparatus, was seriously weakened by the so-called Mingrelian Affair.

DOCUMENT

· 168 ·

Special communication from S. D. Ignat'ev[6] to I. V. Stalin on preparations for the operation of removing hostile elements from Georgia. AP RF, f. 3, op. 58, d. 179, ll. 93–97.

27 November 1951

To the Politburo of the TsK VKP(b)

According to the instructions of the Politburo of the TsK VKP(b), the Ministry of State Security presents herewith the drafts of decisions by the Politburo and Council of Ministers USSR on removal of hostile elements from territory of the Georgian SSR.

Drafts of the decisions have been coordinated with the secretary of TsK KP(b) of Georgia, c. Charkviani.

The MGB USSR is planning to carry out the removal of hostile elements in the second half of December of this year, using the time until then for preparations.

At the same time, in coordination with TsK KP(b) of Georgia, organs of the local MGB will take measures to arrest persons about whom there are sufficient materials concerning their espionage and other hostile activities.

During preparations for the removal operation, the Georgian SSR MGB will file a brief for removal of each family [...]. Agent materials available in the Georgian SSR MGB, testimonies of the arrested, background information of the First Chief Directorate[7] of the MGB USSR, and other documents confirming hostile activities of persons whose families are subject to removal, along with certificates by local authorities about the family structure and relationships, will be collected in the briefs.

A confirmation of removal will be written and approved by the Minister of State Security and the Procurator of the Georgian SSR for each case.

On the basis of these decisions, and on the day established by the MGB USSR, the removal will take place simultaneously all over the republic. Removal will be carried out by the organs of the MGB of the Georgian SSR under the direction of one of the deputy ministers of state security of the USSR, who will be present [in Georgia].

Operational officials of other organs of the MGB, and MGB troops, will be transferred to the MGB of the Georgian SSR for assistance in carrying out the removal operation, at the ratio of one operational official and two soldiers for each family being removed.

At the moment of removal, all those being removed will be told that according to the decision of authorities, they will be moved to residences in the Kazakh SSR. After this, families to be removed, along with their belongings, will be taken to the railroads by automobile and cartage transportation for boarding in echelons. Railroad [collection] points will be determined in advance. Loading will be carried out under protection of convoy troops of the MVD [...].

Cases of the families removed will be considered by the Special Board of the MGB USSR. Extracts from decisions of the latter will be read to the persons being removed, over their signatures.

During the period of time before removal measures are taken, local authorities of the South Kazakhstan and Dzhambul oblasts of Kazakh SSR are to prepare accommodation and employment for those to be removed. For this, special commandants' offices of the MGB will be organized to supervise them.

S. Ignat'ev

The Zionist Plots

Stalin worried constantly about the growth of national separatist groups, especially those with potential ties outside Soviet borders, and this was the background for his suspicions, after the war, of Zionist underground organizations. As an ideology, Zionism was not new, but had gained force and widespread support during and after the war, and coalesced, in large part, around creation of an independent Jewish state in Palestine. These trends, combined with traditional anti-Semitism, made Stalin and other leaders suspicious of any organized Jewish groups, especially if they supported creation of a new state. Such suspicion was enhanced by the close ties that bound the United States to the Zionist cause, since Stalin saw the United States increasingly as a primary enemy. Throughout the postwar period, Stalin received regular reports from the MGB about "anti-Soviet" Jewish activities. In some cases, Stalin decided to act on this information, as in the case of the Soviet based Jewish Antifascist Committee. The JAC was established in 1942, with the full support of the regime, to promote world support for the Soviet war effort. Committee members toured the United States and developed close ties to American and other Allied Jewish organizations. During the war, this kind of activity was encouraged, but afterward, such contacts were grounds for suspicion. In early 1948, the MGB arranged the murder of the JAC head, Solomon Mikhoels, the prominent director of the Moscow State Jewish Theater. Security police staged the murder to look like a car accident. Mikhoels was branded officially as a "nationalist" and, as the following document shows, this led to further "investigation," and eventually to the purge and dismantling of the committee and its activities.[8]

DOCUMENT

· 169 ·

Decision of the Bureau of the Council of Ministers of the USSR on dissolution
of the Jewish Antifascist Committee. RGASPI, f. 558, op. 11, d. 183, l. 51.
21 November 1948

To: *Deviatka* [Ninth Directorate of the MGB—personal security of
Party and government leaders]—for approval.

The Bureau of the Council of Ministers of the USSR charges the MGB
USSR with disbanding immediately the Jewish Antifascist Committee
since, as the facts show, this committee has been a center of anti-Soviet
propaganda, and regularly supplies organs of foreign intelligence services
with anti-Soviet information.

Because of this, close press organs of this committee and confiscate
committee files. Do not arrest anybody, yet.

Stalin, Molotov

At Stalin's behest, further investigation led to the arrest of a number
of committee members and sympathizers. One such person was P. S.
Zhemchuzhina, Molotov's wife. Zhemchuzhina worked as an official
in the Ministry of Food Industry and, as the document below suggests,
police arrested and interrogated her at Stalin's specific order. Enduring
physical torture, Zhemchuzhina admitted her "role" in anti-Soviet,
Jewish nationalist activities associated with Mikhoels. That Stalin was
playing with Molotov is clear, intimidating him and striking at his
wife in order to test his subordinate's loyalty. Molotov remained quiet, while his wife went into exile, to be released only after Stalin's
death in March 1953.

DOCUMENT

· 170 ·

Note from M. F. Shkiryatov and V. S. Abakumov to I. V. Stalin regarding
P. S. Zhemchuzhina. RGASPI, f. 589, op. 3, d. 6188, ll. 25–31.
27 December 1948

To comrade Stalin, I. V.

Fulfilling your assignment, we reviewed available materials about
c. Zhemchuzhina, P. S. As the result of a number of interrogations, and
also from Zhemchuzhina's explanations, the following facts of her politically untrustworthy behavior were established.

After the decisions of the Politburo TsK VKP(b) from 10 August and 24 October 1939, in which she was punished and warned for showing imprudence and unscrupulousness concerning her communications with persons not inspiring political trust, Zhemchuzhina did not fulfill this decision and continued conducting further acquaintance with persons not deserving political trust.

During an extended period of time, Jewish nationalists grouped around her, and she, using her patronage, protected them. According to their statements, she has been their adviser and defender. Some of these persons, who happened to be enemies of the people, both in confronting Zhemchuzhina, and in separate depositions, reported her close relationship with the nationalist, Mikhoels, who was hostile to Soviet power.

At a confrontation with Zhemchuzhina on 26 December of this year, a former secretary of the Jewish Antifascist Committee, Feffer, I. S., said: "Zhemchuzhina was interested in the work of the Jewish Antifascist Committee and the Jewish theater ... Mikhoels told me that 'we have a great friend,' and named Zhemchuzhina. ... Zhemchuzhina, in general, is very much interested in our affairs: about the life of Jews in the Soviet Union and about affairs of the Jewish Ant-fascist Committee; she asked whether we are persecuted. Characterizing Zhemchuzhina's relations to Jews, and also his opinion about her, Mikhoels said: 'She is a good Jewish daughter' ... Mikhoels talked about Zhemchuzhina enthusiastically, declaring that she is a charming person, she helps, and it is possible to seek her advice about the Committee and about the Theater."

A former art director of the Moscow Jewish Theater, Zuskin, V. L., made a similar statement in confrontation with Zhemchuzhina: "Mikhoels was saying that he had great friendly relations with Polina Semenovna. I know that when Mikhoels had some problems, he asked Zhemchuzhina for help ... Mikhoels often met with Zhemchuzhina, called her on the phone, met at receptions."

A former member of the Jewish Antifascist Committee, Grinberg, Z. G., arrested by the MGB USSR, gave similar testimony: "As Mikhoels told those among his inner circle, whenever he turned to the Government with some questions, he discussed these questions with Zhemchuzhina, and received her helpful advice and precepts. ... As a result of all this, the connection between Mikhoels and Zhemchuzhina was important to those of us who surrounded Mikhoels, as we saw in Zhemchuzhina our defender and patron."

[...]

After verifying all these facts, and at the confrontations, Zhemchuzhina conducted herself in a non-Party way, extremely insincere, and, despite Feffer's and Zuskin's statements convicting her, she tried hard to refute factual explanations. At the same time, Zhemchuzhina admitted her connection with Mikhoels, obtaining a letter from him to transfer to government organs, organizing Mikhoels's talk on America in a club, and participating in his funeral.

As a result of a thorough check, and confirmation of all the facts, by a number of persons, we are coming to the conclusion that there is a solid basis to affirm that the accusations brought against her correspond to the facts.

On the basis of all the given materials, we recommend to expel Zhemchuzhina, P. S., from the Party. Protocols of confrontations with Feffer, Zuskin, and Slutsky are attached to this.

M. Shkiryatov

V. Abakumov

Sent to: cc. Stalin, Molotov, Malenkov, Kaganovich, Beria, Voznesensky, Mikoyan, Bulganin, Kosygin

Investigations and arrests in the "affair" of the JAC led to mass media campaigns against "rootless cosmopolitans," a code for Jews, and to the trials and executions of at least thirteen prominent Jewish figures, prison terms for several dozen others, and widespread discrimination against Jews in state and public institutions.

Spies

Stalin's security organs were well practiced at concocting and then uncovering conspiracies and espionage rings against the regime and its leaders. Dealing with real espionage was another matter, and in the early years of the Cold War, there was plenty of that. In the several years after the war, the United States and its allies inserted dozens of spies, if not more, into the Soviet Union, recruited in Western Europe from Soviet refugees and former prisoners of war. They crossed the still weakly protected land frontiers, and were dropped by parachute along the western borders, and from China into eastern regions. Some of these agents took radios with them in order to send information as agents in place. Many, however, were charged with specific assignments, and instructed then to try to leave the country. The report below is about one such agent.

DOCUMENT
· 171 ·

Special communication from S. D. Ignat'ev to I. V. Stalin on an
agent-parachutist, F. K. Sarantsev. AP RF, f. 3, op. 58, d. 263, ll. 62–63.
11 September 1951

Absolutely secret

To comrade Stalin

As already reported to you, on the night of 14 to 15 August of this year, the American intelligence service air-dropped spies with parachutes over the territory of the Moldavian SSR.

One of them, Osmanov, was detained on 15 August of this year at the station of Bendery. Osmanov testified that one more spy was dropped from the same plane.

As a result of follow-up measures, the second spy, Sarantsev, Feodor Kuzmich, was detained on 5 September of this year in the city of Alma-Ata, while he was trying to arrange an overnight stay in a house with a collective farmer. Sarantsev, Feodor Kuzmich, born 1926, native of the village Blagodatnoye of Akmolinsk Oblast, Russian, was mobilized into the Soviet Army in 1943, and in December of the same year was captured by Germans, after the war refused repatriation to the Soviet Union, and remained in the American zone of occupation of Germany.

After he was brought to Moscow, at the interrogation, Sarantsev testified that in June 1951 he was recruited by the American intelligence service, and for a month he prepared for his drop in the Soviet Union. On the instructions of the Americans, he was to go to Semipalatinsk to pinpoint the exact site and configuration of a nuclear plant, which, according to the American intelligence service, is located in the area of Semipalatinsk and Zhana Semey.

As he was told by the Americans, this plant manufactures nuclear bombs or something else connected with atomic energy. Sarantsev was to fix the location of the plant and whatever constructions are next to it, in order to be able to draw a plan for the Americans upon his return.

Also, Sarantsev was to find out how strict is the security of the plant, and what organization is responsible for it.

In addition, the Americans assigned Sarantsev to discover, through local residents, whether there were any explosions or similar phenomena in the area of Semipalatinsk.

After accomplishing this task, Sarantsev was to leave through Armenia, crossing the Soviet-Turkish border illegally. In Turkey, as he was told by Americans, there would be representatives of the American intelligence service, with whom he would be put in contact by local authorities.

The arrested Osmanov testified the following about the character of the espionage assignment he received: he was to make his way to the cities of Kyshtym and Verkhneivinsk, where, according to Americans, nuclear plants are located, and he was to collect data on the precise location of the plants, their exterior, and, in particular, the number of smokestacks, about railroads and other access roads to the plants, the existence of high-voltage lines, whether there are airfields around the plants, and whether there are planes at them.

In addition, Osmanov had the task to cut samples of grass, to cut branches and leaves from trees, and to collect samples of dirt. As Osmanov has testified, the Americans intended to analyze all this in order to define whether, in these areas, work really has been conducted on atomic energy. After accomplishing his assignment, Osmanov was to return to the Americans by illegally crossing the Soviet-Turkish border.

We will be reporting to you on the course of the investigation, and on the results of identification of possible sources of knowledge of Americans about the location of buildings of the 1st Chief Administration of the Council of Ministers of the USSR.[9]

S. Ignat'ev

On the first page, in the top left corner there is a crossed-out note by Stalin: "What is Osmanov's nationality?"

Although many of these spies were caught, the relative ease with which they were able to breach Soviet borders led to the following sharp memorandum on protecting the country's frontiers.

DOCUMENT

· 172 ·

Decision of Politburo of the TsK VKP(b). On search for and detention of agents-parachutists. RGASPI, f. 17, op. 162, d. 47, ll. 18, 118–19.
11 November 1951

To approve the enclosed draft of a telegram.
Absolutely secret
To the Head of the Administration of Border Troops along the Pacific Ocean, Major General Zyryanov
To temporary head of the Administration of Primorie [Maritime] Krai of the MGB, c. Metlenko,
To commander of troops of the Primorie Military District, Colonel General Biryuzov

To commander of troops of the Primorie Frontier Air Defense Raion, Major General Davydov

It became known from our ambassador to China, c. Roschin, that on 2 November an American plane dropped in a violator near the Daduchzhuan village in the Raion Tszinsintsyuy, not far from Hunchun, near the Soviet-Chinese border, that he crossed our border on the same day, and that, on the same day in the same area, ten more American planes were noted that also might have dropped in parachutists.

These facts could have happened only as a result of the extremely unsatisfactory organization of both our border security on our overland border with Manchuria, and of our aviation security there.

It has been more than a week since these disgraceful incidents, but we still have no reports from you about how these incidents took place, or whether the border violators were detained, and what measures you have taken in order to prevent violations of our borders from now on.

We bring this to your attention, and we obligate you:

1. To take serious measures for search and detention of border violators immediately, and to report to us on results.
2. To take measures, and to do all that is necessary, for strengthening our overland and air borders in order to eliminate completely the possibility of their being breached both on the ground and in the air, and to report about the measures you have taken.
3. To give an explanation why you have still not informed about these specific incidents, why the parachutists dropped by the Americans were not found yet, and why you do not show initiative in drawing conclusions on your own from the specific incidents of violation of overland and air borders, without waiting for instructions from above.

Confirm receiving.
Ignat'ev
Vasilevsky
11.11.51

As the document above exemplifies, the Chinese border became a major entering point for spies coming into the Soviet Union, and Stalin and the security police attempted to choke off this channel.

DOCUMENT

· 173 ·

Special communication from V. S. Abakumov to I. V. Stalin on arrests of
Russian emigrants in China. AP RF, f. 3, op. 58, d. 285, l. 90.
16 November 1950

Absolutely secret
To comrade Stalin, I. V.

I am reporting that, at present, over 40 thousand White Russian émigrés live in the territory of the People's Republic of China, mainly in
Shanghai and the cities of Manchuria, a majority of whom were natural-
ized in 1945–47. As a result of processing Japanese archives captured in
1945 in Manchuria by Soviet troops, and also, based on agent materials
and depositions of arrested spies arriving in the USSR from China after
the end of the war under the cover of reemigrants, organs of the MGB
USSR uncovered 470 agents of foreign intelligence services from among
the Russian White emigrants living in China. These agents conducted active subversion against the Soviet Union during the war, on assignment
from the Japanese intelligence service. After the war, a considerable proportion of these were enlisted by American and English intelligence organs, and these days they continue to conduct espionage activity against
the USSR and People's democratic [*sic*] China. The MGB USSR considers
it necessary gradually to arrest the agents of foreign intelligence services
from among Russian White emigrants through the organs of the Ministry
of Public Safety of China, and to extradite them to the territory of the
USSR to conduct detailed investigation.

With this, I present a draft of the resolution of the Politburo TsK
VKP(b) on this question.

I request your decision.

V. Abakumov

The Final Conspiracies

Throughout his life, Stalin obsessed about plots and intrigues against
him, and this tendency continued into the postwar years and became
even more pronounced as he became increasingly ill. In the first half-
decade after the war, Stalin used the security organs to purge key parts
of the Party apparatus, the Leningraders and Georgians, for example,
as a way to maintain his own unassailable power. By 1951, however,
he began to swing the other way, becoming increasingly suspicious of
the security organs' growing power. In classic style, his suspicions
focused on the security minister, Abakumov, appointed in 1946, who

oversaw the Party purges of the postwar years. Stalin set in motion the familiar machinations to set up Abakumov: collecting false reports and allegations of political conspiracy, cover-ups, egregious lapses in duty, and self-aggrandizement.[10] The most incriminating piece of evidence against Abakumov came from M. D. Riumin, a special investigator, whose letter of 2 July 1951 was very likely solicited either by Stalin or by Malenkov. The latter was Abakumov's adversary within the leadership circle and a patron of Riumin, acting for Stalin. Interesting to note, the cut-and-paste repetition of ritualized phrasing, first used in Riumin's letter, that substituted for, and became proof in and of itself, of Abakumov's guilt.

DOCUMENT
· 174 ·

Statement of a senior inspector of the MGB USSR, M. D. Riumin,
to I. V. Stalin. AP RF, f. 3, op, 58, d. 216, ll. 8–11.
2 July 1951

Absolutely secret
To comrade Stalin, I. V. [...]
In November 1950, I was entrusted with conducting an investigation of the case of the arrested professor Etinger,[11] doctor of medical sciences.

At the interrogations, Etinger admitted that he was a confirmed Jewish nationalist, and therefore he had harbored hatred toward the VKP(b) and the Soviet government.

Further, having talked in detail about his hostile activity, Etinger admitted, as well, that in 1945 he used the opportunity of being entrusted to treat comrade Shcherbakov,[12] and did everything to shorten his life.

I reported Etinger's deposition on this matter to comrade Likhachev, a deputy chief of the Investigative Division. Soon after that, myself and comrade Likhachev, together with the arrested Etinger, were called to c. Abakumov's office.

During the "interrogation," or, more precisely, conversation with Etinger, c. Abakumov hinted to him several times that he should retract his testimony about c. Shcherbakov's villainous murder. Then, when Etinger was taken from the office, comrade Abakumov forbade me to interrogate Etinger in the direction of uncovering his practical activities and his plans for terror, explaining this by saying that Etinger "will lead us into a maze." Etinger understood c. Abakumov's hint and, at the next interrogation, he retracted all his confessed testimony, although his hostile attitude to the VKP(b) was incontestably proved by materials of a confidential interception, and by testimonies of his accomplice, the arrested Erozolimsky, who, by the way, told the investigation that Etinger told him about his hostile attitude toward c. Shcherbakov.

Using these and other evidentiary materials, I continued to interrogate Etinger, and gradually he began to return to his previous testimony, about which I was writing daily notes for the report to my supervisors.

About 28–29 January 1951, I was called to the office of c. Leonov, chief of the Investigative Division of Especially Important Cases. He, having referred to comrade Abakumov's instructions, told me to stop working with Etinger and, as comrade Leonov expressed it, "to put his case on a shelf."

In addition to this, I must specify that after the arrested Etinger was called to comrade Abakumov's office, a more severe regime was set up for him, and he was transferred to the Lefortovo prison, into the coldest and dampest cell. Etinger was of an elderly age—64 years old, and he began to have episodes of angina pectoris, about which the Investigative Division received an official medical report on 20 January 1951. It read that "in future each subsequent episode of angina pectoris could lead to [heart] failure."

Considering this circumstance, I several times brought to the attention of the leadership of the Investigative Division the question of allowing me to continue further serious interrogations of the arrested Etinger, but I was turned down. All this came to an end when Etinger suddenly died in early March, and his terrorist activity remained uninvestigated.

However, Etinger had extensive connections, including among his adherents, prominent expert-physicians, and it cannot be excluded that some of them were linked to Etinger's terrorist activity.

I consider it my duty to inform you that according to my observations, comrade Abakumov is inclined to deceive governmental organs by concealing serious defects in the work of the organs of the MGB.

For example, I am at present in charge of an investigative case on a charge against Salimanov, the former deputy director general of a joint-stock company in Germany, "Vismut," who escaped to the Americans in May 1950 and then came back to the Soviet zone of occupation in Germany 3 months later, where he was detained and arrested.

Salimanov testified that in May 1950 he was dismissed from his position, and was ordered back to the USSR, however he did not do this, and, using the absence of surveillance from the organs of the MGB, defected to the Americans.

Then Salimanov said that after betraying the Motherland, he fell into the hands of American intelligence officers, and, while communicating with them, he realized that the American intelligence service has detailed data about activities of the Vismut joint-stock company, which is engaged in the production of uranium ore.

Salimanov's deposition proves that organs of the MGB organized their counterintelligence work in Germany badly.

Instead of informing governmental[ly appropriate] levels about this, and using Salimanov's testimonies for elimination of serious shortcomings in the work of MGB organs in Germany, c. Abakumov forbade the signing of Salimanov's interrogations protocols.

[...]

In summary I dare to express my opinion that comrade Abakumov has been strengthening his position in the government, not always in honest ways, and he is a person dangerous to the state, especially in such a sensitive place as the Ministry of State Security.

He is also dangerous because he put "reliable" people, from his vantage point, in the most key positions in the Ministry, and, in particular, in the Investigative Division. Having secured their careers through his hands, they have been gradually losing their *partiinost'* [party spirit], and have been turning into bootlickers, and obsequiously do everything that comrade Abakumov wants.

(Riumin)

On the basis of Riumin's accusations, a Politburo commission, which included Abakumov's rivals Malenkov and Beria, reviewed and questioned a number of his subordinates. On the basis of their recommendations, the Politburo issued a decision that described chaotic, illegal, and anti-Soviet tendencies within the MGB. Reproduced in part below, the decision enumerated four cases that Abakumov had either quashed or derailed, including those of Etinger and Salimanov. The decision recommended the removal of Abakumov and a number of subordinates.

DOCUMENT

· 175 ·

Decision of TsK VKP(b). On shortcomings in the Ministry of State
Security of the USSR. AP RF, f. 3, op. 58, d. 216, ll. 2–7.
11 July 1951

Strictly secret [...]

On 2 July 1951, TsK VKP(b) received a statement by c. Riumin, a senior inspector of the Investigative Division of Especially Important Cases of the MGB USSR, in which he gave a signal about shortcomings in the MGB in investigations of a number of very important cases of prominent state criminals. He accuses the Minister of State Security c. Abakumov [of creating these shortcomings]. (The statement is included.)

After receiving c. Riumin's statement, TsK VKP(b) created a commission of the Politburo, consisting of c.c. Malenkov, Beria, Shkiryatov, and Ignat'ev, and assigned it to verify the facts reported by c. Riumin.

In the course of the review, the commission interrogated the chief of the Investigative Division of Especially Important Cases of the MGB, c. Lesnov, his deputies—c.c. Likhachev and Komarov, chief of the 2nd Chief Directorate of the MGB, c. Shubnyakov, deputy chief of a subdepartment of the 2nd Chief Directorate, c. Tangiyev, deputy to the chief of the Investigative Division, c. Putintsev, deputy ministers of state security c.c. Ogol'tsov and Pitovranov, and also listened to Abakumov's explanations.

Since the facts stated in c. Riumin's statement were verified during the review, TsK VKP(b) decided to discharge c. Abakumov immediately from his duties as Minister of State Security, and appointed the First Deputy Minister, c. Ogol'tsov, to fulfill duties of the Minister of State Security temporarily. This was on 4 July of this year.

On the basis of the results of the review, the commission of the Politburo TsK VKP(b) established the following indisputable facts.

1. In November 1950, doctor Etinger, a Jewish nationalist exhibiting an extremely hostile attitude to Soviet power, was arrested. At the interrogation by the senior inspector of the MGB, c. Riumin, the arrested Etinger, without any pressure, admitted that when treating c. Shcherbakov, A. S., he had terrorist intentions concerning him, and took all practical measures to shorten his life.

TsK VKP(b) considers Etinger's testimony deserving of close attention. Undoubtedly, among doctors, there is a conspiratorial group of persons who aspire to shorten the lives of Party and government leaders while treating them. It is impossible to forget the crimes of such famous doctors as doctor Pletnev and doctor Levin, who poisoned V. V. Kuibyshev and Maxim Gorky in the recent past, on the instructions of a foreign intelligence service. These villains admitted their crimes in open court, and Levin was shot, while Pletnev was sentenced to 25 years of imprisonment.

However, Minister of State Security c. Abakumov, after receiving Etinger's deposition about his terrorist activity, declared, in the presence of inspector Riumin, the deputy chief of the Investigative Division Likhachev, and also in the presence of the criminal Etinger, that Etinger's testimony was far-fetched, and declared that this case was not worthy, that it would lead the MGB into a maze, and stopped further investigation of the case. Neglecting the MGB doctors' warning, c. Abakumov placed the arrested Etinger, who was seriously ill, in conditions obviously dangerous to his health (in a damp and cold cell), which resulted in Etinger's death in prison on 2 March 1951.

Thus, by extinguishing Etinger's case, c. Abakumov prevented TsK from unmasking what is certainly a conspiratorial group of doctors, who are fulfilling assignments of foreign agents for terrorist activity against the leadership of the Party and the government. Also, it must be noted that c. Abakumov did not consider it necessary to report Etinger's testimony to TsK VKP(b) and thus hid this important case from the Party and the government.

[...]

5. TsK considers it necessary to note that when c. Abakumov was called first to the Politburo, and then to the Tsk VKP(b) commission, he took the path of naked denial of the established facts revealing shortcomings in the work of the MGB. At [his] interrogation, he tried to deceive the Party again, did not exhibit an understanding of his crimes, and did not show any signs of readiness to repent of his crimes.

On the basis of the above, TsK VKP(b) decides:

1. To dismiss c. Abakumov, V. S., from the position of Minister of State Security of the USSR, as a person who has committed crimes against the Party and the Soviet state, to expel him from the VKP(b), and to transfer his case to court.
2. To dismiss c. Leonov from the position of chief of the Investigative Division of Especially Important Cases of the MGB USSR, and c. Likhachev from the position as deputy chief of the Investigative Division, for assisting Abakumov to deceive the Party, and to expel them from the Party.
3. To issue a reprimand to the first deputy minister c. Ogol'tsov, and to deputy minister c. Pitovranov, for not showing the necessary Party spirit, and for not signaling the problems of MGB work to the TsK VKP(b).
4. To obligate the MGB USSR to reopen an investigation of the case of Etinger's terrorist activity, and of the Jewish anti-Soviet youth organization.
5. To appoint Ignat'ev, S. D., member of the Politburo commission to review the work of the MGB, as head of the department of TsK VKP(b) of Party and Komsomol organs, and as a representative of the TsK VKP(b) in the Ministry of State Security.

TsK VKP(b)

As the last point above stipulated, Ignat'ev was appointed as a Central Committee "representative in the MGB." Deputy Minister Ogol'tsov remained acting minister for another month until 9 August 1951, when Ignat'ev's appointment as minister was confirmed. The appointment of Ignat'ev helped shift the balance of power in the MGB back toward Party control, as was (once again) signaled in a decision of December 1952.

DOCUMENT

· 176 ·

From the decision of the TsK KPSS [Communist Party of the
Soviet Union, replacing VKP(b)] on the situation in the MGB.
AP RF, f. 3, op. 22, d. 12, ll. 6–7.
4 December 1952

Absolutely secret
4 December 1952

1. On the situation in the MGB and on wrecking in medical care
    (c. Goglidze):

    a) To approve a draft of the decision "On the situation in the
        MGB," presented by the Commission of the Presidium[13] of TsK,
        with amendments accepted at the meeting of the Presidium TsK
        KPSS
        From the appendix
        On the situation in the MGB
        TsK KPSS decides:
        [...]

2. To obligate the Ministry of State Security of the USSR:

    [...]

    d) In the line of counterintelligence, to organize work of identifica-
        tion and timely elimination of agents of foreign intelligence ser-
        vices and centers of anti-Soviet emigration inside the country.

    e) Raise the quality of investigative work. Unravel to the end crimes
        of participants of the terrorist group of doctors of the Lechsa-
        nupr [the Kremlin sanatorium administration], find the culprits
        and organizers of their malicious deeds. In the shortest time, con-
        clude investigation of the case of wrecking work by Abakumov-
        Shvartsman.[14] [...]

3. To regard control over organs of the Ministry of State Security as the
    most important and urgent task of the Party, of the leadership of the
    Party organs, of all Party organizations. It is necessary to end, reso-
    lutely, the absence of control over activity of organs of the Ministry
    of State Security, and to put their work both in the center and in lo-
    calities under systematic and permanent control of the Party, leading
    Party organs, and Party organizations.

    [...]

After the removal of Abakumov, Stalin pressed Ignat'ev to reopen and expand the investigation of Ya. G. Etinger, the prominent doctor arrested in 1950 as a Jewish nationalist, who had died in prison. Abakumov's downfall had been tied, in part, to his refusal to pursue the Etinger case, and his supposed cover-up of a nationalist conspiracy among a number of prominent Jewish doctors to kill Soviet leaders. Etinger was supposedly a member of this circle, but had died before providing any evidence of conspiracy. This group of "doctor-terrorists" supposedly worked in connection with British and especially American intelligence agencies, and Jewish organizations. According to a number of historians, Stalin threatened Ignat'ev with the same fate as Abakumov—removal and arrest—if he did not produce evidence of a Jewish nationalist–American conspiracy.[15] In early 1952, the case of the "doctor-wreckers" was handed over to the investigator Riumin, whose letter of 2 July 1951 had instigated Abakumov's removal, and who was also charged with bringing to trial the case against the Jewish Antifascist Committee. While the trial against the JAC led to the execution of a number of its leaders, the investigation into the Doctors' Plot dragged on inconclusively to the end of the year. Riumin was relieved of his duties, though not arrested, and a large number of agents continued to pursue leads. Stalin followed the interrogations assiduously, making comments and pushing investigators to follow certain lines. According to historians' accounts, he was obsessed with linking the MGB cover-up with the supposed conspiracy among top Kremlin physicians and other doctors. In Stalin's view, Abakumov and a number of leading security officials had aided and abetted this conspiracy by quashing any investigation of it.

In January 1953, nine prominent physicians were arrested as part of the supposed plot against Soviet leaders. The arrested included Stalin's personal physician P. I. Egorov. In February, Ignat'ev finally provided Stalin what he wanted. The following draft indictment of Abakumov and other MGB officials accused them of a long list of crimes, but of the main crime of covering up the alleged murder of Leningrad Party chief Andrei Zhdanov in 1948. Zhdanov, who had been a prominent Party critic of "rootless cosmopolitanism," had died of heart failure. By 1953, however, MGB investigators, under Stalin's insistent prodding, concluded that Zhdanov's death was not just the result of poor health. It was the result of malicious negligence on the part of Kremlin-assigned doctors, the same Jewish doctors who were arrested as members of the Doctors' Plot. Abakumov had become an accomplice to Zhdanov's murder by deliberately failing to follow up on complaints about Zhdanov's treatment. In Stalin's mind, Zhdanov had been killed both by Jewish doctors and by Abakumov. Stalin then accused Abakumov of killing Etinger in order to hinder further investigation of the Jewish doctors' conspiracy.

DOCUMENT

· 177 ·

Special communication from S. Ignat'ev to I. V. Stalin, with appended draft of the indictment in the case of Abakumov-Shvartsman.
AP RF, f. 3, op. 58, d. 222, ll. 203–43.
17 February 1953

To comrade Stalin

I am presenting to you a draft of the indictment in the case of the dangerous group, Abakumov-Shvartsman.

In addition to Abakumov and Shvartsman, eight more accused will be brought to justice:

Raikhman, L. F.—former deputy chief of the 2nd Chief Directorate of the MGB USSR;

Leonov, A. G.—former chief of the Investigative Division of Investigation of Especially Important Cases of the MGB USSR;

Likhachev, M. T.—former deputy chief of the Investigative Division of Especially Important Cases of the MGB USSR;

Komarov, V. I.—former deputy chief of the Investigative Division of Especially Important Cases of the MGB USSR;

Chernov, I. A.—former chief of the Secretariat of the MGB USSR;

Broverman Ya. M.—former deputy chief of the Secretariat of the MGB USSR;

Sverdlov A. Ya.—former deputy chief of Department "K" of the MGB USSR;

Palkin A. M.—former head of Department "D" of the MGB USSR.

The MGB USSR considers it necessary to try the case of the above criminals by the Military Board of the Supreme Court of the USSR *without defense or prosecution personnel*, [Note in margin: "Need to say: "closed court"] and with a sentence on all arrested of capital punishment—shooting.

A draft proposal on judicial consideration *of others arrested* [Note in margin: "Others who?"] will follow later.

[...]

Minister of state security of the USSR S. Ignat'ev

I. It was established from confessions of the accused, from witnesses' testimonies, and from other evidence collected in this case, that a hostile group around Abakumov-Shvartsman operated for a long time in the MGB USSR with the purpose of undermining the state security of the Soviet Union.

The most serious damage inflicted by Abakumov and his accomplices on the safety of the Soviet state was that they purposely wiped out [Note in margin: "*What is that?*" Literally, the wording here is "greased" or "oiled out," *smazyvali*.] signals arriving in the MGB USSR about terrorist activity by enemies of the Soviet people against Party and government leaders.

In 1948, the MGB USSR received the statement of a doctor Timashuk, L. F., in which she reported about the deliberate application of incorrect treatment methods to a secretary of TsK KPSS, A. A. Zhdanov, which led to fatal consequences for the life of the patient.

As established by the investigation, Abakumov did not take any measures for a Chekist review of this all-important signal about a direct threat to the life of comrade Zhdanov.

Vlasik, the arrested former chief of the MGB USSR Chief Directorate for Protection, testified at the interrogation:

> "I had doctor Timashuk's statement from 29 August 1948 by 30 or 31 August of 1948. I didn't read the statement myself. On the same day that I received it, I took it to Abakumov. He also did not read it, but kept it without giving any instructions to verify the statement."
>
> [...]

Further investigation established that Abakumov and Vlasik consciously were doing nothing to check Timashuk's statement, and took all measures in order to present this statement as untrustworthy, not worthy of attention, and gave up doctor Timashuk, as it were, to be slaughtered by the foreign spy–terrorists Egorov, Vinogradov, Vasilenko, Mayorov, whom she had accused of harmful treatment of comrade Zhdanov, and who are now exposed. Egorov, a member of the espionage and terrorist doctors group, former chief of Lechsanupr [the Kremlin sanatorium administration], arrested by the MGB USSR, testified: "There is no doubt that if Abakumov and Vlasik had conducted a sufficient check of Timashuk's statement right after they received it, we, the doctors guilty of the death of A. A. Zhdanov, would have been exposed in 1948. Acting in our interests, to the advantage of the doctors-wreckers, Abakumov and Vlasik passed over Timashuk's signal indifferently, did not try to verify her statement, and thus helped us to suppress the fact of killing A. A. Zhdanov, and to get rid of Timashuk."

Another participant of the terrorist group of doctors, the English spy Vinogradov, testified on this matter:

"When doctor Timashuk, L. F., tried to expose our criminal treatment of A. A. Zhdanov, I myself, with Egorov, Vasilenko, and Mayorov, took all measures to cover up traces of our crimes. We collectively accused Timashuk of incompetence and finished her career."

Later, Abakumov and his accomplices also prevented, in every possible way, exposure of the group of doctor-poisoners acting in Lechsanupr, by maliciously erasing an investigation of Timashuk's statement.

By the beginning of 1949, as now revealed in materials and terrorist statements by Etinger himself, [Handwritten in ink above the text: "to the murderer of c. Shcherbakov." Marginal note: "Not enough. Need more detail."] who was by then already a member of the gang of doctor-murderers, Abakumov for a long time interfered with the arrest of this declared enemy of Soviet power. When Etinger was arrested and started to give evidence about the harmful treatment of A. S. Shcherbakov, Abakumov, with the help of his accomplices—the accused Likhachev and Leonov—hid these indications from the TsK KPSS, declared them far-fetched, wiped out and extinguished the investigation of Etinger, declaring that it was not trustworthy, and would lead the MGB USSR into a maze.

The accused Likhachev, explaining the circumstances that allowed quashing of the case against the terrorist Etinger, declared:

I aided Abakumov to wipe out and to hide the case against the terrorist Etinger from the Central Committee.

[...]

Abakumov asked Etinger directly: "You concocted all this in prison, didn't you?" Etinger could do nothing else but confirm the answer implied in the question: "Yes, I thought it all up in prison," Etinger declared, understanding that this was an opportunity to retract his testimony admitting to terror." [Marginal note to this crossed-out paragraph: "All this [he has] hidden from Pr-vo" (the government).]

"And [Marginal correction: "Likhachev shows"] further: "When Etinger was taken away, Abakumov told me and Riumin that Etinger was talking nonsense, and that there was not even any need to justify what he said by signing the interrogation protocol, that his deposition would lead us only into a maze.

[...]

In the end, Etinger died [Marginal note in Stalin's hand: "did not simply 'die,' was murdered by Abakumov."] in prison and his criminal activity and contacts ... remained unexposed."

[...]

III. All the materials collected in this case prove that the hostile group of Abakumov-Shvartsman, existing in the MGB, has been attempting for a number of years to tear the Chekist apparatus away from the Party, has conducted subversive work through malicious wrecking in the state security agencies, has been deliberately deceiving the Central Committee of the KPSS, [Marginal note: "To Party and Prav-vo (government)"] ignoring [Overwritten by hand: "systematic violations"] decisions of the Party and the government on strengthening of state security, deliberately covering up cases against spies, terrorists, Jewish nationalists, and other especially dangerous state criminals.

All the accused in the present case, except for Abakumov, acknowledge their guilt in committing these crimes. The hostile activities of all the accused have been exposed by witness testimonies, face-to-face confrontations, and documented evidence.

[...]

Deputy head, Special Investigative Division of Especially Important Cases, Zaichikov

Deputy head, Special Investigative Division of Especially Important Cases, Grishaev

In agreement:

Deputy minister of state security USSR (Goglidze)

As the document above shows, Abakumov never admitted his guilt and refused to acknowledge the existence of a Doctors' Plot.

It has never been clear to what ends Stalin intended to use the Doctors' Plot. In its early stages, the plot bore a striking similarity to the way Stalin had used the death of the young and popular Leningrad Party head Sergei Kirov in December 1934, an assassination by an individual acting alone, as a pretext to begin a purge that culminated in the 1937–38 mass terror. In the early 1950s, Stalin built a conspiracy around the death of another popular Leningrad figure, also popular, Andrei Zhdanov. At the time, rumor had it that Stalin was planning to use the concocted Doctors' Plot as a pretext for mass roundups and exile of Jews and their exile to Siberia, although there is no archival evidence to suggest that Stalin was contemplating such a move. The aging leader probably had more limited goals in mind in 1953, and he certainly used the Zionist plot scenario as a roundabout means to purge and maintain control over the state's security organs.

Whatever plans Stalin had were cut short by the brain hemorrhage that incapacitated him on 1 March 1953. He lingered until the evening of 5 March, when he died. There was probably not a lot that could have been done to save Stalin's life as he lay dying. Still, and ironically, the doctors who knew him best, who could have done whatever was possible, were languishing in prison at the time of Stalin's stroke for supposedly conspiring to kill him. Within days after his death, the other Politburo members quickly and quietly buried the Doctors' Plot and released the arrested physicians. Ignat'ev was dismissed, and Beria presided once again, but only briefly, over a combined MGB and NKVD. His power, and that of the combined ministries, was too threatening for other members of the Politburo, however, and they arrested him in June of 1953. He remained under guard, interrogated and tortured, until December when he was executed for his "crimes" against the Party and the state.

Abakumov remained in prison as well. Although cleared of any connection to the falsified Jewish nationalist conspiracy, he was nonetheless indicted again, in this case for his role in concocting the Leningrad purge of 1949, and for being supposedly a part of the "Beria gang." Abakumov was executed in December 1954. Fearful of the power of the MGB, the new leaders dismantled much of the state security leadership and organizational structure. The MGB was separated from the MVD, and the former was abolished. The Ministry of State Security was reorganized into a Committee of State Security, the KGB, and placed in administrative subordination to the Council of Ministers. The new statutes, drawn up in 1954, remained relatively unchanged until the end of the Soviet Union in 1991.

Conclusion

After Stalin's death and the reorganization of the MGB, the state's security apparatus remained powerful, but never again reached the zenith that it had under Stalin. On the other hand, neither was it wracked by the convulsive purges and reorganizations to which Stalin had subjected it, nor did it ever again serve so completely the power fantasies of a single despotic leader. Stalin could not have ruled as he did without the police and security forces that he did so much to create. Certainly, different leaders of the "organs," as they were called, influenced the institutional culture of the OGPU and its successive incarnations, but the police and security agencies were mainly the product of Stalin's constant manipulations and machinations. He approved or appointed every leader, with the exception of the first, Dzerzhinsky, to their positions. He used these people and agencies for his purposes and, if he felt it necessary, he removed them and reorganized and purged the organs. Stalin was directly or indirectly responsible for killing four of the eight security heads who served under him, along with a significant number of their entourages. As an aging dictator, he let many institutions slide away from his scrutiny, but not the internal security organs. Stalin controlled the affairs of these agencies with the kind of assiduous attention that he devoted only to two other institutions, the Party and the military.

The OGPU, NKVD, NKGB, and MGB were the key to Stalin's power, but not the only one. The secret to Stalin's undisputed authority lay in his ability to manipulate the balance between the Party apparatus and the political police. He played one against the other, at times using the police to purge perceived rivals or groups in the Party, and then using the Party to subdue and purge the police. This swing back and forth was the pattern throughout the dictator's rule.

The function of the police and security organs evolved in different directions from the 1920s to the 1950s. During the 1920s, the OGPU functioned much as we traditionally understand, as a political police that harassed and persecuted Stalin's rivals and perceived enemies. In the early 1930s, the OGPU returned to the role of its predecessor, the Cheka, as a revolutionary arm of the Bolshevik Party. Stalin and the Politburo used the agency to bring revolutionary communist rule to a largely anti-Bolshevik countryside. During the collectivization and dekulakization campaigns, the OGPU returned to the methods of brutal repression and deportation on a mass scale that had characterized Cheka activities during the civil war. After the dekulakization and collectivization campaigns ended, the OGPU and then the GUGB, evolved, again, from a revolutionary force to a state security agency. During the middle years of the 1930s, the NKVD continued to function as Stalin's political police, but it also moved into areas of mass surveillance and repression to protect the social, economic, and political order that Stalin had created. Following Stalin's lead, leaders of the NKVD and the GUGB, specifically, saw the protection of socialist property and the maintenance of social order as primary tasks of state security. Civil policing, enforcement of passport and residence laws, removal and isolation of "socially harmful" populations all fell within the purview of the NKVD. Even the policing of street children and hooliganism became a main responsibility of the state's security organs.

During the 1930s, the organs gained the authority to define social status and citizenship rights through control of the passport system. It was the police, and then the security organs, that ascribed the social status written into passports. That status determined, in turn, where a person could live, work, and travel. And the security organs played a significant role in both determining and enforcing what areas of the country were safe for socialism, what areas would be open to marginalized populations, and where suspect populations would be forced to live out their lives. The regime's leaders related to the Soviet people largely through the police and state security organs during these years. Given nearly unlimited license, political and civil police, in turn, shaped the Soviet body politic in blunt and brutal ways, and in accordance with the ideology of the regime's political leaders and their changing perceptions of danger and state security. The social function of the security forces became brutally clear during the mass operation purges of the late 1930s, and in the continuing deportations of whole ethnic populations during and after the war years.

After the war, Stalin and other leaders employed political police methods—the kind of secret, extrajudicial policing that dominated the 1930s—primarily in the country's new territories, as well as in some regions of the Caucasus. In these areas, leaders perceived that the security of the state was at risk, as local authorities faced serious insurgency movements against Soviet rule all along the country's new borders. Much of the attention of the security and internal police forces focused on these borderland wars, and on the cleansing and "sovietization" of the newly incorporated populations. At the same time, the security organs expanded their expertise to neighboring Soviet-occupied countries, and entered a new era of increasingly pro-fessionalized intelligence gathering and spying operations on an international scale. Still, not everything changed. Stalin continued to use the MGB for the same kind of discrediting and purging of potential rivals that had occupied Chekists since the 1920s. The Leningrad and Mingrelian affairs and the final plots against the Kremlin doctors engaged a great deal of the attention of the MGB.

While Stalin employed mass violence in newly acquired territories, this was no longer the case inside the pre-1939 territories. In these areas, the security forces of the Soviet Union got out of the business of social order policing after the war, although they still played a significant role in domestic spying and monitoring of what was considered anti-Soviet behavior. After Stalin's death, the role of the state's security apparatus diminished still further. More stable, more secure, more professionalized, Soviet security service officials contin-ued to serve the Soviet state until its collapse in 1991.

And what of the documents themselves? Can their language and form tell anything more than the content? Certainly, use of the word "element" dominated the language of the political police during the 1930s. That word belonged to the era of mass social cleansing, and reflected the way police and leaders thought about the population. "Element" simplified the business of categorizing the population in order to act on it. Police used the word uniformly as a negative attri-bute, dehumanizing those who were to be removed, whether geo-graphically or physically.

The language in many of the documents, especially those dealing with repression, is often formulaic, and appears often to have been written in haste. Catchwords and clichéd phrases are thrown together in strings, often without much editorial thought about clarity or precision of meaning. Strings of phrases are separated only by commas or dashes, and there is much repetition of the same clichéd wording. While the documents in this collection do not show it, local officials often had to write to superiors for clarification of orders, especially about whom, exactly, to repress. At the same time, the use of formulaic language allowed local officials great leeway in deciding who fit any particular category to be purged. Documents of Procuracy officials often reflected greater precision than those of the police and security organs. This is understandable, given the concern of these officials to follow and use legal procedure in their various conflicts with the police. The language of documents from Yagoda and Yezhov is the worst, grammatically and stylistically. In many of their orders, and in their correspondence, the language is brutalized, with little regard for grammar and sentence structure. The reader cannot help but feel that the unreflective brutalization of language, expressed in their communications, reflected the same crude and simplistic brutalization that these two brought to their work as Stalin's social engineers. The communications of both of these leaders, especially those dealing with repression, were often written in the passive voice (this action was taken, so-and-so many of the anti-Soviet element were removed or liquidated), as if to distance themselves from what they were doing to real people and their lives.

Feliks Dzerzhinsky, Vyacheslav Menzhinsky, and Lavrentii Beria were the most articulate of the leaders of the political police, judging by the language of their communications. Dzerzhinsky was an Old Bolshevik leader, with education and experience outside the Soviet Union. He was not Stalin's creature, as were Yagoda and Yezhov. Dzerzhinsky's communications were literate and to the point. Lavrentii Beria, perhaps of all the police heads, was the most careful in writing memorandums. With only a few exceptions, he attempted to cover himself with specific and careful language. He wrote in straightforward sentences, free of jargon for the most part. He almost never editorialized, and he almost always justified his activities by reference to Stalin's instructions.[1] Beria's wiliness, in general, may have helped him to survive Stalin, but it did not save him from execution by his compatriots who followed Stalin.

By the postwar period, the language of security and policing documents was beginning to lose the shrill rawness and hypertrophied polemical character of the 1930s. Reports of the security and internal forces on the cleansing of new territories were written in a straightforward and descriptive manner. Some of the prewar scripted language can still be seen in the documents about purging in the Party and the security forces from the late 1940s and early 1950s—in the charges used to justify the Leningrad and Georgian purges, as well as in the indictments against Abakumov and the Kremlin doctors. In these cases, officials fell back on the same tried and true formulas of the 1930s. At the same time, this language did not fit with the new era of a professionalizing and internationally experienced cadre of operatives. Stalin retained sole control over the security and internal affairs ministries until his death, but he, like the language in which he thought, was becoming anachronistic in the very system that he created. Stalin's despotic, martial law version of socialism was giving way quickly to a new kind of socialism and a new kind of state, an oligarchic dictatorship and an authoritarian-bureaucratic kind of socialism. This transition did not occur universally or quickly. Many aspects of Stalinism remained to shape social and state development. Still, Stalin's death in March 1953 hastened the evolution to a new era in the Soviet Union and to a new phase of Soviet socialism.

Biographical Sketches

Abakumov, Viktor Semenovich (1908–54). Finished elementary school; Member of VKP(b) from 1930; 1938–41, head of UNKVD, Rostov Oblast; from 1941, Deputy Commissar of Internal Affairs, USSR, head of Administration of Special Departments; 1943–46, head of counterintelligence administration, SMERSH, under the Commissariat of Defense, and Deputy Commissar of Defense; 1946–51, Minister of State Security, USSR. Arrested 1951 under orders from Stalin for supposed anti-Soviet activities; in 1954, after Stalin's death, tried and executed for his part in the purge of Leningrad Party leaders in 1948. Not rehabilitated.

Agranov (Sorinzon), Yakov Saulovich (1893–1938). 1912–15, member of Socialist Revolutionary Party; 1915, member of Russian Social Democratic Workers Party, Bolshevik faction; 1919, joined the Cheka; 1919–21, head of Special Department; 1922–23 head of Special Bureau for exile of anti-Soviet elements; 1923–31, head of Secret Department, GPU-OGPU SSSR; 1931–33, OGPU plenipotentiary for Moscow Oblast, and head of Special Department for Moscow Military District; 1934–37, First Deputy People's Commissar for Internal Affairs, USSR; 1937–38. NKVD chief, Saratov Oblast. Arrested and executed, August 1938. Not rehabilitated.

Akulov, Ivan Alekseevich (1888–1937). From 1907, member of Russian Social Democratic Workers Party; during the revolution and Civil War, worked in St. Petersburg, Ukrainian, and other oblast Party committees; 1922–29, Chairman of All-Ukrainian Council of Trade Unions; 1930–31, Deputy Chairman, Workers and Peasants Inspectorate; 1931–32, Deputy Chairman, OGPU; 1933–35, Chief Procurator, USSR; 1935–37, Secretary, Central Executive Committee, (TsIK) USSR. Arrested July 1937. Executed. Rehabilitated.

Alekseev, Nikolai Nikolaievich (1893–1937). 1910–18, member of Social Revolutionary Party; 1919 joined VKP(b); 1920, began work in Cheka; 1920–22, plenipotentiary in Foreign Department of Cheka; 1922–25, deputy head of Special Bureau for exile of anti-Soviet elements; 1925–35, OGPU plenipotentiary in Western Siberian Krai; 1935–37, deputy head of GULAG; 1937, arrested and executed. Rehabilitated.

Andreev, Andrei Andreevich (1895–1971). From 1914, Party member; 1920–22, Secretary, Central Council of Trade Union (VTsSPS); 1922–27, Secretary of Railway Union Central Committee; 1927–30, Secretary, North Caucasus Party Committee; from 1930, Chairman Central Control Commission of the TsK VKP(b), and Chairman, Workers and Peasants Inspectorate; 1931–35, Commissar of Transport, USSR; 1935–46, Party Central Committee Secretary; 1943–46, Commissar of Agriculture; 1946–53, Deputy Chairman, Council of Ministers, USSR; 1939–52, Chairman of Party Control Commission of the TsK VKP(b).

Antonov-Ovseenko, Vladimir Aleksandrovich (1884–1939). Russian Social Democratic Workers Party, Bolshevik faction, member since 1917; from 1924, diplomatic work; from 1930, Soviet plenipotentiary in Poland; 1934–37, Russian Republic Chief Procurator; from 1936, General Consul in Barcelona; 1937, recalled to Moscow, arrested, and executed. Rehabilitated.

Artuzov (Frauchi), Artur Khristianovich (1891–1937). From 1917, Bolshevik faction/Party member; 1918, joined Cheka; 1918–22, Special Plenipotentiary and deputy head, Special Department Cheka/GPU; 1922–27, head, counter-intelligence department, OGPU, and one of the organizers of the counterintelligence front organization, *Trest*; 1927–31, deputy head, Secret Operational Administration, OGPU, and deputy head of Foreign [Operations] Department, OGPU; 1931–35, head, INO OGPU-GUGB-NKVD USSR; 1935–37, deputy head of 4th Directorate of the General Staff. May 1937, arrested. Executed. Rehabilitated.

Balitsky, Vsevolod Apolonovich (1892–1937). 1915, joined Russian Social Democratic Workers Party; 1918, member of All-Ukrainian Cheka; 1923–31, OGPU Plenipotentiary in Ukraine; 1924–30, Commissar of Internal Affairs, Ukrainian SSR; 1931–34, Deputy Chairman, OGPU; 1932–34, special plenipotentiary and then head of GPU, Ukrainian SSR; from 1934, Commissar of Internal Affairs, Ukrainian SSR; from 1934, member TsK VKP(b); 1937, transferred to head Far East UNKVD; July 1937, arrested. Executed. Not rehabilitated.

Belen'ky, Abram Yakovlevich (1882–1941). Worked in Cheka from 1917; 1921–28, member Collegium Cheka-GPU-OGPU, and head of personal guard of V. I. Lenin (1921–24); 1930–38, special plenipotentiary; 1938, arrested. Executed. Rehabilitated.

Beloborodov, Aleksandr Grigor'evich (1891–1938). 1907, joined Russian Social Democratic Workers Party, Bolshevik faction; 1917 and the Civil War, worked in regional Party positions; 1912–23 and 1923–27, worked as Deputy Commissar and then as Commissar of Internal Affairs of the Russian Republic; 1927, expelled from the Party as an ally of Trotsky; 1930, reinstated; 1930s, worked in state administrative positions; 1936, arrested. Executed 1938. Rehabilitated.

Bel'sky, Lev Nikolaevich (Abram Mikhailovich Levin) (1889–1941). 1917, joined Russian Social Democratic Workers Party; from 1918, member

Cheka; 1918–20, Chairman, Simbirsk Cheka, and head, Special Department, Eighth Army; 1921–30, Special Plenipotentiary, Tambov Province, Far East, and Central Asia; 1930–31, Special Plenipotentiary, Moscow Oblast; 1931–33, in economic work (Commissariat of Supply); 1933–37, head of *militsiia*; 1936–38, Deputy Commissar, NKVD; 1938, head of NKVD transport department; 1938, arrested. Executed 1941. Not rehabilitated.

Beria, Lavrentii Pavlovich (1899–1953). Born into a peasant family in Tiflis Province, Georgia; finished secondary schooling; from 1917, member of Russian Social Democratic Workers Party, Bolshevik faction; 1920s, worked for the Cheka-GPU-OGPU in Azerbaijan, Georgia, and the Transcaucasus; from 1932, First Secretary of Transcaucasus Party organization; simultaneously, 1931–38, First Secretary, Georgian Party organization; from 1938, First Deputy Commissar of Internal Affairs, USSR, and head of the Main Administration of State Security; 1938–45 and 1953, Commissar and then Minister of Internal Affairs, USSR; 1941–53, Deputy Chairman of Council of People's Commissars and Council of Ministers after 1946; 1953, arrested after Stalin's death. Executed. Not rehabilitated.

Berman, Matvei Davidovich (1898–1939). 1917, joined Russian Social Democratic Workers Party; 1918, joined Cheka; 1920–30, headed Cheka-GPU-OGPU in Ekaterinburg, Tomsk, Buryat-Mongolia, and Central Asia provinces; 1929–32, deputy head, ULAG-GULAG; 1932–37, Deputy Commissar, OGPU-NKVD; 1937–38, Commissar of Transport; 1938, arrested. Executed 1939. Rehabilitated.

Blagonravov, Georgii Ivanovich (1895–1938). 1917, joined Russian Social Democratic Workers Party, Red Guard unit commander, member Petrograd Revolutionary Military Committee, commander Petropavlovsk Fortress; 1918, member, railroad subdepartment, Cheka; 1919–21, head, Cheka transport department Petrograd; 1921–31, head transport department, Cheka-GPU-OGPU; 1929–32, Deputy Commissar of Transport, USSR; 1932–35, First Deputy Commissar of Transport, USSR; 1934, Candidate member, TsK VKP(b); from 1936, head of road construction administration, NKVD USSR; 1937, arrested. Executed. Rehabilitated.

Bliukher, Vasilii Konstantinovich (1890–1938). 1916, joined Russian Social Democratic Workers Party; 1917, member, Military Revolutionary Committee, Samara; 1917–18, head of Red Guards, Chelyabinsk, commander, Eastern Brigade, and commander, Urals Partisan Army; 1921–22, Minister of War and commander, People's Revolutionary Army, Far East Republic; 1924–27, chief military adviser to the Chinese revolutionary government; 1927–29, commander, Ukrainian Military District; 1929–38, commander of special and regular Red Army forces, Far East; from 1934, member, TsK VKP(b); 1938, arrested. Died during interrogation. Rehabilitated.

Bliumkin, Yakov Grigor'evich (1898–1929). 1917, member, Left Socialist Revolutionary Party faction; 1918, head of Cheka Department for Struggle against International Espionage; 6 July 1918, assassinated German ambassador to Russian Republic, sentenced to 3 years prison, escaped; May 1919, amnestied and became member of RKP(b); thereafter worked as Cheka-GPU-OGPU agent in Mongolia, Palestine, Georgia, finally as OGPU resident in Turkey; 1929, met in secret with Trotsky, and arrested for conspiracy on return to USSR. Executed.

Bukharin, Nikolai Ivanovich (1888–1938). From 1906, member of Russian Social Democratic Workers Party; 1911, expelled from Economic Division of Moscow University Juridical Faculty; 1917–34, member of TsK of Russian Social Democratic Workers Party, Bolshevik faction–RKP(b)-VKP(b); "Left" Bolshevik during the Civil War, he opposed the Brest-Litovsk treaty and supported the policies of War Communism, then turned and became a major supporter of and theorist for NEP; from 1924, member of the Politburo of the TsK VKP(b), editor of Party newspaper, *Pravda,* and 1926–29, head of the Communist International organization, Komintern; 1928–29, one of leaders of the so-called Right Deviation, for opposing forced collectivization and grain confiscation; 1929, removed from Politburo and from *Pravda* board; 1934–37, editor *Izvestiia TsIK SSSR;* February 1937, expelled from the Party and arrested. Tried as leading member of so-called Anti-Soviet Right Trotskyist Bloc. Convicted and executed. Rehabilitated.

Bulganin, Nikolai Aleksandrovich (1895–1975). State, Party, and military official; after the Great Patriotic War, worked as Deputy Minister of Defense and Minister of Armed Forces, USSR, Deputy Chairman of Council of Ministers, and from 1955 as Chairman of Council of Ministers; 1958, demoted as part of Khrushchev's rise to power; 1960, forced into retirement.

Chicherin, Georgii Vasil'evich (1872–1936). 1896, finished Historical-Philosophical Faculty, Petersburg University; from 1897, worked in the archive of the Ministry of Foreign Affairs; 1904, emigrated to Germany, where he lived off money inherited from his mother and helped finance the Russian Social Democratic Workers Party; from 1905, member of that party's Menshevik wing; 1908, expelled from Germany for suspicious activity, lived in France; 1914, moved to London and worked with British Socialist Party and newspaper *Golos;* 1917–18, arrested and imprisoned in Britain, then released to Russia where joined the Russian Social Democratic Workers Party, Bolshevik faction; 1918, led Bolshevik delegation at Brest-Litovsk treaty negotiations with Germany, ending Russia's involvement in World War I; 1918, replaced Trotsky as Commissar of Foreign Affairs of the Russian Republic; 1922–23, led Russian delegation to conferences in Genoa and Lausanne, and negotiated German-Russian Treaty of Rapallo; 1923, First Commissar of Foreign Affairs, USSR; from 1925, member of TsK VKP(b); 1930, replaced as Foreign Affairs Commissar by M. M. Litvinov, retired due to illness.

Denikin, Anton Ivanovich (1872–1947). 1918–20, main anti-Bolshevik army commander in southern Russia, head of southern Russian government; 1920, emigrated, lived in Britain, Belgium, France, and United States.

Deribas, Terentii Dmitrevich (1883–1938). 1903, joined Russian Social Democratic Workers Party; 1917–18, one of Bolshevik leaders in Orenburg Province, engaged in Party work; 1918–20, political commissar in Red Army, became well known for mass shootings of "enemies" in Siberia; 1920–21, worked in Secret Department, Cheka; 1921–22, head of Secret Department, took leading role in suppression of Kronstadt uprising of anti-Bolshevik sailors, and of peasant uprisings in Tambov Province; from May 1923, head of Secret Department, OGPU; from 1927, first deputy head of Secret Operational Administration, OGPU; 1931–37, member of OGPU-NKVD Collegium; 1929, OGPU Plenipotentiary for Far East; from 1934, head of Far East UNKVD, 1937, arrested. Executed. Rehabilitated.

Dzerzhinsky, Feliks (1877–1926). Born into Polish noble family; expelled from gymnasium for revolutionary activity; helped organize the Social Democratic Party of Poland and Lithuania; arrested, exiled, and emigrated several times in the first decade of the 1900s, Dzerzhinsky lived and conducted revolutionary activity from Berlin and Capri, and in his native Poland; 1912–17, captured and imprisoned; 1917, joined the Bolsheviks, and worked in the Executive Committee of the Moscow Soviet; elected to the Bolshevik Central Committee, Dzerzhinsky moved to Petrograd, and played an active role in the October seizure of power; 1918, chosen to head the newly founded Cheka; after the Civil War, helped to establish the GPU-OGPU, and worked as Commissar of the Interior and as Chairman of the Supreme Economic Council.

Eikhe, Robert Indrikovich (1890–1940). 1905, joined Russian Social Democratic Workers Party; from 1919, Commissar of Food Supply, Latvia; 1919–24, worked in Commissariat of Food Supply, RSFSR; from 1924, and then 1925–37, deputy head and then First Secretary of Krai Party Committee in Western Siberia, and of the city of Novosibirsk; 1937–38, Commissar of Agriculture, USSR; 1937, deputy for Supreme Soviet USSR; 1938, arrested. Executed 1940. Rehabilitated.

Enukidze, Avel' Safronovich (1877–1937). From 1896, member of Russian Social Democratic Workers Party; 1917, member of Petrograd Military Revolutionary Committee; 1918–22, member of Russian Central Executive Committee (of Soviets); 1922–35, Secretary, Presidium of All Union Central Executive Committee of Soviets; 1935, accused of dereliction of duty in the so-called Kremlin Conspiracy, and excluded from the Party; from 1936, Director of the Kharkov Oblast Transport Trust; 1937, arrested. Executed. Rehabilitated.

Evdokimov, Efim Georgievich (1891–1940). From 1918, member RKP(b); from 1918–19, member, Red Army and Cheka, Special Department for Moscow; 1920–21, deputy head of Cheka Special Department for Southwestern and Southern fronts; 1921–23, head of Special Department for Ukraine; from 1923, OGPU Plenipotentiary for southeastern Russia; 1924–26, OGPU Plenipotentiary for the North Caucasus Krai; 1929, appointed head of OGPU Secret Operational Administration and OGPU Collegium member; 1931–34, OGPU plenipotentiary in Central Asia; 1934, member of TsK VKP(b); 1934–37, First Secretary of VKP(b) in the North Caucasus Krai; from 1937, First Party Secretary Azov–Black Sea and Rostov oblast committees; 1937, elected deputy to Supreme Soviet USSR and Commissar of Water Transport, USSR; 1938, arrested. Executed 1940. Rehabilitated.

Frinovsky, Mikhail Petrovich (1898–1940). From 1918, member of Russian Social Democratic Workers Party, Bolshevik faction, and worked in Cheka; during Civil War and early 1920s, worked as political commissar in various military administrations; 1922–23, headed GPU in Kiev; 1925–27, OGPU deputy plenipotentiary in Northern Caucasus and head of Northern Caucasus Special Department administration; 1930–33, OGPU Chairman, Azerbaijan SSR; from 1933, head of border forces, OGPU USSR, and from 1934, head of border and internal security, NKVD USSR; 1936–38, Deputy Commissar of Internal Affairs. USSR, and second only to Yezhov in organizing and carrying out the great purges; 1938, arrested as part of the purge of Yezhov's leadership group. Executed 1940. Not rehabilitated.

Gamarnik, Yan Borisovich (1894–1937). From 1916, member of Russian Social Democratic Workers Party; from 1929, head of the Red Army Political Administration, member of the Revolutionary Military Council, USSR, and chief editor of the military newspaper, *Red Star;* from 1930, Deputy Commissar of Naval Affairs, USSR; from 1934, Deputy Commissar of Defense, USSR; 1937, committed suicide in anticipation of arrest in the case of the so-called military conspiracy. Rehabilitated.

Ignat'ev, Semen Denisovich (1904–83). Born into a peasant family; from 1926, member of VKP(b); 1935, finished Technical Academy of Industry; throughout the 1930s, worked in various Party positions, including the Industrial Department of the Central Committee; 1937–46, First Secretary of the Buryat-Mongolian Party organization and then the Bashkir Party organization; 1946–51, secretary of Belorussian Party organization and then headed Party organizations in Central Asia; 1951–53, Minister of Internal Affairs, USSR, and a TsK secretary; after 1953, headed the Bashkir and Tatar oblast Party organizations; 1960, retired.

Kaganovich, Lazar' Moiseevich (1893–1991). From 1911, member of Russian Social Democratic Workers Party; 1917, member, Saratov Committee of Bolsheviks; 1918, Commissar, All-Russian Collegium for Red Army Organization; 1918–19, Chairman, Nizhnii Novgorod Province; from 1920, member of the Turkestan Bureau of the TsK RKP(b); 1924–25 and 1928–39, TsK secretary; 1925–28, general secretary of Ukrainian Communist Party; 1930–35, First Secretary, Moscow City Party Committee; 1930–57, member of Politburo of the TsK VKP(b)/KPSS; 1934–35, Chairman, Party Control Commission; 1935–37, 1938–42, 1943–44, Commissar of Transport, USSR; 1937–38, Commissar of Heavy Industry, USSR; 1939–40, Commissar of Petroleum Industry, USSR; 1940–47, Deputy Chairman of Sovnarkom/Sovmin USSR; 1953–57, Chairman, Council of Ministers, USSR; 1957, removed from Presidium (Politburo) and Central Committee of the KPSS; 1962, expelled from Communist Party.

Kamenev (Rozenfel'd), Lev Borisovich (1883–1936). From 1901, member of Russian Social Democratic Workers Party; participated in 1905 revolution; 1908–17, in emigration; 1917, member of All-Russian Central Executive Committee of Soviets; one of the editors of *Pravda;* 1919, special plenipotentiary on the Southern Front; 1922–26, Chairman of the Moscow City Council; 1922–26, Deputy, then First Deputy, Sovnarkom RSFSR, USSR; Chairman of Defense Council; 1923–27, director of Lenin Institute; 1919–25, member of TsK Politburo; implicated in the so-called new opposition bloc; from 1926, ambassador to Italy, Chairman of Scientific-Technical

Administration of the Supreme Economic Council; 1927, expelled from
VKP(b); 1928, reinstated; 1932–33, in exile in Minusinsk; 1934, director of
the Gorky Institute of World Literature; 1935, sentenced to prison as part of
the so-called Moscow Center conspiracy; 1936, sentenced as part of the
"United Trotskyist-Zinovievist Center." Executed. Rehabilitated.

Khrushchev, Nikita Sergeevich (1894–1971). From peasant family; since 1918,
member of Bolshevik faction; 1920s, worked in local Party organizations,
and then the TsK of the Ukrainian Communist Party; 1932–34, Second
Secretary, Moscow city Party organization; from 1934, member of TsK
VKP(b); 1935–38, First Secretary, Moscow city Party organization, and
oversaw the great purges in Moscow; 1938–49, First Secretary, Ukrainian
Communist Party; 1949–53, Secretary in TsK KPSS; 1953–64, First Secretary, Tsk KPSS; from 1958, also Chairman of Council of Ministers; 1964,
removed from office by Central Committee vote, and compelled to retire.

Kobulov, Bogdan Zakharovich (1904–53). Born in Tiflis, Georgia; 1921–25,
served in the Red Army; 1922, started work in the Georgian Cheka-GPU;
1925, joined the Communist Party; from 1931, as a protégé of Beria, worked
in leadership positions in the Secret Political Department of the Georgian
OGPU; from 1936, head of the Georgian UNKVD; from 1938, deputy head
of the GUGB NKVD USSR, and head of the investigative section of the
NKVD USSR; from 1939, candidate then full member of the TsK VKP(b);
from February 1941, Deputy Commissar of the Interior, USSR; from 1943,
Deputy Commissar of State Security, USSR; from 1946, deputy head of the
Administration of Soviet Property Abroad (under the Ministry of Foreign
Trade, and then the Council of Ministers, USSR), and deputy head of the
Soviet military administration in Germany; early 1950s, continued to work
in positions related to Soviet administration in Germany; 1953, First Deputy
Minister of the Interior, USSR; arrested June 1953 in connection with the
purge of Beria's entourage in the state security system. Executed. Not
rehabilitated.

Kosior, Stanislav Vikent'evich (1889–1939). From 1907, member of Russian
Social Democratic Workers Party, active in revolutionary work in Petrograd,
Ukraine; 1917, Commissar of Petrograd Military Revolutionary Committee;
one of organizers of the Ukrainian Communist Party of Bolsheviks; from
1918, Finance Commissar, Ukraine; from 1922, Secretary of the Siberian
Bureau of the TsK RKP(b); 1926–28, Secretary, TsK VKP(b); from 1928,
First Secretary, Ukrainian Communist Party; 1938, Deputy Chairman,
Council of Commissars, USSR, and Chairman, Soviet Control Commission;
from 1924, member of TsK VKP(b); 1927–30 candidate member, Politburo;
from 1930, full member, Politburo, and member of Presidium of the
Central Executive Committee of Soviets; 1938, arrested. Executed 1939.
Rehabilitated.

Kruglov, Sergei Nikiforovich (1907–77). Educated at Moscow Institute of Asian
Studies and Institute of Red Professors; from 1928, member of VKP(b);
1929, began military service; from 1938, worked in the TsK VK(b)
apparatus; 1939, began work as a Special Plenipotentiary in the OGPU;
from 1939, Deputy Commissar of Internal Affairs, USSR, and head of

NKVD Department of Cadres; 1945–53, Commissar, then Minister, of Internal Affairs, USSR; 1953, First Deputy, then again Minister of Internal Affairs, until 1956.

Krylenko, Nikolai Vasil'evich (1885–1938). From 1904, member of Russian Social Democratic Workers Party; 1917, member, Petrograd Military Revolutionary Committee; from 1918, member of Commissariat of Justice Presidium, Chairman of Revolutionary Tribunal under the All-Russian Central Executive Committee, and Procurator of the Russian Republic; 1927–34, member of Central Control Commission of the TsK VKP(b); 1931–36, Commissar of Justice, RSFSR; 1936–37, Commissar of Justice, USSR; member of All-Russian and All-Union executive committees; 1937, arrested. Executed 1938. Rehabilitated.

Kuibyshev, Valerian Vladimirovich (1888–1935). From 1904, member of Russian Social Democratic Workers Party; 1918–19, Commissar and member of Revolutionary Council of the Eastern Front, then Deputy Chairman of Commission of All-Russian (then USSR) Central Executive Committee, on Turkestan; from 1920, member of Central Executive Council, Presidium of Trade Unions; from 1921, Presidium member of Supreme Economic Council, and head of USSR Electrical Administration; from 1926, head of Supreme Economic Council; from 1930, head of Gosplan; from 1934, Chairman of Soviet Control Commission.

Kursky, Dmitrii Ivanovich (1874–1932). From 1904, member of Russian Social Democratic Workers Party; attended higher education institutions; 1919–21, member of Revolutionary Military Council of RSFSR; 1918–28, Commissar of Justice, RSFSR and First Procurator, USSR; 1927–30, member of Central Party Control Commission, head of Institute of Justice; ambassador to Italy.

Litvinov, Maksim Maksimovich (Vallakh, Meer-Genokh Moishevich) (1876– 1951). From 1898, member of Russian Social Democratic Workers Party; 1918–21, member of Commissariat of Foreign Affairs, RSFSR; 1921–23, Deputy Commissar of Foreign Affairs, USSR; from 1923, member of Collegium of Workers and Peasants Inspectorate, USSR; 1930–139, Commissar of Foreign Affairs, USSR; 1934–41, member of TsK VKP(b), and member of VTsIK and TsIK USSR; 1941–46, Deputy Commissar of Foreign Affairs; 1941–43, ambassador to the United States and Soviet representative in Cuba; 1946, retired.

Malenkov, Georgii Maksimilianovich (1901–88). From 1920, member of VKP(b); 1930–34, head of Moscow Party organization; 1934–39, head of Department of Party Organs of the TsK VKP(b); 1939–46, 1948–53, TsK Secretary, and head of Party Cadre Department, 1939–46; 1946–53, 1955–57, Deputy Chairman of Council of Ministers USSR; 1957, expelled from TsK, and in 1961 from KPSS, as part of Khrushchev's rise to power.

Medved', Filipp Dem'yanovich (1889–1937). From 1907, member of Russian Social Democratic Workers Party; before 1917, revolutionary activist, arrested four times, imprisoned for two years; 1917, worked in factory, member of Sokol regional Military Revolutionary Committee, Moscow; from 1918, member of Cheka; 1918–20, member of Collegium of Cheka,

Chairman of Tula Province Cheka, Chairman of Petrograd Cheka, head of
NKVD RSFSR concentration camps, Cheka Plenipotentiary to Western
Front; 1920–21, head of Cheka Special Department for Western Krai;
1921–23, Deputy Chairman, Moscow city Cheka, head of Moscow Province
Cheka, head of Moscow Military District Special Department; 1924–25,
worked in OGPU in Western Territory and Belorussia, and as OGPU
plenipotentiary and head of Special Department in the Far East; 1930–34,
OGPU Plenipotentiary and then head of OGPU administration for Leningrad; December 1934, arrested and convicted in 1935 for lax administration,
and sentenced to three years in prison. Arrested again and executed in 1937.
Rehabilitated.

Menzhinsky, Vyacheslav Rudol'fovich (1874–1934). Born in Poland; from
 1904, member of Russian Social Democratic Workers Party; 1914–17,
 military service in the Caucasus; 1917, Commissar, Petrograd Military
 Revolutionary Committee; 1917–18, Deputy Commissar of Finance; 1918,
 member, Presidium of Petrograd Council, Consul General in Berlin,
 Collegium member, Commissariat of Foreign Affairs; 1919, member,
 Presidium of Cheka, and Special Plenipotentiary of the Cheka Special
 Department; from 1920, head of Special Department Administration, Cheka;
 from 1922, head of Secret Operational Administration; from 1923, Deputy
 Chairman and from 1926, Chairman, OGPU. Died 1934.

Merkulov, Vsevolod Nikolaevich (1895–1953). Son of a tsarist army officer;
 1916–18, served in army; 1921–31, served in Transcaucasus and Georgian
 Cheka-GPU-OGPU; during 1930s, worked in Party apparatus; from 1938,
 head of GUGB USSR, and Deputy Commissar of Internal Affairs, USSR;
 1943–46, Commissar, then Minister, of Internal Affairs, USSR; 1946–53, did
 not work in security organs; 1953, arrested and executed as part of post-
 Stalin purge. Not rehabilitated.

Messing, Stanislav Adamovich (1889–1937). 1917, head of Cheka, Sokol'niki
 Raion, Moscow; 1918, Collegium member and head of Secret Operational
 Department, Moscow Cheka; 1920–21, deputy head and then head of
 Moscow Cheka; from 1921, Chairman, Petrograd Cheka; from 1922,
 commander, GPU forces in Petrograd Military District; from 1923, Collegium member, OGPU; from 1927, head of Foreign Department, OGPU, and
 second deputy head, OGPU; 1931, removed from OGPU and transferred to
 work in various positions in Commissariat of Trade, USSR; 1937, arrested.
 Executed. Rehabilitated.

Mezhlauk, Valerii Ivanovich (1893–1938). Attended Historical-Philological and
 Juridical Faculties, Kharkov University; 1917, Menshevik "Internationalist,"
 then Bolshevik faction member; 1918–20, Deputy Commissar, Finance
 Commissariat, Ukraine, member, Revolutionary Military Committee,
 Southern Front, Deputy Commissar of Defense, Ukraine; 1920–24, head of
 various railroad administrations, and Deputy Commissar of Transport,
 RSFSR-USSR; from 1924, head of Main Metallurgical Administration,
 Commissariat of Heavy Industry, USSR, and member of Supreme Economic
 Council Presidium; from 1931, Deputy Chairman and then Chairman of
 Gosplan); 1937, Commissar of Heavy Industry, USSR, member Central

Executive Committee of Soviets, USSR; 1937, arrested. Executed 1938. Rehabilitated.

Mironov, Lev Grigor'evich (1895–1938). Finished gymnasium and attended three years at Kiev University; from 1918, member of Russian Social Democratic Workers Party; 1918–19, entered Cheka work; 1921–24, conducted political work in Red Army and was Chairman of the Revolutionary Military Tribunal of the Samarkand-Bukhara Forces Group, also Deputy Commissar of Justice for Turkestan; from 1924, entered work in OGPU; 1924–29, department head, then deputy head of Economic Administration, OGPU USSR; 1930–31, OGPU Plenipotentiary in Central Asia; 1931–37, deputy head of Economic Administration, OGPU USSR, then head of Economic Department, GUGB, head of GUGB Counterintelligence Department; 1937, arrested. Executed 1938. Rehabilitated.

Mironov, Sergei Naumovich (1894–1940). Served in the army during World War I, and in the Red Army during the Civil War; worked in the Cheka Special Department and then headed the Foreign Department, GPU, for south-eastern Russia; 1920s, headed OGPU offices in the Black Sea–Azov area, Chechnya, and Vladikavkaz; early 1930s, OGPU deputy plenipotentiary, Kazakhstan; 1933–36, headed OGPU apparatus in Dnepropetrovsk Oblast; 1936–37, head of NKVD in Western Siberian Krai; 1938–39, Soviet envoy to Mongolia; 1939, arrested. Executed 1940. Not rehabilitated.

Molchanov, Georgii Andreevich (1897–1937). Member of Russian Social Democratic Workers Party, Bolshevik faction; 1917–18, served in Red Army, then in various military staff positions; 1919–21, Chairman, Grozny Province Cheka; 1921–23, deputy head of Secret Operational Administration, Cheka and GPU, and of various provincial GPU administrations; 1923–25, head of Secret Operational Administration, OGPU; 1925–31, head of Ivanovo-Voznesensk Province GPU; 1931–36, head of Secret Political Department, OGPU; 1936–37, Commissar of Internal Affairs, Belorussian SSR, and head, Special Department Administration, Belorussian Military District; 1937, arrested and executed. Not rehabilitated.

Molotov (Skryabin), Vyacheslav Mikhailovich (1890–1986). Studied at Petersburg Polytechnic Institute; from 1906, member of Russian Social Democratic Workers Party, Bolshevik faction; 1917, member of Petrograd Soviet Executive Council and Petrograd Committee of Russian Social Democratic Workers Party, Bolshevik faction; from 1918, member of Sovnarkom, and from 1920 of TsK RKP(b) and then VKP(b); from 1921, candidate then full member of Politburo of the TsK RKP(b) and VKP(b); 1930–41, Chairman, Council of People's Commissars; 1937–58, deputy, Supreme Soviet, USSR; 1939–49, Commissar then Minister of Foreign Affairs, USSR; 1941–45, Deputy Chairman, State Defense Committee; 1946–56, held various positions as Chairman or Deputy Chairman of Foreign Ministry, USSR, and Council of Ministers, USSR; 1956, Minister of State Control; 1957, as part of Khrushchev's purge of "Stalinists," removed from post as Deputy Chairman, Council of Ministers, and appointed ambassador to Mongolia; 1962, expelled from KPSS, and retired from politics; 1984, reinstated as member of KPSS.

Ogol'tsov, Sergei Ivanovich (1900–1976). Joined the Cheka at age seventeen, and worked in various positions throughout the 1920s; 1930s and early 1940s, served in various leadership positions in the OGPU border forces, and in the Leningrad and Kuibyshev oblast UNKVD; 1943–45, headed the Kazakhstan UNKGB; 1945–51, First Deputy Minister of State Security, USSR; 1948, given the task of arranging the murder of Solomon Mikhoels, well-known actor and founder of the USSR Jewish Antifascist Committee; 1951, briefly served as temporary Minister of State Security between the removal of V. S. Abakumov and the appointment of S. D. Ignat'ev. After Stalin's death, and on the recommendation of L. Beria, briefly arrested for the murder of Mikhoels, but was released after the arrest of Beria; 1958, expelled from the Party and then stripped of his security rank and forced into retirement.

Ordzhonikidze, Sergo (Grigorii Konstantinovich) (1886–1937). From 1903, member of Russian Social Democratic Workers Party, Bolshevik faction; 1917, member of Petrograd Soviet; 1918–19, Chairman, Council of Defense of North Caucasus; during Civil War served in various Bolshevik military positions on different fronts, one of leading Bolsheviks to help establish Party power in the Caucasus and North Caucasus; 1922–26, First Secretary, Transcaucasus and North Caucasus krai Party committees; 1926–30, Commissar of Central Control Commission and Workers and Peasants Inspectorate; 1930–32, Chairman of Supreme Economic Council; 1932–37, Commissar of Heavy Industry, USSR; 1937, committed suicide.

Pauker, Karl Viktorovich (1893–1937). Born in Austria-Hungary; 1906–14, worked as a barber and a pastry chef apprentice; 1914–15, served in Austro-Hungarian army, captured and interned in Turkestan; 1918–19, Deputy Commandant of Cheka in Samarkand; 1919–20, studied at Sverdlov Communist Academy; 1920–22, worked for Special Department Administration, Cheka-GPU; 1922–37, deputy head and then head of Operational Department, Cheka-GPU-OGPU-NKVD USSR; 1937, arrested and executed 1937. Not rehabilitated.

Pillar, Romual'd Liudwig Pillar von Pil'khau (Pilliar, Roman Aleksandrovich) (1894–1937). Born into Baltic German family; studied in gymnasium in Vil'na, Switzerland, and Russia; 1914, became involved in revolutionary activities; from 1917–19, worked in the Lithuanian and Polish underground revolutionary movements, then transferred to Russia as part of a prisoner exchange; until 1921, Red Army political commissar; after 1921, worked in the counterintelligence and foreign espionage departments, Cheka-GPU-OGPU, including as one of organizers and managers, along with A. Kh. Artuzov, of the counterespionage operation "Trust"; 1925–29, worked in the Belorussian GPU; 1930s, supervised GPU operations in Central Asia, Saratov Krai, and other regions; 1937, arrested and executed as an alleged Polish agent. Rehabilitated.

Piłsudski, Józef (1867–1935). Polish military leader, Chief of State 1918–22, and then de facto military head of the Polish state from 1926 until his death; originally, a socialist and a nationalist, Piłsudski was convinced that Poland would gain independence only through force of arms; 1914–1917, fought under the Austrians against Russia, and then against occupation; 1919–21, commanded Polish forces against Bolshevik domination, attempting, unsuccessfully, to gain control of eastern Ukraine and then defeating Bolshevik armies in 1920 at the siege of Warsaw. As head of state, he attempted to organize a Baltic alliance against the Bolsheviks, and to foster anti-Bolshevik nationalist sentiment among non-Russian populations in western Russia and Ukraine. According to Feliks Dzerzhinsky, a fellow Pole and head of the Russian-Soviet political police, Piłsudski presented the greatest threat to the Soviet Union. 1932, signed the Soviet-Polish Nonaggression Pact.

Poskrebyshev, Aleksandr Nikolaevich (1891–1965). From 1917, member of Russian Social Democratic Workers Party, Bolshevik faction; from 1922, worked in the Central Committee apparatus as deputy head of administration, and as Stalin's deputy; 1929–34, deputy head, then head of the Secret Department of the TsK; 1934–52, head of the Special Sector of the TsK (responsible for all secret communications); from 1931, Stalin's personal secretary and confidant; 1939–56, TsK member; 1953, removed with pension.

Postyshev, Pavel Petrovich (1887–1937). From 1904, member of Russian Social Democratic Workers Party, Bolshevik faction; participated in revolutions of 1905–7 and 1917; one of organizers of Red Army; 1918–19, worked in Irkutsk and Far East Republic; member of revolutionary tribunals and army political commissar; from 1923, engaged in Party work; 1927–38, member of TsK VKP(b) and Organizational Bureau; 1930–34, one of the TsK secretaries; 1933–37, Second Secretary of Ukrainian Communist Party and First Secretary of Kharkov and Kiev oblast Party Committees; Presidium member of Central Executive Committee USSR; Deputy of Supreme Soviet; 1938, arrested. Executed 1939. Rehabilitated.

Prokof'ev, Georgii Evgen'evich (1895–1937). From 1919, member of Russian Social Democratic Workers Party, Bolshevik faction; engaged in revolutionary activity in Kiev, then Red Army volunteer; during Civil War, engaged in political work in cavalry units, and on railroad transport; 1921–24, deputy head of Cheka-GPU Foreign Department; 1924–26, head of OGPU Information Department; 1926–31, head of OGPU Economic Department; 1931–32, member of Supreme Economic Council, deputy head of Workers and Peasants Inspectorate, and head of White Sea Canal construction; 1932–34, third deputy head, OGPU, and head of the USSR *militsiia* administration; 1934–36, Deputy Commissar, NKVD USSR; 1936–37, demoted to Deputy Commissar of Communications, USSR, as part of the purge of Yagoda's leadership circle; 1937, arrested and executed. Not rehabilitated.

Pyatakov, Georgii (Yurii) Leonidovich (1890–1937). Son of a factory manager; studied in Economics Faculty, Petersburg University, expelled 1910; from 1910 member of Russian Social Democratic Workers Party, Bolshevik faction; 1914–17, in emigration in Switzerland; 1918, leading "Left Communist" opposed to treaty with Germany; from 1920, Chairman of Gosplan RSFSR, and worked in Don basin industrial management, close ally of Leon Trotsky; 1923–early 1930s, worked as Deputy Chairman, Supreme

Economic Council, on various trade missions abroad, and in the State Bank administration; from 1932, Deputy Commissar of Heavy Industry; 1923–25 and 1930–36, member of TsK VKP(b); 1937, tried as member of so-called Parallel Anti-Soviet Trotskyist Center. Convicted and executed. Rehabilitated.

Radek (Sobel'son), Karl Bernardovich (1895–1939). Studied in the History Faculty, University of Cracow; 1902, joined the Polish Social Democratic Party, and the Russian Social Democratic Workers Party in 1904. Worked as a journalist and in the socialist press in Poland, Switzerland, and Germany; expelled from the German Social Democratic Party; after the 1917 February revolution, worked as a representative for the Russian Social Democratic Workers Party in Stockholm; helped negotiate the return of Bolshevik leaders, including Lenin, to Russia through Germany; 1918, member of Bolshevik delegation at Brest-Litovsk negotiations, but also a "Left Communist," opposed to a separate peace with Germany; 1919, one of founders of German Communist Party, and participant in failed communist uprising; 1920, arrested and returned to Russia; 1919–24, member of TsK RKP(b), active in the Communist International organization, and a close ally of Leon Trotsky; 1927, expelled from the Party as a Trotskyist, and sentenced to three years in exile; 1929, freed from exile and reinstated in Party in 1930. Early 1930s, worked abroad, especially in Poland, for Stalin; 1937, arrested and sentenced to ten years in a labor camp. Murdered in prison. Rehabilitated.

Rakovsky, Khristian Georgievich (1873–1941). Born in Bulgaria; doctor by profession; worked in social democratic movements in Bulgaria, Romania, and France. 1917, joined Russian Social Democratic Workers Party, Bolshevik faction, worked in communist revolutionary movement in Romania and Ukraine; 1919–23, Chairman of Council of Commissars, Ukraine; 1923–27, Soviet ambassador in Britain and then France, Deputy Commissar of Foreign Affairs, member of TsK RKP(b); 1919–27, close ally of Trotsky; 1927, expelled from Party as Trotskyist and exiled to Central Asia; 1934, returned from exile; 1935–37, Chairman of Red Cross Society; 1938, tried as member of "Right-Trotskyist Bloc," and sentenced to twenty years in labor camp. Died in 1941. Rehabilitated.

Redens, Stanislav Frantsevich (1892–1939). From 1914, member of Russian Social Democratic Workers Party, Bolshevik faction; from 1918, worked for the Cheka during the Civil War, and then in the Crimea and Transcaucasus during the 1920s; from 1931, OGPU Plenipotentiary in Belorussia; 1932–33, Chairman, OGPU in Ukraine, oversaw collectivization and dekulakization; 1933–38, OGPU Plenipotentiary in Moscow, member of purge troika in 1937–38; 1938–39, Commissar of Internal Affairs, Kazakhstan SSR; 1938, arrested 1938. Executed 1939. Rehabilitated.

Rudzutak, Yan Ernestovich (1887–1938). 1904, joined Russian Social Democratic Workers Party, Bolshevik faction; from 1917, engaged in Party, government, trade union, and diplomatic work; in early 1920s, worked in trade union movements, member of TsK RKP(b); throughout the 1920s, engaged in high-level Party work, in Secretariat, in Central Asia, as Soviet

delegate to the 1922 Genoa Conference; early and mid-1930s, Deputy
Chairman of the Council of People's Commissars, member of the Council of
Labor and Defense, and Commissar of the Workers and Peasants Inspector-
ate; May 1937, arrested for supposedly spying for Germany and being a
Trotskyist. Executed 1938. Rehabilitated 1956.

Rykov, Aleksei Ivanovich (1881–1938). Studied in Juridical Faculty, Kazan
University; 1908, joined Russian Social Democratic Workers Party, Bolshevik
faction; participated actively in revolutions of 1905–7 and 1917; throughout
the 1920s, held high-level government and Party positions, most importantly
as Chairman of the Council of People's Commissars; 1931–36, Commissar
of Communications and member of Central Executive Committee of Soviets,
USSR; 1937, expelled from Party as member of so-called Right Deviation;
1938, tried and executed. Rehabilitated.

Ryutin, Martem'yan Nikitich (1890–1937). Born in Irkutsk Province; 1914,
joined Russian Social Democratic Workers Party, Bolshevik faction; fought in
World War I and helped establish Bolshevik power in Siberia; 1920s,
engaged in Party work in a number of provinces; 1927–30, candidate then
full member of TsK, RKP(b); member of Presidium of Supreme Economic
Council; early 1930s, organized the Union of Marxists-Leninists and agitated
for removal of Stalin as general secretary; author of programmatic letter
critical of Stalin, and distributed among Party leaders; 1932, arrested and
imprisoned; 1937, arrested again and executed. Rehabilitated.

Semashko, Nikolai Aleksandrovich (1874–1949). 1901, finished Medical
Faculty, Kazan University; participated in 1905–7 revolution, arrested, freed
on bond, fled abroad, and lived in Switzerland and France; 1917, returned to
Russia; from 1918, Commissar of Health, RSFSR; from 1930, Chairman of
Children's Commission, RSFSR.

Shcherbakov, Aleksandr Sergeevich (1901–45). Party functionary and founding
member of Soviet Writers Union; 1934–38, deputy to Andrei Zhdanov in
the Leningrad Party organization, then transferred to head the Moscow
Oblast Party organization; during the war, served as head of the Political
Administration of the Soviet army; 1945, died of a heart attack, later
claimed as a murder by anti-Soviet Zionist agents.

Sokol'nikov, Grigorii Yakovlevich (Brilliant, Girsh Yankevich) (1888–1939).
Son of a doctor's family; finished Juridical Faculty, University of Paris; 1905,
joined Russian Social Democratic Workers Party, Bolshevik faction; 1917,
active in revolutionary affairs; member of TsK, VKP(b); 1918, member of
Bolshevik delegation to Brest-Litovsk negotiations, and signed treaty for the
Bolsheviks; during 1920s, worked in high-level positions in Soviet banking;
1923–26, First Commissar of Finances, USSR; 1926, demoted to work in
other positions; 1930s, member of Collegium of Commissariat of Foreign
Affairs; 1936, expelled from Party and arrested; 1937, convicted and
sentenced to ten years in labor camp as member of "Parallel Anti-Soviet
Trotskyist Center." Murdered in prison.

Sol'tz, Aron Aleksandrovich (1872–1945). Born into prosperous merchant
family; 1898, joined Russian Social Democratic Workers Party 1898; 1917,

worked in Moscow Committee of the party's Bolshevik faction; 1920s and
1930s, worked in various positions in the Russian Republic and USSR
judicial system and the USSR and RSFSR Procuracy, including the RSFSR
Supreme Court; 1923–38, member of Central Control Commission of Party.

Stalin, Iosif Vissarionovich (Ioseb Besarionis Dze Jugashvili) (1878–1953).
From the 1890s, active in revolutionary politics in Georgia, and then with
the Leninist Bolshevik faction of the Russian Social Democratic Workers
Party; member of the Bolshevik Central Committee during the 1917 revolutionary year; from 1922 until his death in 1953, general secretary of the
Communist Party of the Soviet Union; from the late 1920s, undisputed
dictator of the Soviet Union.

Tomsky (Efremov), Mikhail Pavlovich (1880–1936). 1904, joined Russian
Social Democratic Workers Party; engaged in revolutionary activity in
Russian Estonia, arrested and exiled to France, returned to Russia, arrested
again, and freed from prison in 1917 by the Provisional Government; 1917,
member of Petrograd Executive Committee of Bolsheviks; 1920s, head of the
Central Council of Trade Unions, RSFSR and then USSR; from 1927,
member of Politburo; one of leaders of so-called Right Deviation, supporting
NEP and opposed to the Stalinist policies of forced collectivization and
industrialization; 1930, expelled from Politburo and headed the State
Publishing House; 1936, committed suicide when implicated in supposed
anti-Soviet terrorist activities.

Trilisser, Meer Abramovich (1883–1940). 1901, joined Russian Social Democratic Workers Party, Bolshevik faction; participated in revolutionary underground in Finland, arrested numerous times; 1917 and in Civil War, worked
in Siberia and the Far Eastern Republic as a Bolshevik Party functionary, and
in the Cheka, actively engaging in the "Red Terror" in Siberia; from 1921,
deputy head and then head of Foreign Department, Cheka, as one of key
organizers of foreign spy work in Russia and the early Soviet Union; 1926,
Deputy Chairman, OGPU; 1930–34, deputy head of the Workers and
Peasants Inspectorate; 1935, work in the Komintern Executive Committee
under the name Mikhail Aleksandrovich Moskvin, responsible for the Spanish
Communist Party; 1938, arrested. Executed 1940. Rehabilitated.

Trotsky (Bronshtein), Lev Davidovich (1879–1940). Since 1908, involved in the
Russian Social Democratic movement; first associated with the Mensheviks,
headed the Petersburg Soviet in 1905; 1907–17, lived in emigration; 1917,
returned to Russia, changed to Bolshevik faction, Chairman of Petrograd
Soviet; one of the founders of the Soviet state, commander of Red Army
forces during the Civil War, Commissar of War and, briefly, of Foreign
Relations; Politburo member; after Lenin's death in 1924, a major rival for
political power against Bukharin, Kamenev, and Stalin; 1927, expelled from
the Party and exiled to Alma-Ata; 1929, deported from the USSR, lived in
emigration in Turkey, France, Norway, and finally Mexico; 1938, founded
the Fourth International; 1940, murdered in his home in Coyoacán by an
NKVD hired assassin, Ramón Mercader.

Tukhachevsky, Mikhail Nikolaevich (1893–1937). During the Civil War,
commander in the Red Army; helped defeat Kolchak's forces in Siberia and

Admiral Denikin in the Crimea; 1920, defeated by at the siege of Warsaw, and came into conflict with Stalin over the defeat, each blaming the other; Tukhachevsky went on to become a prominent military strategist and, in 1935, Marshal of the Soviet Union; 1937, long distrusted by Stalin, Tukhachevsky was arrested, tried, and executed along with other leading military officers as supposed German agents working to overthrow the Soviet government. Rehabilitated.

Uglanov, Nikolai Aleksandrovich (1886–1937). 1907, joined Russian Social Democratic Workers Party, Bolshevik faction; from 1917, worked in trade union movement and administration, and in provincial Party administrations; 1924–29, Secretary, TsK RKP(b), and Moscow Party Committee; 1928–30, Commissar of Labor USSR; 1933, arrested for supposed anti-Party activities; 1936, arrested again. Tried and executed 1937. Rehabilitated.

Unshlikht, Iosef Stanislavovich (1879–1938). 1900, joined Polish and Lithuanian Social Democratic Party; 1906, member, Russian Social Democratic Workers Party, Bolshevik faction; Deputy Chairman, Cheka-GPU; early and mid-1920s, as deputy to Feliks Dzerzhinsky, Unshlikht was aggressive and a crucial player in preserving and then expanding GPU-OGPU authority and activities, especially in organizing foreign disinformation apparatus; from 1925, TsK member RKP(b); 1925–30, Deputy Commissar for Military and Naval Affairs, USSR; 1933–35, head of civilian shipping administration; 1935, Secretary of Central Executive Committee of Soviets; 1937, arrested. Tried and executed 1938. Rehabilitated.

Voroshilov, Kliment Efremovich (1881–1969). From 1903, member Russian Social Democratic Workers Party, Bolshevik faction; 1921–60, member TsK and then Politburo RKP(b); 1925–34, Commissar of Military and Naval Affairs; 1934–40, Commissar of Defense, USSR, close ally of Stalin; 1940–53, Deputy Chairman, Sovnarkom-Sovmin, and Chairman of Defense Committee of Sovnarkom-Sovmin; 1953–60, Chairman of Presidium of the Supreme Soviet.

Voznesensky, Nikolai Alekseevich (1903–50). 1920s, worked in the Communist Youth League; 1924, entered Party work; 1931–34, taught in the Economic Institute of Red Professors, and simultaneously in Party Control Commission; from 1934, also worked in the Soviet Control Commission; from 1935, worked in the Leningrad Party administration, and from 1937, as Deputy Chairman of the People's Council of Commissars, USSR, in Moscow; from 1939, member of Party TsK, and from 1941, member of the Politburo; 1942–45, member of State Defense Committee; 1942–48, Chairman, Gosplan; from 1943, member of USSR Academy of Sciences; 1949, removed from Gosplan, Politburo, and TsK; arrested for supposed anti-Party activities. Executed 1950. Rehabilitated.

Vrangel', Petr Nikolaevich (1878–1928). Born into a Baltic German noble family; during the Civil War, one of main military and political opponents of the Bolsheviks as commander of White armies in southern Russia; 1920, after evacuation from the Crimea, lived abroad; 1924–28, organizer and leader of the Russian All-Military Union. Died in Brussels.

Vyshinsky, Andrei Yanuar'evich (1883–1954). From 1903, member of Russian
Social Democratic Workers Party, Menshevik faction; 1913, finished
Juridical Faculty, University of Saint Vladimir, Kiev; from 1920, Bolshevik
Party member and made his career within the Soviet judicial and then
Procuracy administration; 1925–28, Rector of Moscow University; 1928,
chief prosecutor in Shakhty trial; 1930, chief prosecutor in the Industrial
Party trial; from 1931, Procurator of the Russian Republic and Deputy
Commissar of Justice; 1935–39, Deputy and then Chief Procurator, USSR;
1939–40, Chairman of Council of People's Commissars; from 1940, Deputy
Commissar of Foreign Affairs; after World War II, worked in diplomatic
apparatus.

Yagoda, Genrikh Grigor'evich (Yenokh Gershenovich) (1891–1938). From
1917, member of Russian Social Democratic Workers Party, Bolshevik
faction; 1917, participated in revolutionary events in Moscow; from 1920,
worked in the Cheka, as deputy head then head of Special Department
administration, and as head of the Secret Operational Department; 1923–29,
Second Deputy Chairman, OGPU; 1929–34, First Deputy Chairman, OGPU;
1934–36, Commissar of Internal Affairs, USSR; 1936–37, Commissar of
Communications, USSR; 1937, arrested. Convicted as member of supposed
"Right Trotskyist Bloc" and executed 1938. Not rehabilitated.

Yakovlev (Epshtein), Yakov Arkad'evich (1896–1938). Born in Poland; from
1913, member of Russian Social Democratic Workers Party; from 1926,
Deputy Commissar, Workers and Peasants Inspectorate; 1929–34, Commissar of Agriculture, USSR, and member of Council of Labor and Defense;
1937, First Secretary of Belorussian Communist Party TsK. Repressed.
Rehabilitated.

Yezhov, Nikolai Ivanovich (1895–1940). From 1917, member of Russian Social
Democratic Workers Party, Bolshevik faction; 1920s, worked in provincial
Party apparatus, and from 1927, in the Party TsK administration; 1929–30,
Deputy Commissar of Agriculture; 1933, designated as head of commission
to purge the Party; from 1934, member of TsK; from 1935, TsK Secretary
and Chairman of Party Control Commission; 1936–38, Commissar of
Internal Affairs, USSR; 1938, Commissar of Water Transport, USSR; 1939,
arrested. Executed 1940. Not rehabilitated.

Zakovsky, Leonid Mikhailovich (Shtubis, Genrikh Ernestovich) (1894–1938).
From 1913, member of Russian Social Democratic Workers Party; during
Civil War, worked as a spy for the Cheka and as a political commissar and
head of several Special Department administrations; 1920s, headed GPU-
OGPU organizations in Siberia and Odessa, and headed the Special Department of the Siberian Military District; 1932, OGPU plenipotentiary in
Belorussia, then head of Belorussian SSR OGPU; 1934–38, headed the
Leningrad UNKVD, and oversaw the purges of Leningrad in 1935 and in
1937–38; 1938, designated Deputy Commissar of Internal Affairs USSR, and
head of State Security Main Administration for Moscow Oblast. Arrested
and executed 1938. Not rehabilitated.

Zhdanov, Andrei (1896–1948). From 1934, First Secretary of Leningrad Party
organization, after the assassination of Sergei Kirov; 1940, in charge of

establishing Soviet government in newly annexed Estonia; during the Great Patriotic War, in charge of the defense of Leningrad; 1938–47, Chairman of RSFSR Supreme Soviet; after the war, led the official campaign against "cosmopolitanism," which signaled a return to cultural isolation, a form of Russianized Bolshevism, anti-Semitism, and a rejection of modernism in its various forms. Died of heart failure in 1948.

Zhemchuzhina, Polina Semenovna (Karpovskaya, Peri Semenovna) (1897–1960). From 1918, member of Bolshevik faction; attended Moscow University and Moscow Economics Institute; worked as regional Party functionary; 1921, married V. Molotov; during 1920s and 1930s, worked in various enterprise administrations; from 1939, Commissar of Fisheries, USSR, and candidate member TsK; from 1942 worked in the Jewish Antifascist Committee, USSR; 1949, arrested for her association with the committee, and especially with Solomon Mikhoels, committee founder and supposedly an anti-Soviet Zionist-nationalist and American spy; exiled to Kustanaisk Oblast; 1953, after Stalin's death, released and rehabilitated.

Zinoviev, Grigorii Evseevich (Radomysl'sky, Ovsei-Gersh Aronovich) (1883–1936). From 1901, member of Russian Social Democratic Workers Party, Bolshevik faction; 1908–17, lived in emigration; participated in revolutionary events in Petrograd; 1912–27, member of Party TsK; 1921–26, member of Politburo; during the 1920s, one of leaders of the "New Opposition" and the "Trotsky-Zinoviev Bloc" against Stalin; 1927 and 1932, expelled from Party for factional activity, then reinstated, and finally expelled in 1934; in the 1930s, worked as an editor of the journal *Bolshevik;* 1935, sentenced to prison as member of supposed "Moscow Center" group; 1936, convicted and executed as organizer of supposed "Anti-Soviet United Trotskyist-Zinovievist Center." Rehabilitated.

Zof, Vyacheslav Ivanovich (1889–1937). From 1913, member of Russian Social Democratic Workers Party, Bolshevik faction; during Civil War and early 1920s, worked in military administration of the Baltic fleet; deputy commander of naval forces of the Russian Republic; in the late 1920s, Deputy Commissar of Water Transport, USSR, and Commissariat of Communications, USSR; 1937, arrested and executed. Rehabilitated.

Documents

1. Note from I. S. Unshlikht to V. M. Molotov on delivery to the Politburo of statutes of the GPU, its province-level and transport departments, and its district-level plenipotentiaries. 6 March 1922. AP RF, f. 3, op. 58, d. 2, ll. 49–62.
2. Decision of the Politburo of TsK RKP(b) [Political Bureau of the Central Committee of the Russian Communist Party (of Bolsheviks)]. On coordination of decisions of the Presidium of VtsIK, related to the State Political Administration, with the Politburo. 15 February 1922. RGASPI, f. 17, op. 3, d. 266, l. 5.
3. Decision of the Politburo of TsK RKP(b). On extraordinary powers of the GPU for struggle against banditry. 27 April 1922. RGASPI, f. 17, op. 3, d. 290. l. 4.
4. Note from I. S. Unshlikht to I. V. Stalin on additions to Statutes of the State Political Administration. 10 May 1922. AP RF, f. 3, op. 58, d. 2, l. 92.
5. Letter of F. E. Dzerzhinsky to I. V. Stalin on the difficult conditions of GPU personnel, with letter from V. N. Mantsev appended. 6 July 1922. RGASPI, f. 76, op. 3, d. 245, ll. 4–5.
6. V. I. Lenin's proposal for a Politburo directive in connection with N. A. Semashko's letter appraising the congress of medical doctors. With a TsK cover letter. 23 May 1922. AP RF, f. 3. Op. 58. d. 2, ll. 3–4.
7. Note from F. E. Dzerzhinsky to the Politburo of TsK RKP(b), with attachment of the GPU report about anti-Soviet groupings among the intelligentsia. 3 June 1922. AP RF, f. 3, op. 58, d. 175, ll. 7–12.
8. Decision of the Politburo of TsK RKP(b). On anti-Soviet groupings among the intelligentsia. 8 June 1922. RGASPI, f. 17, op. 3, d. 296, ll. 2–3.
9. Appendix to Politburo session No. 59, 29.III.23. Protocol of meeting, 22.III.23, on the question of measures to struggle against Mensheviks, in accordance with instructions from the Chair of the GPU, c. Dzerzhinsky. AP RF, f. 3, op. 59, d. 3, ll. 78–80.

10. Decision of the Politburo of the TsK RKP(b) on authority of the GPU. 28 September 1922. AP RF, f. 3, op. 58, d. 2, ll. 99–100.

11. Memorandum of N. V. Krylenko to I. V. Stalin on authority of the GPU to impose extrajudicial sentences. 9 October 1922. AP RF, f. 3, op. 58, d. 2, l. 112.

12. Letter from F. E. Dzerzhinsky to I. V. Stalin on measures against malicious speculators. 22 October 1923. TsA FSB RF, f. 2, op 1, d. 56, l. 99.

13. Memorandum from F. E. Dzerzhinsky to the Politburo of TsK RKP(b) on the necessity to strengthen the struggle against banditry. 29 January 1924. AP RF, f. 3, op. 58, d. 197, l. 78.

14. G. V. Chicherin's memorandum to the Politburo of the TsK RKP(b) concerning c. Dzerzhinsky's recommendations concerning the struggle against banditry. 30 January 1924. AP RF, f. 3, op. 58, d. 197, l. 80.

15. Memorandum of N. V. Krylenko to the Politburo of the TsK RKP(b) concerning F. E. Dzerzhinsky's recommendations on the struggle against banditry. 1 February 1924. AP RF, f. 3, op. 58, d. 197, ll. 79–79ob.

16. Decision of the Politburo of TsK RKP(b). On the struggle against banditry. 14 February 1924. RGASPI, f. 17, op. 3, d. 418, l. 3.

17. Decision of the Politburo of TsK RKP(b). On struggle against thefts in Moscow. 27 June 1924. RGASPI, f. 17, op. 162, d. 2, l. 6.

18. Note from N. V. Krylenko to the Politburo TsK RKP(b) about creating extraordinary courts within the OGPU of the USSR. 1 July 1927. AP RF, f. 3, op. 58, d. 3, l. 113.

19. Memorandum from I. S. Unshlikht to I. V. Stalin and L. D. Trotsky on disinformation. 22 December 1922. AP RF, f. 3, op. 58, d. 2, ll. 131–32.

20. Statement from M. M. Litvinov to I. V. Stalin regarding the bureau of disinformation, with cover letter from the TsK RKP(b). 15 January 1923. AP RF, f. 3, op. 58, d. 2, ll. 135–36.

21. Letter from I. S. Unshlikht and R. A. Pilliar to I. S. Stalin concerning M. M. Litvinov's letter regarding the disinformation bureau. 17 January 1923. AP RF, f. 3, op. 58, d. 2, l. 133.

22. Memorandum from I. S. Unshlikht to I. V. Stalin to concentrate all lines of intelligence activity in the GPU. 28 March 1923. AP RF, f. 3, op. 58, d. 2, l. 140.

23. Memorandum of M. Litvinov to the TsK RKP(b). Late January or early February 1925. RGASPI, f. 76, op. 3, d. 349, l. 2–2ob.

24. Memorandum, F. Dzerzhinsky to M. Trilisser. February 1925. RGASPI, f. 76, op. 3, d. 349, ll. 2–2ob.

25. Note from F. E. Dzerzhinsky to I. V. Stalin with the suggestion to include V. R. Menzhinsky on the Board of NKID. 23 May 1925. RGASPI, f. 76, op. 3, d. 349, l. 3.

26. Memorandum from V. I. Zof to L. D. Trotsky. 15 October 1922. AP RF, f. 3, op. 58, d. 2, l. 117.

27. Memorandum from L. D. Trotsky to F. Dzerzhinsky. 15 October 1922. AP RF, f. 3, op. 58, d. 2, ll. 114–15.

28. Memorandum from F. Dzerzhinsky to L. D. Trotsky. 17 October 1922. AP RF, f. 3, op. 58, d. 2, ll. 121–22.

29. Note from L. D. Trotsky to the Secretariat of TsK related to the Morved case, in connection with F. E. Dzerzhinsky's answer. 17 October 1922. AP RF, f. 3, op. 58, d. 2, ll. 121–22.
30. Decision of the Politburo of TsK RKP(b). On work of the GPU. 26 October 1922. RGASPI, f. 17, op. 3, d. 17, l. 4.
31. Memorandum of F. E. Dzerzhinsky to I. V. Stalin on the reasons for not sending a report on GPU activities for May 1922. 6 July 1922. RGASPI, f. 76, op. 3, d. 253, l. 1.
32. From the decision of the Politburo of TsK VKP(b) on security of factories of the military industry. 3 March 1927. RGASPI, f. 17, op. 162, d. 4 l. 70.
33. Decision of the Politburo of TsK VKP(b) on measures of struggle against subversive actions. 31 March 1927. RGASPI, f. 17, op. 162, d. 4, ll. 89, 94–96.
34. Coded telegram from I. V. Stalin to V. M. Molotov on hardening punitive measures in relation to the murder of the plenipotentiary of the USSR to Poland P. L. Voikov. 8 June 1927. RGASPI, f. 558, op. 11, d. 71, ll. 2–3.
35. Decision of the Politburo of the TsK VKP(b). On measures in connection with White Guardist actions. 8 June 1927. RGASPI, f. 17, op. 162, d. 5, l. 35.
36. Coded telegram from I. V. Stalin to V. P. Menzhinsky on tasks of the OGPU. 23 June 1927. RGASPI, f. 558, op. 11, d. 71, l. 29.
37. Decision of the Politburo of TsK VKP(b) following c. M[enzhinsky]'s information. 30 June 1927. RGASPI, f. 17, op. 162, d. 5, l. 55.
38. Answer of I. V. Stalin to foreign worker delegates on the role and place of the GPU in the Soviet state. 5 November 1927.
39. Decision of the Politburo of TsK VKP(b) on the Shakhty case. On arrests of Germans. 8 March 1928. RGASPI, f. 17, op. 162, d. 6, ll. 37–38.
40. Special communication from G. G. Yagoda to I. V. Stalin on the counter-revolutionary organization in the Donugol system [The Don Basin Coal Administration]. 12 March 1928. AP RF, f. 3, op. 58, d. 328, ll. 20–25.
41. Memorandum from L. M. Kaganovich to I. V. Stalin on investigation of economic counterrevolution in the Donbass. 26 April 1928. AP RF, f. 3, op. 58, d. 329, ll. 28–31.
42. Decision of the Politburo commission of TsK VKP(b). On the Shakhty case. 11 April 1928. AP RF, f. 3, op. 58, d. 329, ll. 10–12.
43. Memorandum from Ya. Rudzutak to the Politburo of the TsK (VKP(b) on purging specialists working in Moscow factories. 1 June 1928. AP RF, f. 3, op. 58, d. 332, l. 27.
44. Decision of the Politburo of the TsK VKP(b). On specialists. 2 August 1928. RGASPI, f. 17, op. 162, d. 6, l. 118.
45. Memorandum from I. V. Stalin to members and candidate members of the Politburo of the TsK VKP(b) on the case of the group of specialists in military industries. 12 May 1928. AP RF, f. 45, op. 1, d. 170, l. 40.
46. Memorandum from I. V. Stalin to members and candidate members of the Politburo, TsK secretaries, and members of the TsKK Presidium, with appended report by the OGPU on wrecking in railroad transport. 16 June 1928. AP RF, f. 3, op. 58, d. 372, ll. 25–41.

47. Decision of the Politburo of TsK VKP(b). On the work of INO OGPU [Foreign Department of the OGPU]. 5 February 1930. AP RF, f. 3, op. 50, d. 32, l. 115.

48. Letter from I. V. Stalin to V. R. Menzhinsky on future directions of testimony of the leaders of the TKP [Labor-Peasant Party] and of the Promparty [Industrial Party]. October 1930. TsA FSB RF, f. 2, op. 9, d. 388, ll. 270–71.

49. Decision of the Politburo of TsK VKP(b). On use of the wreckers' depositions about intervention. 25 October 1930. RGASPI, f. 17, op. 162, d. 9, l. 53.

50. Decision of the Politburo of TsK VKP(b). On the trial of the Promparty. 25 November 1930. RGASPI, f. 17, op. 162, d. 9, l. 81.

51. Proposal of the commission on the case of the Promparty. 25 November 1930. RGASPI, f. 17, op. 162, d. 9, ll. 81–82.

52. Decision of the Politburo of TsK VKP(b). On kulak terror. 26 September 1929. RGASPI, f. 17, op. 162, d. 7, l. 158.

53. Note telegraphed from Tiflis, from S. F. Redens to G. G. Yagoda, with TsK cover letter to members and candidate members of the Politburo of TsK VKP(b) and of the Presidium of TsKK. 11 March 1930. AP RF, f. 3, op. 30, d. 146, ll. 74–77.

54. Decision of the Politburo of TsK VKP(b). On Ukraine and Belorussia. 15 March 1930. AP RF, f. 3, op. 30, d. 193, l. 154a.

55. Note from G. G. Yagoda and G. E. Evdokimov to I. V. Stalin on political moods in Siberia in connection with collectivization and dekulakization. 20 March 1930. AP RF, f. 3, op. 30, d. 147, ll. 117–23.

56. Telegram from M. O. Razumov, first secretary of Tatar *Obkom* [oblast committee] of VKP(b) to the Secretariat of TsK VKP(b) regarding peasant riots. 22 March 1930. AP RF, f. 3, op. 30, d. 146, ll. 124–25.

57. Report from G. G. Yagoda and E. G. Evdokimov on counterrevolutionary activity in the Didoevsk District of Andiisk Okrug, Dagestan. 4 April 1930. AP RF, f. 3, op. 30, d. 147, ll. 15–17.

58. Coded telegram from M. M. Malinov to I. V. Stalin regarding mass peasant demonstrations. 1 March 1931. AP RF, f. 3, op. 58, d. 200, l. 132.

59. Decision of the Politburo of TsK RKP(b). On increasing the number of OGPU employees. 10 August 1930. RGASPI, f. 17, op. 162, d. 9, ll. 16, 20.

60. Regarding kulaks. (PB from 11.III.31, protocol No. 29, point 2/6-c). (cc. Andreev, Yagoda, Postyshev.) 25 March 1931. RGASPI, f. 17, op. 162, d. 9, l. 174, 176–78.

61. Special report from G. G. Yagoda to I. V. Stalin on completion of kulak exile operation. 15 October 1931. AP RF, f. 3, op. 30, d. 195, l. 163.

62. Report of V. M. Burmistrov to Commissar of Justice, Siberian Territory, Yanson. 7 January 1930. GANO, f. 47, op. 5, d. 104, l. 10.

63. Extract of report of the USSR Procuracy to the Presidium of TsIK [Central Executive Committee] USSR on supervision of the OGPU for 1931. 20 December 1931. GARF, f. 8131, op. 37, d. 20, ll. 50–51.

64. Protocol of the Andreev Commission from 15 May 1931, on organization of a *Spetspereselenie* Administration, and on productive use of special settlers. RGASPI, f. 17, op. 162, d. 10, ll. 46, 51–54.

65. Regarding a special plenipotentiary representative of the OGPU in Ukraine. 25 November 1932. RGASPI, f. 17, op. 3, d. 907, l. 20.

66. Sabotage of grain collection in Orekhovo region of Ukraine. 7 December 1932. AP RF, f. 3, op. 58, d. 380, ll. 94–97.

67. Special communication from G. G. Yagoda to I. V. Stalin on operations to cleanse areas along the western border of the USSR. 26 March 1933. AP RF, f. 3, op. 58, d. 201, ll. 75–87.

68. Memorandum from G. G. Yagoda on cadre conditions of the GUGB NKVD and cadre dynamics for the period 1.VII.31 to 1.I.35. GARF, f. 9401, op. 8, d. 41, ll. 11–37.

69. Letter of I. V. Stalin to L. Kaganovich. 4 August 1932. RGASPI, f. 17, op. 3, d. 896, l. 260.

70. V. R. Menzhinsky's report to I. V. Stalin on the struggle against hooliganism, homeless children, and theft on transportation. 31 August 1932. TsA FSB RF, f. 2, op. 10, d. 145, ll. 3–7.

71. Extract of letter from I. V. Stalin to L Kaganovich, 15 July 1932.

72. Instructions on implementing the law on protection of socialist property (PB from 8.IX.32, pr[otocol]. No. 115, p[oint]. 5). 16 September 1932. AP RF, f. 3, op. 57, d. 60, ll. 13–.

73. Memorandum of G. E. Prokof'ev and L. G. Mironov to I. V. Stalin on the number of those prosecuted by the OGPU for theft of public property. 20 March 1933. AP RF, f. 45, op. 1, d. 171, ll. 87–89.

74. TsK VKP(b) and SNK USSR directive on prevention of mass departure of starving peasants. 22 January 1933. RGASPI, f. 558, op. 11, d. 45, ll. 109–1090b.

75. Report of G. E. Prokof'ev to I. V. Stalin on measures taken in the struggle against mass departures from Ukraine and SKK [North Caucasus], with attached notes by V. A. Balitsky and E. G. Evdokimov. 23 January 1933. AP RF, f. 3, op. 30, d. 189, ll. 3–10.

76. Memorandum from G. G. Yagoda to I. V. Stalin on results of operational measures to curb mass flight of peasants. 17 February 1933. AP RF, f. 3, op. 30, d. 189, ll. 36–37.

77. Memorandum from G. G. Yagoda and M. D. Berman to I. V. Stalin on the organization of special settlements. 13 February 1933. AP RF, f. 3, op. 30, d. 196, ll. 127–38.

78. Directive-instructions of the TsK VKP(b) and SNK USSR on cessation of mass exile of peasants, regulating arrests, and reducing prison populations. 8 May 1933. AP RF, f. 3, op. 30, d. 196, ll. 163–1630b.

79. Decision of the Politburo of the TsK VKP(b). 20 March 1933. RGASPI, f. 17, op. 162, d. 14, l. 96.

80. Memorandum from N. I. Krylenko to I. V. Stalin, V. M. Molotov, D. E. Sulimov, G. G. Yagoda, and A. Ya. Vyshinsky on the illegality of OGPU instructions. 14 July 1933. AP RF, f. 3, op. 57, d. 60, l. 55.

81. OGPU circular on organizational and operational measures in connection with passportization. 21 May 1933. GARF, f. 9401, op. 12, d. 137, document 46 (l. 200).

82. OGPU Order No. 009. On Chekist measures to introduce the passport system. 5 January 1933. GARF, f. 9401, op. 12, d. 137, doc. 1.

83. OGPU circular on the use of measures of extrajudicial repression in relation to citizens violating the law on passportization of the population. 13 August 1933. GARF, f. 9401, op. 12, d. 137, ll. 202–4.
84. Memorandum from G. E. Prokof'ev and L. G. Mironov to I. V. Stalin on the number of those "brought in" [subjected to *privod*] for speculation, as of 1 April, by OGPU organs. 2 April 1933. AP RF, f. 45, op. 1, d. 171, l. 90.
85. Decision of the Politburo TsK VKP(b). On the struggle against criminal and déclassé elements in the city of Moscow. 20 January 1934. RGASPI, f. 17, op. 162, d. 15, l. 161.
86. Decision of the Politburo TsK VKB(b). On deportation from Kharkov Oblast of the déclassé element. 20 January 1934. RGASPI, f. 17, op. 162, d. 15, l. 164.
87. Decision of the Politburo TsK VKP(b). On measures of struggle against hooliganism and train wrecks on railroads. 9 June 1934. RGASPI, f. 17, op. 3, d. 946, l. 65.
88. Memorandum from G. G. Yagoda to I. V. Stalin requesting confirmation of the statute of the NKVD USSR and the Special Board. 24 August 1934. AP RF, f. 3, op. 58, d. 4, ll. 60–77.
89. Report from St. Kosior to I. V. Stalin on strengthening border zones. 23 December 1934. AP RF, f. 3, op. 58, d. 130, ll. 162–66.
90. Report from P. P. Postyshev to I. V. Stalin on the need to resettle counter-revolutionary elements. 31 July 1935. AP RF f. 3, op. 58, d. 131, ll. 106–7.
91. Note from G. G. Yagoda and A. Ya. Vyshinsky to Stalin. 20 April 1935. AP RF, f. 3, op. 58, d. 158, l. 150. Published in Istochnik 6/1997, p. 109.
92. NKVD Order 00192: Instructions to NKVD troikas for reviewing cases of criminals and déclassé elements, and on malicious violations of passport laws. 9 May 1935. GARF, f. 8131, op. 38, d. 6, ll. 62–64.
93. From a circular letter of the NKVD USSR to all local organs of the Commissariat. January 1935. AP RF f. 3, op. 58, d. 51, ll. 15, 18, 19.
94. Special report from G. G. Yagoda to I. V. Stalin regarding a counterrevolutionary group in the Kremlin. 20 January 1935. AP RF, f. 3, op. 58, d. 231, ll. 1, 14.
95. Note from Ya. S. Agranov to I. V. Stalin regarding more arrests among personnel in the Kremlin. 2 February 1935. AP RF, f. 3, op. 58, d. 231, ll. 15–17.
96. Report from G. G. Yagoda to I. V. Stalin on the course of investigation of the Kremlin case. 5 February 1935. AP RF, f. 3, op. 58, d. 231, ll. 22–26.
97. Letter of Ya. S. Agranov to I. V. Stalin with appended protocol of interrogation of L. B. Kamenev (Kremlin case). 21 March 1935. AP RF, f. 3, op. 58, d. 234, l. 1.
98. Protocol of interrogation of Kamenev, Lev Borisovich, from 20 March 1935. AP RF, f. 3, op. 58, d. 234, ll. 1–6.
99. Decision of the Politburo of TsK VKP(b). On the apparatus of TsIK USSR and c. Enukidze. 3 April 1935. AP RF, f. 3, op. 58, d. 234, ll. 47–53.
100. Report of L. G. Mironov to I. V. Stalin and N. I. Yezhov about results of operational actions of the Tatar Republic UNKVD in connection with

verification of Party documents [membership cards]. 15 February 1936. TsA FSB RF, f. 3, op. 3, d. 62, ll. 144–76.

101. Coded telegram from I. V. Stalin to members of the Politburo of TsK of VKP(b) on appointment of N. Yezhov as Commissar of Internal Affairs. 25 September 1936.

102. Decision of the Politburo of Tsk VKP(b). On deprivation of decorations of former executives of the Narkomat of Internal Affairs of the USSR. 1 June 1937. RGASPI, f. 17, op. 3, d. 987, ll. 100–101.

103. Memorandum of M. P. Frinovsky to I. V. Stalin on V. A. Balitsky's statement. 21 July 1937. AP RF, f. 3, op. 24, d. 316, ll. 8–12.

104. Decision of the Politburo of the TsK VKP(b). On anti-Soviet elements. 2 July 1937. AP RF, f. 3, op. 58, d. 212, l. 32.

105. Decision of the Politburo of the TsK VKP(b). On anti-Soviet elements. 5 July 1937. AP RF, f. 3, op. 58, d. 212, l. 33.

106. Decision of the Politburo of the TsK VKP(b). On anti-Soviet elements. 9 July 1937. AP RF, f. 3, op. 58, d. 212, l. 34.

107. Report of S. N. Mironov, Head of the UNKVD [local NKVD administration] of the West-Siberian Territory to the kraikom VKP(b). On the case of a S-R [Socialist-Revolutionary]-monarchist conspiracy in Western Siberia. 17 June 1937. GANO, f. R-4, op. 34, d. 26, ll. 1–3.

108. Coded telegram from A. S. Zimin to I. V. Stalin on "insurgency" groups in Yaroslavl Oblast. 16 July 1937. RGASPI, f. 558, op. 11, d. 65, l. 53.

109. Memorandum from M. I. Frinovsky to the Politburo TsK VKP(b) with appended Operational Order NKVD USSR No. 00447. 30 July 1937. AP RF, f. 3, op. 58, d. 212, ll. 55, 59–78.

110. Decision of the Politburo of the TsK (VKPb). On the question of the NKVD. 31 July 1937. AP RF, f. 3, op. 58, d. 212, ll. 52–54.

111. Coded telegram from G. F. Gorbach to N. I. Yezhov on increasing the limit for the "kulak" operation in Omsk Oblast. 15 August 1937. AP RF, f. 3, op. 58, d. 212, l. 87b.

112. Decision of the Politburo of the TsK VKP(b). On the NKVD, with appended draft for Operational Order No. 00593. 19 September 1937. AP RF, f. 3, op. 58, d. 254, ll. 223–28.

113. Report of January 26 1938 from Procuracy transport investigator of the 5th Kirov railroad, Vorob'ev, to Deputy Procurator of the Kirov railroad, Shapiro. GARF, f. 8131, op. 37, d. 69, ll. 8–10, 114.

114. Memorandum from I. V. Stalin to N. I. Yezhov concerning SRs. 17 January 1938. AP RF, f. 3, op. 24, d. 330, l. 18.

115. Decision of the Politburo of the TsK VKP(b). On anti-Soviet elements. 31 January 1938. AP RF, f. 3, op. 58, d. 212, ll. 155–56.

116. Decision of the Politburo of the TsK VKP(b). On continuing repression among populations according to their nationality. 31 January 1938. AP RF, f. 3, op. 58, d. 254a, l. 90.

117. Decision of the Politburo of the TsK VKP(b). On refugees. 31 January 1938. AP RF, f. 3, op. 58, d. 6, l. 53.

118. Coded telegram from Ia. A. Popok to I. V. Stalin regarding an additional limit for review of cases of anti-Soviet elements. 2 February 1938. RGASPI, f. 558, op. 11, d. 65, l. 108.

119. Coded telegram from Iu. M. Kaganovich to I. V. Stalin and N. I. Yezhov on increasing the limit for Gorky Oblast. 4 February 1938. AP RF, f. 3, op. 58, d. 212, l. 158.
120. Decision of the Politburo of the TsK VKP(b). On the question of the NKVD. 17 February 1938. AP RF, f. 3, op. 58, d. 212, l. 161.
121. Special communication from N. I. Yezhov to I. V. Stalin with appended copy of telegram by S. I. Lebedev on progress of the foreign nationalities operations. 24 March 1938. AP RF, f. 3, op. 58, d. 254, ll. 200–205.
122. Decision of the Politburo of the TsK VKP(b). On the question of the NKVD. 26 May 1938. AP RF, f. 3, op. 58, d. 212, l. 177.
123. Decision of the Politburo of the TsK VKP(b). On arrests, procuratorial supervision, and the conduct of investigations. 17 November 1938. RGASPI, f. 17, op. 3, d. 1003, ll. 85–87.
124. Letter from N. I. Yezhov to the Politburo TsK VKP(b) [and to] I. V. Stalin. 23 November 1938. RGASPI, f. 17, op. 3, d. 1003, ll. 82–84.
125. Coded telegram from I. V. Stalin to Party organ leaders on the unsatisfactory situation in the NKVD. 25 November 1938. RGASPI, f. 558, op. 11, d. 58, l. 61.
126. I. V. Stalin's note to A. Ya. Vyshinsky on organizing public trials of NKVD officials. 3 January 1939. AP RF, f. 3, op. 57, d. 96, l. 110.
127. From the decision of Politburo TsK VKP(b) on the work of the Bashkir Obkom [Oblast Committee] of the VKP(b). 9 January 1939. RGASPI, f. 17, op. 3, d. 1005, ll. 12–13.
128. Coded telegram from I. V. Stalin to secretaries of obkoms, kraikoms and to the leadership of the NKVD-UNKVD [local NKVD administrations] on using measures of physical coercion in relation to "enemies of the people." 10 January 1939. AP RF, f. 3, op. 58, d. 6, ll. 145–46.
129. Special communication from L. P. Beria and A. Ya. Vyshinsky to I. V. Stalin on removal of criminal records of those people who had been convicted by extrajudicial organs of the NKVD USSR, with appended draft of the decree of the Supreme Council of the USSR. 5 February 1939. AP RF, f. 3, op. 58, d. 212, ll. 207–9.
130. Special communication from L. P. Beria, A. Ya. Vyshinsky and N. M. Rychkov [Commissar of Justice] to I. V. Stalin, with a draft order appended about implementation of the decision of SNK USSR and TsK VKP(b) of 17 November 1938, on arrests, procuratorial supervision, and conducting investigations. 21 February 1939. AP RF, f. 3, op. 58, d. 6, ll. 172–75.
131. Decision of the Politburo of the TsK VKP(b). On bringing to trial members of the Right-Trotskyist organization. 16 February 1939. AP RF, f. 3, op. 24, d. 373, l. 1.
132. Decision of the Politburo of the TsK VKP(b). On conviction of counter-revolutionary elements. 8 April 1939. RGASPI, f. 17, op. 162, d. 25, l. 7.
133. Special communication of L. P. Beria to I. V. Stalin with appended statement by L. S. Frinovsky. 13 April 1939. RGASPI, f. 17, op. 3, d. 1009, l. 34.
134. Memorandum from L. P. Beria to I. V. Stalin regarding N. I. Yezhov, with appended protocol of interrogation. 27 April 1939. AP RF, f. 3, op. 24, d. 375, ll. 122–64.

135. Note from A. Ya. Vyshinsky to I. V. Stalin on violations of arrest procedures. 31 May 1939. AP RF, f. 3, op. 58, d. 6, l. 185.
136. Note of A. Ya. Vyshinsky to I. V. Stalin regarding the Special Board of the NKVD USSR. 31 May 1939. RGANI, f. 89, op. 18, d. 2, l. 1.
137. Decision of the Politburo of the TsK VKP(b). On camps of the NKVD USSR. 10 June 1939. RGASPI, f. 17, op. 162, d. 25, ll. 54–55.
138. Decision of the Politburo of the TsK VKP(b). On securing a labor force for work carried out by the NKVD USSR in 1939. 16 June 1939. RGASPI, f. 17, op. 3, d. 1011, l. 4.
139. Circular of NKVD USSR, the Procuracy of the USSR, and Narkomiust USSR on investigative work. 25 July 1939. AP RF, f. 3, op. 58, d. 7, ll. 18–.
140. Special communication from L. P. Beria to I. V. Stalin on results of the operation to remove *osadniki* and forest guards from the western oblasts of Ukraine and Belorussia. 12 February 1940. AP RF, f. 3, op. 30, d. 199, ll. 50–51.
141. From the decision of the Politburo of TsK VKP(b) on resettlement of citizens of foreign nationalities from the city of Murmansk and the Murmansk Oblast. 23 June 1940. RGASPI, f. 17, op. 162, d. 27, ll. 166–67.
142. Report of L. P. Beria to I. V. Stalin on imprisoned Polish military and police personnel. 5 March 1940. RGASPI, f. 17, op. 166, d. 621, ll. 130–33.
143. Decision of the Politburo of the TsK VKP(b). On removal of counterrevolutionary organizations in the western oblasts of the UkSSR. 14 May 1941. RGASPI, f. 17, op. 162, d. 34, l. 156.
144. Special communication from V. N. Merkulov [then head of the NKGB] to I. V. Stalin regarding the results of the operation to arrest and remove "anti-Soviet" elements from the western oblasts of Belorussia. 21 June 1941. RGANI, f. 89, op. 18, d. 7, ll. 1–3.
145. Draft of a decision of TsK VKP(b) on reorganization of the Commissariat of Internal Affairs of the USSR. January 1941. RGASPI, f. 17, op. 163, d. 1295, ll. 103–6, 109.
146. Resolution of the GKO [State Committee of Defense] approving the operational and administrative charter of the GUKR [Main Administration of Counterintelligence] "Smersh" of the NKO [People's Commissariat of Defense] USSR. 21 April 1943.
147. Report of S. R. Milshtein to L. P. Beria on the number of arrested and executed military personnel who were separated from their units and fled from the front. October 1941. RGANI, f. 89, op. 18, d. 8, ll. 1–3.
148. Special communication of L. P. Beria to I. V. Stalin with appended draft of a decision of the SNK USSR and TsK VKP(b) about procedures for resettling Germans from the Republic of Germans of the Volga Region, Saratov Oblast, and Stalingrad Oblast. 25 August 1941. AP RF, f. 3, op. 58, d. 178, ll. 6–9.
149. Special communication of L. P. Beria to I. V. Stalin and V. M. Molotov on conducting the resettlement operation of people of the Kalmyk nationality. 3 January 1944. GARF, f. 9401 s/ch [secret section], op. 2, d. 64, l. 1.
150. Telegram of L. P. Beria to I. V. Stalin regarding preparations for the eviction of Chechens and Ingush. 17 February 1944. GARF, f. 9401 s/ch, op. 2, d. 64, l. 167.

151. Special communication of L. P. Beria to I. V. Stalin, V. M. Molotov, and G. M. Malenkov regarding work of operational-Chekist groups in cleansing the Crimean ASSR [Autonomous Soviet Socialist Republic]. 1 May 1944. GARF, f. 9401 s/ch, op. 2, d. 64, ll. 385–89.
152. Special communication from L. P. Beria to I. V. Stalin on the expediency of removing Bulgarians, Greeks, and Armenians from the territory of Crimea. 29 May 1944. GARF, f. 9401s, op. 2, d. 65, ll. 161–63.
153. Special communication of L. P. Beria to I. V. Stalin on removal of *spetspereselentsy* [special resettlers] from the Crimea. 4 July 1944. GARF, f. 9401s, op. 2, d. 65, l. 275.
154. Special communication of L. P. Beria to I. V. Stalin, V. M. Molotov, and G. M. Malenkov on the conduct of Chekist-military operations to liquidate armed groups of the OUN. 5 August 1944. GARF, f. 9401 s/ch, op. 2, d. 66, ll. 130–31.
155. Special communication from L. P. Beria to I. V. Stalin, V. M. Molotov, and G. M. Malenkov on the struggle against the "anti-Soviet" underground in the Belorussian SSR. 12 December 1944. GARF, f. 9401 s/ch, op. 2, d. 68, ll. 103–7.
156. Special communication from L. P. Beria to I. V. Stalin, V. M. Molotov, and G. M. Malenkov on results of work to liquidate bandit formations in 1944. 14 March 1945. GARF, f. 9401 s/ch, op. 2, d. 94, ll. 39–40.
157. Special communication from L. P. Beria to I. V. Stalin on cleansing the rear area of Red Army operations. 17 April 1945. RGANI, f. 89, op. 75, d. 5, ll. 1–3.
158. Special communication from L. P. Beria to I. V. Stalin, V. M. Molotov, and G. M. Malenkov on the work of filtration points for Soviet citizens. 2 January 1945. GARF, f. 9401 s/ch, op. 2, d. 92, ll. 6–8.
159. Special communication from L. P. Beria to I. V. Stalin, V. M. Molotov, and G. M. Malenkov on the course of struggle against an armed underground in the western oblasts of Belorussia. 17 September 1945. GARF, f. 9401 s/ch, op. 2, d. 99, ll. 167–69.
160. Liquidation of anti-Soviet nationalist organizations and gangs linked to them, as well as of others of the anti-Soviet element, on the territory of the Western Oblast of Ukraine SSR, 1944–47. GARF, f. 9478, op. 1, d. 764 ll. 1–15.
161. From a special communication of V. S. Abakumov to I. V. Stalin on the work of state security organs of the UkSSR to liquidate anti-Soviet church-sectarian groups. 30 November 1950. TsA FSB RF, f. 40s, op. 8, d. 11, ll. 354–62.
162. Decision of Politburo TsK VKP(b). On organizing trials of American and English agents. 23 October 1950. RGASPI, f. 17, op. 162, d. 44, l. 132.
163. Decision of the Politburo of the TsK VKP(b). On assistance to organs of state security of the People's Republic of China. 6 November 1950. RGASPI, f. 17, op. 162, d. 44, l. 138.
164. Decision of the Politburo of the TsK VKP(b). On sending MGB advisers to Czechoslovakia. 21 December 1950. RGASPI, f. 17, op. 162, d. 45, l. 16.

165. Special communication from V. S. Abakumov to I. V. Stalin on arrests in the city of Leningrad and the Leningrad Oblast. 14 January 1950. TsA FSB RF, f. 40s, op. 8, d. 1, l. 124.

166. Special communication from V. S. Abakumov to I. V. Stalin on the need for expulsion of the unreliable element from the city of Leningrad and the Leningrad Oblast. 14 January 1950. TsA FSB RF, f. 40s, op. 8, d. 1. 125–27.

167. From special communication from V. S. Abakumov to I. V. Stalin on replacement of UMGB officials of the Leningrad Oblast. 10 January 1950. TsA FSB RF, f. 40s, op. 8, d. 1, ll. 61–62.

168. Special communication from S. D. Ignat'ev to I. V. Stalin on preparations for the operation of removing hostile elements from Georgia. 27 November 1951. AP RF, f. 3, op. 58, d. 179, ll. 93–97.

169. Decision of the Bureau of the Council of Ministers of the USSR on dissolution of the Jewish Antifascist Committee. 21 November 1948. RGASPI, f. 558, op. 11, d. 183, l. 51.

170. Note from M. F. Shkiryatov and V. S. Abakumov to I. V. Stalin regarding P. S. Zhemchuzhina. 27 December 1948. RGASPI, f. 589, op. 3, d. 6188, ll. 25–31.

171. Special communication from S. D. Ignat'ev to I. V. Stalin on an agent-parachutist, F. K. Sarantsev. 11 September 1951. AP RF, f. 3, op. 58, d. 263, ll. 62–63.

172. Decision of Politburo of the TsK VKP(b). On search for and detention of agents-parachutists. 11 November 1951. RGASPI, f. 17, op. 162, d. 47, ll. 18, 118–.

173. Special communication from V. S. Abakumov to I. V. Stalin on arrests of Russian emigrants in China. 16 November 1950. AP RF, f. 3, op. 58, d. 285, l. 90.

174. Statement of a senior inspector of the MGB USSR, M. D. Riumin, to I. V. Stalin. 2 July 1951. AP RF, f. 3, op, 58, d. 216, ll. 8–11.

175. Decision of TsK VKP(b). On shortcomings in the Ministry of State Security of the USSR. 11 July 1951. AP RF, f. 3, op. 58, d. 216, ll. 2–7.

176. From the decision of the TsK KPSS [Communist Party of the Soviet Union, replacing VKP(b)] on the situation in the MGB. 4 December 1952. AP RF, f. 3, op. 22, d. 12, ll. 6–7.

177. Special communication from S. Ignat'ev to I. V. Stalin, with appended draft of the indictment in the case of Abakumov-Shvartsman. 17 February 1953. AP RF f 3, op. 58, d. 222, ll. 203–43.

Notes

INTRODUCTION

1. Stuart Finkel, "An Intensification of Vigilance: Recent Perspectives on the Institutional History of the Soviet Security Apparatus in the 1920s," *Kritika: Explorations in Russian and Eurasian History* 5, no. 2 (Spring 2004): 299–320.
2. For example, V. N. Khaustov, V. P. Naumov, and N. S. Plotnikova, *Lubianka: Stalin i VChK-GPU-OGPU-NKVD, ianvar' 1932–dekabr' 1936* (Moscow, 2004).
3. There is a limited but rich literature on the history of the Cheka and the Soviet political and security police. On the Cheka, see: O. I. Kapchinskii, "VChK: Organizatsionnaia struktura i kadrovyi sostav, 1917–1922" (Candidate diss., Moscow State Pedagogical University, 2005); George Leggett, *The Cheka: Lenin's Political Police* (New York, 1986); S. P. Mel'gunov, *Krasnyi terror v Rossii, 1918–1923* (Moscow, 1990), translated as *The Red Terror in Russia* (London, 1995); A. A. Plekhanov and A. M. Plekhanov, *Vserossiiskaia chrezvychainaia komissiia SNK (7 (20) dekabria 1917–6 fevralia 1922): Kratkii spravochnik* (Moscow, 2011); Igor Simbirtsev, *VChK v leninskoi Rossii, 1917–1922* (Moscow, 2008); V. Vinogradov and N. Peremyshlennikova, eds., *Arkhiv VChK: Sbornik dokumentov* (Moscow, 2007); M. A. Iakovlev, *MChK: Moskovskaia chrezvychainaia komissiia* (Moscow, 2011). For the most comprehensive history of the Soviet political police, see V. M. Chebrikov, *Istoriia Sovetskikh organov gosudarstvennoi bezopasnosti: Uchebnik* (Moscow, 1977); O. I. Cherdakov, *Formirovanie pravookhranitel'noi sistemy Sovetskogo gosudarstva v 1917–1936 gg.: Istoriko-pravovoe issledovanie* (Saratov, 2001); Paul Gregory, *Terror by Quota: State Security from Lenin to Stalin (an Archival Study)* (New Haven, 2009); V. N. Khaustov, V. P. Naumov, and N. S. Plotnikova, *Lubianka, Stalin i VChK-GPU-OGPU-NKVD, ianvar' 1922–dekabr' 1936* (Moscow, 2003); V. N. Khaustov, V. P. Naumov, and N. S. Plotnikova, *Lubianka: Stalin i Glavnoe upravlenie gosbezopastnosti NKVD. Arkhiv Stalina. Dokumenty vysshikh organov partiinoi i gosudarstvennoi*

345

vlasti, 1937–1938 (Moscow, 2004); V. N. Khaustov, V. P. Naumov, and N. S. Plotnikova, *Lubianka: Stalin i NKVD-NKGB-GUKR "Smersh," 1939–mart 1946* (Moscow, 2006); V. N. Khaustov, V. P. Naumov, and N. S. Plotnikova, *Lubianka: Stalin i MGB SSSR, mart 1946–mart 1953. Dokumenty* (Moscow, 2007); V. S. Izmozik, *Glaza i ushi rezhima: Gosudarstvennyi politicheskii kontrol za naseleniem Sovetskoi Rossii v 1918–1928 godakh* (Moscow, 1995); O. B. Mozokhin, *Pravo na repressii: Vnesudebnie polnomochiia organov gosudarstvennoi bezopasnosti. Statisticheskie svedeniia o deiatel'nosti VChK-OGPU-NKVD-MGB SSSR, 1918–1953* (Moscow, 2011); Michael Parrish, *The Lesser Terror: Soviet State Security, 1939–1953* (Westport, 1996); L. P. Rasskazov, *Karatel'nye organy v protsesse formirovaniia administrativno-komandnoi sistemy v Sovetskom gosudarstve, 1917–1941 gg.* (Ufa, 1994); Nicolas Werth and Alexis Berelowitch, *L'État soviétique contre les paysans: Rapports secrets de la police politique. Tcheka, GPU, NKVD, 1918–1939* (Paris, 2011). For a major collection in Ukrainian, see Iurii Shapoval, Volodymyr Prystaiko, and Vadym Zolotar'ov, *ChK—HPU—NKVD v Ukraïni: Osoby, fakty, dokumenty* (Kiev, 1997).

4. Donald Rayfield, "The Exquisite Inquisitor: Viacheslav Menzhinsky as Poet and Hangman," *Slavonic Journeys Across Two Hemispheres: Festschrift in Honour of Arnold McMillin,* special issue of *New Zealand Slavonic Journal* 37 (2003): 91–109.

5. For biographies of the various heads of the political police and state security forces see: Donald Rayfield, *Stalin and His Hangmen: The Tyrant and Those Who Killed for Him* (New York, 2005); Nikita Petrov and Marc Jansen, *Stalin's Loyal Executioner: People's Commissar Nikolai Ezhov, 1895–1940* (Stanford, 2002); Michael Parrish, *The Lesser Terror: Soviet State Security, 1939–1953* (New York, 1996); J. Arch Getty and Oleg V. Naumov, *Yezhov: The Rise of Stalin's "Iron Fist"* (New Haven, 2008); Amy Knight, *Beria: Stalin's First Lieutenant* (New Brunswick, 1993); A. N. Iakovlev, ed., *Lavrentii Beriia: 1953 g. Stenogramma iul'skogo plenuma TsK KPSS i drugie dokumenty* (Moscow, 1999); B. V. Sokolov, *Beriia: Sud'ba vsesil'nogo narkoma* (Moscow, 2011); N. V. Petrov and K. V. Skorkin, *Kto rukovodil NKVD, 1934–1941: Spravochnik* (Moscow, 1999).

6. OGPU was the name of the political police until late 1934, when it was incorporated into the Commissariat of the Interior, the NKVD. On collectivization, see the monumental document collection V. Danilov, R. Manning, and L. Viola, eds., *Tragediia sovetskoi derevni: Kollektivizatsiia i razkulachivanie. Dokumenty i materialy v 5 tomakh, 1927–1939,* 5 vols. in 6 (Moscow, 1999–2004). In English, the most comprehensive account of collectivization is in Lynne Viola, *Peasant Rebels under Stalin: Collectivization and the Culture of Resistance* (New York, 1996), and Lynne Viola, V. P. Danilov, et al., *The War Against the Peasantry, 1927–1930* (New Haven, 2005). See also R. W. Davies, *The Socialist Offensive: The Collectivisation of Soviet Agriculture, 1929–1930* (Cambridge, 1980); R. W. Davies and Stephen G. Wheatcroft, *The Years of Hunger: Soviet Agriculture, 1931–1933* (London, 2004); Moshe Lewin, *The Making of the Soviet System: Essays in the History of Interwar Russia,* especially pt. 2, "Collectivization—Or Something Else?" (New York, 1985), 91–190. For the role of the OGPU during collectivization, see also

Lynne Viola, "The Role of the OGPU in Dekulakization, Mass Deportations, and Special Settlements in 1930," The Carl Beck Papers in Russian and East European Studies, No. 1406 (Pittsburgh, 2000).

7. Histories of repression and political police under Stalin usually overlook the social order policing campaigns of the 1930s, perhaps because these campaigns were not overtly political, Robert Conquest, for example, leaves out social order policing in his two studies of Stalinist repression. *The Great Terror: A Reassessment* (New York, 1990). More recent studies by J. Arch Getty and Oleg Naumov also pass over such repression. J. Arch Getty and Oleg Naumov, *The Road to Terror: Stalin and the Self-Destruction of the Bolsheviks, 1932–1939* (New Haven, 1999), and J. Arch Getty, " 'Excesses Are Not Permitted': Mass Terror and Stalinist Governance in the Late 1930s," *Russian Review* 61 (January 2002): 113–38. For exceptions, see the brief discussions of repression of social marginals in V. N. Zemskov, *Spetsposelentsy v SSSR, 1930–1960* (Moscow, 2003), 45–46, and N. Vert and S. V. Mironenko, eds., *Istoriia stalinskogo Gulaga: Konets 1920-kh–pervaia polovina 1950-kh godov: Sobranie dokumentov v 7-mi tomakh,* vol. 1: *Massovye repressii v SSSR* (Moscow, 2004), 68–69. For more extensive coverage, see Paul Hagenloh, *Stalin's Police: Public Order and Mass Repression in the USSR, 1926–1941* (Washington, DC, 2009), " 'Socially Harmful Elements' and the Great Terror," in *Stalinism: New Directions,* ed. Sheila Fitzpatrick (London, 2000), 286–308, and " 'Chekist in Essence, Chekist in Spirit': Regular and Political Police in the 1930s," *Cahiers du Monde russe* 42, nos. 2–4 (April–December 2001): 447–76; Gabor Rittersporn, "Vrednye elementy, 'opasnye men'shinstva' i bol'shevistskie trevogi," in *V sem'e edinoi: Natsional'naia politika partii bol'shevikov i ee osushchestvlenie na Severo-Zapade Rossii v 1920–1950-e gody. Sbornik statei,* ed. Timo Vihavainen and Irina Takala (Petrozavodsk, 1998), 101–19; David Shearer, *Policing Stalin's Socialism: Social Order and Mass Repression in the Soviet Union, 1924–1953.* (New Haven, CT: Yale University Press, 2009), "Social Disorder, Mass Repression, and the NKVD during the 1930s," *Cahiers du Monde russe* 42, nos. 2–4 (April–December 2001): 505–34, and "Crime and Social Disorder in Stalin's Russia: A Reassessment of the Great Retreat and the Origins of Mass Repression," *Cahiers du Monde russe* 39/1–2 (1998): 119–48.

8. Hagenloh, *Stalin's Police;* Gabor Rittersporn, *Stalinist Simplifications and Soviet Complications: Social Tensions and Political Conflicts in the USSR, 1933–1953* (New York, 1991); Shearer, *Policing Stalin's Socialism.*

9. On the role of ideology and the change in views of deviance from the 1920s to the 1930s, see, especially, David L. Hoffmann, *Stalinist Values: The Cultural Norms of Stalinist Modernity, 1917–1941* (Ithaca, 2003), 177–78; David Priestland, *Stalinism and the Politics of Mobilization: Ideas, Power, and Terror in Inter-war Russia* (Oxford, 2007). For an overview of Stalin's socialist offensive, see, especially, R. W. Davies, *The Socialist Offensive: The Collectivisation of Soviet Agriculture, 1929–1930* (Cambridge, 1980), and *Soviet Economic Development from Lenin to Khrushchev* (Cambridge, 1998).

10. On militarization of police forces in general in European states after World War I, see Gerald Blaney Jr., ed., *Policing Interwar Europe: Continuity, Changing, and Crisis, 1918–1940* (Basingstoke, 2007), 3–7.

11. Neither the civil nor the political police under Stalin were subordinated to the military, as were most gendarme forces during the nineteenth century, and the civil police, at least, did not live in barracks. Many units of the Soviet political police, and especially the units of the internal forces, did live in barracks, and were organized by military rank. Both the civil and the political police under Stalin were subordinated to military law and discipline. On Western European gendarme forces, see Clive Emsley, *Gendarmes and the State in Nineteenth-Century Europe* (Oxford, 1999); Herbert Reinke, " 'Armed as if for War': The State, the Military, and the Professionalisation of the Prussian Police in Imperial Germany" in *Policing Western Europe: Politics, Professionalism, and Public Order, 1850–1940*, ed. Clive Emsley and Barbara Weinberger (New York, 1991), 55–73; David H. Bayley, *Patterns of Policing: A Comparative International Analysis* (New Brunswick, 1985); Howard C. Payne, *The Police State of Napoleon Bonaparte, 1851–1860* (Seattle, 1966). On the Russian gendarmerie, see V. S. Izmozik, *Zhandarmy Rossii* (St. Petersburg, 2002); Z. I. Peregudova, *Politicheskii sysk Rossii, 1880–1917* (Moscow, 2000); E. I. Shcherbakova, *Politicheskaia politsiia i politicheskii terrorizm v Rossii (vtoraia polovina XIX–nachalo XX vv)* (Moscow, 2001); M. I. Siznikov, A. V. Borisov, and A. E. Skripilev, *Istoriia politsii Rossii (1718–1917)* (Moscow, 1992); E. P. Sichinskii, ed., *Istoriia pravokhranitel'nykh organov Rossii: Sbornik nauchnykh trudov* (Cheliabinsk, 2000).
12. Khaustov et al., *Lubianka: Stalin i VChK-GPU-OGPU-NKVD*, 821 n. 159.
13. Leonid Naumov, *Bor'ba v rukovodstve NKVD v 1936–1938 gg.: Oprichnyi dvor Iosifa Groznogo* (Moscow, 2006); Rayfield, *Stalin's Hangmen*, 281–89.
14. Terry Martin, *An Affirmative Action Empire: Nations and Nationalism in the Soviet Union, 1923–1939* (Ithaca, 2001).
15. Shearer, "Social Disorder." See also Hiroaki Kuromiya, "Accounting for the 'Great Terror,' " *Jahrbücher für Geschichte Osteuropas* 53, no. 1 (January 2005): 86–101, and Getty, " 'Excesses Are Not Permitted.' "
16. Oleg Khlevniuk, "Prichiny 'Bol'shogo Terrora': Vneshnepoliticheskii aspekt" (unpublished manuscript), and "The Reasons for the 'Great Terror': The Foreign-Political Aspect," in *Russia in the Age of Wars, 1914–1945*, ed. S. Pons and A. Romano (Milan, 2000), 159–69. Based on his review of current literature, Kuromiya agrees with this assessment, "Accounting for the 'Great Terror,' " 87.
17. For works focused primarily on the mass purges of 1937 and 1938, see: Andrei Artizov et al., *Reabilitatsiia: Kak eto bylo. Dokumenty prezidiuma TsK KPSS i drugie materialy*, 3 vols. (Moscow, 2000); E. A. Bakirov et al., *Butovskii poligon, 1937–1938: Kniga pamiati zhertv politicheskikh represii*, 8 vols. (Moscow, 1997–2003); Robert Conquest, *The Great Terror: A Reassessment* (New York, 2007); Mark Iunge and Rol'f Binner, *Kak terror stal 'bol'shim': Sekretnyi prikaz No. 00447 i tekhnologiia ego ispolneniia* (Moscow, 2003); Mark Iunge, Gennadii Bordiugov, and Rol'f Binner, *Vertikal' bol'shogo terror* (Moscow, 2008): Mark Iunge, *Cherez trupy vraga na blago naroda: "Kulatskaia operatsiia" v Ukrainskoi SSR, 1937–1941*, 2 vols. (Moscow, 2010); Mark Iunge, G. Zhdanov, V. Razgon, and Rol'f Binner, *Massovye represii v Altaiskom krae, 1937–1938 gg: Prikaz 00447* (Moscow, 2010); V. A. Ivanov, "Mekhanizm massovykh represii v sovetskoi Rossii v kontse

20-kh–40kh gg." (Doctoral diss., Sankt-Peterburgskaia Akademiia MVD, Rossii, St. Petersburg, 1998); V. N. Khaustov and Lennart Samuel'son, *Stalin, NKVD, i repressii, 1936–1938 gg* (Moscow, 2009); Leonid Naumov, *Stalin i NKVD* (Moscow, 2010); Hiroaki Kuromiya, *The Voices of the Dead: Stalin's Great Terror in the 1930s* (New Haven, 2007); Barry McLoughlin and Kevin McDermott, eds., *Stalin's Terror: High Politics and Mass Repression in the Soviet Union* (London, 2003); Vadim Z. Rogovin, *Stalin's Terror of 1937– 1938: Political Genocide in the USSR* (Oak Park, 2009); Karl Schlögel, *Terror und Traum: Moskau 1937* (Munich, 2008), translated as *Moscow 1937* (Cambridge, 2012); Sergei Tepliakov, *Mashina terrora: OGPU-NKVD Sibiri v 1929–1941 gg.* (Moscow, 2008); Aleksandr Vatlin, *Terror raionnogo masshtaba: Massovye operatsii NKVD v Kuntsevskom raione Moskovskoi oblasti 1937–1938 gg.* (Moscow, 2004); Vert and Mironenko, *Istoriia stalinskogo gulaga*, vol. 1; Nicolas Werth, "Les 'opérations de masse' de la 'Grande Terreur' en URSS, 1937–1938," *Bulletin de l'Institut d'histoire du temps présent* 86 (2006): 6–167; V. N. Khaustov, N. V. Naumov, and N. S. Plotnikova, *Lubianka: Stalin i Glavnoe upravlenie gosbezopasnosti NKVD, 1937–1938* (Moscow, 2004).

18. I. I. Alekseenko, *Repressii na Kubani i na Severnom Kavkaze v 30-e gg. XX veka* (Krasnodar, 1993); K. Chomaev, *Nakazannyi narod* (Cherkessk, 1993); A. E. Gur'ianov, ed., *Repressii protiv poliakov i pol'skikh grazhdan* (Moscow, 1997); V. N. Nikol'skii, A. N. But, et al., *Kniga pamiati grekov Ukrainy* (Donetsk, 2005); Pavel Polian, *Ne po svoei vole: Istoriia i geografiia prinuditel'nykh migratsii v SSSR* (Moscow, 2001); J. Critchlow, *Repressirovannye narody Sovetskogo Soiuza: Nasledie stalinskikh deportatsii. Otchet Khel'sinkskoi gruppoi po pravam cheloveka, Sentiabr' 1991* (Moscow, 1991); I. L. Shcherbakova, ed., *Nakazannyi narod: Repressii protiv rossiiskikh nemtsev* (Moscow, 1999).

19. For general works, see Andres Küng, *Communism and Crimes against Humanity in the Baltic States* (Stockholm, 1999); Elena Zubkova, *Pribaltika i kreml'* (Moscow, 2008).

20. On Soviet nationality deportations, see: N. F. Bugai, *Deportatsiia narodov Kryma* (Moscow, 2002), and *Deportatsiia narodov Rossii: Chechentsy i ingushi* (Moscow, 1994); *Materialy k serii "Narody i kultury,"* no. 12: *Deportatsiia narodov v SSSR, 1930–1950-e gody* (Moscow, 1992); N. F. Bugai, *Ssylka kalmykov: Kak eto bylo* (Moscow, 1993), and *L. Beriia–I. Stalinu: "Soglasno vashemy ukazaniiu"* (Moscow, 1995); N. F. Bugai, T. M. Broev, and R. M. Broev, *Sovetskie kurdy: Vremia peremen* (Moscow, 1993); A. M. Gonov, *Kavkaz: Narody v eshelonakh: 20–60-e gody* (Moscow, 1998); A. N. Iakovlev, *Stalinskie deportatsii 1928–1953* (Moscow, 2005). On the Katyn massacres, see: Anna M. Cienciala, Natalia S. Lebedeva, and Wojciech Materski, eds., *Katyn: A Crime Without Punishment* (New Haven, 2007); Stanislaw Swianiewicz, *In the Shadow of Katyn*, trans. and annotated by Witold Swianiewicz (Pender Island, BC, 2002), originally published as *W cieniu Katynia* (Paris, 1976); Polish Cultural Foundation, *The Crime of Katyn: Facts and Documents* (London, 1989); Natalia S. Lebedeva, *Katyn: Prestuplenie protiv chelovechstva* (Moscow, 1994); Rudolf G. Pikhoia, Natalia S. Lebedeva, Aleksander Gieysztor, Wojciech Materski, et al., eds., *Katyn: Plenniki*

nieob'iavlennoi voiny (Moscow, 1997); Allen Paul, *Katyn: Stalin's Massacre and the Triumph of Truth* (Chicago, 2010); George Sanford, *Katyn and the Soviet Massacre of 1940: Truth, Justice and Memory* (London, 2005); J. K. Zawodny, *Death in the Forest: The Story of the Katyn Forest Massacre* (Notre Dame, 1962). For the original German investigation of the Katyn site, see Deutsche Informationsstelle, *Amtliches Material zum Massenmord von Katyn* (Berlin, 1943).

21. On the borderland wars, see A. N. Artizov et al, eds., *Ukrainskie natsionalisticheskie organizatsii v gody Vtoroi mirovoi voiny, 1939–1945*, 2 vols. (Moscow, 2012); Aleksandr E. Gur'ianov, ed., *Repressii protiv Poliakov i pol'skikh grazhdan* (Moscow, 1997); A. Kentii et al., *Borot'ba proty UPA i natsionalistichnoho pidpillia: Dyrektivni dokumenty CK KP(b)U, obkomiv partii, NKVS-MVS, MDB-KDB 1943–1959* (Kiev, 2002–3); Volodimir Kosyk, *Spetsoperatsii NKVD-KHB proty OUN: Borot'ba Moskvy proty ukraïns'koho natsionalizmu 1933–1943: Doslidzhenniametodiv borot'by* (L'viv, 2009); S. M. Mechnyk, *Sluzhba bezpeky revoliutsii noï OUN u borot'bi z NKVD-NKHB-MHB-KHB* (Ternopil', 1994); I. E. Nadol'skii, *Deportaciïna politika stalins'kogo totalitarnogo rezhimu v zahidnih oblastiah Ukraïni, 1939–1953 rr.* (Luts'k, 2008); Timothy Snyder, *Bloodlands: Europe between Hitler and Stalin* (New York, 2010); N. I. Vladimirtsev and A. I. Kokurin, *NKVD-MVD v bor'be s banditizmom i vooruzhennym natsionalisticheskim podpol'em na zapadnoi Ukraine, v zapadnoi Belorussii i pribaltike (1939–1956): Sbornik dokumentov* (Moscow, 2008); Amir Weiner, "The Empires Pay a Visit: Gulag Returnees, East European Rebellions, and Soviet Frontier Politics," *Journal of Modern History* 78, no. 2 (2006): 333–76.

CHAPTER 1. EXPANDING POWER, INFILTRATING THE STATE

1. On these conflicts, see especially Stuart Finkel, "An Intensification of Vigilance: Recent Perspectives on the Institutional History of the Soviet Security Apparatus in the 1920s," *Kritika: Explorations in Russian and Eurasian History* 5, no. 2 (Spring 2004): 309; George Lin, "Fighting in Vain: The NKVD RSFSR in the 1920s" (Ph.D. diss., Stanford University, 1997); Nicholas Werth, "L'OGPU en 1924: Radiographie d'une institution à son niveau d'étiage," *Cahiers du Monde russe* 42, nos. 2–4 (April–December 2001): 397–422; Vladimir N. Haustov, "Razvitie sovetskikh organov gosudarstvennoi bezopasnosti, 1917–1953 gg," ibid., 357–74; A. M. Plekhanov, *VChK-OGPU v gody novoi ekonomicheskoi politiki, 1921–1928* (Moscow, 2006), esp. 99–115; Paul Hagenloh, "Police, Crime, and Public Order," 21–32, and " 'Chekist in Essence, Chekist in Spirit': Regular and Political Police in the 1930s," *Cahiers du Monde russe* 42, nos. 2–4 (April–December 2001): 451–53; S. A. Krasil'nikov, "Vysylka i ssylka intelligentsii kak element Sovetskoi karatel'noi politiki 20-kh–nachala 30-kh gg.," in *Diskriminizatsiia intelligentsii v poslerevoliutsionnoi Sibirii (1920–1930-e gg): Sbornik nauchnykh trudov*, ed. S. A. Krasil'nikov and L. I. Pystina, *Minuvshee*, no. 21 (1997): 179–239. Hagenloh, Werth, and Lin stress the intensity of these conflicts, while other authors downplay the seriousness of the threat to the OGPU. See also A. Ia. Malygin, "Organy vnutrennikh del v periode provedeniiia novoi

ekonomicheskoi politiki (1921–1929)" in Borisov et al., *Politsiia i militsiia Rossii*, 114–39 and Rasskazov, *Karatel'nie organy v protsesse formirovaniia administrativno-komandnoi sistemy v Sovetskom gosudarstve, 1917–1941 gg.* (Ufa, 1994), 162–230.

2. AP RF, f. 3, op. 58, d. 52.

3. RGASPI, f. 76, op. 3, d. 305, l. 64.

4. Semashko refers here to a perceived return to polite etiquette and social deference to the educated upper classes, a lessening of revolutionary sensibilities as a result of the partial retreat to capitalism, and a revival of old ways under the NEP. He opposed this tendency, believing this kind of deference was misplaced and should be eradicated as dangerous.

5. Many in the Black Hundreds and similar groups viewed Bolshevism as a front for a worldwide Jewish conspiracy.

6. In 1922, the various Soviet republics united under Moscow's control and became known as the Union of Soviet Socialist Republics. With republic unification came organizational unification of the various republic police organs. Control over the various republic GPU organs came under a new "Unified [centralized] State Political Administration," (*Ob"edinennoe gosudarstvennoe politicheskoe upravlenie*, OGPU). The designation GPU remained for republic-level political police.

7. On Bolshevik-intelligentsia relations, see Michael David-Fox, *Revolution of the Mind: Higher Learning among the Bolsheviks, 1918–1929* (Ithaca, 1997); Stuart Finkel, *On the Ideological Front: The Russian Intelligentsia and the Making of the Soviet Public Sphere* (New Haven, 2007).

8. Stuart Finkel, "Purging the Public Intellectual: The 1922 Expulsion from Soviet Russia," *Russian Review* 62 (October 2003): 589–613.

9. For a classic study, see Leopold H. Haimson, *The Mensheviks: From the Revolution of 1917 to the Second World War* (Chicago, 1975). On the anti-Menshevik campaigns, see Vladimir N. Brovkin, *The Mensheviks after October: Socialist Opposition and the Rise of the Bolshevik Dictatorship* (Ithaca, 1991).

10. Diane Koenker, *Republic of Labor: Russian Printers and Soviet Socialism, 1918–1930* (Ithaca, 2005).

11. On the early Soviet legal system, see Peter H. Solomon Jr., *Soviet Criminal Justice under Stalin* (Cambridge, 1996), esp. chap. 2, "Criminal Justice under NEP."

12. This was a bold statement, made numerous times throughout the 1920s and the 1930s, to justify the frequent and usually ineffective campaigns against "speculators."

13. During the 1920s, the criminal investigations organs and the civil police were separate agencies.

14. Krylenko referred to "numerous" letters and telegrams, for example, from British socialist individuals and organizations, criticizing the Soviet Union for engaging in punishment without trial. AP RF, f. 3, op. 58, d. 281, l. 105. The executions resulted from the mass arrests of supposed monarchists and other counterrevolutionaries in 1927. For further discussion and references, see chapter 3.

15. Dzerzhinsky died of a heart attack on 20 July 1926.

16. Ievhen Petrushevych (1863–1940). Ukrainian lawyer and national activist, President of the Western Ukrainian National Republic, 1918–1919, and a diplomat in Austrian and German exile throughout the 1920s. Initially anti-Bolshevik, Petrushevych sought Soviet support for Western Ukrainian independence when, in 1923, the Entente governments officially recognized the 1919 annexation of eastern areas of Galicia by Poland. The Soviets, initially suspicious of Petrushevych as a British agent, financed his organization in exile. Christopher Gilley, "A Simple Question of 'Pragmatism'? Sovietophilism in West Ukrainian Emigration in the 1920s," Kozsalin Institute of Comparative European Studies, Working Paper No. 4 (March 2006), 18–21. For GPU claims that Petrushevych was working in collusion with the British, see V. N. Khaustov, V. P. Naumov, and N. S. Plotnikova, *Lubianka: Stalin i VChK-GPU-OGPU-NKVD, ianvar' 1922–dekabr' 1936* (Moscow, 2003), 75.
17. Khaustov et al., *Lubianka: Stalin i VChK-GPU-OGPU-NKVD*, p. 792 n. 42.
18. Ibid.
19. Donald Rayfield, *Stalin and His Hangmen: The Tyrant and Those Who Killed for Him* (New York, 2005), 140. Rayfield notes that Dzerzhinsky later became wary of Stalin, and began to move back toward Trotsky.
20. V. A. Antonov-Ovseenko, an ally of Trotsky, headed the Political Administration of the Revolutionary Military Council, and had been dispatched to Petrograd to investigate tensions between the military and the political police.

CHAPTER 2. THREATS FROM ABROAD, INFILTRATING THE ECONOMY

1. V. N. Khaustov, V. P. Naumov, and N. S. Plotnikova, *Lubianka, Stalin i VChK-GPU-OGPU-NKVD, ianvar' 1922–dekabr' 1936* (Moscow, 2003), 111–13, 117–18.
2. In 1924, Baldwin's Conservatives unseated the Labour government of Ramsay MacDonald, and took a harder line against the Soviets than had the Labourites.
3. For good accounts of these events, see the following: Keith Neilson, *Britain, Soviet Russia and the Collapse of the Versailles Order, 1919–1939* (Cambridge, 2006), 54–55 on the Arcos raid; also, Harriette Flory, "The Arcos Raid and the Rupture of Anglo-Soviet Relations, 1927," *Journal of Contemporary History* 12, no. 4 (October 1977): 707–23. On Soviet international relations and the war scare of the late 1920s, see Alastair Kocho-Williams, *Russia's International Relations in the Twentieth Century* (New York, 2013), esp. chap. 3, "Soviet Foreign Policy in the 1920s"; Gabriel Gorodetsky, *The Precarious Truce: Anglo-Soviet Relations, 1924–1927* (1977; Cambridge, 2008); Edward Hallett Carr, *Foundations of a Planned Economy, 1926–1929*, vol. 3, pt. 1 (New York, 1976), 18–26; Kocho-Williams focuses on Comintern policy versus Soviet diplomatic policies. For a discussion of OGPU activities, see Christopher Andrew, "The British Secret Service and Anglo-Soviet Relations in the 1920s, Part 1: From the Trade Negotiations to the Zinoviev Letter," *Historical Journal* 20, no. 3 (1977): 673–706; Leonid Nezhinskii, ed., *Sovetskaia vneshniaia politika, 1917–1945 gg: Poiski novykh podkhodov* (Moscow, 1992).

4. There are many studies of Party politics and debates during this period. One of the most succinct and accessible, still, is that of the Czechoslovak Michal Reiman, *The Birth of Stalinism: The USSR on the Eve of the "Second Revolution"* (Bloomington, 1987), originally in German, *Die Geburt des Stalinismus: Die UdSSR am Vorabend der "zweiten Revolution"* (Frankfurt/Main, 1979). See also the classic account by Edward Hallett Carr, *Foundations of a Planned Economy, 1926–1929*, vol. 2 (New York, 1971), 3–147.
5. In 1922, with the formation of the Union of Soviet Socialist Republics, the Russian Communist Party was dissolved into a new structure incorporating the parties of all the republics. The new, united, organization became the All-Union Communist Party of Bolsheviks, or VKP(b).
6. The lists of undesirable populations were compiled, essentially by political police, and those entered in them were to be removed by special transport police under OGPU command.
7. Voikov was murdered by an anti-Soviet political émigré. For Chicherin's response, see Gorodetsky, *The Precarious Truce*, 236.
8. Sarajevo is a reference to the assassination of the Austrian Archduke and his wife, July 1914, which precipitated World War I. Vorovsky was a Soviet delegate to the Lausanne international conference of 1923, murdered by a self-proclaimed White Guardist.
9. Born as either Georgii or Salomon Rosenblum, in Odessa or elsewhere in Ukraine in 1873, Reilly left imperial Russia sometime in the early 1890s. By various unclear and most likely unscrupulous means, he ended up in Britain, where he began working for the British Secret Intelligence Service (SIS), spying on radical émigré groups. It was in Britain that Rosenblum took the pseudonym Sidney George Reilly. After a number of intelligence exploits, he was smuggled into Russia as a British agent at the time of the revolution in order to work against the Bolsheviks. Andrew Cook, *Ace of Spies: The True Story of Sidney Reilly* (London, 2004); Michael Smith, *MI6: The Real James Bonds, 1919–1939* (London, 2011); Richard B. Spence, *Trust No One: The Secret World of Sidney Reilly* (Port Townsend, 2003).
10. Published also in Donald Rayfield, *Stalin and His Hangmen: The Tyrant and Those Who Killed for Him* (New York, 2004), 145.
11. A. Kh. Artuzov headed the OGPU's counterespionage unit.
12. Georgii El'vengren was a Russian military officer of Karelian origin who emigrated to Finland after the Civil War. An anti-Soviet White Guardist, he worked with Reilly, and entered the Soviet Union in 1925 with a false Romanian passport, in connection with activities of the Trust, a supposedly anti-Bolshevik underground organization that was, in fact, an OGPU front organization. He was discovered and arrested in Tver, and executed as one of "the 20" prominent monarchists/White Guardists in retaliation for the murder of Voikov.
13. At the time of his capture, Reilly was no longer working actively for the British secret service, having officially retired from SIS in 1921. Reilly was contacted informally to sneak into Russia to assess the Trust's legitimacy. OGPU agents, working undercover as part of the Trust, organized Reilly's entrance into the Soviet Union through Finland, and then arrested him. Known as a British agent, and already sentenced in absentia in Russia in 1918, Reilly was

executed in 1925. Reilly's capture, interrogation, and execution no doubt confirmed Stalin's suspicions about British malevolent intentions.

14. Eduard Operput, a leading OGPU counterespionage agent, had defected to Finland early in 1927, and had secretly returned to the USSR in the summer to conduct sabotage against the Soviet government. He and several others were killed as they attempted to flee capture.

15. *Trest* was the designation used for a merging of several economic or industrial entities, like the English word "trust." Unlike "trust," however, the word *trest* does not signify confidence or belief.

16. On Savinkov, see *Boris Savinkov v Lubianke: Dokumenty* (Moscow, 2000), and Richard B. Spence, *Boris Savinkov: Renegade on the Left* (New York, 1991). Donald Rayfield attributes organization of the Trust to Vladimir Dzunkovsky, the head of the tsarist political police, the Okhrana, who worked for the Soviets in the 1920s, and who supposedly modeled the Trust on the Okhrana's successful infiltration organizations that operated during the pre-revolutionary period. Rayfield, *Stalin and His Hangmen*, 142. Pamela K. Simpkins and K. Leigh Dyer trace the origins to an earlier successful GPU operation from 1920 called *Maiak* (Beacon), also designed to penetrate émigré anti-Bolshevik circles. Prepared originally for the CIA, Simpkins and Dyer's work, published under the Freedom of Information Act, contains the best discussion of the leading figures involved in the Trust operations, including and especially information on real names and backgrounds. Pamela K. Simpkins and K. Leigh Dyer, *The Trust*, The Security and Intelligence Foundation Reprint Series (Alexandria, VA, 1989). See also John Costello and Oleg Tsarev, *Deadly Illusions: The KGB Orlov Dossier Reveals Stalin's Master Spy* (New York, 1993).

17. Khaustov et al., *Lubianka: Stalin i VChK-GPU-OGPU-NKVD*, p. 796 n. 60.

18. From I. Stalin, *Interview with Foreign Workers' Delegations* (Moscow, 1927), 44–48.

19. "Versaillers" refers to the official French government and its sympathizers, based at the Palace of Versailles so long as the revolutionary Commune controlled Paris.

20. Marie Joseph Louis Adolphe Thiers, president of France 1871–73, came to power after the defeat of France by Prussia and the collapse of the Second Empire under Napoleon III. Thiers oversaw the bloody suppression of the Paris Commune in 1871.

21. Reference to military intervention by Allied armed forces during the Russian Civil War.

22. On the Shakhty trial and issues surrounding it, see Edward Hallett Carr and R. W. Davies, *Foundations of a Planned Economy, 1926–1929* vol. 1, pt. 2 (New York, 1969), 574–604; Sabine Dullin, "Rol' mezhdunarodnogo voprosa v politicheskikh protsessakh v SSSR: Shakhtinskoe delo i sovetskaia vneshniaia politika," in *Sudebnie politicheskie protsessy v SSSR i kommunisticheskikh stranakh Evropy: Sravitel'nyi analiz mekhanizmov i prakhtik provedeniia. Sbornik materialov rossiiskogo-frantsuskogo seminara, Moskva, 11–12 sentiabria, 2009*, ed. S. A. Krasilnikov and Alan Blum (Novosibirsk, 2010), 66–74. See also Gordon W. Morrell, *Britain Confronts the Stalin Revolution: Anglo-Soviet Relations and the Metro-Vickers Crisis* (Ontario, 1995).

23. The Workers' and Peasants' Inspectorate (RKI) was the government inspectorate agency, as opposed to the Central Control Commission (TsKK), which was the Party's internal inspectorate. E. A. Rees, *State Control in Soviet Russia: The Rise and Fall of the Workers' and Peasants' Inspectorate, 1920–34* (London, 1987).

24. In fact, Efim Georgievich Evdokimov, one of the most ruthless of the high OGPU officials.

25. Politburo member, USSR transport commissar, and assistant head of the Council of Labor and Defense.

26. M. L. Rukhimovich, assistant head of the VSNKh USSR, the Supreme Economic Council.

27. For further reading on the Industrial Party trial, see Kendall E. Bailes, *Technology and Society under Lenin and Stalin: Origins of the Soviet Technical Intelligentsia, 1917–1941* (Princeton, 1978), esp. pt. 2, "The Old Specialists and the Power Structure, 1928–1931."

28. Also published in *Kommunist*, no. 11 (1990): 99–100, and in English in Rayfield, *Stalin and His Hangmen*, 166–67.

29. One of the first indications that the conspiracy was concocted by Stalin, and the OGPU was the connection that was supposed to exist between the conspirators in the USSR and P. P. Ryabushinsky, a former industrialist, who had immigrated to France after the Bolshevik seizure of power. Ryabushinsky was supposedly a key link connecting Ramzin et al. to French government circles. According to OGPU materials, he was supposed to become the interior minister in a new Russian government after supposed intervention and destruction of the Soviet regime. Apparently unknown to the OGPU, Ryabushinsky died in 1925, before the conspiracy supposedly coalesced.

30. V. G. Groman, an internationally known economist of balanced planning, opposed to the accelerated tempos of Stalinist industrialization. Groman was held and tried as part of the Menshevik trial of 1931. See Naum Jasny, *Soviet Economists of the Twenties: Names to Be Remembered* (Cambridge, 1972), esp. chap. 6, "Vladimir Gustavovich Groman," 89–124, and pt. 2, "The Trial," 60–88, on the Menshevik trial.

31. N. D. Kondrat'ev, economist, founder of the analysis of long cycles, also opposed to forced industrialization. For a biographical sketch, see Jasny, *Soviet Economists*, 158–78. A. V. Chayanov was known for his studies of agrarian subsistence economy and rural households. He leaned toward the moderate Socialist Revolutionaries' idea of rural cooperative development.

32. Pavel Miliukov, lawyer, prominent Constitutional Democrat, and foreign minister under the Provisional Government of 1917, emigrated and lived abroad after 1917.

33. Lars Lih, Oleg Naumov, and Oleg Khlevniuk, eds., *Stalin's Letters to Molotov, 1925–1936* (New Haven, 1995), 200.

34. In addition to Jasny's work on economists, see also Bailes, *Technology and Society;* Loren R. Graham, *The Ghost of the Executed Engineer: Technology and the Fall of the Soviet Union* (Cambridge, 1993).

CHAPTER 3. SUBDUING THE COUNTRYSIDE

1. For recent histories of the Gulag, see Iu. N. Afanas'ev et al., eds., *Istoriia stalinskogo gulaga: Konets 1920-kh–pervaia polovina 1950-kh godov. Sobranie dokumentov*, 7 vols. (Moscow, 2004–5); Anne Applebaum, *Gulag: A History* (New York, 2004); Steven Barnes, *Death and Redemption: The Gulag and the Shaping of Soviet Society* (Princeton, 2011); Oleg Khlevniuk, *The History of the Gulag: From Collectivization to the Great Terror*, trans. Vadim Staklo (New Haven, 2004); Fyodor Vasilevich Mochulsky, *Gulag Boss: A Soviet Memoir*, trans. Deborah Kaple (New York, 2012). See also the classic works: Evgeniia Ginzburg, *Journey into the Whirlwind* (New York, 1967); and Aleksandr Solzhenitsyn, *The Gulag Archipelago, 1918–1956: An Experiment in Literary Investigation* (New York, 1997), originally published as *Arkhipelag GULAG: Khudozhestvenno-istoricheskoe proizvedenie* (Paris, 1973).
2. RGASPI, f. 17, op. 3, d. 761, l. 17.
3. V. N. Khaustov, V. P. Naumov, and N. S. Plotnikova, *Lubianka: Stalin i VChK-GPU-OGPU-NKVD, ianvar' 1922–dekabr' 1936* (Moscow, 2003), 226–29.
4. Category 2 kulaks were subject to exile to penal work colonies, as opposed to category 1 kulaks, who were slated for execution or imprisoned in labor camps.
5. Said Bek Shamil: One of the founders and leaders of the Mountain Republic of the Northern Caucasus (MRNC), which existed briefly from 1917 to 1920, when MRNC forces were defeated by the Bolsheviks. Shamil escaped, settled in Berlin, and there led the émigré organization Committee of Independence of the Caucasus. Shamil was the grandson of Imam Shamil, the Dagestani sheikh who rallied the population to resist Russian occupation in the 1850s. Nazhmutdin Gotsinsky: Anti-Bolshevik Islamic revolutionary leader who led uprisings in the Caucasus during the period 1917 to the early 1920s. Gotsinsky was caught and executed in 1925. On the Caucasus region during the revolutionary period, see Edward Hallett Carr, *The Bolshevik Revolution, 1917–1923*, vol. 1 (New York, 1951), 339–50; S. Mural, "The Jihad of Said Shamil and Sultan Murad for the Liberation of the Caucasus," *Central Asian Survey* 10, nos. 1–2 (1991): 181–87; Michael A. Reynolds, *Shattering Empires: The Clash and Collapse of the Ottoman and Russian Empires 1908–1918* (Cambridge, 2011); Ronald J. Suny, *The Baku Commune: Class and Nationality in the Russian Revolution* (Princeton, 1972), *Armenia in the Twentieth Century* (1983), and *The Making of the Georgian Nation* (Bloomington, 1994); Ronald Suny, ed., *Transcaucasia, Nationalism, and Social Change: Essays in the History of Armenia, Azerbaijan, and Georgia* (Ann Arbor, 1996). See also Ronald Suny and Terry Martin, eds., *A State of Nations: Empire and Nation-Making in the Age of Lenin and Stalin* (New York, 2001); Vera Tolz, *Russia's Own Orient: The Politics of Identity and Oriental Studies in the Late Imperial and Early Soviet Periods* (London, 2011).
6. On the special settlements, see, among others, S. A. Krasil'nikov, *Serp i molokh: Krest'ianskaia ssylka v Zapadnoi Sibiri v 1930-e gody* (Moscow, 2003); Lynne Viola, *The Unknown Gulag: The Lost World of Stalin's Special Settlements* (New York, 2007); V. N. Zemskov, *Spetsposelentsy v SSSR,*

1930–1960 (Moscow, 2005). See also the document collection V. P. Danilov and S. A. Krasil'nikov, eds., *Spetspereselentsy v Zapadnoi Siberii: Vesna 1931-nachalo 1933* (Novosibirsk, 1993), and their edited volume of essays, *Spetspereselentsy v Zapadnoi Sibiri, 1933–1938* (Novosibirsk, 1994).

7. V. M. Burmistrov, Procuracy official in Western Siberia and then deputy chief procurator of the Russian republic chief, arrested in 1938.

8. The other major cause of attrition was escape.

9. See the remarkable account of conditions, written by the propaganda instructor Belichko, in Danilov and Krasil'nikov, *Spetspereselentsy v Zapadnoi Sibiri, 1933–1938*, 89–100. See also Nicolas Werth, *Cannibal Island: Death in a Siberian Gulag.* trans. Steven Rendall (Princeton, 2007).

10. R. W. Davies et al., eds., *The Stalin-Kaganovich Correspondence 1931–1936* (New Haven, 2003), 179–81.

11. In communes, all property and produce was held in common, whereas kolkhozes were cooperatives in which some private property was permitted. Most farms were organized as kolkhozes.

12. Symon Petliura (1879–1926) headed the anti-Bolshevik government of the Ukrainian National Republic, 1919–20. He made an alliance with Poland in 1920 during the Polish-Soviet War, and was assassinated in Paris in 1926.

CHAPTER 4. ORDERING SOCIETY

1. RGASPI, f. 17, op. 2, d. 514, ll. 14–17.

2. There is a large literature on the famine, especially on the famine in Ukraine. In English, see especially the journal *Holodomor Studies*. More generally, see Robert Conquest, *The Harvest of Sorrow: Soviet Collectivization and the Terror-Famine* (New York, 1986); R. W. Davies and Stephen G. Wheatcroft, *The Years of Hunger: Soviet Agriculture, 1931–1933* (London, 2004). See also the memoir account by Miron Dolot, *Execution by Hunger: The Hidden Holocaust* (New York, 1987). Articles in several languages are included in V. Vasil'ev and Y. Shapoval, *Komandiri velikogo golodu: Poizdki V. Molotova i L. Kaganovicha v Ukrainu ta na Pivnichnii Kavkaz, 1932–1933 rr.* (Kiev, 2001). See also exchanges about causes, issues of genocide, and demographic discussions: Mark B. Tauger, "Natural Disasters and Human Actions in the Soviet Famine of 1931–1933," The Carl Beck Papers in Russian & East European Studies, No. 1506 (Pittsburgh, 2001); Jacques Vallin, France Meslé, Serguei Adamets, and Serhii Pyrozhkov, "A New Estimate of Ukrainian Population Losses During the Crises of the 1930s and 1940s," *Population Studies* 56, no. 3 (2002): 249–64; and exchanges in *Europe Asia Studies* vols. 51, no. 8 (1999); 57, no. 6 (2005); 58, no. 4 (2006); 59, no. 4 (2009).

3. For migration figures and patterns, see S. N. Golotik and V. V. Minaev, *Naselenie i vlast': Ocherki demograficheskoi istorii SSSR 1930-kh godov* (Moscow, 2004); V. B. Zhiromskaia, *Demograficheskaia istoriia Rossii v 1930-e gody: Vzgliad v neizvestnoe* (Moscow, 2001). On marginals, see S. A. Krasil'nikov, *Na izlomakh sotsial'noi struktury: Marginaly v poslerevoliutsionnom obshchestve (1917–konets 1930-kh gg)* (Novosibirsk, 1998); S. A. Krasil'nikov, ed., *Marginaly v Sovetskom obshchestve 1920–1930-godov: Istoriografiia, istochniki. Sbornik nauchnykh trudov* (Novosibirsk, 2001).

4. David Hoffmann, *Peasant Metropolis: Social Identities in Moscow, 1929–1941* (Ithaca, 1994); Gijs Kessler, "The Peasant and the Town: Rural-Urban Migration in the Soviet Union, 1929–40" (Ph.D. diss., European University, Florence, 2000).
5. RGASPI, f. 17, op. 2, d. 514, l. 17.
6. Paul Hagenloh, *Stalin's Police: Public Order and Mass Repression in the USSR, 1926–1941* (Washington, DC, 2009); George Lin, "Fighting in Vain: The NKVD RSFSR in the 1920s" (Ph.D. diss., Stanford University, 1997); David Shearer, *Policing Stalin's Socialism: Social Order and Mass Repression in the Soviet Union, 1924–1953* (New Haven, 2009).
7. Published in O. V. Khlevniuk et al., *Stalin i Kaganovich: Perepiska, 1931–1936* (Moscow, 2001), 260. For an English-language version of this document, see R. W. Davies, Oleg V. Khlevniuk, et al., eds., *The Stalin-Kaganovich Correspondence, 1931–1936* (New Haven, 1003), 175.
8. Published in V. P. Danilov et al., *Tragediia sovetskoi derevni: Kollektivizatsiia i raskulachivanie. Dokumenty i materially, 1927–1939*, vol. 3: *Konets 1930–1933* (Moscow, 2001), 419.
9. First published in Danilov et al., *Tragediia Sovetskoi derevni*, 3:634–35.
10. SPO, Secret Political Department.
11. AP RF, f. 3, op. 30, d. 189, l. 43.
12. Published in Danilov et al., *Tragediia sovetskoi derevni*, 3:746–52.
13. Molotov's real name.
14. RGASPI, f. 17, op. 162, d. 15, l. 2.
15. Informal courts made up of citizens and local officials who could censure and fine an individual, and impose community sanctions, but could not impose criminal responsibility or prison penalties.
16. V. N. Khaustov, V. P. Naumov, and N. S. Plotnikova, *Lubianka: Stalin i VChK-GPU-OGPU-NKVD, ianvar' 1922–dekabr' 1936* (Moscow, 2003), 811 n. 117.
17. Golfo Alexopoulos, *Stalin's Outcasts: Aliens, Citizens, and the Soviet State, 1926–1936* (Ithaca, 2003).
18. GA RF, f. 1235, op. 141, d. 1650, ll. 30–32.
19. Registration in police precinct for disorderly conduct, but without arrest.
20. The final charter of the NKVD was approved 5 November 1934.
21. Khaustov et al., *Lubianka: Stalin i VChK-GPU-OGPU-NKVD*, #467.
22. Published in *Istochnik* 6 (1997): 109.
23. The paragraph that defined "regime" areas.
24. GA RF, f. 9401, op. 12, d. 135, doc. 119. We are grateful to Paul Hagenloh for help in reconstructing Yagoda's speech. For a more complete description of this speech, see Paul Hagenloh, " 'Socially Harmful Elements' and the Great Terror," in *Stalinism: New Directions*, ed. Sheila Fitzpatrick (New York, 2000), 299.
25. RGASPI, f. 17, op. 2, d. 598, ll. 12, 41–43. See also Yagoda's directive to operational departments of the GUGB, as well as the civil police, in March 1936, to free themselves from unnecessary tasks and to "focus on priorities of aggravated robbery, murder, and theft of socialist property." GA RF, f. 9401, op. 12, d. 135, doc. 31, l. 4.
26. GA RF, f. 5446, op. 26, d. 18, l. 195, and d. 50, l. 5.

27. GA RF, f. 5446, op. 18a, d. 904, l. 6.
28. GA RF, f. 5446, op. 16a, d. 591, l. 21.
29. GA RF, f. 1235, op. 2, d. 2032, l. 26.

CHAPTER 5. THE GREAT PURGES

1. See the introduction.
2. Lenin's testament: a statement drawn up by Lenin, in failing health, intended to guide the Party after his death, included critical statements about the other Party leaders. Lenin recommended, allegedly, that Stalin be removed as general secretary, but there is controversy surrounding this aspect of the testament. The Russian historian V. A. Sakharov has argued that the anti-Stalinist parts of the testament were forged, largely by Trotsky and Krupskaia, Lenin's wife. See Hiroaki Kuromiya, *Stalin* (Harlow, UK, 2005), 60–61.
3. Anti-Bolshevik government during the civil war.
4. Ernst Röhm, head of the National Socialist Storm Troopers (SA), murdered 30 June 1934 as part of the mass purge of the SA. Kurt von Schleicher, last chancellor of Germany before Adolph Hitler, also assassinated at the time of the SA purge.
5. V. N. Khaustov, V. P. Naumov, and N. S. Plotnikova, *Lubianka: Stalin i VChK-GPU-OGPU-NKVD, ianvar' 1922–dekabr' 1936* (Moscow, 2003), 824 n. 175.
6. RGASPI, f. 671, op. 1, d. 118, ll. 1–33.
7. Published in O. V. Khlevniuk et al., *Stalin i Kaganovich: Perepiska, 1931–1936 gg.* (Moscow, 2005), 682–83.
8. Still serviceable is John Erickson, *The Soviet High Command: A Military-Political History 1918–41* (London, 1962); see also Harold Shukman, *Stalin's Generals* (New York, 1993).
9. I. V. Iakir (1893–1937), Commander of the Kiev Military District during the 1930s, Central Committee and Politburo member of the Ukrainian Communist Party, arrested as a supposed member of the Tukhachevsky plot.
10. Ian Gamarnik (1894–1937), birth name Iakiv Borysovych Pudykovych, a political activist and senior military and defense official, supported Tukhachevsky's innocence and committed suicide after Tukhachevsky's execution. Implicated in the Anti-Soviet Military Organization plot.

CHAPTER 6. SOCIAL AND ETHNIC CLEANSING

1. Li U Khe (Vladimir Fedorovich Li) and Kim Yen Un, *Belaia kniga o deportatsii koreiskogo naseleniia Rossii v 30-40-kh godakh* (Moscow, 1992).
2. Published in V. Danilov et al., *Tragediia sovetskoi derevni: Kollekivizatsiia i raskulachivanie. Dokumenty i materialy*, vol. 5, bk. 1: *1937–1938* (Moscow, 2004), 256–57.
3. Aleksei Rykov, (1881–1938), an early Party leader, former head of Sovnarkom, arrested and executed as "right deviationist" in 1937–38.
4. First published, in fragmentary form, in *Trud*, no. 88, June 4, 1992, 1, 4. For the full text in English, see J. Arch Getty and Oleg V. Naumov, *The Road to*

Terror: Stalin and the Self-Destruction of the Bolsheviks, 1932–1939 (New Haven, 1999), 473–79.

5. Dashnak (Dashnaksutyun, Armenian Revolutionary Federation): an anti-Soviet socialist organization, founded in the 1890s, dedicated to an independent and socialist Armenia. Mussavatists: members of the Azerbaijani nationalist political party Mussavat, the majority party in the short-lived Azerbaijan Democratic Republic, 1918–20. Ittihadists: members of the radical Islamic party Ittihad, formed in response to the more secular Mussavat party.

6. Published in *Istoricheskii arkhiv* 1 (1992): 125–28.

7. Published ibid., 129–30, and in English in Getty and Naumov, *The Road to Terror*, 538–40.

8. For discussion of the purges as a changing series of Party "scripts" and "transcripts," see ibid.

9. V. N. Khaustov, V. P. Naumov, and N. S. Plotnikova, *Lubianka: Stalin i glavnoe upravlenie gosbezopastnosti NKVD, 1937–1938* (Moscow, 2004), 612–15.

10. Ibid., 663.

CHAPTER 7. THE SECURITY ORGANS AT WAR

1. The statute used to convict people of counterrevolutionary and anti-Soviet crimes.

2. V. N. Khaustov, V. P. Naumov, and N. S. Plotnikova, *Lubianka: Stalin i NKVD-NKGB-GUKR "Smersh," 1939–mart 1946* (Moscow, 2006), 564 n. 11.

3. The antiterrorist law, cases under which were tried in camera, without right of appeal, and carried a mandatory death penalty.

4. On the United Front and the German-Soviet agreement, see Mieczyslaw B. Biskupski and Piotr Stefan Wandycz, *Ideology, Politics, and Diplomacy in East Central Europe* (Woodbridge, UK, 2003); Robert Boyce and Joseph A. Maiolo, *The Origins of World War Two: The Debate Continues* (London, 2003); Edward Hallett Carr, *German-Soviet Relations between the Two World Wars, 1919–1939* (1951; New York, 1979); Jonathan Haslam, *The Soviet Union and the Struggle for Collective Security in Europe, 1933–1939* (London, 1984); Gabriel Gorodetsky, *Grand Delusion: Stalin and the German Invasion of Russia* (New Haven, 1999); Igor Lukes and Erik Goldstein, eds., *The Munich Crisis, 1938: Prelude to World War II* (London, 1999); Werner Maser, *Der Wortbruch: Hitler, Stalin und der Zweite Weltkrieg* (Munich, 1994); Aleksandr Nekrich, Adam Ulam, and Gregory L. Freeze, *Pariahs, Partners, Predators: German—Soviet Relations, 1922–1941* (New York, 1997); Frank McDonough, ed. *The Origins of the Second World War: An International Perspective* (London, 2011); Alfred. J. Rieber, "Stalin as Foreign Policy–Maker: Avoiding War, 1927–1953," in *Stalin: A New History*, ed. S. W. Davies and J. R. Harris (Cambridge, 2005), 140–58; Geoffrey Roberts, *The Soviet Union and the Origins of the Second World War* (London, 1995), and *Stalin's Wars: From World War to Cold War, 1939–1953* (New Haven, 2006); Izidors Vizulis, *The Molotov-Ribbentrop Pact of 1939: The Baltic Case* (New York, 1999).

5. Alexander Chubaryan and Harold Shukman, eds., *Stalin and the Soviet-Finnish War, 1939–1940* (New Haven, 2002); Robert Edwards, *White Death:*

Russia's War on Finland 1939–40 (London, 2006); Eloise Engle and Lauri Paananen, *The Winter War: The Russo-Finnish Conflict, 1939–1940* (1973; Boulder, 1985); David Glanz, *Stumbling Colossus: The Red Army on the Eve of World War* (Lawrence, 1998); Philip Jowett and Brent Snodgrass, *Finland at War 1939–45* (Oxford, 2006); William R. Trotter, *A Frozen Hell: The Russo—Finnish Winter War of 1939–40* (1991; London, 2006); Carl Van Dyke, *The Soviet Invasion of Finland, 1939–40* (Frank Cass, 1997).

6. On policies of sovietization, see Jan Gross, *Revolution from Abroad: The Soviet Conquest of Poland's Western Ukraine and Western Belorussia* (1988; Princeton, 2002); Alfred J. Rieber, ed., *Forced Migration in Central and Eastern Europe, 1939–1950* (London, 2000); Timothy Snyder, *Bloodlands: Europe between Hitler and Stalin* (New York, 2010).

7. Khaustov et al., *Lubianka: Stalin i NKVD-NKGB-GUKR "Smersh,"* 568 n. 28.

8. For histories of the Katyn massacre, see above, Introduction, note 20.

9. B. Z. Kobulov (1904–53), Beria's protégé, candidate member of the Central Committee, and head of the NKVD Investigative Department. V. N. Merkulov (1895–1953) at this time was deputy head of the GUGB. Both Kobulov and Merkulov were arrested and executed when Beria fell from power in 1953. L. F. Bashtakov, one of the officers responsible for the Katyn executions of Polish military officers, survived until his natural death in 1970. On Kobulov, Merkulov, and Bashtakov, see Michael Parrish, *The Lesser Terror: Soviet State Security, 1939–1953* (Westport, 1996).

10. Terry Martin, *An Affirmative Action Empire: Nations and Nationalism in the Soviet Union, 1923–1939* (Ithaca, 2001), 362–72.

11. Published in A. I. Kokurin and N. V. Petrov, *Lubianka: Organy VChK-OGPU-NKVD-NKGB-MGB-MVD-KGB, 1917–1991: Spravochnik* (Moscow, 2003), 623–26.

12. In addition to the works cited above (introduction, note 21), see V. A. Berdinskikh, *Spetsposelentsy: Politicheskaia ssylka narodov Sovetskoi Rossii* (Moscow, 2005); N. Bugai, *Iosif Stalin–Lavrentiu Berii, "Ikh nado deportirovat": Dokumenty, fakty, kommentarii* (Moscow, 1992); Diakhat Ediev, "Demograficheskie poteri deportirovannykh narodov SSSR," *Naselenie i obshchestvo* 79 (2004); Terry Martin, "The Origins of Soviet Ethnic Cleansing," *Journal of Modern History* 70, no. 4 (1998): 813–61; Norman Naimark, *Stalin's Genocides* (New York, 2011); O. J. Pohl, *Ethnic Cleansing in the USSR, 1937–1949* (Westport, 1999), and *The Stalinist Penal System: A Statistical History of Soviet Repression and Terror, 1930–1953* (Jefferson, NC, 1997).

13. Friedrich Paulus (1890–1957), German field marshal, commander of the German Sixth Army, encircled and surrendered at the battle of Stalingrad, 1943.

CHAPTER 8. BORDER WARS, PLOTS, AND SPY MANIA

1. *Istrebitel'nie otriady*: locally recruited "extermination" units.

2. Rudolf Slánský, general secretary of the Communist Party of Czechoslovakia.

3. Slánský was purged as a part of a sweep of East European communist leaders out of favor with Stalin. He was accused of trying to infiltrate Trotskyist and "Zionist" sympathizers into the Czechoslovak Communist Party and government. Karel Kaplan, *Report on the Murder of the General Secretary* (Columbus,

1990); Igor Lukes, "The Rudolf Slánský Affair: New Evidence," *Slavic Review* 58, no. 1 (Spring 1999): 160–87.

4. For background information on the postwar period, we rely on two works: Yoram Gorlitsky and Oleg Khlevniuk, *Cold Peace: Stalin and His Ruling Circle, 1945–1953* (Oxford, 2004); and Oleg Khlevniuk, *Master of the House: Stalin and His Inner Circle* (New Haven, 2009). For foreign policy, see Jonathan Haslam, *Russia's Cold War: From the October Revolution to the Fall of the Wall* (New Haven, 2010); Vladimir Pechatnov, *Stalin, Ruzvelt, Trumen: SSSR i SShA v 1940-kh godakh. Dokumental'nye ocherki* (Moscow, 2006); Geoffrey Roberts, *Stalin's Wars: From World War to Cold War, 1939–1953* (New Haven, 2006); Vladislav Zubok and Constantine Pleshakov, *Inside the Kremlin's Cold War: From Stalin to Khrushchev* (Cambridge, MA, 1996).

5. V. N. Khaustov, V. P. Naumov, and N. S. Plotnikova, *Lubianka: Stalin i MGB SSSR, mart 1946–mart 1953* (Moscow, 2007), 599.

6. S. D. Ignat'ev, then Minister of State Security, replacing Abakumov, arrested in July 1951. See further discussion of Abakumov's arrest, below.

7. In keeping with convention, *Glavnoe upravlenie* is translated as Chief Directorate, when referring to the organizational structure of the MGB. Otherwise *upravlenie* is translated as "administration."

8. See Arno Lustiger, *Stalin and the Jews: The Red Book. The Tragedy of the Jewish Anti-Fascist Committee and the Soviet Jews* (New York, 2003); G. V. Kostyrchenko, *Tainaia politika Stalina: Vlast' i antisemitizm* (Moscow, 2000); Joshua Rubenstein and Vladimir P. Naumov, eds., *Stalin's Secret Pogrom: The Postwar Inquisition of the Jewish Anti-Fascist Committee*, trans. Laura Esther Wolfson (New Haven, 2001); Yehoshua A Gilboa, *The Black Years of Soviet Jewry, 1939–1953* (Boston, 1971).

9. The administration responsible for nuclear energy development.

10. For greater detail, see Gorlitsky and Khlevniuk, *Cold Peace*, 113–20.

11. Ya. G. Etinger, prominent cardiologist, medical professor, and consultant for the Kremlin's rest sanatorium, often referred to as the first victim of the so-called Doctors' Plot.

12. A. S. Shcherbakov, Oblast Party Secretary, Party Central Committee member, and head of the Red Army Chief Political Administration; died of a heart attack on the night of 9–10 May 1945.

13. Alternative name for the Politburo after the war.

14. L. L. Shvartsman, a career Chekist, deputy director of the Investigative Division of Especially Important Cases, implicated in the supposed plot with Abakumov.

15. Gorlitsky and Khlevniuk, *Cold Peace*, 155.

CONCLUSION

1. We are grateful to Stephen Kotkin for first making this observation.

Index

The Stalin-Kaganovich Correspondence, 1931–36, compiled and edited by R. W. Davies, Oleg V. Khlevniuk, E. A. Rees, Liudmila P. Kosheleva, and Larisa A. Rogovaya

Stalin's Letters to Molotov, 1925–1936, edited by Lars T. Lih, Oleg V. Naumov, and Oleg V. Khlevniuk

Stalin's Secret Pogrom: The Postwar Inquisition of the Soviet Jewish Anti-Fascist Committee, edited by Joshua Rubenstein and Vladimir P. Naumov

The Unknown Lenin: From the Secret Archive, edited by Richard Pipes

The Voice of the People: Letters from the Soviet Village, 1918–1932, by C. J. Storella and A. K. Sokolov

Voices of Revolution, 1917, by Mark D. Steinberg

The War Against the Peasantry, 1927–1930, edited by Lynne Viola, V. P. Danilov, N. A. Ivnitskii, and Denis Kozlov